THE HUMAN PERSPECTIVE
in Sociology

The Methodology of Participant Observation

SEVERYN T. BRUYN
Boston College

Prentice-Hall, Inc.   Englewood Cliffs, New Jersey

To my mother and father

PRENTICE-HALL SOCIOLOGY SERIES
Herbert Blumer, editor

Current printing (last digit):
10   9   8   7   6   5   4   3

Prentice-Hall International, Inc., *London*
Prentice-Hall of Australia, Pty. Ltd., *Sydney*
Prentice-Hall of Canada, Ltd., *Toronto*
Prentice-Hall of India (Private) Ltd., *New Delhi*
Prentice-Hall of Japan, Inc., *Tokyo*

Library of Congress Catalog Card Number: 66–10114

PRINTED IN THE UNITED STATES OF AMERICA
C–44520

Foreword

Professor Bruyn's book is a signally penetrating discussion of the most important problem confronting social and psychological sciences, namely, how to study man.

We must acknowledge that many social scientists and psychologists do not regard the problem as significant, much less that it is the most vital problem in their fields. Their position is easily understood. They believe that the problem has been already largely solved, in that the essential character and principles of scientific procedure have by now been firmly established. In their eyes, the steady development of the physical and biological sciences over the past four centuries has forged, under the test of exacting experience, the basic rudiments of the method of science. The social and psychological sciences have the good fortune of being the beneficiaries of this legacy; they are spared the need of having to work out the nature of scientific method through their own efforts. They have a different task, namely, to apply the already established knowledge of scientific procedure to the areas of their respective interests. This application, to be true, gives rise to a variety of specific technical problems as social scientists and psychologists encounter one or another area of concern in their fields. But such technical problems are of a different *genre* than that of the problem of scientific method as such—they represent the translation of scientific method into specific procedures suitable for the identification and handling of divergent sets of empirical data. They are not seen as challenging the known nature of scientific method as such. Indeed, an opposite relation exists between such technical problems, on one hand, and scientific method, on the other, in that the principles of scientific method provide the guidance and set the standards for the devising of techniques. In this sense, technical problems are of subsidiary importance; they are met, one by one, as experience and in-

iii

genuity lead to the development of techniques appropriate to given types of subject matter. The handling of technical problems is under the control of the known criteria of scientific method. The objective is to bring the techniques which are devised into the closest possible conformity with the criteria. This focusing of interest and effort on the innovation and perfection of techniques signifies that, in the study of man, no special problem is seen other than to work out appropriate applications of the scientific method. It is for this reason that the interest in "methodology" in the social and psychological sciences is so predominantly preoccupied with the development and use of techniques. The motivation in this interest is to devise techniques that come closest to meeting and expressing the "true" character of scientific procedure.

This view, held by so many, that the only real task in social and psychological science is to apply the established principles and criteria of scientific procedure needs to be critically examined. Obviously, the model of scientific method that is used to supply the principles and criteria is derived from the physical and biological sciences. This seems to be entirely appropriate in that the whole idea of scientific study is solely a product of their experience. Further, the demonstrated and impressive record of their accomplishments over time attests the value of the model of scientific method which they have developed. The method of science is seen fundamentally as the scientific method which has been worked out in the physical and biological sciences. This line of reasoning seems to be incontestable. But one is forced to pause when he asks what is the model of scientific method which has been developed and established in the so-called natural sciences. Here we enter into an area of difference, ambiguity, confusion, and indeed, controversy. If we turn, first, to the conceptions of scientific method held by social scientists and psychologists, restricting ourselves to their conceptions of scientific method in the natural sciences, we discover that these conceptions do not reflect in any sense a unitary and firmly established view. Instead, they show significant differences along many different lines. Some see scientific method in terms of a set of logical procedures, such as are outlined in conventional treatises on logic or scientific method. Others identify scientific method with given forms of general procedures, such as quantification or the use of laboratory experimentation. Others feel that its essence is to lie in certain special procedures, such as "operationalism" or the use of "input-output" models. Others view it in terms of the presumed composition of the "world" addressed by science, as in the case of a probabilistic model, a mechanical model, a "system" model, or an aggregate of variables. One scarcely needs to note that such diverse perspectives of scientific method may be combined in many different patterns with considerable ranges of difference in emphasis.

A little reflection should make clear that there is really no consensus as to what constitutes "scientific method." There is disagreement as to the logical steps in scientific procedure; there is difference as to the extent and form in which scientific procedure is said to be quantitative or experimental in a strict controlled sense; there is disagreement as to whether scientific method can be reduced to special procedures such as "operationalism"; there is conspicuous variation in the type of "world" presupposed by the nature of scientific study—whether it is mechanical or probabilistic, or whether it is configurational or an aggregation of disparate units. The lines of diversity in the conceptions of scientific method far exceed the few that are mentioned here. This picture of extensive difference is obscured by the tendency at one or another period of time for a particular conception to acquire prestige and relative dominance—as in the case of the current identification of scientific procedure with "research design" cast in the form of a relationship between independent and dependent variables under conditions of a control group. One should not be deceived by such a seeming approximation to consensus at any given time. A review of the ways in which scientific method has been portrayed reveals over time a more or less running picture of difference, change, shift, and displacement—a most interesting and significant story in itself. Nor should one assume that this picture of divergency and change in how scientific method is seen is due merely to an inability of unsophisticated social scientists and psychologists to grasp the true nature of scientific method as developed in the physical and biological sciences. The history of the portrayals of scientific method over the past two centuries by natural scientists and sophisticated interpreters shows a comparable picture of differences, change, shifts, and new versions. The nature of scientific method has not been, and is not now, a fixed, established datum.

The import of these few observations is that the problem of how to study human beings and their group life cannot be handled by the simple dictum to apply the true and tested principles of scientific study as they have been developed by physical and biological science. Such "principles" have not been clearly and firmly established. They cannot be wrapped up in a neat, packaged scheme, ready to give universally acceptable guidance to social scientists and psychologists. Instead, it is clear that social scientists and psychologists select, construct, and work with divergent and frequently inconsistent conceptions of the essence of scientific procedure. And the answer to this divergency is not to be sought by a more meticulous scrutiny of scientific procedure in the physical and biological sciences since such procedure, itself, is marked by variation, change, shifts, and different perspectives. The question of how to study human conduct and group life goes far beyond a problem of how to apply an established body of tested knowledge of scientific procedure.

It is with this recognition that we can appreciate the thrust of Professor Bruyn's thoughtful and careful discussion. His approach might be said to stem from the proposition that the cardinal requirement of an empirical science is to respect the nature of its subject matter. In place of applying to human life an imported scheme of scientific procedure, he stresses the need of recognizing in the first instance the peculiar character of human beings, their behavior, and their group life. And he persistently develops the thesis that scientific study in these areas must be grounded on an appreciation of this peculiar character. In doing so, he brings the topic of "methodology" in the social and psychological sciences into proper focus, shifting it away from preoccupation with "scientific method" as derived from the natural sciences to the basic concern with method that reflects the nature of human life.

Professor Bruyn is obviously not the first scholar to have noted and to have discussed the difference. Indeed, he has joined company with a large number of distinguished scholars who in one or another way have recognized and appreciated the fundamental importance of gearing social and psychological science to fit what is distinctive in the case of human beings. One thinks immediately of such a variety of scholars as Auguste Comte, William Graham Sumner, John Dewey, George Herbert Mead, W. I. Thomas, Florian Znaniecki, Clyde Kluckhohn, Robert E. Park, Max Weber, C. H. Cooley, and Robert MacIver. The merit of Professor Bruyn's treatment is that he has discussed the topic systematically, with meticulous care, with a searching examination of the appropriate historical and philosophical background, with a thoughtful coverage of current views, with a refreshing analysis of the major concepts in contemporary sociology and social psychology, and with a perceptive consideration of the form which research inquiry has to take in dealing with human behavior.

Professor Bruyn has used the concept of "participant observation" to cover his extensive discussion and systematic analysis because the concept brings neatly into focus the position of the scholar and researcher who proposes to study human group life. The concept signifies the relation which the human observer of human beings cannot escape—having to participate in some fashion in the experience and action of those he observes. Professor Bruyn has sought to isolate the nature of this participation and to draw out its implications for the actual observation and study of human group life. In doing this, he has appropriately covered a far wider range of matters than is suggested when the concept of "participant observation" is restricted to a mere field technique. It is indeed this broader and richer treatment that makes his discussion of prime value to the research student who may be concerned with participant observation in the narrower conventional sense.

Anyone who is sensitive to currents of thought and sentiment in sociology and social psychology today is aware of the restiveness of many, particularly younger, scholars with regard to research inquiry. They sense deep inadequacy in the nature and directions of present work, feeling somehow that despite the growth in technical excellence scientific study is not coming to grips with our social world. I am sure that such scholars will find the reading of Professor Bruyn's book to be exciting and highly rewarding. The book will provide a new perspective, open new doors to understanding, and sketch out a new orientation to the study of human beings and their group life. They will have a feeling of entering into the main channel in the study of man.

HERBERT BLUMER

Preface

When Sir Charles P. Snow's Rede Lecture was published as *The Two Cultures and the Scientific Revolution* in 1959, it created quite a stir. In fact, the book went through four printings in a year. Snow had unwittingly taken the lid off a pot that was already simmering to a boil in the circles of academe. Soon letters were flowing to him and articles were appearing which both agreed and disagreed with his thesis.

Snow asserted that two distinctly opposing cultures have evolved in the intellectual life of modern man. One culture is that of the literary intellectual and the other is that of the scientist. One culture is represented in the humanities and the other in the sciences and technologies of our modern era. Each culture has its own common denominators, Snow said, its own familiar symbols which distinguish it, but each culture is a world apart from the other. Men of letters have no basis for conversation with men of science and technology. A work of Shakespeare, it seems, does not compare with the Second Law of Thermodynamics.

In a later, expanded version of the lecture (*The Two Cultures: And a Second Look*) Snow comments on the reaction of his wide audience, mentioning the emergence of a "third culture" which he had failed to recognize in his earlier lectures. This third culture is now developing in a number of fields, Snow reflected, such as social history, sociology, demography, political science, economics, and psychology. "It seems a mixed bag," he said, "but there is an inner consistency." Snow then explained apologetically why he had failed to see this. He had been a "prisoner of...English upbringing, conditioned to be suspicious of any but the established intellectual disciplines. . . ."

This "mixed bag" in the form of the social sciences is already established in the curricula of American universities. In fact, these new sciences are burgeoning in ways comparable to the other sciences, producing a third culture which is understood neither in the category of the humanities nor in the category of the sciences in the traditional sense. They stand complexly and uniquely between. Although the social sciences do have some resemblances both to the so-called "hard sciences," from which much of their own culture derives, and to the humanities, from which they still have much to learn, in essence, they are in neither category, and they often suffer from a lack of identity.

The social scientist's claim to recognition in the academic world has in the past rested on the "scientific" character of his field of study. Thus, the social scientist has tended to identify himself with the scientific pole of the "two cultures." To be scientific has been to be associated with new worlds of progress, precision, control, objectivity, laboratory magic, prediction, power—desirable things in the scientific culture of modern society. But the social scientist's claim to be scientific in the traditional sense has not rested on firm ground, for the culture of the social scientist is not the culture of the natural scientist.

Most social scientists have long recognized this fact, but few have understood completely how the social scientist's culture differs and what truly constitutes that culture. However, more social scientists are now recognizing the distinctiveness of their area of knowledge as having a special character and integrity of its own. There are signs that social scientists are genuinely beginning to understand the human character of their science, and are also beginning to see its implications for theory and method.

The inadequacy of the naturalistic orientation of the physical and biological sciences when applied to the study of social phenomena is evident in many fields of study, of which a number are discussed in this book. Among these fields is included the field of community studies. My own experiences in this particular area will introduce the reader to how I personally realized the diversity of method in the social sciences—and thus came to write this book. Let me recount briefly the pattern of my experience.

About fourteen years ago I was conducting some research on the processes of social change in communities of midwestern United States. My previous experience in research had involved working with problems of another order —those related to actuarial devices used in predicting success and failure of prison parolees. The sudden change from a quantitative type of approach to one of a basically different order made apparent the complexity of study in the social sciences. The research questions I began to ask were fundamentally different from those of a quantitative nature and I had to seek ways to treat the special problems they produced.

My fieldwork was aimed at discovering the basis for social action and change in community life. There seemed to be no precedents to follow. The statistical approach was not fully applicable, nor could the experimentalist approach be applied effectively for this purpose. The case-study approach helped, but fell short in many ways. The armchair approach of the grand theorists was obviously inappropriate. Qualitative analysis, too, was not adequate to grapple with the special problems I had to solve.

I finally realized that the special problems confronting me involved research in what was called "participant observation." Slowly, as a result of my inquiry into this field, I discovered a body of literature that was quietly accumulating in social research with its own distinctive methodology. Some authors identified their research work with participant observation while others never mentioned it as such, and yet their work was clearly in that growing tradition. Actually, participant observation had not yet become commonly recognized in social research as a methodological approach or tradition with its own principles and procedures. Yet, as I read these works I found that the procedures were quite applicable in my own fieldwork.

In my observations of social processes I realized that what I was studying was not human behavior so much as the inner collective life of people who were deeply involved personally in changing their community and in being changed by it. This inner life revealed itself symbolically in the dialogues between people on street corners, in committees, in back rooms, and in assemblies. It had visible counterparts in the statue on the square, the cemetery, and the new industry moving into the community. The evidence of this life generally appeared in equivocal terms not very conducive to the methods of a scientist aiming for prediction, precision, and control. At times it seemed as though it might be better for a novelist or a playwright to represent the subtleties of these terms in community life. And yet I realized that the social scientist *must* apprehend the original meanings of these terms with all their subtleties, for they were clearly an essential part of what was determining the course of social action.

If I was to get to the basis of social action in the community, then, I had to interpret the terms in these dialogues at the symbolic levels at which they were expressed. This meant, first, accepting these terms (I call them *concrete concepts*) as they were understood in the context in which people lived with them. This was more than a journalistic effort, for although I had to get the facts straight in my stories of community action, I also had to relate these facts to theory and history; furthermore, I had to discover the human "ground" of being in the expression of these facts in order fully to understand them. To reach the ground for their expression I found I had to "get personal" with the people who expressed these terms. "Getting personal" with people in a scientific study was not in the textbooks on methodology.

I found, for instance, that I had to provide a place in my method of study where I could live close to where my subjects lived *as persons*. I did not fully achieve this end. Moreover, since there were no clear precedents to follow and no standards by which to judge the validity of my findings, I considered my work to be only another exploratory effort to reach beyond the traditional methods of study. What was needed was a more systematic statement about this kind of method and its implications for social scientific theory and method.

There were opposing elements in this method of study that kept reappearing with implications for what has recently been called the "new sociology." These opposing elements seem to represent part of the differences that C. P. Snow describes in the two cultures. Their co-existence in the social sciences is clearly like a "third culture" that is developing with an "inner consistency."

This book is about those opposing elements and about the inner consistency that is developing. It does not contain a new system of theory. Instead, it points to some of the nonsystem features of this kind of science. It purposely pokes at the sensitive areas of the social scientist's culture and would push the scientist to his limits in an effort to see where he lives as a human being in that culture. It does not build from a preconceived plan, but builds, instead, from the ruins of the expectations I shared with others to study the human community solely from the traditional standards of science. This book builds, too, from ideas contained in books that are not scientific in the traditional sense and yet have contributed immeasurably to our systematic knowledge of man. Social science, it seems, is building a culture that is very difficult to compare accurately with any set forms in the history of science. Perhaps in these remarks we can supplement this effort by indicating something of its nature by means of a rhetorical form found in the humanities.

While reading James Thurber's delightful story "The Thirteen Clocks," I was struck by how an allegorical interpretation of it could illustrate a number of themes about the third culture which we will be discussing. Such an interpretation should introduce our discussion of the role of social science among the major fields of learning, and at the same time tell us something of the perspective of the participant observer when he attempts to be "interpretive" of human reality.

"The Thirteen Clocks" is a fairy tale for adults that has all the characters one would expect, with one exception—the Golux. He wears an "indescribable hat" and his "eyes were wide and astonished, as if everything were happening for the first time." Then, somewhat more true to classic form, but having a special twist to his character, is the "cold Duke" who has killed time and stopped the thirteen clocks in his castle with .his cruel, frozen ways. There is a Princess (whose beauty resembles the delicate rose) whom the Duke has trapped in his castle. Her fate would seem to be in the hands of the cold Duke, so the story goes, except for the possibility of being discovered and saved by a Prince.

It so happens that a Prince is traveling by the castle yearning to find the maiden of his dreams. He hears of the trapped Princess and also of the impossible tasks set by the Duke for her suitors to win her in marriage. As the Prince contemplates these matters outside the castle he is tapped gently on the shoulder from behind. He turns to meet the indescribable Golux, who offers his services to the Prince. The Prince thinks at first that the Golux is a "mere Device" but the Golux denies the resemblance. "I resemble only half the things I say I don't," the Golux says. "The other half resembles me." The Prince finds that the Golux has strange ways but an honest heart, and so he accepts his services in the interest of defeating the Duke. Then they set out together to rid the castle of the cold Duke.

The task the Duke sets before the Prince is really impossible. He is to bring back a thousand jewels in 9 and 90 hours, before the clocks strike 5. There are no jewels within walking distance, it seems, and the clocks are frozen silent at ten minutes before 5 o'clock. Nevertheless, aided by the special powers and uncommon methods of the Golux, the Prince obtains the jewels just in time. When they return to the castle together, they slip past the guards to start the clocks moving again. The Golux asks the Princess to unfreeze the clocks by touching them with her warm hands (for she has the only warm hands in the castle). She touches one but it will not start. In despair the Princess cries to the Golux, "Use magic!" The Golux replies, "I have no magic to depend on." The Princess cries again, "Use logic, then!" But the castle guards were almost upon them.

"Now let me see," the Golux said. "If you can touch the clocks and never start them, then you can start the clocks and never touch them. That's logic, as I know and use it. Hold your hand this far away. Closer. Now a little farther back. A little farther. There! I think you have it! Do not move!" And the clocks began to whir and tick.

Thurber does not indicate in any way that he wrote this delightful tale as an allegory. He says he wrote it only for escape and self indulgence, and to maintain his sanity. To suggest that there might be allegorical elements in it may be to prejudice Thurber's interest in having fun. If we err here (and we surely intend to) then we must call upon the spirit of this tale and claim the allegory to be a "mere Device" to get our story told just as the Golux helped complete the story of the thirteen clocks.

Our other story would go like this: the Duke represents the great frightening shadow of science in the modern world which has trapped the Princess, who represents the humanities. The Prince is science in its true value and character. It would seek to conquer the inhuman powers that have developed in its wake—atomic powers that could make the clocks stop around the world and end all that is beautiful and human in the world.

The odd-looking Golux represents the social scientist who, as a participant observer, is not understood by any of the major characters in the story, for no one has ever seen anything like him before. He looks at the world phenomenologically, as we say in the ensuing chapters, as though things were happening to him for the first time. The Duke mistakenly employs him as one of his spies, but the Golux has his own ends and makes himself invisible in the Duke's employment. The Duke can talk to the Golux, but he cannot really see him. As the Duke's spy, the Golux is called "Listen"—

and that is exactly what he does to discover what is going on inside the castle. The Duke has heard about the Golux from those outside the castle even though he cannot see him in the castle, and he warns the Prince against trusting the Golux because, as the Duke said, "He cannot tell what can be from what can't. He seldom knows what should be from what is."

In the story, after listening to the advice of the Duke, the Prince momentarily distrusted the Golux. When the Prince next saw the fellow he did not appear so strange; his hat suddenly looked "describable" as though he were capable only of foolishness and deception as the Duke had depicted him. Nevertheless, the more the Prince came to know the Golux, the more he respected his unusual powers in their common effort to defeat the Duke. In the end the Golux proved worthy of his trust.

We cannot stretch our allegory much more or the reader will disclaim our Device and we would do an injustice to Thurber's fun piece. Thurber's story is complete in itself, but our real-life story is not yet finished. The modern scientist of society is still developing his uncommon methods and the story is therefore just beginning. The point of our unfinished story is that the social scientist is the means to help destroy the cold Duke, science's shadow of impersonality and dehumanization in society. It is the belief of many social scientists that they can do much to bridge the deepening chasm between science and humanity.

This is one interpretation of the story. It can be called the "dramatic" view that is associated with the personal perspective of the involved "participant" who dreams of the constructive possibilities of social science in the modern world. This dramatic view is important, but without the undramatic, cool perspective of the "observer," it is insufficient. The observer views the personal perspective of participants with some detachment; if he is wise in his work, he can create an overall rational design, the "forms" of knowledge which contain the concrete details. Unless he is sympathetic to these details, however, he cannot see their authentic relation to his design.

The detached observer could conclude that the real story about the schools of learning in the modern world is too complex to be told in the simplified imagery of an allegory. The differences between the technical scientist and the literary artist are overdrawn in the allegorical interpretation. In reality, a great deal of overlap and interpenetration exist within each field of learning.

For one thing, scientists have human values, as do artists, which are expressed through professional organizations as well as individually. Moreover, the creative (rather than the destructive) applications of a science such as physics or chemistry may prove to be a deciding factor in the achievement of peace in the new world of the future, a factor at least as important as the poet's or the social scientist's contribution. Furthermore, from the wholistic viewpoint of the observer, those novelists, poets, artists, and university faculty who are identified with the humanities (the beautiful Princess) can be as destructive or as creative as the scientist and the technical engineer with regard to bringing about a peaceful world. Then the observer would say that either the literati or the scientists can be instrumental in closing serious intellectual gaps that C. P. Snow claims have developed academically between the extremes of the two cultures. Although elements of the opposing cultures are integrated in the social sciences, the field does not represent a higher synthesis in the Hegelian sense. That is, when a synthesis is being formed in the social sciences, it merely represents another approach to knowledge which is neither more nor less important than the natural sciences or the humanities.

From the observer's standpoint the problems of the modern world are much too complex to be represented fairly by the intellectual divisions of learning that we call the sciences, the humanities, and the social sciences. It is not that some disciplines of learning do not logically fall into any one of these divisions—a fact which, in itself, is critically noteworthy. Rather, it is that the solutions of modern world conflicts are not normally the province of the intellectual. The solutions are made by creative legislators, statemen, executives, administrators, educators, and religious leaders, whereas the intellectual is only a part of this immense enterprise. Why then trouble with an allegory about social science as a helpmate in the marriage of beauty and power?

The answer is that dramatization of empirical reality in an allegory allows sympathetic insight for the observer into the motive-meanings and cultural world of participants. Dramatization is essential to see personally how particular meanings function to shape the objective world and create the realities which the observer must understand and untangle in his analysis. We do not claim that our allegorical interpretation of the story as a representation of three cultures of learning fits actual meanings that are empirically present in the minds of social scientists (*i.e.*, meanings based on research into the culture of their work), but such a rhetorical device *could* do this. It could serve as a methodological medium for communicating such meanings if they were found to have allegorical qualities. We have used the device of the allegory here only to describe a social scientific dream, which has no higher level of reality than a fairy tale. Yet it is a dream which we believe is latent within the developing third culture, one which could become a forceful reality as this third culture unfolds in the modern world. Our concern in this preface is not with the message of the dream so much as with the illustration of the method we are using to reach a human perspective—of which dreams are an important part. The method of the social scientist, we are saying, must take dramatic account of the sociocultural world—the complex of actors and their plots as they live and dream on the stage of society—as a breathing part of his theoretical design

This is the task of the social scientist who works in a world of troubled

societies full of dreams and myths which are a part of the continuing creation of human reality. These societies may dramatically witness the close
of one era and the opening of another in this century, and the social scientist
is in a position to help people make the transition with a new cultural
perspective. The cultural perspective of social science is still in the making,
but we already know that the images which comprise it are basically different from the traditional images of science because the social scientist is
both a participant in and an observer of the society he studies.

Thus, the social scientist finds that the concrete, the ideal, and the simple
images that are frequently a part of the "participant" perspective are as
important to understand as are the formal, the realistic, and the complex
images that are frequently a part of the "observer" perspective. Neither
perspective could be complete without the other. If the social scientist
assumed only the formal perspective of a Georg Simmel, for example, he
would achieve a level of generality that would permit him enlightened
judgments about social forms that lacked the concrete particulars that shape
these forms. Then he could not understand an important part of what
makes people human, and he would misinterpret the nature of man in
society.

In the knowledge world of the social scientist, particulars can be as important as generalities; realism can be as important to his outlook as
idealism; a personal explanation can be as important as an objective explanation. The understanding of such basic differences in man's perception
of the world is the basis of the human perspective. The systematic description of the relationships between such differences and how they conjoin
to explain social and cultural reality is the basis of the third culture. This
third culture has the impossible task of understanding these differences
within itself while at the same time transcending them with new interpretations. (It has this task whether or not it wants to start the clocks
moving in the castle.) Its task, in effect, is to explain itself in the process of
making itself. Only a character with an indescribable hat could do that.

A few comments about the organization of the book should be made.
The opening chapters are intended to set forth a methodological basis for
participant observation as instrumental in developing human perspectives
in field studies and the implications these studies have for developing a
general perspective in theory. The two final chapters continue to develop
operational assumptions and procedures of the method, which may be
examined for their usefulness and applicability to field research in the future.
The middle two chapters (*Toward a Human Perspective* and *The Rhetoric
of Sociology*), however, constitute a somewhat excursive discussion of fields
in the humanities, which involves a shift in function and purpose from the
other chapters somewhat more systematically and logically constituted.
(The topics in Chapter 5, for example, are organized on the basis of

alliteration, a principle of rhetoric, rather than of logic.) Such a discussion has the purpose of discovering concepts which may be helpful in the development of a human perspective in sociology. The sequential order of these chapters in the book reflects my own journey in pursuit of the scientific and human implications of research in participant observation. And yet the presence of these two chapters in the center of the book suggests a basic point: that the craftsmen who work at the center of this developing third culture must take account of the variegated ways of understanding man—must, in other words, be conscious of the standards and techniques of work used in the humanities—when they construct their scientific theories about man in society.

Much of this book is necessarily about abstract theories and philosophical problems. The method of participant observation, we believe, has reached a stage where it contains so many contradictions in the interpretation and analysis of data that the researcher can no longer ignore the philosophy behind the method. The researcher can no longer shrug off philosophical problems as "unrelated" to his work in collecting human data. He must now resolve these contradictions by developing a systematic viewpoint of the phenomenon of man; and where it is not possible to resolve contradictions, he must understand how they function in the interpretation of his data.

Sections of the manuscript have been read by individuals representing different fields in different parts of the country. Suggestions have been made by each of the following people, who to some degree influenced the terms used or the ideas in certain sections of the manuscript: Dr. William McBride in philosophy at Yale University, Dr. Cornelius Krusé in philosophy at Wesleyan University in Connecticut, Dr. Howard S. Becker in sociology at Northwestern University, Dr. Fred Davis in social research at the San Francisco Medical Center of the University of California, Dr. J. E. Hulett, Jr. in sociology at the University of Illinois, Dr. Richard Palmer in the humanities and Dr. Robert Guthrie in sociology, both at MacMurray College in Illinois, and Dr. Maurice Schwartz at Brandeis University. In particular I wish to acknowledge the helpful criticisms of Dr. Herbert Blumer at the University of California at Berkeley who read the entire manuscript. The final editing at Prentice-Hall was done by Miss Dorothy L. Green, whose labors are deeply appreciated. I must stress, however, that the ideas contained in the book are entirely my own responsibility.

Finally, my wife's patience with my preoccupations in writing the draft has been more than I deserve. Her graces did much to contribute perceptive ideas on clarity in the draft while she typed sections of it. My children are unconscious of the patience they displayed. I must say that their spontaneity in the face of my efforts to concentrate is a tribute to their own independent lovely selves.

SEVERYN T. BRUYN

Contents

1

The

Background

Introduction

In every scientific discipline there is need for continuous dialogue among researchers and theorists about methodology. Methods and techniques are constantly changing as scientists seek firmer grounds for explaining reality. Sometimes new methods arise spontaneously out of the scientist's own determination to pursue—or even hound—an unanswered question to whatever limits he can. In this determined pursuit of knowledge, the scientist often creates unstandardized techniques in field experimentation to overcome whatever obstacles lie in his path to truth. Even though these techniques do not always fit scientific standards, with repeated application they continue to reveal their value to the scientific discipline, in time acquiring wider acceptance and definitiveness through repeated practice, eventually developing a rigor which meets technical expectations of scientists everywhere. One such technique has been in the throes of development within the social sciences for the last half-century, having begun essentially as a technique to obtain data that could not be obtained otherwise. It has grown in its value to the field where today it constitutes a distinct, yet evolving, method of social research. This is the technique or method of participant observation.

Because this method is far from being clearly defined, our function is partly to describe it more fully, first by reviewing how researchers in the past have defined and used it, and second by discussing some of the implications which it has for research and theory in social science. Nevertheless, even without clear definition, this method has already proven to be an independent, productive approach to the acquisition of knowledge in the social sciences through many studies which have utilized it in the past.

In reviewing the nature and implications of any social research of such increasing significance as this, we must re-examine the basic books on

methodology to determine the link of participant observation with the past
before we can assess its role in the future. There are many works of note to
which we could refer, but three "classics" set the background of this study:
Emile Durkheim's *The Rules of Sociological Method* (1895), Max Weber's
The Methodology of the Social Sciences (a recent collection of essays written
originally between 1903 and 1917), and Florian Znaniecki's *The Method
of Sociology* (1934).[1] These small but protean texts contain the social scientific issues of the last hundred years—issues that are basic to the history of
social thought. They deal with the place of values in the context of social
theory and research; the problem of causality and human freedom; and the
"rules" or principles of sociological analysis, finding it necessary to relate
research to social theory, particularly with regard to concept construction
and typologies in social scientific research. Such items also concern us today
in the method of participant observation.

Aside from touching on the major issues of methodology, these three
studies each present us with a period of thought and a viewpoint which sets
the stage for our approach to contemporary methods. We find that the works
of Durkheim and Znaniecki form separate foundations upon which two
pillars of research methodology have been built, one of which we will investigate in our treatment here and the other of which clarifies our task by
virtue of the contrasts it presents to the former. Weber's book functions in
another way: it indicates the direction in which theory may move in order
to provide the necessary archway between these two pillars of research
methodology and to house them with some reasonably consistent architec-
tural design. The construction of this house is not our problem here. The
analogy is made only to indicate the task which ultimately lies ahead for
sociological inquiry and about which we will comment after examining the
differences in research approaches to the study of society. Our concern
throughout will be the methodological aspects of these dimensions of inquiry.

The Two Major Research Approaches

The two major research approaches are distinguished from each other
rather clearly in the classic works of Durkheim and Znaniecki. It was
Durkheim who first considered how we should proceed in order to discover
empirical knowledge. In his book on *Rules* he begins by saying: "The first

---

[1] Emile Durkheim, *The Rules of Sociological Method* (8th ed.) (New York: Free
Press of Glencoe, Inc., 1950); Florian Znaniecki, *The Method of Sociology* (New
York: Holt, Rinehart & Winston, Inc., 1934); Max Weber, *The Methodology of the
Social Sciences,* trans., eds. Edward Shils and Henry A. Finch (New York: Free Press
of Glencoe, Inc., 1949). See also H. H. Gerth and C. Wright Mills, eds., *From Max
Weber: Essays in Sociology* (New York: Oxford University Press, Inc., 1946).

and most fundamental rule: Consider facts as things."[2] In the preface to his second edition he seeks to clarify what is meant by "things," expressing a point which sets the theme for our subsequent chapters:

> What, precisely, is a "thing"? A thing differs from an idea in the same way as that which we know from without differs from that which we know from within.[3]

In fact, for Durkheim, "every object of science is a thing,"[4] a proposition which presents the fundamental issue in social research today most clearly, and makes the difference between the two research approaches we are about to describe most evident.

Durkheim continues to elaborate on his first rule by introducing corollaries. The first is: "All preconceptions must be eradicated,"[5] to which we must add that Durkheim meant medieval theology and mysticism. The second corollary, however, sets up new preconceptions:

> The subject matter of every sociological study should comprise a group of phenomena defined in advance by certain common external characteristics, and all phenomena so defined should be included in this group.[6]

In this corollary Durkheim has stated the essence of nineteenth-century naturalism in its social form, triggering the beginning of one major line of research and setting the standard for empirical-statistical studies in the first half of the twentieth century. Durkheim himself set the example for such research in one of the most outstanding advances in controlled statistical research of his day (*Le Suicide*),[7] a work which is still a classic in contemporary studies of suicide, as well as a basic theoretical orientation to the entire field of social problems.

Florian Znaniecki, writing in the 1930's, sees some value in quantitative studies, but states that the data of the "cultural student are always 'somebody's' never 'nobody's' data." The essential character of this data he called the "humanistic" coefficient. If this "coefficient" were withdrawn, Znaniecki declared, that is, if the scientist tried to study the cultural system as he studies a material or natural system as though it existed separately from human experience, "the system would disappear and in its stead he

---

2 Durkheim, *Rules*, p. 14. Durkheim's general method was to move from the outer to the inner realities of man. However, his approach is too complex to discuss here. For recent interpretations by Robert Bellah, Harry Alpert, and Bruce Donrenwend, see *American Sociological Review*, **24**, No. 4 (August 1959).

3 Durkheim, *Rules*, p. xliii.

4 *Ibid.*, p. xliv.

5 *Ibid.*, p. 31.

6 *Ibid.*, p. 35. Durkheim's methodology is transitional; in special ways its form is idealistic and even on the threshold of phenomenology. See p. 93.

7 Emile Durkheim, *Le Suicide* (Paris: F. Alcan, 1897), trans. John A. Spaulding and George Simpson, *Suicide* (New York: Free Press of Glencoe, Inc., 1951).

[the scientist] would find a disjointed mass of natural things and processes, without any similarity to the reality he started to investigate."[8] This statement is a pole apart from Durkheim's rules. As if he were pointing his criticism directly at Durkheim, Znaniecki proceeds to elaborate his point: "We call natural objects *things,* cultural objects *values,* in view of their essential practical determination with reference to human activity."[9]

Znaniecki identified two basic ways of viewing scientific data; one he called the *natural* and the other the *cultural.* The latter approach involved what he termed the *humanistic coefficient,* and was the basis for sociological investigation:

> One is the way of the naturalist who, even while recognizing that cultural objects are human values and that cultural systems are constructed by human activity, believes that human activity can nevertheless be studied as a natural process given to him (like other natural processes) without any reference to how it appears to anybody else; and also that a human value viewed in the light of a naturalistic theory of activity can be simply analyzed into a natural thing. . . . The other way of obtaining an inductive knowledge of human activity would be to use consistently the humanistic coefficient in dealing with it and take it as it appears to the agent himself and to those who cooperate with him or counteract him.[10]

These two approaches to the inductive process of research have been the basis of a long series of research studies which have, over the years, added content to the work of social theorists. Znaniecki's exemplary cultural study, *The Polish Peasant in Europe and America,*[11] written in collaboration with William I. Thomas, has become a classic reference, still relevant to both researchers and theorists in social organization and social problems fields.

We find the works of Durkheim and Znaniecki to be hallmarks in the history of sociological research, one representing the quantitative and the other the qualitative study of human phenomena. In the time since these studies were made, research has ranged productively between these polar modes of inquiry, both of which have contributed valuable materials for the workshop of the social theorist. Within the one mode, which tends toward quantitative research, are varieties of tradition, including those of the positivist and the behaviorist, which are designated here as *traditional empiricism.* Within the other mode, which tends toward qualitative research, are the more interpretive types of inquiry, including that which we now describe as *participant observation.*

---

8 Znaniecki, *The Method of Sociology,* p. 37.

9 *Ibid.,* p. 41.

10 *Ibid.,* pp. 44–45.

11 William I. Thomas and Florian Znaniecki, *The Polish Peasant in Europe and America,* 5 Vols. (Chicago: University of Chicago Press, 1918–20). The studies of Durkheim and Znaniecki are cited here to illustrate opposing trends in research; their separate works are not in total opposition.

One expression of traditional empiricism is experimental behaviorism, a method of inquiry which contrasts most distinctly with the method of participant observation. As we shall see, however, the distinctive features of participant observation contrast so markedly with the entire tradition of scientific empiricism as it has developed historically that we must make this tradition the comparative basis for our analysis.

It is true, of course, that empiricism has assumed many shapes since its modern history began with Francis Bacon and then was systematically developed by the British empiricists. (It was the Englishman John Locke who set forth the epoch-making polemic against the rationalist position of innate ideas, *An Essay Concerning Human Understanding,* 1690.) The philosophic emphasis in scientific *research,* as distinguished from scientific *theory,* can be traced to its origins in the works of those British empiricists who stressed sense experience as the source of all viable knowledge. Since that time, science has taken its major philosophic orientation from Immanuel Kant who, at the end of the eighteenth century, sought to integrate the positions of empiricism and rationalism. But even the Kantian position, as we will contend later in some detail, is not sufficient to account for the complexities of social research which are becoming evident in modern cultural studies.

The use of the term empiricism in modern social scientific circles essentially means experimental procedures which involve sense-data that ultimately can be quantified.[12] While social scientists have broadened the term to some extent by including within it what is called *qualitative analysis,* certain facts of qualitative analysis simply do not fit the traditional requirements of scientific empiricism, and the weight of this tradition on social researchers has caused confusion and has tended to curb many creative possibilities of their work. Therefore, it is necessary to elaborate a methodology which can no longer be explained by this tradition and yet which will stand in its own right and earn a legitimate place in the scientific study of man.

In the social sciences the term empiricism must have a broader, more

---

12 Traditional empiricism includes a number of specific research orientations which have had different names at different times. Among these orientations are: *behaviorists* who traditionally insist that the only data admissible to scientific study are those which are observable to the senses; *experimentalists* who demand that all studies be rigorously controlled and employ only operationally defined variables; *social actionists* who would translate all observable phenomena into stimulus-response or materialistic terminology; and *neo-positivists, group dynamicists, sociometrists,* and *ecologists* who emphasize for purposes of verification that all data be definitive to the point of being quantified.

In contrast, the participant observer would hold that not all knowledge need be quantified to be verifiable; knowledge may be acquired without resorting to rigorous controls over variables in the traditional sense; not all scientific knowledge ought to be reduced to a stimulus-response or physical orientation; and, in fact, not all knowledge significant to social research can or should be derived directly from the five senses.

complex meaning than it has in the physical sciences; otherwise, it should be restricted to traditional usage or totally abandoned as inappropriate to social research. If it is retained and broadened, empiricism must include much that goes beyond what is presently permitted by professional use in social scientific research. It must include a wider range of experiential data; assimilate new research techniques which deviate radically from tradition; be ready to accept and adapt new tools from the humanities as well as the physical sciences; be capable of producing a richer descriptive vocabulary; and adjust to a basically different perspective of man than has been the case in its scientific past. This new perspective suggests itself through the qualitative research studies of participant observation. This method of observation is showing that a new empiricism which cannot be fully explained by the traditions of the past is being formulated.

There are three task roles among those working in the sociological enterprise which are becoming increasingly more clear. They are represented in the diagram below.

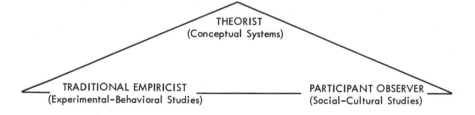

THEORIST
(Conceptual Systems)

TRADITIONAL EMPIRICIST
(Experimental–Behavioral Studies)

PARTICIPANT OBSERVER
(Social–Cultural Studies)

Both the traditional empiricist and the participant observer derive scientific knowledge from their research experiences guided by professional rules for investigating human phenomena. However, the differences between the rules and their experiences are great, and have extensive implications for social theory. Social theory today must construct a coherent, comprehensive body of knowledge that is consistent with the findings from these two polar, yet basic, research orientations.

Max Weber presents the third point of orientation, the theoretical, in which we find some insight into the enormous task of integrating the divergent findings of these two research orientations. Theory construction, to be fruitful, must allow for some creative interplay between these polar research approaches to the study of human reality. In Max Weber's methodology, one finds some signs of an integrating temper, which may very well be the starting point for theoretical inquiry.

Weber was a man who could accept what was valuable in each research category on the basis of what it could contribute to the pursuit of knowledge; he wrestled with contradictory positions existing in the pursuit of a historical, as contrasted with a scientific reality, a problem not dissimilar to the two basic research positions represented by the participant observer and the traditional empiricist, respectively. Weber saw what was so important in Durkheim's naturalistic position, the objectification of social phenomena, but he rejected its extremes. He questioned the applicability of the concept of "law," as conceived in the physical sciences, to the social sciences. From this perspective as a social historian he was inclined to state:

> The more comprehensive the validity—or scope—of a term, the more it leads us away from the richness of reality since in order to include the common elements of the largest possible number of phenomena, it must be as abstract as possible and hence *devoid* of content.[13]

Social "laws," he felt, cannot be conceived as ends in themselves, but as instruments with which we can better comprehend social reality. Knowledge of social reality can be judged by the significance it provides in understanding concrete situations. Even though Weber's historical training led him to accept what came to be Znaniecki's humanistic position on subjective understanding, he maintained an empirical-analytical position similar to Durkheim's in his study of typologies.[14]

The social sciences were to remain value-free in that the scientist was to refrain from basing his conclusions on value judgments. Nevertheless Weber saw the importance of the scientist's entering into the lives of the people he studied to seek personal understanding (*Verstehen*) of their position. While certain features of the theoretical position he took on some scientific issues may today be questionable, his work as a whole represents one of the most masterful attempts to date to integrate the divergencies apparent in his time within the science of sociology. Weber's concern for both "causal adequacy" and "human meaning" and his attempt to find them both in his own studies is suggestive of the kind of theoretical task which must still challenge the social scientist today.

Weber's statement regarding the critical stage of historical inquiry of his time with which he dealt in his *Methodology* is relevant to sociological inquiry at the present time:

> Only by laying bare and solving *substantive problems* can sciences be established and their methods developed. On the other hand, purely epistemological and methodological reflections have never played the crucial role in such developments. Such discussions become important for the enterprise of science only when, as a result of considerable shifts of the "viewpoint" from which a datum becomes the object of analysis, the idea emerges that the new "viewpoint" also requires a revision of the logical forms in which the "enterprise" has heretofore operated, and when, accordingly, uncertainty about the "nature" of one's own work arises.[15]

---

[13] Weber, *The Methodology of the Social Sciences*, p. 80.
[14] *Ibid.*, p. 92.
[15] *Ibid.*, p. 116.

It is our purpose here to indicate the considerable "shifts of the viewpoint from which the datum becomes the object of analysis" in the work of the participant observer and the necessity for a "revision of the logical forms in which the enterprise has heretofore operated."

The most significant attempt to build from the works of Max Weber in recent decades is that of Talcott Parsons. His systematic effort to bring together the divergent philosophies which lay behind the relatively unsystematic and yet integrative work of Max Weber is one of the most important developments of sociology in the United States. In his book *The Structure of Social Action* Talcott Parsons took a mammoth step toward the resolution of those major philosophic issues that burned on the European continent during the nineteenth century. However, he left many problems unsolved, among them what kind of methodology would help formulate the subjective categories of sociological theory. Subjective categories such as "justice," "freedom," "trust," "beauty," "community," and "purpose" which are fundamental to the nature of society could not be explained by the controlling categories of "structure," "function," "action," "system," and "role-expectations." Without a method, the resulting "action theory" which was formulated could not fully realize the possibilities of the philosophic foundation which Parsons had begun to lay in his original effort.[16] For this reason

---

16 The basis of action theory is that social action must be understood from the subjective viewpoint of people who initiate action. (Cf. Talcott Parsons, *The Structure of Social Action* (New York: Free Press of Glencoe, Inc., 1949); Talcott Parsons and Edward Shils, *Toward a General Theory of Action* (Cambridge, Mass.: Harvard University Press, 1951); Talcott Parsons, *The Social System* (New York: Free Press of Glencoe, Inc., 1951).) However, as action theory has become delineated in these works it has become clear that the dominant explanatory concepts of structure and function are not derived from subjective orientations of people toward the world. The choice of concepts reflects instead the impersonal, objective world of the scientist. The key concept of *action system* parallels the perspective of the physical and biological scientist so that the scientific framework may remain consistent and interdisciplinary exchange of information may take place. Terms such as *human encounter, conduct,* or *meeting* of people in action are less workable for they limit the possibility of connecting social theory with physical theory. Social scientists analyze human society in a physical perspective partly because the terms have universal references for all sciences. (The physical scientist would not accept the reverse analogy and analyze the physical world in human terms; such a viewpoint would smack of anthropormorphism and lack reality.) Therefore, the key concepts of science are physical.

For Max Weber, however, social scientific concepts carry subjective meaning. We must understand the social and personal meaning of Calvinism in order to explain the institutional changes that were occurring when it arose in Europe. Such subjective concepts, of course, must be grounded in fact as they exist in the culture. Weber was saying, in effect, that even though subjective terms may function ideologically in society, the social scientist can employ them instrumentally in his effort to understand the workings of that society.

Since Weber was working at what is sometimes referred to in theory as "middle range," a general theory of human action would require a higher level of analysis. If we were to move back to follow Weber's reasoning, the next step toward a general

we must again confront the philosophic underpinnings of the social sciences in order to explore the basis for studying those subjective categories of knowledge which Max Weber said required *Verstehen*. The methodological basis, we would contend, has already begun to be drawn in those studies employing participant observation.

The Method

The beginning of the participant observer approach to research can be traced back through the many early anthropological field studies produced just before, and ever since, the turn of the twentieth century to Frederick LePlay (*Les Ouvriers Européens*, 1855). It is not our purpose to trace the history of this approach, but we must indicate that social and cultural studies, in which participant observation plays a central role, have played an important part in sociological research since the turn of the century. By social and cultural studies we mean qualitative, systematically conceived descriptions and explanations of the symbolic modes of life among distinct human groups.

The study of Thomas and Znaniecki (*The Polish Peasant in Europe and America*) represents a turning point in the history of sociological research. Concentrating as it did upon the qualitative analysis of personal and public documents this study introduced new elements into research and new techniques to study these elements which were not standard to empirical investigation in the traditional sense. The study recognized the fact that

---

theory would include terms with subjective meanings. The post-Socratic Greek concepts of truth, justice, and beauty could serve as a starting point if we recognize their influence and importance in shaping western culture. These concepts have generalizing sources in human experience just as do structure and function. People in every society have an idea of what is right and wrong and an idea of what is beautiful and ugly to them. Of course ideas are relative and therefore various, but there are surely as many variations in social structure and function in societies throughout the world as there are variations on what is conceived to be true, fair, or beautiful.

An exploration of the meanings of such basic concepts which the Greeks considered of importance would very likely lead to a general theory with some relevance to human history and some significance in human experience. Structure and function, then, would become techniques of analysis (not the primary descriptive fact) of society, illuminating other important instrumental categories of knowledge. The controlling instrumental concepts, we would contend, should at best be those categories having reference to both objective and subjective dimensions of the human world. The master concept, *human order*, for example, would serve better as a basic category than *social system* since the former has reference to the realities of both *system* as an objective category and *justice* as a subjective category. These problems are further explored in Chapter 3 on polarities. Our task, however, is methodological rather than substantive: we must point to substantive issues clearly but then move toward developing a method by which appropriate categories may be formulated and studied.

significant social research could take place without reducing data to quantitative terms.

Other similar but smaller cultural studies were produced in the 1920's.[17] Those studies initiated by Robert Park and Ernest Burgess at the University of Chicago included works which were given added significance because the authors contributed sensitive insight to their analyses, insight drawn from their personal knowledge of the people and their way of life in the areas studied. It would follow that the significance of such studies to theory was *not* found in the results of statistical analyses or through the authors' exercising of experimental controls over carefully defined variables. Some of these works are: Frederick Thrasher's *The Gang;* Clifford Shaw's *Brothers in Crime* and *The Jack Roller;* Harvey Zorbaugh's *The Gold Coast and the Slum;* and Louis Wirth's *The Ghetto.*

The Lynds' study of *Middletown* in the 1920's and the follow-up study, *Middletown in Transition,* ten years later, together represent a significant stimulus for the use of informal interviewing in many later community studies. Roethlisberger and Dickson's *Management and the Worker* (1930) represents a major stimulus for later industrial studies to employ participant observation for gathering data. These early studies did not refer to the role of the participant observer as such but rather to an "informal interviewer" and how he should conduct himself to obtain the most accurate information. In certain cases it was obvious to investigators that the use of the schedule and the questionnaire disrupted the social processes which needed to be

---

[17] The field studies conducted in the Department of Sociology at the University of Chicago were heavily influenced by the works of Georg Simmel. This meant that the formative beginnings of participant observation in sociology were socially rather than culturally oriented. Observations focused upon the ways people related to one another and the positions they took in social organization, concentrating on forms of social interaction and processes in community life such as competition, communication, and accomodation. However, there was a personal element added to the content of these field studies which Simmel did not assume in his studies—the social feeling expressed in attitudes and sentiments of subjects recorded in personal documents or actual dialogues as an expressive part of the data.

The history of participant-observer studies shows that researchers in general directed their attention to both cultural and social phenomena. The professional distinction which developed between anthropology (culture) and sociology (social) was not upheld by researchers in their respective fields. The fieldwork of many American anthropologists working abroad shows evidence of a distinct interest in culture. The fieldwork of British anthropologists, however, shows an emphasis on the social and structural aspects of primitive societies. On the other hand, some American anthropologists such as W. Lloyd Warner have also dealt with the social features of community life. William Whyte's study, *Street Corner Society,* was socially oriented and emphasized the structure of the gang and positions of gang members in that structure. Conversely, the studies of sociologist Clifford Shaw of personal attitudes and beliefs of delinquent subcultures in Chicago show cultural interests, as do those of William I. Thomas. In myriad ways, observers have cut across the formal distinctions currently made between social and cultural theory. We must conclude that participant observation harbors no theoretical bias on this point and may serve as a basis for relating these two theoretical modes of interpreting society.

examined; hence, the use of the informal participant observer became important in gathering information that otherwise could not have been obtained.

In the "Yankee City" series, W. Lloyd Warner notes how the use of the questionnaire was inadvisable at certain stages since a participant observer usually did not know the local situation well enough to know how to frame questions and obtain valid results. Schedules and questionnaires were used only in specific instances in *The Social Life of a Modern Community* and instead of the formal approach there is a liberal use of informal interviews. Warner's introduction of the essentials of participant observation into his studies of the community must be understood in part to be a result of his anthropological training. He notes how his approach involved a transfer from field work methods developed to study primitive societies to the study of a New England community:

> The combination of the techniques of observation and interviewing may be illustrated by an ethnographical example. Certain members of an Australian tribe paint themselves, then dance and sing a song (which is a secret ritual) under the direction of a ceremonial leader. The fieldworker, if he knows what is going to occur: (1) interviews the participants before the rite takes place in order to ascertain what they think is about to happen, what the participants themselves ideally expect, what their physical actions are, the words of their song, and the interrelations of the words and actions; (2) becomes, during the ritual event, an observer and records what he sees of the ceremony; and (3) reviews, with participants and others after the performance is over, what has taken place. Thus the interviewer accumulates a knowledge of what the participants say the relations should be, what he observes them to be at a given moment in a rite, and what the several individuals say of them after the event has occurred. A comparison of the several accounts and an analysis, combined with later interviewing for discrepancies, are always most illuminating and rewarding.
>
> Substitution of the leader of an American Legion Memorial Day parade for the Australian ritual leader and his totem dancers does not essentially alter the situation as far as the interview technique is concerned.[18]

If we were to trace the history of participant observation in anthropology we would find that participant observation constitutes a distinct method in itself, one which characterizes all field studies. And even though the study of complex modern communities has involved much more, including the amassing and organizing of a great deal of empirical data drawn from demographic and statistical records of communities, the technique of participant observation gained in definition and grew in significance in sociological research through these early community studies.

---

[18] W. Lloyd Warner and Paul S. Lunt, *The Social Life of a Modern Community* (New Haven: Yale University Press, 1941), p. 46.

One of the first important sociological studies of a community which stressed participant observation as its primary methodology was *Street Corner Society*. The author, William Whyte, discussed his role as a participant observer in the third edition of his book and recalled how be began his training in participant observation in 1937. Other studies followed which made extensive use of the participant observer as the primary source for obtaining data in hospitals, prisons, city neighborhoods, factories, and other settings, to which we will have occasion to refer in the ensuing discussion. Social scientists who have contributed toward the development of this field technique have been Robert Redfield, Conrad Arensberg, Everett Hughes, Alvin Gouldner, Arthur Vidich, Joseph Bensman, Buford Junker, Herbert Gans, Melville Dalton, Howard S. Becker, and Morris Schwartz, among others.

For our purposes we will examine participant observation as a methodology, *i.e.*, in terms of its principles, its procedures, and its philosophy as a basic orientation to the study of human society. We will compare it with traditional empiricism, which has its own underlying principles, procedures, and philosophy. The differences between these two methodologies will be developed as we proceed in Chapter 2, but some can be introduced here.

For example, the methodological emphases that researchers exhibit in initial approaches to subjects differ on basic points. The traditional empiricist considers himself (as a scientist) to be the primary source of knowledge, and trusts his own senses and logic more than he would trust that of his subjects. The participant observer, on the other hand, considers the interpretations of his subjects to have first importance, and initially the observer may not want to understand these interpretations objectively; he may want to understand them subjectively through his own involvement with the culture before he can understand them from any other viewpoint. Thus, the two methods differ in emphasis; however, as we shall continue to point out, both approaches do not entirely ignore the methodological interests represented so well in their opposite.

What is especially distinctive about the method of participant observation is the manner by which the researcher gains knowledge. By taking the role of his subjects he re-creates in his own imagination and experience the thoughts and feelings which are in the minds of those he studies. It is through a process of symbolic interpretation of the "experienced culture" that the observer works with his data and discovers meanings in them. The perspective of the symbolic interactionist in social theory is perhaps best suited to describe the initial importance of this process in gaining accurate knowledge in research. Herbert Blumer brings this point into sharp focus:

> To catch the process, the student must take the role of the acting unit whose behavior he is studying. Since the interpretation is being made by the acting unit in terms of objects designated and appraised, meanings acquired, and

decisions made, the process has to be seen from the standpoint of the acting unit.... To try to catch the interpretive process by remaining aloof as a so-called "objective" observer and refusing to take the role of the acting unit is to risk the worst kind of subjectivism—the objective observer is likely to fill in the process of interpretation with his own surmises in place of catching the process as it occurs in the experience of the acting unit which uses it.[19]

The intent of the participant observer is to "catch the process as it occurs in the experience" of those he studies. With this in mind, let us now examine the principles which define participant observation as they have developed in the experience of researchers.

We shall follow the lead of Durkheim and set down some rules and corollaries which distinguish participant observation field studies. Since this approach has already been in the making for many years, at this point we shall translate what could be considered "rules" into axioms that represent the facts of research experience. Rules set down in a normative sense are introduced at the end of this work, after we have had an opportunity to examine the implications surrounding the facts inherent in the approach today. The axioms which follow are interpretations of the field researcher's experience and anticipate the major issues and problems that we will deal with in more detail in later chapters.

Axiom 1:   The participant observer shares in the life activities and sentiments of people in face-to-face relationships.[20]

Florence Kluckhohn has provided the original and now somewhat classic statement on this fact about participant observation, derived from her field-work in a Mexican village.[21] She describes participant observation as:

---

[19] Herbert Blumer, "Society as Symbolic Interaction," in *Human Behavior and Social Processes: An Interactionist Approach,* ed. Arnold Rose (Boston: Houghton Mifflin Company, 1962), p. 188.

[20] Pp. 13–15 adapted from Severyn T. Bruyn, "The Methodology of Participant Observation," *Human Organization,* 22, No. 3 (Ithaca, N.Y.: Society for Applied Anthropology, Fall 1963), 224–25.

[21] Although Florence Kluckhohn's statement is a standard reference in the literature on participant observation, her work had precedents. Probably the first American to devise the term and describe the observer's role in scientific studies of human groups was Eduard C. Lindeman at Columbia University:

"For experimental purposes the cooperating observers have been called 'participant observers.' The term implies not that the observers are participating in the study but that they are participating in the activities of the group being observed.... There are few such persons available and those who are must be trained. Such training involves its own difficulties. Shall the participant observer be trained to look for exactly the same factors which are sought by the observer from the outside? This method would inevitably lead to error for the participant observer should be free to see many things which the outside observer can never see." (Eduard C. Lindeman, *Social Discovery: An Approach to the Study of Functional Groups* (New York: Republic Publishing Co., 1924), p. 191.)

...conscious and systematic sharing, insofar as circumstances permit, in the life activities, and on occasion, in the interests and affects of a group of persons.[22]

Thus, we may observe at the outset that while the traditional role of the scientist is that of a neutral observer who remains unmoved, unchanged, and untouched in his examination of phenomena, the role of the participant observer requires sharing the sentiments of people in social situations; as a consequence he himself is changed as well as changing to some degree the situation in which he is a participant. The situation which is created is not unlike that created by the famous Heisenberg Uncertainty Principle in physics where the instruments used to measure the *velocity* and *position* of an electron alter the accuracy of measurement. That is, by the very act of observing the position of the electron its velocity is changed, and the more accurately its velocity is determined, the more indefinite its position becomes. In our case of participant observation the effects are reciprocal for observer and observed. The participant observer seeks, on the one hand, to take advantage of the changes due to his presence in the group by recording these changes as part of his study, and on the other hand, to reduce the changes to a minimum by the manner in which he enters into the life of the group.

Researchers have noted that although they become changed through their participation it is important that the change not be total in character, that some part should remain unchanged and detached. Therefore, even though they "share" the experience, they are not entirely "of it." Herein lies a second significant descriptive trait of the researcher's role.

Corollary: The role of the participant observer requires both detachment and personal involvement.

In a report on their experience as participant observers in a mental hospital, Morris and Charlotte Schwartz point out that the personal involvement of the researcher should be accepted and recognized as part of the research process:

> The issue is not whether he [participant observer] will become emotionally involved, but rather the nature of the involvement. The involvement, whether it is closer to one end of the continuum (*sympathetic identification*) or the other end (*projective distortion*), is very little a function of an observer's role. Rather, it is primarily a function of his experience, awareness, and personality constellation and the way these become integrated with a particular situation. ...

---

[22] Florence Kluckhohn, "The Participant-Observer Technique in Small Communities," *American Journal of Sociology*, **46** (November 1940), 331.

Sympathetic identification includes empathic communication and imaginative participation in the life of the observed through identification and role-taking. In this type of involvement the observer is both detached and effectively participating; he feels no need to moralize or judge the interaction; his attitude is one of interested curiousity and matter-of-fact inquiry directed toward understanding the observed.[23]

In seeking to share something of the experience of the observed the researcher must not only become personally involved, but must also acquire a role which can function within the culture of the observed. There is no standard role which he can assume, but the general requirements for the role have become evident from the experience of researchers.

Axiom 2: The participant observer is a normal part of the culture and the life of the people under observation.

The role of the participant observer may take many forms but in any case it is designed to be a normal part of the life of the people being studied. It has not been the intent of participant observers to create roles which are "forced" on or considered artificial to the ways of the people under study. Such roles may prove in the future to have some research value, but this has not been the practice of researchers up to now. The type of role which is taken is affected by the research design, the framework of the culture to be studied and the abilities of particular researchers to assume tasks which can be accepted as a natural part of a culture. Buford Junker, in his excellent review of fieldwork methods, describes four different kinds of roles which the participant observer may assume according to the design and purpose of his study. Portions of this very useful typology of participant observation are described below:

1. *Complete Participant.* In this role, the observer's activities as such are wholly concealed. The fieldworker is or becomes a complete member of an in-group, thus sharing secret information guarded from outsiders. The fieldworker's freedom to observe outside the in-group system of relationships may be severely limited, and in such a role tends to block perception of the workings of the reciprocal relations between the in-group and the larger social system, nor is it easy to switch from this to another role permitting observation of the details of the larger system.

2. *Participant as Observer.* In this role, the fieldworker's observer activities are *not* wholly concealed, but are "kept under wraps" as it were, or subordinated to activities as participant, activities which give the people in the situation

---

23 Morris S. Schwartz and Charlotte G. Schwartz, "Problems in Participant Observation," *American Journal of Sociology*, **60** (January 1955), 350–51.

their main bases for evaluating the fieldworker in his role. This role may limit access to some kinds of information, perhaps especially at the secret level; precisely how he "rates" as a pseudo-"Member of the Wedding" will affect the fieldworker's ability to communicate below the level of public information.

3. *Observer as Participant.* This is the role in which the observer's activities as such are made publicly known at the outset, are more or less publicly sponsored by people in the situation studied, and are intentionally *not* "kept under wraps." The role may provide access to a wide range of information and even secrets may be given to the fieldworker when he becomes known for keeping them, as well as for guarding confidential information. In this role the social scientist might conceivably achieve maximum freedom to gather information but only at the price of accepting maximum constraints upon his reporting. . . .

4. *Complete Observer.* This describes a range of roles in which, at one extreme, the observer hides behind a one-way mirror, perhaps equipped with sound film facilities, and at the other extreme, his activities are completely public in a special kind of theoretical group where there are, by consensus, "no secrets" and "nothing sacred."[24]

The types of roles we are chiefly reviewing here are the "observer as participant" and the "participant as observer" types, which are jointly referred to as the participant observer. However, it must be recognized that researchers are all to some degree both observers and participants in all situations. These two functions, as we shall note in more detail later, are complementary aspects of all human activity.

Florence Kluckhohn originally made the distinction between general, specific, and complementary roles. In her study of a Mexican village she took the role of a local storekeeper (a role complementary to her customers) and thus came to understand reflectively the kind of life led by the villagers in this role. She also took the role of a local housewife, which she conceived as a general role similar to that of other women in the village. Examples of general roles which in Junker's terms would be "complete participants" would be the researcher's role as prisoner in studying prison socialization,[25] and the role of an Air Force recruit which a researcher undertook to study a military program.[26]

The researcher's interest in observing and participating in the natural life

---

24 Buford H. Junker, *Field Work: An Introduction to the Social Sciences* (Chicago: University of Chicago Press, 1960), pp. 35–38. Reprinted by permission of The University of Chicago Press. Copyright 1960 by The University of Chicago Press.

25 Hans Reimer, "Socialization in the Prison Community," *American Prison Association Proceedings* (1937), pp. 151–55.

26 Mortimer A. Sullivan, Jr., Stuart A. Queen, and Ralph C. Patrick, Jr., "Participant Observation in a Military Program," *American Sociological Review*, **23** (December 1958), 660–67.

of the group is not unrelated to the naturalistic philosophy of his scientific approach. It is true that he disturbs the natural behavior of the group to some extent by the introduction of his own presence, but he seeks to minimize the amount of disturbance which he might create in order to interpret more adequately the natural functions or principles governing the life of the group. He may introduce variables other than himself into the group, and still treat the phenomenon naturalistically, but this increases the complexity of problems with which he must contend.

The natural way in which participant observers have sought to become a part of the social setting which they seek to study can be illustrated in different ways. In *Deep South* a white fieldworker and his wife and a Negro fieldworker and his wife lived in the community they studied for a little over one and one-half years. The roles of the researchers are described as follows:

> In Old City they conformed to the behavioral modes of their respective castes;...after about six months of residence, they appeared to be accepted as full-fledged members of their caste and class groups, and dropped their initial roles of researchers. Their observations of group behavior were therefore made in the actual societal context, in situations where they participated as members of the community, within the limits of their caste and class roles. The interviews were also obtained in this normal context, and except where matters of fact, such as factory or plantation management were concerned, few questions were asked. Every effort was made to adapt the principles of "free associative" interviewing to intimate social situations, so that the talk of the individual or group would not be guided by the fieldworker, but would follow the normal course of talk in that part of the society.[27]

In his study, *Street Corner Society*, William Whyte became a member of a gang. He describes one phase of his activities with the gang:

> At one time I was nominated as secretary of the Italian Community Club. My first impulse was to decline the nomination, but then I reflected that the secretary's job is normally considered simply a matter of dirty work—writing the minutes and handling correspondence. I accepted and found that I could write a very full account of the progress of the meeting as it went on under the pretext of keeping notes for the minutes.
>
> While I sought to avoid influencing individuals or groups, I tried to be helpful in the way a friend is expected to help in Cornerville. When one of the boys had to go downtown on an errand and wanted company, I went along with him. When somebody was trying to get a job and had to write a letter about himself, I helped him to compose it, and so on.[28]

---

[27] Allison Davis, Burleigh Gardner, and Mary Gardner, *Deep South* (Chicago: University of Chicago Press, 1941), p. viii.

[28] William F. Whyte, *Street Corner Society* (2nd ed.) (Chicago: University of Chicago Press, 1955), p. 305.

George Homans reports on the efforts of a researcher to become a normal part of an industrial setting in his description of the bank wiring observation room:

> ...The research staff believed that it would be hard to get the men's cooperation in continuing to work just as they had been working. It did not turn out to be. Habit may be too strong for people even when they know they are being watched. In the background, moreover, were the earlier researches, in which the staff had made pretty intimate studies of workers' lives without once violating a confidence. No promises had been broken; no person hurt. After all, the observer did not in the least resemble a spy. The operators had been told just what he was in the room to do, and he did just that. After a period of constraint and misunderstanding, they first became used to the observer, then friendly with him, and they drew him into their conversations. The clearest sign that they had lost all suspicion of him was their willingness to do and say things in front of him that broke or implied breaking various rules of the company. There is little evidence, either in output and earnings, or in general activities and conversations, that the workers' behavior was unlike what it had been in the main department.[29]

The kind of role which is assumed by the researcher is also determined by his abilities (*i.e.,* whether he is able to speak the language, socially adjust to the environs, etc.) and the norms of the culture itself. The participant observer must be able to find a satisfactory entrée, develop and maintain a role adequate to meet his scientific needs, and finally be able to terminate relationships in a way reasonably consistent with cultural expectations. These requirements have of course varied markedly from case to case; an American business firm poses considerably different requirements from a primitive tribe in Africa. The general principles which may guide the researcher are still being formulated, but it does seem clear that if he has sought to find a role that is natural to a culture, he will consequently find that his scientific objectives and techniques are interdependent with the cultural role he assumes in the social setting.

Corollary: The scientific role of the participant observer is interdependent with his social role in the culture of the observed.

In his scientific role the participant observer seeks to apprehend, register, interpret, and conceptualize the social facts and meanings which he finds in a prescribed area of study. He is interested in people as they are, not as he thinks they ought to be according to some standard of his own; he is interested in the lack of uniformity as well as the uniformities of their cul-

---

[29] George C. Homans, *The Human Group* (New York: Harcourt, Brace & World, Inc.. 1950), pp. 53–54.

ture, in the unpredictable as well as the predictable state of human existence. He finds that those interests which are embodied in this, his scientific (observer) role, coincide in many ways with his social role as participant. He finds his social role an interdependent and indispensable part of the scientific process.

This social interdependence is often not seen or ignored by scientists who are hidden away in their laboratories, but it becomes a distinguishing characteristic of the role of the participant observer,[30] causing many problems and nonscientific repercussions in terms of confidences, commitments, and other personal involvements which penetrate the life of the fieldworker. The participant observer assumes he can make these commitments and become involved without ignoring scientific standards or the interests of the people he is studying.

The researcher may even take into consideration the interests of his subjects in formulating his hypotheses and designing his study. William Whyte describes the replanning of his study as growing out of a gang leader's interest in a recreation project.[31] Similarly, Whyte's planning of an "action-research project" grew out of a concern with personal problems which gang members were facing. Thus, the personal lives of the people the participant observer studies often become of special importance to him in the fulfillment of both his scientific role and his social role in the culture he studies. Without this primary interest in his subjects as persons the data would become liable to distortion. He must assume that, in this state of interdependence, one role makes the other possible.

It should be evident what kinds of problems this fact about participant observation raises: problems both of how to become a natural part of the life of the observed; and thereafter, how to maintain scientific integrity while affectively involved in the research. If scientific integrity is maintained, there may be problems of ethical integrity in terms of personal obligations and commitments which develop in the process of research. These and other problems are subjects for our discussion in the ensuing part of the book.

In view of suggesting something of the depth to which the facts of participant observation carry us in our analysis, we will state one more axiom which exists at still another level of interpretation of facts about this research. In truth, it is an assumption which takes us one step beyond the more apparent facts of the case.

---

[30] The close interdependence of scientific and social roles and the problems it raises have been noted in the reports of many researchers. Cf. Alvin Gouldner, *Patterns of Industrial Bureaucracy* (New York: Free Press of Glencoe, Inc., 1954), Appendix; Melville Dalton, *Men Who Manage* (New York: John Wiley & Sons, Inc., 1959), pp. 282–84.

[31] Whyte, *Street Corner Society*, pp. 325–28.

Axiom 3: The role of the participant observer reflects the social process of living in society.

In a very real sense, the researcher participates in a social process which has meaning for people in groups outside the group he studies, since the processes of living in any society are similar for people everywhere. If the researcher reveals insight into the collective symbols of people in one group in one community, his conclusions can be understood and have significance for people in other communities, even in an entire nation living with the same symbols. Research into the culture of a particular family (*e.g.,* Oscar Lewis' *The Children of Sanchez*) can provide a basis for understanding the meaning of the politico-economic transition of a whole nation over a given period of time. Research into the culture and organization of a local factory (*e.g.,* Alvin Gouldner's *Patterns of Industrial Bureaucracy*) can provide insight into the nature of corporate organization at the national level. The more the researcher shows perception into the universality and relevance of the culture in the particular group he studies, the more likely his conclusions will have significance beyond the local setting.

The same principle applies to the novelist working in the context of society. Thomas Mann's story of one family *(Buddenbrooks)* perceptively reveals the changing social realities of capitalism in Europe at the turn of the century. Albert Camus' story of a community in crisis *(The Plague)* sensitively reveals the heroic character of people that transcends the boundaries of any single community or any single nation. The setting for a novelist or a scientific researcher may be local, but the work as a whole can clarify and explain the cultural character of man or the social trends in society. One major difference between the artist and the social scientist, at this point, is that the latter seeks certainty outside himself by following rules and procedures for verifying his findings.

The epistemological basis for interpreting these collective symbols is an intuitive process (as much as rational) and, as we contend in later chapters, is a process that can be scientifically verified. Charles Cooley was one of the first American sociologists to see this special element in the research process when he spoke of how the mind which studies social processes interprets symbols differently from the mind which studies physical and organic processes:

> The human mind participates in social processes in a way that it does not in any other processes. It is itself a sample, a phase, of those processes, and is capable, under favorable circumstances, of so far identifying itself with the general movement of a group as to achieve a remarkably just anticipation of what the group will do. Prediction of this sort is largely intuitive rather than intellectual. . . .[32]

---

[32] Charles Cooley, *Sociological Theory and Social Research* (New York: Holt, Rinehart & Winston, Inc., 1930), p. 308.

George Herbert Mead takes us one step further into the meaning of this axiom about social process. He suggests that there are elements in the social process common to man in society—common to any person who would live in any society. All people, Mead has said, must engage in social interaction and symbolic communication with one another to be members of society. In order to engage in symbolic communication, Mead insisted, man must engage in the process of role-taking. All people must learn to take the roles of others at some time in their lives in order to communicate in any human sense. This is a social fact universal to man in society.

Essential to the method of participant observation, in fact, making the method possible, then, is the process of role-taking. The researcher's understanding of this process should give him a basis for knowing man in the most fundamental sense in the light of Meadean theory. A full understanding of the method should give him potential access to the symbols of any society. If the researcher is aware of the hazards and the rules of the method of participant observation, then he should be able accurately to find the cultural meanings contained in any group he studies—some meanings of which may lie at the root of man's existence in society.

Mead states that the end of the role-taking process is the complete self, which "reflects the unity and the structure of the social process as a whole."[33] While Mead never seriously examined the tensions and disharmonies involved in the process of role-taking, which we would contend are also a part of the research process of participant observation, we must recognize that the aim of the researcher is to take part in the socialization process, but as do the other true members of a culture, to the point where his inner experience can reflect the "unity and structure of the whole."

Up to this point the participant observer generally has been conceived of as an outsider who seeks to take part in a culture unlike his own. It is

---

[33] Anselm Strauss, ed., *The Social Psychology of George Herbert Mead* (Chicago: University of Chicago Press, 1956), p. 221. Mead's theory leads us to observe how the poet's work can be visible in the content of social research as much as that of the novelist or the playwright. While the symbols of the novel and the play tend to be bound by a particular time and place and by individual characterizations in a social context, the symbols of a poem tend to be spiritual, timeless, and universal. Although it is true that the subject of a poem may have a societal context, as in the American poetry of Carl Sandburg ("Chicago") or Walt Whitman ("I Hear America Singing"), nevertheless, the trend in symbolism is toward universality. The more powerful poems (such as William Bryant's "Thanatopsis" on the subject of death) need not contain any extended reference to historical time or place or to any special societal context. In the Meadean sense, the social researcher also need not be time-bound or place-bound in some of his descriptive interpretations of the people he studies, so long as he is accurate in his work. If he finds that the timeless symbols of love, hate, or loneliness are expressed culturally in what he observes, he may record them poetically. As a social scientist, of course, he has limits that a poet would not have. He must first be true to the cultural reality he finds outside himself. Then, he must communicate his symbolic interpretations in ways that colleagues can understand professionally, including the relation such symbols have to social and cultural theory.

now apparent that at another level certain elements that comprise the participant observer method are fundamental to the social act (in the Meadean sense) and therefore are, to some degree, part of all research and human activity. This is why a study of the role of the participant observer must go to the heart of methodology in the social sciences.

Summary

Since the observer plays a natural, interdependent role in the culture he studies, sharing in the life and becoming involved in the activities of the people he observes, new methodological problems are necessarily set up to be solved which have not been previously encountered. Unlike the traditional empiricist, the participant observer must view a culture just as the people he is studying view it, including reflecting on the social process in which he is inwardly engaged. This means he sees goals and interests of people in the same way that the people see them, not as functions or experimental causes as would the traditional empiricist; it means that he sees people in the concrete reality in which they present themselves in daily experiences, not as abstractions as would the traditional empiricist; it means he senses that these people act freely within the scope of what they see as the possible, not as determined agents of social forces as the traditional empiricist would see them. These are matters which must be examined in more detail before we can shift our concern to the implications that these differences have for social theory.

2

Polar Orientations
in Research

The role which the participant observer has taken in his research orientation presents certain methodological contrasts to that of the social scientist who follows the more traditional principles of empirical research. We must, therefore, trace some of these differences in detail to determine more exactly what implications the role of the participant observer may have in sociological theory and method. To do this we will examine six dimensions of research methodology in which the contrasts are most evident: (1) the perspective of the observer (inner and outer); (2) the mode of interpretation (concrete and operational); (3) the mode of conception (sensitizing and formalizing); (4) the mode of description (synthesis and analysis); (5) the modes of explanation including principles (telic and causal); and (6) models (voluntarism and determinism).

The Perspective: Inner and Outer

Auguste Comte, in formulating the new field he called sociology, described three stages or levels of man's explanation of the world. He said that in the first stage ("theological"), man sought to explain the world in terms of his inner feelings which he projected outward as manifestations of the physical world. Rivers, mountains, trees, and stars were given life-like characteristics; they were either gods or were controlled by gods who had feelings and a spirit like man himself. But man, Comte said, was able to transcend this primitive stage of explanation to where he was able to treat the world about him abstractly, as though the stars, for example, were controlled by abstract forces, such as attraction and repulsion rather than human feelings. This stage ("metaphysical"), Comte noted, was transcended as man entered a third stage ("Positivist" or scientific) in which the world was explained in terms of laws. Man's explanation of society was now passing through its second stage and entering into its third and final stage. Society, he felt, was to be understood through laws in the same way the outer world had come to be understood by the physical scientists.

One major point which Comte missed in his perceptive account of man's developing ability to explain the world was that the explanatory process did not necessarily begin with man projecting his inner world outward to explain the physical world, but rather involved a creative alternation between the two worlds as man gradually came to interpret one by the other. That is, the signs and symbols man created to explain one reality were used to describe the newly sensed or felt reality of the other. The many words which man came to select to explain his inner life were derivatives of the signs and symbols (words) which he formulated to describe the outer world. Thus, the word *spirit* in Greek, Hebrew, and Chinese may be traced to its original association with the physical "breath" of man. Those words which seem to stand as independent representations of our inner perspective can be traced back to those words which originally represented an outer reality. Arthur Waley notes how certain conceptions took on meaning in this way over two thousand years ago in China:

> But in the period centering around 300 B.C. the question was asked (Mencius, VI), is not the conduct that we call *i* (moral) merely the outward expression of a feeling about what is right and wrong, and is it not this feeling, rather than the outward manifestation of it, that we ought to call morality? Thus just as the words for soul, spirit, etc., had begun their careers as names for outside things, and ended by being names for parts of man's interior, psychological equipment, so the word *i*, which at first meant little more than sensible, reasonable conduct, came in the end to mean something very like "conscience."[1]

Down through the literate history of man one finds a basic polarity evident between what may be called the outer perspective and the inner perspective. What man has come to know about himself and the world has developed out of the gradual, creative alternation between these two perspectives. Man has appeared to explore one in terms of the other until he finds in various ways that he has reached the productive limits of the symbols in one perspective and then proceeds in the other direction.

Philosophy has conceptualized the differences between these two perspectives into two major systems of thought roughly distinguished as naturalism and idealism. Naturalistic philosophies have maintained an outer perspective of observation while idealistic philosophies have maintained an inner

---

[1] Arthur Waley, *The Way and Its Power: A Study of the Tao Te Ching and Its Place in Chinese Thought* (New York: Grove Press, 1958), pp. 32–33.

perspective. Both philosophies have undergone considerable change since their origin in the seventeenth century.[2]

The terms "inner" and "outer" perspective are used here as our basic terms because idealism and naturalism have existed in such variety and have been subject to so many special emphases and prejudices that they are helpful only from a historical viewpoint. Idealism and naturalism represent philosophic currents which have run their courses in history, sometimes colliding and re-forming, sometimes merging into a new stream of thought, as particular philosophers have managed to bring together selected elements in them. In each case, however, the new philosophic formations have resulted in a special metaphysics which we wish to avoid in our present formulation of the method of participant observation.

Much of twentieth-century philosophy, for example, is a revolt against idealism. Included in this revolt would be Marxism, positivism, British analytic philosophy, pragmatism, and existentialism. Pragmatists and existentialists would normally fall within the broad province of idealism in philosophy, except that they both rejected its traditional forms. William James rejected the "a priori reasons, fixed principles, closed systems, pretended absolutes, and origins" in favor of facts with "concreteness" and

---

[2] The formulator of the modern variant of naturalism was Thomas Hobbes, who conceived all of nature to be basically materialistic. He believed that all man's actions, thoughts, and feelings could be reduced to their true state as small particles in motion. A later naturalistic interpretation is illustrated in Jeremy Bentham's philosophy that all man's actions could be determined and understood by weighing the gains and losses people felt existed between pleasureful and painful consequences. A still later development is the theory of Karl Marx, who broadened the particle theory of Hobbes and the physiological theory of Bentham to a sociological base in economic determinism. The changing economic forces became the mechanism through which all culture was determined. Still later, neo-positivists broadened the position further to include man's *general behavior* (not simply economic) as the foundation for understanding and predicting man's actions. Throughout this development, however, the deterministic-mechanistic image of man was retained and it was assumed that all behavioral phenomena could be quantified. The foundations of modern science have been built from this philosophy.

The modern expression of idealism took form with Bishop George Berkeley who held the radical view that the external world had no real existence outside of mental processes. He felt that physical properties could not be known outside the mind, and therefore the mind itself was the source of all knowledge. Later developments such as German idealism (as in Fichte and Hegel) accepted physical reality but insisted on the supremacy of the mind as a source and creator of knowledge. A still more recent variety, called personal idealism, focuses upon personality as the source of knowledge. The modern conceptions of idealism base the source of knowledge in experience, with its many dimensions, thus broadening to a position which, while emphasizing the importance of the mind to produce knowledge independent of external factors, does not ignore the place of these factors in the experience of man.

Some philosophers would today interpret naturalism so broadly as to see it threading its way across the whole pattern of western thought, including strains of idealism. (See **Vergilius Ferm**, "Varieties of Naturalism," *A History of Philosophical Systems*

"adequacy" in his formulation of pragmatism.[3] Existentialists rejected ideal-ism for devaluing the "particular" and for its failure to respond to the personal realities of living in a confused world. Idealism therefore, has these historical complexities which, at this point of inquiry, we do not wish to introduce into our discussion of participant observation.

The terms inner and outer, then, are intended only to be rough approxi-mations of these polar tendencies in the intellectual cultures of man. Our use of them is not to suggest that they are ultimately real, but only that they are convenient categories which are descriptive of these opposing tendencies, within which the method of participant observation may find some status. The status of the method appears to fall most logically within the inner perspective, for in many respects participant observation has shown itself to be in almost cataclysmic opposition to the scientific outlook in which it emerged; but it nevertheless cuts complexly across the traditional categories of idealism and naturalism as much as did pragmatism when it appeared.[4] The method of participant observation functions as a method for discovering human meanings in culture, one of which could be the meaning of tradi-tional empiricism as it exists in the values and operations of the social scientist.

The basic methodological scheme of the scientist stemmed originally from

---

(New York: Philosophical Library, Inc., 1950), pp. 429–40.) Other philosophers would define naturalism and idealism as two distinctly different traditions whose differences have yet to be systematically integrated in modern terms. (For this view-point and an exploratory synthesis, see D. W. Gotshalk, *Metaphysics in Modern Times* (Chicago: University of Chicago Press, 1940).)

René Descartes, generally recognized as the father of modern philosophy, is responsible for introducing the mind-body dichotomy about which so much philo-sophical discussion has revolved. The Cartesian solution of the dualism (the famous pineal gland account of the interaction of mind and body) proved to be wholly untenable. Thus, the two philosophic systems of which we speak began in an unhappy alliance. It is important to note, too, that there are two problem areas implied in these philosophic traditions: epistemology and ontology. Our primary reference here is to epistemology but the two areas are closely related. Descartes' epistemology was idealistic, but his ontology was not. Hobbes and Berkeley represent the dichotomous traditions (naturalism and idealism) most consistently in their philosophies. We shall later distinguish the ontological perspective of society that issued from these philo-sophic traditions.

3 For further reading where these points are treated in detail, see William Barrett, "The Twentieth Century in Its Philosophy," in *Philosophy in the Twentieth Century: An Anthology*, eds. William Barrett and Henry D. Aiken (New York: Random House, Inc., 1962), Vol. I, pp. 19–43.

4 The method of participant observation is close to the American tradition of pragmatism, the development of which was furthered by Charles Pierce, William James, and John Dewey. Participant observation and pragmatism are difficult to com-pare because special theories of pragmatism have existed in such variety. Nevertheless, they are similar insofar as they both hold that the acquisition of knowledge con-stitutes "progressive approximations" to reality and is based broadly in man's experi-ence, in contrast to the more narrow interpretations of positivism and behaviorism. Participant observation and pragmatism are both interested in the theory of meaning

early conceptions of naturalism. The scientist traditionally has taken an outside view of his subject, and through his systematic observations of the behavior of his data, has discovered regularities which are translatable into quantitative terms. The positions of the physicist, chemist, biologist, and empirical sociologist have been the same or very similar in this respect. Each observes the behavior of his subjects with varying degrees of control over them. The social scientist has carried this naturalistic tradition into the study of man.

As this tradition was applied to man, however, certain problems arose in method and theory. Many sociologists and theorists of other fields in the history of social science have stressed the importance of adding idealistic elements to the naturalistic foundation of social science. The additions have advanced slowly but steadily in patchwork fashion. The work of Talcott Parsons, for example, has been a major effort to break away from crude naturalistic interpretations and introduce subjective elements, but his resulting theory emphasized a severe analytic standpoint and retained physical metaphors in key concepts. The work of British anthropologists such as Bronislaw Malinowski and Radcliffe-Brown was a break from viewing man in a physiological perspective to a "functional" perspective which stressed the *human* needs of man. Early functionalism, however, retained strong physiological overtones while gaining in a human perspective. Robert Merton was able to transform the physiological perspective of functionalism into a pragmatic perspective more broadly based on social experience. Merton defined "functions" as the "consequences" of social structures, and the focus of research and theory shifted toward the realities of human organization. Slowly, a human standpoint has been emerging, showing signs of becoming the dominant theme of the social sciences.

The method of participant observation is, in part, another step in the direction of completing this picture. It adds more of the human perspective to sociocultural theory, and further, adds principles of method which make it more possible to study society in the light of the added perspective. A theoretical element that gains in importance in this perspective is culture.

The participant observer is concerned with the inner character of culture

---

and in making statements of fact with "warranted assertibility" in the pursuit of truth. However, pragmatism has emphasized certain aspects of truth and truth-finding as more important than other aspects, in contrast to the participant observer who recognizes that these other aspects can take precedence in the minds of people whom he studies. The participant observer is interested in verifying the existence and ascertaining the nature of these other aspects. He does not try "to interpret each notion by tracing its respective practical consequences," as William James once said of pragmatism. The participant observer does not see truth-finding solely as a process of trial and error, as do many pragmatists. Rather, the participant observer is interested in discovering different "right ways" to find truth, as defined by different peoples without his own philosophic judgment about them, and also in finding how these ways compare to one another through his separate observations of cultures.

and its meaning in man's life, but he does not ignore the external manifestations. He assumes that knowledge can be derived beyond the outer manifestations of culture, from active, albeit controlled, participation in the life
of the observed, and that by means of direct communication and empathic
relationships with those he is studying he can gain important insight into
the nature of the culture he studies. The aim of the participant observer
is to understand people from their own frame of reference. He cannot accept
the Comtean assumption that one perspective (the inner) is to be explained
solely in terms of another (the outer). He believes that the inner can be
explained in terms of itself.

If he works with the inner perspective the participant observer finds that
his data are different from those of the traditional empiricist. That is, the
participant observer does not initially explain his data in impersonal categories or definitive concepts; rather, he usually finds it more cogent to
express his data in personal terms in the form of a portrait or an illustrative
story—although he seeks to place any such record in an objective context.
He finds he can explain his findings more adequately through rhetorical
devices and cultural symbols which he expects to be related to the theoretical
development of his field.

Different types of thought operate within these two viewpoints. The inner
and outer perspectives of man are visible in his modes of interpretation,
conception, description, and explanation of sociocultural phenomena. The
dualistic tendencies operative in these two perspectives are treated separately
here for analytical reasons but they interpenetrate in actual research.

Modes of Interpretation :   Concrete and Operational

By *mode of interpretation* we mean how the researcher initially appre-
hends and records his data. Two contrasting initial approaches to data
have developed in social research: one is closely associated with traditional
empiricism and the other with participant observation.

The experimentalist has traditionally used procedures which he calls
operationalizing—i.e., defining and identifying the outer visible conditions
under which he conducts an experiment.[5] These procedures have been
fundamental to all quantitative research. A term may be called an *operational concept* when it implicitly sums up all the procedures that measure the

---

[5] While operational procedures are often thought to be based purely upon sense
experience, this is clearly a fiction which the operationalist must knowingly tolerate
in his work. That is, any particular experiment must have some logical and social
inferences made at crucial points which are not based directly upon sense experience.
Nevertheless, this procedure with its special emphases has proven itself useful and
represents an important part of the pattern of social research.

phenomenon the term identifies. An example would be the operational concept *intelligence* when its meaning is assumed to be based upon the procedures used to obtain an IQ. That is, intelligence in this case would be the measured results of the application of specific psychological tests under specific conditions and graded in a specific manner.

The participant observer has more frequently followed procedures which may be termed *concretizing—i.e.,* illustrating and identifying particular symbolic meanings which are significant to the culture being studied. Like the work of the experimentalist, the work of the participant observer is a record of procedures but of a different kind. The participant observer must carefully describe how he personally came to understand the particular meanings he studies. These meanings can be expressed in a term which we will call a *concrete universal*—when it is explained by particular experiences through which it can be understood and when it refers to a phenomenon which is shared by everyone in the context of the culture under study. These experiences generally function at a symbolic level of meaning which cannot be simply inferred from observing external behavior. The meaning is conveyed to outsiders through such rhetorical means as metaphors, analogies, allegories, parables, and paradoxes. Since the concrete universal is not a part of the language of empirical research, we will discuss it here in more detail.

Every culture has symbols which are personally meaningful to members of that culture. A criminal reacts most strongly to the term *stoolie* or *rat* and members of a gang may fight to the death over what that symbol represents to them. The members of one Christian sect are deeply moved by their interpretation of the "blood of Christ" and may sacrifice their lives guided by that image. Understanding the personal meaning such symbols have for people may be the key to understanding their culture and anticipating their actions under certain conditions. Some personal symbols are very complex and vary in their meaning under different circumstances, but in any case the observer must comprehend the meaning as members of the subculture comprehend it. He must then communicate it to colleagues rhetorically by illustration and comparison, describing those particular events or experiences that insiders and outsiders have in common.

This is how human understanding is achieved in the ordinary course of living in society. The meaning of agony, for example, is communicated by one person to another person by illustrating the totally helpless and generally hopeless feeling which overcomes people when in great physical or psychological pain. The agony may be a collective phenomenon as described and dramatized in Euripides' play *The Trojan Women* or as felt and recorded by Jews who saw their members slaughtered by Nazis under Hitler's regime. The personal meaning of such complex cultural experiences as these may be the vital focal point of a study of a society from which one is seeking to draw scientific knowledge. Many cultural experiences are explained best through subjective symbols—an area of study usually restricted to the arts, religion, and the humanities—or sometimes explained in everyday words such as agony which carry their meaning personally to communicants. While the qualitative character and spirit of collective experiences have not been a traditional part of empirical research because of the problem of subjectivity, we know they can be a legitimate part of cultural studies in participant observation.

Sociological studies of people in communities or societies struck by calamity can provide the beginning for a study of the larger meaning of the human condition reflecting agony or despair. Learning from such studies, the theorist, in his ineluctable way, would analyze such states of being. He would then, at best, familiarize himself with literary studies of tragedy and formulate the basic principles explaining tragedy as a master concept. Taking some lessons from the literary critic who has applied theories of tragedy to the drama and the novel to illuminate the character of man, the social scientist would apply these theories to historical studies of societies and sociocultural realities revealed through studies in participant observation. While it cannot function as an operational or ideal concept in the traditional sense, a concept of tragedy can still be described definitively so that we can understand better the concrete meaning of agony or despair.[6]

There are different levels of adequacy in understanding which must be clarified in any such effort. The level which is adequate depends upon the purposes involved. The concept of agony, for example, may be differentiated readily for most people from experiences of delight or happiness, but it requires special efforts to distinguish its relation to frenzy, frustration, worry, or anxiety. The interpretation may only approximate the meaning held by those originally experiencing the agony observed, but it may still be sufficient to provide a crucial understanding of the culture from which generalizations may be drawn.

The term *concrete universal* may sound clumsy or difficult to use here, but it is appropriate for our purposes. We use *universal* in the same sense that a social statistician would use the term to refer to that group of people from which a sample is drawn. The universe may be as small as a street corner gang or as large as society itself. And, as is now evident, social observations may identify those basic human elements in culture which refer directly to what is experienced by people in every society. Elementary forms of social life may be found universally in any community in which people daily live. These forms are found through experiences of authority, dominance, status, and kinship, or they may be found through experiences of social or personal needs such as recognition, mastery, security, and new

---

6 For a description of the meaning of tragedy as it is revealed through the comparative literature of different societies, see Herbert J. Muller, *The Spirit of Tragedy* (New York: Washington Square Press, Inc., 1965).

experience, to use W. I. Thomas' selection of types of intercultural wishes.[7] The universal forms of group life can be understood by different ethnic groups if procedures for identifying the meaning of the terms are translated into the language or communication system of the separate groups.

It is in the concrete experience that man's understanding of tragedy is rooted; it is also in the concrete experience that man's understanding of comedy develops. Patterns of comedy and tragedy are sociological phenomena which grow out of a common inner life and a common culture and which constitute part of the human perspective of man. If the theorist is to understand these types of human reality, he must be able to understand them in a concrete sense. If such concepts are to find their significant place in the systematic explanation of man in society, the theorist must have data from which to build his theoretical forms. The participant observer is in a unique position to supply this data.

Social experience can be both concrete and universal at the same time. We have said that it is *universal* if the particular experiences have the same or similar meanings among all those in the culture studied; particular experiences are *concrete* if they are felt personally. In this sense concrete universal has a different meaning from that formulated by Georg Friedrich Hegel, in whose philosophy the particular was lost in the rational form or the universal idea. The universal idea was the ultimate truth for Hegel. In the framework of social science, however, the ultimate truth can only emerge through the entire pattern of knowledge which unfolds through the combined work of the researcher and the theorist. If the symbols of abstraction were widely believed to be the "real" in the Hegelian sense of ultimately replacing the symbols of sense and personal meaning, we would conclude that the results would be a gross distortion of the nature of human society.

Modes of Conception: Sensitizing and Formalizing

While the researcher makes his original interpretations of data by concretizing and operationalizing his procedures, he inevitably engages in some

---

7 William I. Thomas and Florian Znaniecki, *The Polish Peasant in Europe and America* (Chicago: University of Chicago Press, 1918–20), p. 73. It is impossible to imagine that the elemental fact of social recognition does not exist universally in the experience of every human being who can communicate, for a form of recognition occurs in the act of communicating. It is likely that if one studied the reports of anthropologists carefully one would find as much universality of social and cultural form as anthropologists have found diversity and relativity. Because of his interest in describing diversity in cultures the anthropologist sometimes overlooks the unanimity. The very fact that the language of one people can be translated into the language of another people involves a recognition of the universality of cultural experience along with its diversity.

degree of higher concept construction in the process. The kinds of concepts most closely associated with these two modes of interpretation differ dualistically, and the ultimate effects are in different kinds of theorizing.

Two types of concepts which have been considered important in social research are the sensitizing and the formalizing concepts. The latter may be illustrated by the *ideal type* which Max Weber so aptly describes—*i.e.*, a generalized concept which does not describe a concrete case but rather serves as a model from which a number of concrete cases may be compared and analyzed. The ideal type contains no statements of empirical fact as does the operational concept, and while its elements are independently variable, they necessarily must have a fixed relation to one another within the definition of the type. The modern use of the term *bureaucracy* as an ideal type is drawn from Weber's analysis,[8] and consists of a hierarchy of offices, official rules, and specialization of skills, among other important criteria. This is an example of a formally defined concept from which empirical studies have traditionally been made.

Another basic type of concept appears to be more closely associated with participant observation and is called the *sensitizing concept*. This phrase was coined by Herbert Blumer some years ago to indicate those kinds of terms which give a sense of reference, a general orientation, rather than a precise definition, to a phenomenon under study. Blumer suggests that the meanings of sensitizing concepts are not communicated by formal definitions, but are communicated "by means of exposition which yields a meaningful picture, abetted by apt illustrations which enable one to grasp the reference in terms of one's own experience."[9] This statement describes the kind of illustrative interpretations which participant observers are prone to make and which lead to the sensitizing concept. An example could be the concept of intelligence if it were broadly defined with concrete illustrations as to how it functions in particular cases.

Mores is another example of a frequently used sensitizing concept. Although they exist in every society as a social form, mores can be understood only in personal terms, that is, by concrete illustrations of how strong sanctions are placed upon certain types of conduct. Let us suppose an average American citizen were asked to take up the tabooed practice of cannibalism or, let us say, to practice nudism in some public place in an American city. The strength of the sanctions against these practices is commonly and personally conveyed to those who would imagine themselves engaging in such practices. The image of oneself walking nude across a

---

[8] Max Weber, *The Theory of Social and Economic Organization*, trans. A. M. Henderson and Talcott Parsons (New York: Free Press of Glencoe, Inc., 1947), pp. 329–41.

[9] Herbert Blumer, "What Is Wrong with Social Theory?" *American Sociological Review*, **19** (February 1954), 9.

public shopping square or eating the flesh of a fellow citizen at a banquet is enough to educate the socialized American as to what mores refers in a society. The image is concrete and particular, the feeling personal and yet shared almost universally among American citizens. The specific nature of the feeling which is associated with social practices of these kinds, that is, mixtures of revulsion, fear, anger, and shame (concrete concepts) need not be depicted further, for the strength of the feeling is all that is necessary to illustrate the social meaning of the concept mores.

Contrary to the opinion of some experimentalists and behaviorists, sensitizing concepts do not have to become operational to be scientific. Such a position would deny the authenticity of the original meanings and function these concepts have in research; it would omit the reality they represent. This is true of other types of concepts as well.

When a concrete, sensitizing or formal concept becomes operationalized, its meaning changes. While it may be argued that all data can be measured, it is nevertheless true that when an attempt is made to measure certain concepts, the distinctive original character that provides an understanding of the concept at a particular level is lost. Let us say that defining a concrete emotion such as hate or fear as that which is measured by certain visceral responses to stimuli cannot convey the true meaning of such feelings as they are socially perceived. And one's social perceptions of these emotive conditions may have everything to do with understanding human behavior. Each of the concepts we have described, therefore, has a right to its own level of understanding without being reduced to the so-called "real facts" which presumably lie at the operational level.[10]

Each different concept has a place in the larger aims of social science. The sensitizing concept is flexible in its usage and finds a certain virtue in its inexactness. Since it reflects the more permanent forms in society which itself has many social forms that are constantly changing, this concept gains a certain continuous and widespread use in the field. In time, concepts that

---

[10] There are "real facts" existing at different levels of knowing, not all of which are at the level of the senses. If we want to prove or ascertain the existence of the "self" as a "fact," for example, we cannot do it on purely sense grounds, for the self is not a phenomenon to be verified directly by the senses. If we take George H. Mead's definition of the self as that object which has the "characteristic that it is an object to itself," we cannot touch it or see it and thus prove its existence. Rather, the self must be ascertained intuitively, that is, by the sheer act of introspection upon one's own existence as a separate social being. Other definitions of the self make testing its existence still more complex. One does not "see" one's self physically and understand its essence; rather, one sees one's self socially by using interior language built up through social interaction. Other types of concepts are still more complex than the self and escape the traditional methods of empirical study. As we shall indicate later, many of the verities of social life must be ascertained through other means including rhetorical analysis and symbolic consensus. Our task here is to explore the problems involved in achieving intuitive certainty.

are carefully fixed in definition can lose their fixed references and their significance. Formal concepts, however, lend themselves to more rigorous study, whereas sensitizing concepts could not. Formal concepts have significance to the traditional aims of science—measurement and prediction of phenomena—and, along with operational concepts, lend themselves to these ends.

The more concrete and sensitizing concepts, however, contribute to the clarification of key values and social structures and encourage a more sensitive understanding of them. They also provide the observer with a special knowledge of the future in ways that statistical studies cannot. The participant observer, for example, who functions within a prison setting anticipates success or failure of an inmate's being paroled on a different basis than an actuarial device may predict. The two kinds of knowledge—statistical and social—differ in kind, and along with their respective aims—prediction and sensitive understanding—are in many ways in tension with one another. In the long run, however, they both contribute to the larger aims of the social sciences.

Modes of Description: Synthesis and Analysis[11]

Not only must the researcher interpret and conceptualize his data in distinctive ways, he must also describe them, both analytically and synthetically. Analyzed data are taken apart intellectually—*i.e.,* events, beliefs, and patterns of conduct are separated in order to see new relationships among them. The researcher then puts these parts together in a new way, inventing categories to contain them or relating them to some theoretical viewpoint. When the parts are put together and the concepts integrated into a meaningful relationship, the synthetic process becomes more evident. These two modes of description are active in all cases of reflective study, but one or the other type may appear dominant, depending upon the observer and his interests.

Analysis and synthesis differ in the emphasis the observer gives to the general process by which he acquires knowledge and the kind of knowledge he acquires. The kind of knowledge he acquires through concrete illustrations and sensitizing concepts is a social knowledge which has a personal dimension to it. It tends to be synthetic in character insofar as the observer adds insight that unifies (or reveals uniformities in) the separate forms of personal knowledge he acquires in the field. The kind of knowledge which

11 Adapted from Severyn T. Bruyn, "The Methodology of Participant Observation," *Human Organization,* 22, No. 3 (Ithaca, N.Y.: Society for Applied Anthropology, Fall 1963), 230.

the observer acquires through operational and formal concepts is intellectual and if systematized, becomes theoretical. Theoretical knowledge tends to be analytic in character insofar as the observer abstracts from his social data and examines the parts separately and critically.[12]

If by synthetic process, we mean discovering an element of unity or uniformity within disparate elements of data that relates them into a coherent whole, we are certain that this process may function at any level of knowledge. However, we want to note especially how the operation of the synthetic process functions at the personal-social level of knowledge in significant ways that the analytical process does not. To the participant observer, the synthetic process is in part intuitive and involves grasping the essence of personal meanings which inhere in the cultural context being studied. In describing events, the researcher engages in a kind of intuitive reconnaissance of the character and spirit of the people engaged in those events. This process is different from a logical analysis of observable data in the following ways:

First, the participant observer seeks to identify with the people he is observing without analyzing them. Analysis, he believes, at certain stages may prove to be a barrier to his understanding. The researcher seeks a certain kind of communion with what he observes; therefore, any efforts to comment analytically about a situation prevent this communion. In fact, there is no place for either rational or emotional comments at the point of intuitive contact. Charles Cooley has stressed this point with regard to reflective emotions:

> Sympathy in the sense of compassion is a specific emotion or sentiment, and has nothing necessarily in common with sympathy in the sense of communion. It might be thought, perhaps, that compassion was one form of sharing feeling; but this appears not to be the case. The sharing of painful feeling may precede and cause compassion, but is not the same with it. When I feel sorry for a man in disgrace, it is, no doubt, in most cases, because I have imaginatively partaken of his humiliation; but my compassion for him is not the thing is shared, but is something additional, a comment on the shared feeling. I may imagine how a suffering man feels—sympathize with him in that sense—and be moved not to pity but to disgust, contempt, or perhaps admiration. Our feeling makes all sorts of comments on the imagined feeling of others.[13]

Second, since the participant observer is interested in knowing intimately the essence of that way of life which he is studying, he normally tends to

---

[12] The distinction William James once made between "knowledge of" and "knowledge about" is similar to the distinction we are making here. Knowledge *of* people is personal and social, whereas knowledge *about* people is intellectual and theoretical.

[13] Charles Cooley, *Sociological Theory and Social Research* (New York: Holt, Rinehart & Winston, Inc., 1930), p. 102.

interpret his data synthetically rather than analytically. That is, he seeks the central symbols around which a culture is organized—symbols which are not necessarily publically visible or socially acclaimed, but which neverthe-less explain the foundation upon which people have built their lives. Thus, the participant observer's description of a culture need not have an analyti-cal emphasis; it may be simply socially descriptive but in an essentially penetrating, meaningful way. The writings of some field anthropologists have a descriptively synthetic form to them. For example, Ruth Benedict's reference to Apollonian and Dionysian principles is an attempt to find central principles which describe the character and the spirit of the people in the cultures she studied.[14]

Synthetic description may oversimplify or overemphasize a few key elements while minimizing variability within cultures. On the other hand, analysis fails to see the whole for the parts, fails to see the larger meaning or significance of data. Together these polar modes of description comple-ment one another and provide a broad, firm basis for approaching the study of man.

Interrelatedness of Modes: In Retrospect

These dualities allow for more adequate knowledge in social research than if one or the other mode were encouraged to develop by itself. These dual processes of knowing human reality together clarify the totality of human experiences of man in their basic varieties—*i.e.,* the totality is understood through different forms of knowledge which express man in his essence, his relatedness, his abstractness, and his concreteness in society.

These dualities reflect the independent modes of knowledge necessary to know man as a human being. Yet each independent mode is dependent in certain ways on the other modes. In order to clarify the nature of the relationships between these modes in our effort to understand the whole man in society, we will now explore somewhat further the nature of these research processes.

We have said that the operational concept consists of carefully defined procedures which the observer performs in order to know the nature of a particular phenomenon. That is, in order for the observer to know "factually" he conducts himself in those ways in which he can control variables and observe specified social activities. In such cases the experi-mentalist observes and records what he sees through his physical senses and infers meaning logically from that data. He then seeks to relate his data

---

14 These principles refer to basic differences in the ethos of two Indian cultures; the Pueblos and the northwest Indians. Ruth Benedict, *Patterns of Culture* (Balti-more: Penguin Books, Inc., 1934).

to the ideal type. All the traits of an ideal or formal concept, however, cannot be immediately visible in his study. Yet, if enough traits can be inferred as logically reflected in the data, a conceptual bridge is made and the experimentalist gains confidence that the data and the formal concept together represent a scheme of reality.

The building of scientific knowledge does not stop with formal concepts, for these concepts merely bridge the gap between operational concepts and what we shall later designate on a higher level of abstraction as theoretical principles; from this viewpoint formal concepts mediate between very abstract and operational levels of knowledge.

At the middle level of abstraction we also find sensitizing concepts which are rationally, but not formally, oriented. These concepts link the discipline to the less definitive language of the conventional world and orient scientists to what is important in that world. Many of the frequently used sensitizing concepts in sociology such as primary group, mores, or institutions are formed especially to point to significant areas of social life the influence of which might otherwise be ignored by those who seek to study society. Those sensitizing concepts which are culturally oriented, such as beliefs, values, or myths, lead the observer closer to the sentiments of man.

The traditional empiricist and the participant observer may both do research on the same concepts, each obtaining a different perspective of these concepts, but together producing a more comprehensive knowledge of the concepts. The experimentalist, for example, may formulate high-level crosscultural generalizations about certain sentiments of man, a province which may also be investigated by the participant observer. The experimentalist may generalize in the following way: "All men learn the pleasure of eating food at some time in their lives in every society," or "All people learn frustration in the process of socialization," or "All people learn affection in the process of growing up in any society." He would then seek to study these generalizations in an experimental way, *operationalizing* "pleasure," frustration," and "affection." His findings and the interpretive process he uses would be very much different from that of the participant observer even though the subject area would be the same.

The participant observer would seek to convey the concrete reality of pleasure, frustration, and affection as they are found in the communicative life of the people he studies, first interpreting these experiences in terms the people can understand. He would begin to authenticate his interpretation by communicating it to the people and obtaining their assent or lack of assent. Then, when he feels he has understood the experience in their terms, he would look for elements in the culture of his fellow social scientists which are comparable to those he has studied in order to provide the basis for his colleagues' own understanding of the cultural data. He may do this by minting special metaphors or creating analogies from his original experience in both cultures in order to create a unity of understanding between them.

The participant observer, then, moves from his original apprehension of the concrete reality to locating appropriate words and illustrations with comparable intent, connotation, and meaning in the experiences of fellow scientists. His next step may be to move through this reproducible experience toward concepts couched in the language of formal theory.

Concrete concepts are direct expressions rather than scientific formulations of cultural life. In some cases they are more "direct" than in others. For example, when the word *love* is expressed concretely by someone in our society, such as in "I love you," the feeling of love can be created and experienced directly through the expression of the words. Similarly, the expression "You are free" can create the experiential reality of being free. In this sense some words are nonrepresentational, that is, their meaning is produced through their expression without reflection and cannot be represented accurately in other forms. Concrete concepts such as *democracy* involve expressive beliefs which have more rational form, yet are nevertheless linked to the sentiments of people in that culture. The researcher must be able to experience the meaning of these concepts in his role as participant and formulate theory about them in his role as observer.

Concrete concepts differ from sensitizing concepts in two ways. First, the concrete concept is derived indigenously from the culture studied; it takes its meaning solely from that culture and not from the scientist's special definition of it. Sensitizing concepts, however, are formulated by the scientist who sees significant areas of social life that require definition. He takes the conventional meaning into account in his own definition but he is not ruled by it. The social scientist may seek to sharpen the meaning in his own interest, to define it from a more objective standpoint. He will distinguish *custom* from *tradition* and both from *convention,* whereas the average person would confuse the terms and use them interchangeably in everyday speech. Sensitizing concepts are often a combination of a scientific need for precision and a necessity to have the term represent cultural reality. The same conditions hold for the more formal, ideal type of concept (as we shall note later in discussing Max Weber's definition of it) except that the objective requirements of definition are more rigorously followed in the ideal type.

Second, the concrete concept is linked more clearly with particular cultural sentiments than is the sensitizing concept, which is more rational so that objectivity can be maintained in the scientist's vocabulary. The meaning of a concrete concept such as *free* has a different group of connotations from that group related to the concept *freedom.* The concrete meaning expressed in being free is not simply a rational expression of man, nor is it simply an expression of the normative structure of society. Rather, it directly expresses the process of man's becoming released from the normative traditions of his society or some past society, sometimes with reason and sometimes without. The concept of freedom, on the other hand, elevates the experiential meaning of being free to an "idea" about it.

The idea of freedom can serve as a sensitizing concept if it is studied objectively. A systematically conducted crosscultural study of the meaning of freedom in the ideologies of modern societies could result in finding common elements among them so that a definition with both scientific and cultural requirements could be formulated.[15] The cultural requirements are fulfilled simply because these common elements have real referents to particular cultures in the way people in these cultures define the idea of freedom. The scientific requirements are found in the rigor of method and the representativeness of the sampling involved in the research for common elements.

There are complicated beliefs associated with the experience of being free (e.g., as with capitalism or socialism) as there are complicated beliefs associated with being in love (e.g., as with Christianity or Hinduism) which have their institutional expressions in societies. Social scientists have been more willing to study institutions in the abstract than the beliefs or concrete realities in which these institutions have their collective origins and their source of power. The procedural description of concrete concepts and their relation to beliefs and institutions, however, has been accomplished through the aid of participant observation in anthropology where excellent source materials can be located in research monographs.[16]

Our point here is that the basic forms of sociological analysis must be

---

[15] The meaning of freedom as conceived in the traditional literature of the United States has involved beliefs about a culturally diverse, pluralistic social order with opportunities for people to achieve voluntarily individual purposes in institutions independent of government control. However, this concept requires considerable historical research of its variety of meanings in western literature before common elements can be scientifically ascertained.

[16] The term concrete universal is intended to cover a variety of cultural expressions from a shared state of mind to a social belief people have about the world. However, this term is a procedural concept similar to the operational concept. The concrete concept is known by the researcher's description of how he was able to understand its existence in the culture he studies. For an example of how this is done, see Bronislaw Malinowski's depiction of the Kiriwina's belief in *Baloma,* the spirit of the dead among the Trobriand Islanders. Note how he describes his personal participation in particular events which led to his conclusions; how he searches for shades of meaning and the variety of interpretations that can be expressed by the Islanders; how he compares and contrasts this belief in *Baloma* with European beliefs in ghosts and generally sets up the basis for outsiders to come to a personal understanding of native beliefs. *Baloma* is a concrete concept in the lives of these natives—it is understood personally and universally among the members of their society. See Bronislaw Malinowski, *Magic, Science, and Religion* (Garden City, N.Y.: Doubleday Anchor Books, 1948), pp. 149–90.

able to express as well as explain the fundamental meanings which exist in society, some of which are outside the traditional vocabulary of science. Since this vocabulary has been built on sense and logic, we need to delineate especially those basic forms in culture which are, to all appearances, lacking in sense and logic. The concrete concept must be translated in cultural studies, for it represents just these nonobjective forms of human life. In other words, the social scientist must study the spirit of man as it is expressed through the symbolic imagery of society which is expressed in part through folklore, myths, and songs. These images are understood concretely by the scientist through such mediums as allegory, metaphor, and paradox, forms we shall discuss later as part of the rhetoric of sociology. Here we will simply stress the difference in conceptual forms as well as the epistemological sources necessary to grasp these forms in their variety. (See diagram.)

EPISTEMOLOGICAL SOURCE	SENSE	REASON		INTUITION
CONCEPTUAL FORM	Operational (e.g.,"IQ")	Formal (e.g., "Bureaucracy")	Sensitizing (e.g., "Mores")	Concrete (e.g.,"Free")

The operational and concrete concepts are at opposite ends of a continuum and are distinctly different in character. The process of "knowing" the operational concept involves maximizing sense experience even though this cannot eliminate rational or intuitive processes from entering into knowing. The concrete concept maximizes the expressive meaning of particular sentiments through the explication of procedures for knowing them intuitively even though it cannot disregard the senses or reason as an important part of the process. (We shall discuss the intuitive process in detail later.) Between the concepts at the extremes lie the more rationally oriented concepts, the formal and sensitizing concepts. In these special ways the dimensions of man are coming to serve as the basis for a more adequate conception of man in society.[17]

---

17 This position is represented in Pitirim Sorokin's sociocultural theory that the basic facts of society must be understood in three-dimensional terms. He describes what he calls "super-systems" of man's sociocultural life which have been built around ideational, idealistic, and sensory truth. Integral truth, however, is not identical with any one of these truths but embraces them all. "The empirico-sensory aspects of it is given by the truth of the senses; the rational aspect, by the truth of reason; the superrational aspect by the truth of faith." Pitirim Sorokin, *Social and Cultural Dynamics* (New York: American Book Company, 1941), Vol. IV, pp. 762–63.

Modes of Explanation: Descriptive Metaphysics

Principles: Telic and Causal

At the point where the researcher must ask why a particular phenomenon occurs the way it does, he becomes involved in the processes of explanation. An explanation of why any event occurs is made on a basis which includes two contrasting metaphysical principles called the *telic* (or *teleological*) and *causal* principles. The former refers to the purposes, means, and ends of man, the latter, to the causes and effects operating man's life. Both principles are basic to the full explanation of man as he exists in society.

Even though the observer would deny making any metaphysical judgments in his explanations of data, these are nevertheless implied in his work and cannot be avoided entirely. People inevitably try to apply the observer's findings and scientific orientation to their own lives, so the observer does become involved. However, the social scientist is not making an explanation so much as a description of data within a set of logically related propositions which are not normally a part of the conventional world of the people being studied. These propositions thus evince a truth beyond the everyday realities and open a new reality. The propositions of a Marx or a Freud become the "explanation" of what is real, for propositions take on metaphysical character in people's lives because they allow people to see conceptions *after* (*meta-*) the everyday explanations of events.

The participant observer does not normally apply his theoretical propositions initially in his work. Rather, he encounters both telic and causal principles as they are reflected in the commonsense realities of those he studies. Since people have their own explanations of events on the basis of cause and effect, the participant observer must try to understand their explanation.

However, the participant observer, in contrast with the traditional empiricist, is newly concerned with purpose as a scientist. He must not only treat purposes as data, but must also act within the purposes he holds as data. He does more than simply study the purposes people have in working, governing, and worshiping within the context of their community; he knowingly adopts these purposes as his own. The observer may intentionally allow the purposive values of the people he studies to invade and infuse his descriptions of their everyday life—he may allow their ethics to guide his own conduct. These purposive factors, he finds, become not only part of his data but also part of his methodology.

The causal principle has long been the official trademark of the scientist. The telic principle, however, has suffered low status and at best has maintained a rather ambiguous position. During the rise of science in western Europe, teleology was associated with medieval theology and early scientists and philosophers rejected it as fully incompatible with the study of scientific laws based upon cause and effect. Yet whenever the scientist discusses *cause* he must reckon with human purpose. The social scientist must therefore come to terms with the fact that purpose is a basic part of human reality.

When Aristotle first analyzed the meaning of cause he found it necessary to include *purpose* as a basic part of his explanation. When a modern social scientist, Robert M. MacIver, recently analyzed scientific causation, he too found it necessary to include purpose as a basic part of his explanation of the causal principle. Although modern science has abandoned Aristotelian metaphysics, the social sciences must find a new way of studying and treating purpose as part of the scientific framework for studying society. Cause and purpose are still intertwined, as MacIver's study so aptly demonstrates.[18]

The scientific observer today may explain human events by emphasizing either the causal or the telic principle if he is aware of the limitations of his work. However, if one or the other principle is the sole basis for a descriptive analysis and the observer assumes that the theoretical principle he chooses is adequate to explain the whole of the human reality that he investigates, his assumption is incorrect.

---

[18] Robert MacIver's study of the concept of "cause" illustrates (as did Aristotle's) how this term ramifies into a teleological explanation of man. In pursuing the "modes of the question why," MacIver asserts that scientific answers can take four different paths. First, there is the question of physical causality which is answered in terms of the "invariant order" of things—*i.e.*, the answer involves describing the invariant sequence and concomitance of certain properties under defined conditions. Second, there is the causality of organic being which involves an explanation in terms of function. For example, the question: Why does the liver secrete bile? would be answered with: It has a role in the digestion of food. In other words, the functional significance of organs and organic processes are explained in relation to the organism as a whole. Third, there is the causality of conscious being which involves an explanation in terms of objectives (goals), motives, and design. For example, the questions: Why do people follow this road? Why did you sell that stock? Why do people marry in church? would be answered in terms of specific objectives, motives, and designs. It is as scientifically correct to explain the reasons why men act the way they do on the basis of their purposes and motives as it is on the basis of culturally determined designs. MacIver points out that a "design" is like Aristotle's formal cause; the design exists prior to the construction of a house by an architect. Therefore, people marry in a church or wear a certain cut of clothes with certain motives in mind but also *because* it is the custom or the style of that society. Fourth, there is causality of "social nexus" which involves an explanation in terms of the "social conjuncture" of different social patterns which result in unforeseen consequences. For example, the questions: Why are ground values high in the center of the city? Why is a greater division of labor a concomitant of advancing technology? would be answered partly in terms of an explanation of how different types of factors are involved in the particular resultant. Ground values are high because of such factors as a competitive market, special zoning laws, the aims of speculative landlords. In these ways MacIver's study of scientific causation leads eventually to human purposes as a fundamental part of the explanation of human events. See Robert M. MacIver, *Social Causation* (Boston: Ginn & Company, 1942).

The causal framework generally has led to a conception of determinism in which man is seen solely as the product of outside forces, the telic framework, to a conception of freedom in which man's individual choice is not determined by the forces of the past. The former conception (absolute determinism) is evidenced in the writings of many social scientists and the latter (absolute freedom), in the writings of many existentialists.

Either conception in its extreme form produces a distorted image of man. At the same time, we are wont to say, each position expresses a principle with much validity about the nature of man. Our contention here is that both principles and the basic orientations associated with them must be a comprehensive part of a theory of man in society.

The meaning of freedom cannot be understood by the social scientist who follows the older traditions of science. Freedom, the traditional empiricist would say, is a subjective idea, not an objective concept—it is not a part of the scientist's vocabulary. It is the subject of philosophy, not science.

Such a position is untenable today in the light of participant observer research which contains such subjective meanings as part of its data. The meaning of freedom is as important to the culture of the university student at Berkeley, California as it is to the culture of tribal politicians of Nigeria, and the social scientist must be in a position to understand and conceptualize this meaning.

Models: Voluntarism and Determinism

When Robert and Helen Lynd functioned as participant observers in a midwestern community called Middletown three decades ago, they struggled with the paradoxical character of two contrasting perspectives of human nature: their own deterministic perspective as scientists and their subjects' voluntaristic perspective as citizens. In *Middletown in Transition* they reflect upon their initial study:

> Middletown tends to regard human nature as "rational," "free," and "responsible," and there is large precedent for so doing. . . . But, again, the student of comparative culture takes the view that any institutional form in a given setting is simply a product of a given set of conditions. . . .[19]

Social scientists who study society with a predominately behavioristic or positivistic perspective of man cannot view concepts such as *free will* as having any basis in fact. Under such conditions it is easy to see how some

---

[19] Robert S. Lynd and Helen M. Lynd, *Middletown in Transition* (New York: Harcourt, Brace & World, Inc., 1937), pp. xv–xvi.

social scientists reach the conclusion that free will has no reality. Actually, what is considered "fact" by the traditional scientist is only that which he selectively interprets from within his own explanatory model, and this model is only part of a wider factual reality. The broader historical fact is that scientific determinism is the legacy of a cultural rebellion against medieval thought, a legacy which now excludes any viewpoint or concept (such as free will) which helped to support the special metaphysics and closed theological outlook of the times. Science emerged through the rebellion as the more powerful and effective voice, replacing medieval metaphysics by scientific metaphysics which screened out the personal realities of man. Social scientists, in turn, have adopted much of this metaphysics, and the impact of this scientific outlook on European thought has been, of course, tremendous. So have been its intellectual consequences, one of which, existentialism, rejects virtually everything science stands for.

If the social scientist were to examine the intellectual history of Europe in the last century he would find existentialism appearing as a counter-rebellion, a rebellion directed against the closed, one-sided emphasis science has given to its own interpretation of the world. That one-sided interpretation has lingered on in the methodology of social scientists, obscuring the truth about man in society. Nevertheless, that scientific perspective characterizable as causal-determinism continues to dominate the methodology of social research. In a recent debate with Arthur Schlesinger on humanism and empirical research George Homans said:

> The sociologist and the historian are, moreover, both determinists. Indeed I think any effort at explanation implies a deterministic assumption.... Our knowledge is always going to be inadequate in some degree, and we shall never be able to demonstrate universal determinism, for even if we got to the place where we thought that in principle we would predict everyone's behavior, it would cost more to do it than the result would be worth. Money, not doctrine, will be the savior of free will.[20]

Only in recent times have theories of voluntarism been given some legitimacy in social-scientific explanations of social action. These theories have contributed a new dimension to social theory, but they have not expressed the full character of man as he exists in society. As they now stand, such theories cannot serve as adequate theories of social action, but they do have importance when taken as methodological models which typify select features of human culture. The development of other models which express man in his true variety must await further studies in participant observation. The problem so far has been that the social scientist has too

---

[20] George Homans, "Schlesinger on Humanism and Empirical Research," *American Sociological Review*, **28**, No. 1 (February 1963), 100.

readily defined human reality from his position as a theoretical "observer" drawing upon the older metaphysics of science; thus he has failed to see the human complexities of social life in his other somewhat forgotten role as "participant."[21]

A monumental effort to integrate a theory of voluntarism into sociological theory was made by Talcott Parsons in his work *The Structure of Social Action*.[22] In this work the theories of Alfred Marshall, Vilfredo Pareto, Emile Durkheim, and Max Weber were combined into a new "voluntaristic theory" which sought to replace the old "positivistic theory of action." The essential characteristic of voluntarism was seen by Parsons to be a "ration-

---

[21] The limits to which the deterministic and voluntaristic models can be carried separately can best be seen in their clashes in the field of criminology. These clashes also reveal the possibilities which may develop from the dialectical exchange that is produced by them.

The academic criminologist, for example, in his search for causal determinants, has been led in the past to conclude that the criminal is not responsible for his acts. The causes, he finds, are located in the general culture or environment which produces the criminal. The psychologist has also found the criminal to be a product of external forces, of libidinous drives and familial frustrations. Such deterministic interpretations come into direct conflict with the voluntaristic perspective of the legal theorist who observes the criminal acting freely, making his own decisions and thus being causally responsible for his actions.

Through the years of intellectual conflict, the arguments of each theorist have penetrated the opposition, somewhat altering the positions previously held by each opponent. The cultural determinist, for his part, now recognizes that for all practical purposes the criminal must be held "accountable" for his actions even if he is still not primarily causally responsible. (Cf. Donald Taft, *Criminology* (New York: The Macmillan Company, 1947), pp. 14–15, 192, 290–95.) Furthermore, it is possible to view the criminal himself as a causal factor of a self-determining type; he is one part of a causal-purposive network of relationships generating crime. The legal theorist, for his part, has come to recognize the wider causal web of "responsibility" functioning outside the individual criminal, and as a result of his influence, the law and the courts have adjusted accordingly. The law has increasingly taken into account extenuating circumstances outside individual consciousness which cause the individual to commit his crimes. Perhaps even more significant for practical purposes is the development of Youth Correction Authorities under the influence of revised legal theory which has broadened conceptions of causation. The individual criminal is now considered to be only a part of the problem of correction; the causal conditions existing in the neighborhoods which the determinist argued originally helped produce the criminal are acted upon by these Youth Authorities through local programs enacting social change. The changes in corrective services are practical outcomes of changes in social theory, since theorists have been developing a new theoretical base to fit reality. While the conflicts may appear to represent only normal differences between normative (legal) and scientific theories, we shall argue later that these differences are accentuated to the point of conflict because scientific theory has not taken into account the realities of everyday life.

[22] Talcott Parsons, *The Structure of Social Action* (New York: McGraw-Hill Book Company, 1937). For a simplified statement of the Parsonian position on voluntarism, see Kingsley Davis, *Human Society* (New York: The Macmillan Company, 1949), pp. 121ff.

ality of action" which related means to ends. The introduction of such a theory which recognized the reality of voluntary, rational action as a central principle guiding human action must be considered as a major advance in sociological theory. This theory did not, however, fully incorporate a *theory of freedom*—i.e., still another type of reality and an additional step to be taken beyond the recognition of rationality in man.

The participant observer can accept the voluntaristic model as a methodological guide for his study more readily than he can the deterministic model, for the former expresses more accurately what he observes in the daily lives of people who make decisions. The subtleties of decision-making are great however, and often involve something different from a rational consideration of means and ends. Rationality is only a construct from which man often deviates and which by itself cannot serve to explain the actions of man. The observer, then, is in a position to document where rationality does not apply empirically in the subjective lives of his subjects and to develop other key constructs which may be incorporated into a theoretical viewpoint more compatible with what we now know is a very complex human reality.

In order to explain this complex reality sufficiently the observer may need to examine the culture that is interbound with social action. In so doing he may find that cultures are something more than linear—i.e., social action cannot be adequately explained by merely looking for causal or telic factors in action taken by people in a sequential line of events. (The voluntaristic and deterministic perspectives both require sequences of events examined either through cause and effect or through means and ends.) The observer may find other principles functioning in culture that are independent of these causal-telic principles. Or he may find that cultures consist of layers of reality which unfold in action only gradually and perhaps embryonically, for perhaps the development of cultures, like embryos, is controlled by elements beyond his normal visibility and requires special techniques for interior observation and verification.

Cultures have revealed circularity as well as linearity but they have also revealed something more than can be described by geometric or biological figures—images without analogy. Many of these images have meanings which have not been encountered by the conceptual vocabulary of social science. Sensitive observers of society have encountered and described them but not as social scientists. The cultural meanings in humor, for example, the *ribald* as observed by Honoré de Balzac, the *whimsical* as observed by James Thurber, and the *macabre* as observed in the interpretive movies of Ingmar Bergman affect human behavior but are not a part of behavioral studies. These meanings may be imposed upon situations by the artistic observer or they may exist inherently in the situation, felt by the participants. In either case, the cultural basis for social action of people in these situations is not explained by causal analysis in the traditional sense or even by a rational model of voluntarism.

The participant observer explains social action in such cases by bringing himself and other observers into the situation so they can observe and understand it symbolically for themselves. Once understood, the meanings of a culture complex such as humor can enlighten the realities of other scientific studies. Other studies often take such meanings for granted, creating their own meanings and often ignoring those meanings actually contained in the subject studied.

The purpose of participant observation is to study human meanings and how they are revealed in the context of society. The observer is interested in the design of these meanings and the processes by which this design is interpreted. Meanings are expressed through all the components of society, including social organization, language, philosophies, artifacts, actions, and attitudes of people, and methodologies of social scientists. The methodological perspectives of determinism and voluntarism are thus only two ways of revealing meanings.

The contrasting methodological models of determinism and voluntarism represent different states of man's view of the world, each emphasizing one side of a subject-object dichotomy which has puzzled man in the modern era ever since Descartes' original mind-body dichotomy. The participant observer is not interested in subscribing to either position for its methodological priority over the other, nor does he want to judge the metaphysical validity of either one. He is interested only in examining how these meanings arise and take shape in man's sociocultural world.

There are other observers besides the social scientist who are interested in the interpretation of meaning in the context of society.[23] There are similarities in their approaches but there are differences too. The novelist, the playwright, the theologian, or the poet may have a dozen or more purposes in mind which shape his interpretation. These observers may want to create an emotional effect, perpetuate a tradition, produce some dramatic insight into the nature of human tragedy, or effect some social reform by the presentation of the design. In so doing, they add new meanings which

---

[23] Students of the sociology of knowledge, for example, have been concerned with the development of ideas in the context of society. Their emphasis, however, has been upon how ideas are influenced by the social structure. Our emphasis is upon meanings themselves (ideas are only one form of their expression) without necessarily being concerned with causal relations between ideas and social life. Students in the field of hermeneutics are also concerned with the problems of interpreting meaning. (Cf. James M. Robinson and John B. Cobb, Jr., eds., *The New Hermeneutic* (New York: Harper & Row, Publishers, 1964). Students in the field of existential phenomenology have also treated these problems. (Cf. Maurice Merleau-Ponty, *Phenomenology of Perception*, trans. Colin Smith (London: Routledge & Kegan Paul, Ltd.; New York: Humanities Press, 1962).

shape their interpretations. On the other hand, for accuracy, the participant observer interprets a meaning as an end in itself, a methodological requirement he must follow even though he knows he cannot achieve perfection in every respect. He is interested in the process of interpretation, in the meanings interpreted, and in the design of these meanings in the culture studied. The processes and forms of culture which the participant observer interprets as an end-value in the context of his work, in turn become a means toward systematizing knowledge of society. But systemization functions after the fact rather than as a guiding interest of the observer in the throes of his study, for otherwise his inside interpretation is affected by his outside interests. Artists may or may not subject themselves to this requirement.[24]

Therefore, the purpose of the participant observer in exploring meanings in society is not simply to observe how actions are determined by causes, as George Homans would stress it, or to observe how people perceive the ends and means of action as Talcott Parsons would stress it. It has a much more fundamental purpose than these methodological perspectives would express, involving the studying of cultural meanings for their own sake as a methodological process of gaining accurate knowledge of man in society.

Theory and methodology in social science must be structured to encompass a phenomenon which includes the telic and causal perspectives, but still goes well beyond their tendency to be enclosed in the subject-object dichotomy in order to see *how different meanings emerge and take focus in society*. To detect these meanings in society, social scientists must develop sensitive tools, for they cannot be guided by a partial perspective of man. They must seek a human perspective, a perspective which is partial only to man himself. Then the groundwork for building a unified theory of man in society can begin.

Summary

The two research orientations we have described as traditional empiricism and participant observation generate two basically different kinds of social reality, which are expressed in what we have termed the inner and outer perspectives. These two perspectives characterize, but do not determine altogether, the kinds of procedures used in research orientation. Each orientation is based upon different philosophical foundations and different modes

---

24 Another requirement of the scientific observer, we repeatedly stress, is that he report with accuracy that human reality he studies outside himself. Artists need not be so obligated in their reporting. Thus, Marcel Proust's depiction of the aristocratic styles of families in Paris (*Remembrance of Things Past*) need not be verifiable to be appreciated, but Seeley, Sim, and Loosely's depictions of the styles of family life in a Canadian suburb (*Crestwood Heights*) must be verifiable to be acceptable to social science.

of interpretation, conceptualization, description, and explanation. These separate components (including the different aims of each orientation) are summarized in the table below.

The Human Perspective: Methodological Dimensions (Basic Research Orientations)*

	Inner Perspective (*Participant Observer*)	*Outer Perspective* (*Traditional Empiricist*)
Philosophical background	Idealism	Naturalism
Mode of:		
Interpretation	Concrete procedures	Operational procedures
Conceptualization	Sensitizing concepts	Formal concepts
Description	Synthesis	Analysis
Explanation		
Principles	Telic	Causal
Models	Voluntarism	Determinism
Aims	Sensitively accurate interpretation and explanation of man's social and cultural life	Accurate measurement and prediction of man's behavior

* Adapted from Severyn T. Bruyn, "The Methodology of Participant Observation," *Human Organization*, **22**, No. 3 (Ithaca, N.Y.: Society for Applied Anthropology, Fall 1963), 231.

Merging Reality

Anyone accustomed to the discipline of social research knows that these polar types are only abstractions of what, in reality, tend to combine in various ways which this dichotomy fails to express. How this dichotomy does not fit reality is as important to understand as the abstractions themselves.

A complete statement of how divergent perspectives have crossed in the configuration of particular research projects and in philosophy would involve a lengthy dissertation. A few basic points, however, will illustrate some crossings for the reader:

1. The participant observer is sometimes a part of a larger quantitative study and then may enumerate his findings rather than sensitively describing them in order to contribute to the purposes of the larger study.
2. The history of idealism in philosophy has also included theories of idealistic determinism.
3. Sensitizing concepts have been reduced to operational concepts.
4. Formal concepts involve a process of synthesis (combining elements) as well as analysis (breaking down elements).
5. A descriptive *analysis* may take on telic features, that is, it may become

oriented toward explaining the purposes of man and yet be supported by an otherwise quantitatively oriented methodology.

6. Sociological analysis need not be solely deterministic.

While these and other apparent exceptions to the two types of research orientations we have presented here could be listed, the types will stand on the basis of the emphasis that is given to each research perspective and procedure.

1. While the participant observer may be employed to enumerate data which could not be obtained in other ways, this is not the usual role he assumes in social research.

2. While at times idealism has included deterministic perspectives, its emphasis in the history of philosophy has been toward the explanation of man's purposes and freedom.

3. While some sensitizing concepts may be quantified, many other concepts lose their meaning in the process, thus destroying the original insights.

4. While to some degree all conceptualization involves both synthesis and analysis, the synthetic emphasis as we have described it is especially visible in the works of participant observers.

5. While some statistical studies such as *The American Soldier*[25] include quantitatively obtained attitudes and opinions, meaningfully interpreted by the authors as part of an empirical investigation, any qualitative interpretation of data includes the technique of participant observation, a point we shall explore in detail later.[26]

6. While sociological studies need not be deterministically oriented, as we have indicated, they are generally so oriented when traditional rules of empirical investigation are followed.

The basis for interpreting the polar refractions of these two research orientations in sociological theory will be discussed in the following chapter. It will suffice to say that the dualities evident in the history of social research, which we have indicated in this chapter, are in any case oversimplifications, and to that extent, distortions of the nature of social research. Therefore, once the observer is able to understand the tendencies he should forget the typology and begin to determine the foundation underlying these differences. This must be considered the central task for social scientists in the future: to take into serious account the findings from these contrasting instrumentalities of research and then shape the logical structures of theory in order to comprehend these structures as part of human reality. This process requires a special methodology in itself which we shall discuss in the next chapter.

---

[25] For a short commentary on this study, see Robert K. Merton and Paul F. Lazarfeld, eds., *Continuities in Social Research: Studies in the Scope and Method of "The American Soldier"* (New York: Free Press of Glencoe, Inc., 1950).

[26] Arthur J. Vidich, "Participant Observation and the Collection and Interpretation of Data," *American Journal of Sociology,* **60** (January 1955), 385.

3

Polarities
in Theory

The tendency to polarize perspectives, concepts, and modes of interpretation in these approaches to research has many implications in social theory. The first major implication lies in the meaning of the tendency itself, and its roots run to the core of the scholarly tradition in the humanities as well as in the social sciences. Polarity is eminently evident in the entire history of social and literary thought. If one were to trace the history of such dualities in major scholarly works, beginning, let us say, with Plato's distinctions between appearance and reality and the Chinese conception of Yin and Yang, and move historically forward, the list would demonstrate our point quite convincingly: this tendency to see the world in opposites, whether real or not, lies deep in man's culture. The problem of how to deal with this tendency is a major challenge to the modern theorist, for he too is still caught in the polar dilemmas already defined by the recent past.

For example, if we look back to such recent, masterful, and world-shaping theories of human nature as may be found in the writings of Charles Darwin, Karl Marx, and Sigmund Freud, we can locate the origins of some major polar conceptions of reality which modern theorists still struggle to reconcile. In Darwin, we see the duality which arose between the natural and divine orders of existence, a problem which still, at new levels, challenges scholars; in Marx, it was the conceptualized conflict between two social classes set forth by him as the fundamental explanation of how society functioned in history; in Freud, it was the division he saw between the unconscious and the conscious operations of the mind, or perhaps more significantly, the duel between the id and the superego. Such legacies in polarized thought still confront modern theory with many dimensions, seemingly immune to efforts to integrate their parts. Yet the polarizing instinct is not dead; the tendency to search for new opposites goes on in the work of social theorists as well as in empirical research as we continue into the twentieth century.

The modern sociologist, no matter how much he may dress himself in his scientific armor, is not invulnerable to this same intellectual instinct to see reality from two sides. A brief look at the theoretical and empirical works of this century reveals the same tendency. For example, social scientists have been impelled to look behind the public or official descriptions of social reality for the real or "true" conception of what exists. This tendency has been so consistently revealed in sociological studies that it has led Peter Berger to refer to it as constituting "debunking" and "unrespectable" motifs which seem to be a continuing part of sociological analyses. In his classic study *The Protestant Ethic and the Spirit of Capitalism,* Max Weber seeks to validate empirically a position that is in opposition to the prevailing Marxian conception. The same polarizing tendency may be found in Thorstein Veblen's analysis of the leisure class. Veblen took a rather disrespectful look at the underside of the American leisure class, exposing its interest in conspicuous consumption as the "fact" in opposition to the public conception of this "finer way of life." The proclivity to look on the opposite side of the official definitions of reality is evident in the empirical studies of the "Chicago Ecological School" under Robert Park, studies which tended to reveal unexamined, less desirable sectors of city life. It was the same disposition to look for opposites, we would say, that led the Lynds to expose the contradictions in the cultural life of Middletown. Similarly, C. Wright Mills, at the level of society, and Floyd Hunter, at the community level, sought to study the power structure that lay behind official councils of power.

The predominance through history of an intellectual tendency to look for opposites leads the observer to wonder whether this is not one of the major strategems underlying all human studies, one which should be the subject for its own studies. Its timeless presence suggests that it may be an inherent part of the structure of all social thought, peculiar to no one single culture. The polarizing tendency, like other human instincts, may produce problems if given unguided reign, but if studied and understood for its place in the larger human perspective, it can be an instrument toward scientific and human understanding.

Our analysis in Chapter 2 suggests that there are two basic polar research methods existing in the study of social phenomena, but such an analysis can be misleading. The polarities are introduced in this way only because there is no better alternative than to move through this stage of recognizing certain realities of social research and their rational implications before theory, in turn, can proceed to take the necessary steps to eliminate or reconcile the contradictions in the two approaches. We would contend that these dualities contain less distortion at this point than that which would result from a conception of only one side of social reality.

The methodological problem of reaching that perspective within which these polar conceptions can be understood in their fundamental and proper relationships with each other is indeed large, and not likely to be accomplished in any one grand sweep. Our present aim is simply to indicate some of the complexities of this problem and to suggest some methodological guides which may lead to theoretical integration. We want to begin by examining major works in the history of social thought.

Since the problem of polarities is a familiar one in the history of philosophy, we shall first turn to selected works in this field of inquiry before we examine the polarities which are evident in selected works of sociological theory. After surveying certain key theorists in philosophy and sociology for what information we can extract (and admittedly oversimplifying certain ideas), we shall suggest general rules which may be useful to theoreticians in treating the problem of polarities.

Polar Thought in Review

Polarities in Philosophy

The Greeks were among the first to treat the problem of polarities analytically. The Pythagoreans in ancient Greece dealt with conceptual opposites at some length. They listed ten familiar opposites—*e.g.*, odd and even, square and oblong, male and female, good and bad, etc.—and suggested that these opposites actually had mathematical relationships to each other. Later, Plato and Aristotle continued the discussion of opposites in human experience. Plato advocated a kind of esthetic harmony of opposites in rational balance as the criterion for solving the problem of man's striving for justice. Aristotle examined the problems evident in man's search for moral conduct, and elaborated a scheme of opposites between which man might choose the "mean" or the right conduct. Some scholars would contend that all that is basic to know about the nature of polarities may be traced through Greek thought.[1]

Still later in the history of social thought, philosophers again confronted the reality of opposites—but this time more significantly for our purposes—by developing whole metaphysical systems of analysis around them as key explanatory principles. Immanuel Kant, for example, confronted the polar

---

1 A review of these and other philosophic positions may be found in Louis W. Norris, *Polarity* (Chicago: Henry Regnery Co., 1956), pp. 1–33. This text examines philosophical polarities as the basis for developing a system of ethics.

epistemological problem of empiricism and rationalism, and sought a synthesis in practical reason. The relations that exist between growing facets of these two major approaches to objective knowledge are still being worked out in detail as science advances in its exploration of the world.

Then Fichte, Schelling, and Hegel, in major works having complexities we cannot take time to explore, developed the theory of the dialectic to explain how polar opposites struggle with one another toward that end in which the opposing ideas become united in a still higher and more inclusive concept. They felt that everything in nature generates its own opposite, and that in the ensuing struggle a transcendence of the limitations of each contradictory idea is achieved. However, in pursuing particular notions in their theories to their logical limits, each philosopher tended to overemphasize the idealistic features of the dialectic process. For example, Schelling examined the material principles operative in physics, chemistry, and biology, and developed a position of "absolute idealism" in which he concluded that the whole of nature has the same essential form as conscious experience and can be perceived through introspective analysis. Everything that is known in experience, according to Schelling's view of the dialectic, is a composite of opposites mixed and compounded in different degrees. Opposites such as ideal and real, subjective and objective are ultimately fused in a realm of "indifference" which is "absolute reason." This idealistic realm itself, we may say in retrospect, was to become still another opposite pole which philosophy has struggled to reconcile dialectically with other equally important dimensions of knowledge.

The Hegelian dialectical idealism was subjected to criticism, particularly from the Marxian position which has maintained that Hegel interpreted the struggle for truth as existing only at the spiritual level of ideas (*Geist*); Marx frankly and intentionally contradicted this position by maintaining that ideas were merely an epiphenomenon of the material world, an intellectual superstructure created by men rationalizing their own class privileges. The basis for understanding how a man explained the world was to be found in his social location with reference to sectors of economic power and influence, for a man formed his religious and political beliefs, said Marx, to fit his place in the hierarchy of economic order. For Marx, in contrast to Hegel, the dialectical struggle was based upon material, rather than the ideational, foundations.

Marx convincingly demonstrated that the dialectic cannot simply be explained in ideational terms—*i.e.*, that opposites do not originate simply from the process of reason, or from the workings of a spiritual absolute, as Hegel would ultimately define it, but from non-ideational and non-spiritual factors. For Marx, the economic factor was most important, whereas for Buckle, LePlay, and many other human geographers, the topographical or climatic factor took precedence—*i.e.*, the type of land and climate, helps determine the creation of particular thought systems and social systems.

We would add: so do other physical and biological forces. Thus, we may say that different spheres of human inquiry create different polar perspectives which somehow must be reconciled as new knowledge about man emerges. And, as we shall note further in a discussion of scientific rationale, the kind of knowledge with which the theoretician deals is largely ideational, but he must somehow relate it to the structured sense-data of the empiricist and the distinctive knowledge of the participant observer in forming a well-balanced conceptual system.

If one stays at the ideational or rational level of understanding, the dialectic appears valid in its methodological form. The Marxian position may be interpreted as another basic idea contradicting that part of the Hegelian position which asserts that the dialectic is to be understood solely as the product of reason. The dialectic pattern, as conceived by Hegel, reveals a basic truth about the theoretical process which may even be seen in twentieth-century sociology and philosophy.

Nevertheless, it is also true that not all theoretical knowledge manifests itself in the shape of polarities or dualities. Furthermore, it is not in the best interests of history to represent ideas in the form of a dialectic, for if a history of ideas is confined to dialectic formulations, it would certainly oversimplify major works and necessarily overlook important elements in complex theories which should be understood in their full context. At the same time, we must conclude that under certain circumstances the dialectic may be fruitfully employed, and basic truths may thus be found. The dialectic theme may be the first step towards clarifying alternative facts in a given theoretical problem. Our point here is that the recognition of polar differences is not the end of inquiry, but it may be a constructive beginning.

A definition of polarity which suggests the usage which we are making of the term was given in 1944 by philosopher W. H. Sheldon in his book *Process and Polarity*. He said:

> In sum, polarity means a relation between two opposites, each of partly independent status, asymmetrical, and productive because of the cooperation, and also just because each has already a being, power, and efficacy of its own which enables it to contribute something in the cooperation.[2]

In a short treatment of the problem of polarities we cannot be as specific and as extensive in our definition as would be a more systematic work. But this use of the term in philosophy suggests that we understand polarities as those kinds of ideational opposites which may contain the possibility of either contradiction or complement, depending upon how the specific formulations of them are made. In any case, polarities are independent conceptions of the world in the sense that one pole cannot be interpreted in terms of

---

[2] W. H. Sheldon, *Process and Polarity* (New York: Columbia University Press, 1944), p. 108.

the other pole without doing some injustice to the meaning of this other pole. Examples of particular sociological polarities will be discussed later in some detail.

The concept of polarities in philosophy has long been a characteristic of basic problems in that field. Morris Raphael Cohen suggests its importance as a principle of rationalism expressed in the scientific method:

> The foregoing considerations are all applications of a wider principle, viz. the principle of polarity. By this I mean the opposites such as immediacy and mediation, unity and plurality, the fixed and the flux, substance and function, ideal and real, actual and possible, etc., [which,] like the north (positive) and the south (negative) poles of a magnet, all involve each other when applied to any significant entity. Familiar illustrations of this are: that physical action is not possible without resistance of reaction and that protoplasm, in the language of Huxley, cannot live except by continually dying.[3]

Certain major trends in modern philosophy, however, have rejected in toto the rationalism and the methodology that arose primarily from German idealism. Philosophers have moved in two other important directions. One is known as *existentialism*, a form of philosophy which includes writers who reject the creation of thought systems altogether and emphasize the importance of meaning found through each man's personal encounter with the world. The other direction is known as *logical positivism*, a philosophy which would eliminate the personal dimension entirely and insist upon stressing the more definitive and mathematical nature of truth. The basic premises of these two approaches to knowledge in philosophy would appear today to be irreconcilable polarities.

These two splinter trends in modern philosophy are not unlike the methodological differences represented in sociological studies. The two approaches we have examined in social research of traditional empiricism and participant observation represent comparable, but perhaps less severe differences. The traditional, empirical approach stresses definitive, operational language which has reference to sense data, while the participant-observer approach stresses sensitizing terms which refer to human meanings interpreted within cultural settings.

In contemporary social thought, the study of symbolic forms seems to come closest to establishing some rapprochement of these two positions. The philosopher and the sociologist who seek to move toward some degree of theoretical integration of these polar positions in their respective disciplines may find a common focal point of interest in the symbol. That is, the position of the logical positivist and the existentialist in philosophy and that

---

[3] Morris Raphael Cohen, *Reason and Nature: An Essay on the Meaning of Scientific Method* (2nd ed.) (New York: Free Press of Glencoe, Inc., 1959), p. 165.

of the traditional empiricist and the participant observer in sociology may be linked systematically through a study of symbols.[4]

The philosopher who has done the most extensive and original work in this area of symbolism has been Ernst Cassirer. In discussing the problem of dualism in philosophy he says, significantly:

> For metaphysics and the doctrine of dualism, "soul" and "body," "inner" and "outer" signify two spheres of being strictly cut off from each other. . . . They are able to influence each other, even though this influence becomes ever more mysterious and problematic the more metaphysics draws its own consequences. But the radical distinction between them is not to be overcome. . . .
>
> For the critical interpretation, even this alternative dissolves into a dialectical illusion. For our interpretation seeks to show that the inner and outer experience are not two foreign and separate things, but that they subsist by virtue of common conditions, and that they can come to be only in conjunction and in continuous interrelation. Instead of *separation of substances,* there is *correlativity of relationship* and of *fulfillment.*[5]

The problem of modern philosophy and sociology, we may surmise, is to recognize and study the correlativity of relationships between the two positions. In esthetic theory, for example, the methodological problem is to study how *form* may correspond and be mutually related to *expression* and under what conditions each may fulfill the other. We will suggest later that there is a parallel problem in sociological theory in terms of the dualities which it confronts today.

In Cassirer's work, *Philosophy of Symbolic Forms,*[6] we find the closest approximation to a system which makes intelligible the relationships of major philosophical dualities in human understanding. Some philosophers have suggested that Cassirer has provided the basis for a fundamentally new philosophical perspective which integrates the long debated metaphysical dualism of idealism and naturalism.[7] Whether or not a "naturalistic idealism" or an "idealistic naturalism" will eventually emerge from Cassirer's theory of symbolic systems, at this point it does seem true that the spirit in which Cassirer has approached his task gives him a vantage point. Philosophy, he says, cannot give up its search for fundamental unity:

---

4 For the study of signs and symbols in logical positivism, see the works of Rudolf Carnap, C. W. Morris, and Leonard Bloomfield. The branch of philosophy leading to phenomenology and existentialism may be found in the works of Edmund Husserl, Martin Heidegger, and Gabriel Marcel.

5 Ernst Cassirer, *The Logic of the Humanities,* trans. Clarence S. Howe (New Haven: Yale University Press, 1961), p. 81.

6 Ernst Cassirer, *The Philosophy of Symbolic Forms,* trans. Ralph Manheim (New Haven: Yale University Press, 1953–57), Vols. I–III.

7 Cassirer, *The Logic of the Humanities.* See translator's foreword.

But it does not confound this unity with simplicity. It does not overlook the tensions and frictions, the strong contrasts and deep conflicts between the various powers of man. These cannot be reduced to a common denominator. They tend in different directions and obey different principles. But this multiplicity and disparateness does not denote discord or disharmony. All these functions complete and complement one another. Each one opens a new horizon and shows us a new aspect of humanity. The dissonant is in harmony with itself; the contraries are not mutually exclusive, but interdependent: "harmony in contrariety, as in the case of the bow and the lyre."[8]

Polarities in Sociology

Sociology emerged with Auguste Comte and his contemporaries as an effort to apply the scientific method of physicists and biologists to the study of society; the subject matter of society took on the characteristics of the physical and organic world. For the first theorists such as Comte, Spencer, Ward, and Tonnies, society had "structure" like a stone building, and grew like the "cells" of an organism.

Sociological theory began in the creative synthesis of two sets of theoretical poles. The model of society, a synthesis of the organic and physical dimensions of knowledge whose terms were applied to society, was combined with a method for studying society, a synthesis of the empirical and rational modes of knowing, called by Comte the positive, or scientific method.

Historically, the elements of what Comte came to call the positive method can be traced back to the Greeks, but it rose to a special importance with the iconoclastic writings of Francis Bacon, who exposed the fallacies of the medieval "idols" in his *Novum Organum* of 1620. Bacon noted two "ways of searching into and discovering truth." One way, he said, begins with "general axioms, and...proceeds to judgments and to the discovery of middle axioms." And this, Bacon noted, was fashionable in his time. "The other derives axioms from the senses and particulars, rising by a gradual broken ascent, so that it arrives at the most general axioms last of all."[9] It was the latter way that Bacon recommended be developed more systematically; it became known as *empiricism*, while the former method continued to be developed as *rationalism*. As we noted earlier, these polar forms of knowing were reconciled by Immanuel Kant as two independent, yet interdependent, orders of knowing truth, and together came to be known as the scientific method.

It is interesting to recall historically that what was integrated in the

---

8 Ernst Cassirer, *An Essay on Man* (New Haven: Yale University Press, 1944), p. 288.
9 Francis Bacon, "Novum Organum," in Benjamin Rand, *Modern Classical Philosophers* (Boston: Houghton Mifflin Company, 1936), p. 27.

model of society (*i.e.*, physicalism-organicism) and in the method (empiricism-rationalism) later divided again into separate theories which emphasized the separate principle contained in each system which had been originally integrated. The limits of the organic model were explored by Social Darwinists such as Scheffel and Lilienfeld, and by Oswald Spengler who formulated a historical perspective in addition to the organic model. However, the physical model came to be accepted as primary in the explanation of society by such students as George Lundberg and Stuart Dodd, and the emphasis of the physical model as the guide for studying social phenomena is still much in evidence today among articles in major professional journals. It seemed as if each system of thought—organic and physical—had not yet been thoroughly explored independently before the synthesis, and that each contained special meanings in itself which could continue to dominate the work of social scientists.

At the turn of the century, the theoretical trends turned toward the exploration of elements which had been separately combined to define the scientific method—rationalism and empiricism. At the rational pole of knowing, a theoretical trend, of which Georg Simmel and Leopold von Wiese were well-known proponents, arose in Europe and eventually influenced American sociologists belonging to the *formalist* school of thought. Within this theoretical framework, the subject matter of sociology was to be found in forms of "sociation" (Simmel's *Vergesellschaftung*) or in formal relations of terms (von Wiese). The polar character of the formalist school—*i.e.,* its capacity to study society independently—is illustrated by the following interpretation of its approach, which makes no reference to concrete human purpose:

> Sociology...must deal with interhuman relations without immediate reference to ends, norms, or purposes; it involves a wholly different kind of abstraction.[10]

Empiricism, however, began to flourish indigenously in the United States in the ecological studies of Park and Burgess and their students. For this school of thought, the empirical procedure and data gathered from it were emphasized and valued over the more abstractly rational form of approach to subject matter conceived to be appropriate to sociology in European schools.

While the organic-physical model has continued to be a dominant one in sociological theory even up to the present time, there were significant by-roads which the history of social theory reveals that must be indicated. They represent polar problems to be resolved in future developments.

---

[10] Howard Becker, *Systematic Sociology on the Basis of* Beziehungslehre *and* Gebildelehre *of Leopold von Wiese* (New York: John Wiley & Sons, Inc., 1932), pp. 72–73, quoted in Don Martindale, *The Nature and Types of Sociological Theory* (Boston: Houghton Mifflin Company, 1960), p. 256.

An early significant departure from the original Comtean tradition may be seen in the conflict or crisis theories of the nineteenth century. The polarity here was on a point which was basically human in character, rather than simply physical or organic: whether society was to be explained and understood primarily on the basis of consensus or on the basis of conflict. Comte held that all societies were based upon some consensus, some human agreement about important values which held the society together, and without which, there would be no society.

The conflict theories can be traced historically to Thomas Hobbes, Friedrich Hegel, and others, but the first significant theory for our purposes was that of Karl Marx. Marx held that society was to be explained on the basis of class conflict; it was through such conflict that society was formed and evolved through history. Society was to be characterized by a lack of consensus; it was fundamentally dynamic, not static.

It is interesting that although Marx was taken seriously in European thought, in American sociology he was never accepted in the same way. That is, Marx's theory served as a contrast for American sociological theorists, a point to be debated, but never a point of orientation for the systematic development of a theoretical system. His work was never incorporated into sociological theory or research in the same way that the works of Comte, Spencer, Durkheim, and Weber were utilized, for both sociological and professional reasons. Sociologically, we can say that Marx's ideological formulations were not consonant with American culture, for American society was not suffering from the crises of European societies, and therefore the Marxian interpretation did not have a personal impact upon social thought. Professionally (and somewhat less convincingly), we could argue that Marx' thought carried strong ideological overtones and moral imperatives which sociologists seeking to maintain a scientific perspective could not tolerate.

The implications of the greater weight of the sociological reason must be considered within social theory today. The history of social theory in the United States demonstrates that conflict theorists were evident here only in the form of Social Darwinists and social evolutionists who emphasized the "blood, tooth, and claw" philosophy implicit in nineteenth-century capitalism. The explanation for the survival power of Social Darwinism over Marxism must be that Marxian theory was simply not compatible with the reality of existing social arrangements of American society. We must make this conclusion because evolutionists such as Herbert Spencer and William Sumner enunciated their beliefs in laissez faire capitalism as clearly and as bluntly as did Marx in rebelling against it.

If we based our interpretation of these differences on the sociology of knowledge, which owes its origins largely to Marxian theory, we would conclude that the direction social theory took in the United States was dependent upon the functional position of social scientists living within a relatively stable political order, and reflecting in their ideas the "natural" conditions of the society about them. We mention this departure in American social theory in detail because it represents one of the basic polar problems yet to be reconciled between American and European social theory in the future.

Another significant departure from the Comtean tradition is to be found in social phenomenology. Professor Don Martindale includes *phenomenology* in his survey of sociological theories as a branch of the formalist school because of "the possibility it offered for a special kind of formalism in which intuited essences are assumed to supply the elements of generality in social life."[11] But the phenomenological school never became a legitimate part of American sociology. In fact, phenomenology as a method of explaining and understanding human society would probably be considered incompatible with the mainstream of American theory today by many sociologists. Only by indirect references or by means of a single concept has the phenomenological viewpoint entered American sociological theory.

In American sociological theory, Max Weber's concept of *Verstehen* is disputed by some as to whether it has any relevance to methodology, and interpreted by others to be important; but never has the principle which underlies the *Verstehen* concept been the basis for a systematic way of studying society.[12] Gidding's "consciousness of kind" comes close to serving as a key theoretical construct, but it was never developed systematically in any way similar to the development of European schools of thought. Similarly, Znaniecki's "humanistic coefficient" and MacIver's "dynamic assessment" are special terms that refer to the human perspective, which although felt to be significant, was never developed into a systematic viewpoint.

Probably the trend in social thought in the United States which most closely parallels the phenomenological trend in Europe may be categorized as *symbolic interactionism*. Writers in American sociology such as Charles Cooley, W. I. Thomas, Florian Znaniecki, and George Mead continued to incorporate something of value from the idealistic tradition in philosophy into the scientific temper of the times. This tradition is being carried on today in the work of Herbert Blumer, Arnold Rose, and others, and has recently shown promise of developing into a more systematic approach to

---

[11] *Ibid.*, p. 268.

[12] The terms *consciousness of kind, sympathetic introspection, teleology, end,* and *principle* were scattered throughout the works of early writers such as Ward, Ross, Giddings, Small, Cooley, Thomas, and others, but they took a secondary role to the terms derived from nineteenth-century naturalism and organic evolution. For a discussion of the background of this train of thought, see Roscoe Hinkle, "Antecedents of the Action Orientation in American Sociology Before 1935," *American Sociological Review,* **28,** No. 5 (October 1963), 705–15.

the study of human interaction.[13] The men of this theoretical bent have sought, more clearly than those in any other tradition, to study something of what we have termed the *inner perspective*. In no case, however, did the history of sociological theory evidence a comprehensive school of thought based upon Weber's *Verstehen* idea.

Social action theory as represented in the work of Talcott Parsons requires special reference here because of the key role it has played in modern theory. The conception of *Verstehen* and the notion of creative, free choice in social action was an early conception of the Parsonian scheme. However, it never took a central role in Parsons' work, and as years went by, took an increasingly lesser role, at times being dismissed entirely. In a perceptive review of Parsons' thinking on this subject, John Scott evaluates the place of *voluntarism* and *Verstehen* in this influential approach to social action:

> Since the subjective and normative aspects of action were the means by which voluntarism was given its salience and necessity in the action scheme of 1935 and 1937, they are the parts most changed in the scheme of 1951, where voluntarism has been obscured and reduced to a wholly hypothetical role.[14]

In general, Scott concludes, the subjective reference was rejected on "a priori" grounds, but retained for practical reasons "if ever it might be needed." Thus, we must say that the main line of American theory brought in *Verstehen* theory as an added thought, or an extra "rudder" to guide the boat when the main steering mechanism failed to perform adequately.

At midcentury, the elaboration of functionalism and its wide application in sociological studies was evidence that many sociologists were interested in exploring still further the organic and physical dimensions of society. Functionalism, of course, has its roots in the organic model, and represents an extension of this seminal, yet polar view of society. Its major conceptual terms, *structure* and *function*, which were originally used by Comte and Durkheim in fusing the physical and organic model, are clearly extended in great detail by modern macro-theorists such as Talcott Parsons, Marion Levy, and others, and by middle-range theorists such as Robert Merton and his colleagues. In low-range or micro-theory the physical model has served as the major point of orientation, with organic overtones in specialized

---

[13] While this trend of sociological theory has advanced considerably since the turn of the century, a continuing lag in its development lies in the fact that it has stayed primarily in the area of social psychology. The future developments of this important dimension of theory may be anticipated in the work of European phenomenologists who see the significance of symbolic meanings in wider sociological levels. For a brief systematic statement and criticism of the stage of this work in the United States, see Arnold Rose, *Human Behavior and Social Processes* (Boston: Houghton Mifflin Company, 1962), pp. 3–19.

[14] John Finley Scott, "The Changing Foundations of the Parsonian Action Scheme," *American Sociological Review*, **28** (October 1963), 716–35.

fields such as sociometrics and group dynamics. This includes the theoretical work of Lewin, Moreno, Lippitt, Cartwright, Zander, Bales, and many others.

At midcentury the trend was to explore to the maximum other facets of these original models of society, and to give emphasis to the physical dimension as the more fruitful and fundamental model of scientific inquiry. In the 1950's, Parsons joined his concept of pattern variables with Bales' four functional problems in a way suggestive of classical mechanics. Human action was thus conceived to be in a state of moving equilibrium and adjustment in space. The quantification of the system and the conceptual references to *action-space, inertia,* etc., represented another reconceptualization of the physical model with certain features of the organic model setting the basis for strengthening the foundation of the action scheme of analysis.[15]

There are signs of change in the basic orientation of sociological inquiry, in the second half of the twentieth century, but before we can hazard a look ahead, we should pause to examine the differences between polar *principles* of analysis and polar *typologies.*

Major Polar Principles

We use the term *major polar principle* to refer to that abstract concept which sums up a system of thought that is fundamental to explaining the character of society. For example, the organic principle and the physical principle which have guided social theory in the past may be considered to be polar principles.

Major polar principles can be identified by their ability to generate coherent analytical systems for explaining social data that are relatively complete in themselves. Their level of abstraction and capacity to provide insight into social relations are so profound that they become pivotal points or basic principles of special inquiries into the nature of society. Their opposites, however (and this is the salient point), cannot be made wholly subordinate to these principles without distortion; that is, one polar perspective cannot be explained from the framework of another without changing the meaning of that type of fact which is found through the independent functioning of the other principle. This means of course, that they are each ultimately involved in the complete explanation of social data, and also that they are not wholly independent and self-sufficient in their capacity to explain social data.

Some methodological polar principles about which we have had occasion

---

15 Talcott Parsons, Robert Bales, and Edward Shils, *Working Papers in the Theory of Action* (New York: Free Press of Glencoe, Inc., 1953).

to refer in this book have been teleology-causality, freedom-determinism, physicalism-organicism, quality-quantity, and analysis-synthesis. If we were to use these polarities to explain what happened in a social event, such as a man fleeing from a crowd (to use the classic illustration of the Lundberg-MacIver debate),[16] we would find all these polar principles and the explanatory concepts they generate quite applicable within their own framework of analysis. The situation can be interpreted quantitatively or qualitatively. It can be understood in terms of the causes of the man's behavior or in terms of his purposes and interests. As we indicated earlier, a causal analysis will tend to lead to a deterministic explanation, and an explanation of man's purpose will lead to some conception of freedom. The scene can be broken down methodologically into abstract parts and thus "analyzed," or it can be described according to its significant common elements that lead to synthesizing judgments about the data.

From this viewpoint, then, the researcher or theorist has the option of choosing the basis upon which he intends to explain the phenomena. This does not necessarily mean that he has an either-or choice between principles, but he must judiciously employ the concepts associated with each major principle in such a way as to maintain the authenticity of the principle in his explanation. Sociological theory has already demonstrated that organic and physical principles can be employed in the analysis of an event without serious contradiction of terms. In fact, as we have just indicated, this has been most significant achievement of sociological analysis up to the present time. The major polar problem today lies in another direction.

The emerging problem is that no matter how carefully and accurately a situation is described in modern analytical terms, its analysis still keeps the observer outside the scene itself, resulting in the observer's inability to fully or accurately understand the nature of his data. This is one of the major polar problems to be considered in greater detail after we review another facet of polarity.

Major Polar Typologies

Sociological typologies are introduced as opposites, and since they have been a basic part of sociology since its inception, they require special attention here. There are, for example, such typologies as Tonnies' *Gemeinschaft-*

---

16 This illustration may be examined in the following works: Robert M. MacIver, *Society: A Textbook of Sociology* (New York: Holt, Rinehart & Winston, Inc., 1937), pp. 476–77; G. A. Lundberg, *Foundations of Sociology* (New York: The Macmillan Company, 1939), pp. 12–14; Robert M. MacIver, *Social Causation* (Boston: Ginn & Company, 1942), pp. 299–300; Robert M. MacIver and C. H. Page, *Society: An Introductory Analysis* (New York: Holt, Rinehart & Winston, Inc., 1949), p. 628.

Gesellschaft, Sorokin's sensate-ideational, Parsons' pattern variables, Red-field's folk-urban, Maine's status-contract, and Weber's charismatic-bureau-cratic. There are many other sociological terms, which are somewhat similar to typologies, such as primary-secondary group and social organiza-tion-disorganization; although they are often applied with less rigor than typologies, they do contain oppositional characteristics.

Typological dichotomies are intentionally designed to refer to specific empirical referents at a middle-range level of generalization, although they may approach the level of an operational concept in some cases. Typologies may be distinguished from major polar principles in that polar types are designed to be mutually exclusive and to apply to a concrete case in an either-or fashion. In other words, they exist below the level of the *principle* and above the level of the *operational concept.*

Polar typologies are sometimes difficult to distinguish from polar principles because the latter are involved in the description of typologies. For example, Howard Becker's sacred-secular typology is based largely upon the polar principles of *permanence* and *change.*[17] What Becker has done in this par-ticular typology is to break down two independent principles into a series of parts which reveal a continuous graduation of concrete situations, which are in a state of fixity at one end of a continuum, and in a state of flux or rapid change at the other end. Becker's empirical types run from a maximum state of reluctance to accept change, a condition Becker terms "holy," to other fixed conditions he calls (in the order of their openness to change) "loyalty," "intimacy," "moralistic," "fitting," "appropriate"; at the latter stage, zero is reached, and types of secularity are described as "principial evaluation," "expediency," and finally "nonrational secularity," which ex-presses the condition wherein people embrace all change for the thrill of it. These types are intended to refer to specific social situations and to be mutually exclusive in their application. A particular situation, for example, must be characterized by the researcher as either being "expedient," or "holy"; it cannot be both at the same time.[18]

Typologies are seldom defined so explicitly as to be wholly operational, although at first it would seem to be the case with Becker's subtypes. Becker states clearly that the continuum may be applied to "any society or part thereof," which allows, we must say, considerable room for estimation when applied at the level of whole societies. What is lost by the lack of precision, however, is offset by what is gained by the insight produced at

---

17 Howard Becker and Alvin Boskoff, *Modern Sociological Theory* (New York: The Dryden Press, 1957), pp. 133–85.

18 The polar principles of permanence and change are also evident in other typologies such as Vilfredo Pareto's *rentier* and *speculator* and the residues of *com-bination* and *persistence of aggregates,* as well as in W. I. Thomas' personality types, *Philistine* and *Bohemian,* and his analysis of man's basic wishes.

the rational level. The typology characteristically adds descriptive criteria which go beyond operational visibility and are a middle-range expression of polar principles.

What distinguishes polar principles from polar typologies, then, is the fact that the principles are actually high-level abstractions which reflect universal traits of social phenomena, whereas typologies are restricted to a class of empirical instances. Applying the universality test to those polar principles we have considered so far would lead us to conclude the following: the observer should never be able to find any social situation where there is no human purpose involved in it; no social situation which is not causally determined; no situation without some degree of social change taking place within it; and no situation which does not have some degree of fixity or permanence evident in it also. In other words, major polar principles express a deeper, more pervading truth about human social action than do lower-level generalizations. When we posit, for example, that every human act has something unique in it which is discoverable and demonstrable in the universal fact of social change, we also posit that every human act has something of tradition (structure) in it, that people cannot act completely separated from their past—which structures their action in ways that are discoverable and empirically really there. The many research studies of typologies which are associated with these principles continue to validate their existence.

It seems fairly clear now which major polar principles and typologies have yet to be given their proper focus in twentieth-century theory. These principles can be summed up in the still larger concept of "the human perspective" which has yet to be adequately defined and related to what in the past has been a combination of the organic and physical perspectives. Some of the principles and types contained within the human perspective which must be examined for their meaning and their articulation with their counterparts in present sociological theory are: human purpose, human order, human freedom, human crisis, human trust, human conflict, human justice, and other cultural terms such as capitalism, communism, Christianity and Buddhism, which must be applied to, and conversely, must develop from a concrete, historical reality. Concepts explaining the inner perspective of society are out of focus in the second half of the twentieth century because they still carry nineteenth-century misconceptions which are no longer applicable or relevant. The concept of purpose, caught up as it was in the welfare-oriented sociology of the last century is out of focus for good reason. The problem today really is one of refocusing and redefining these concepts in the light of modern theory.

This is no small task for sociological theory. It is less likely to be accomplished in any single stroke of theoretical genius than through the gradual, continuous outpourings of creative researchers and theoreticians who become conscious of the problems in technical jargon and begin to develop a vocabulary which fits the problems immediately before them. Individual efforts should together begin to lay a foundation into which alien principles and typological concepts can be gradually incorporated.

If any systematic effort were made to facilitate the process of incorporating basic concepts associated with the human perspective into sociological theory, certain methodological steps would have to be taken. These steps would need to be guided by the wisdom of past works in both philosophy and sociology. In a preliminary way, we may suggest a few methodological guides which do take into account works and ideas we have reviewed so far in this chapter.

Methodological Guides

1: Theoretical principles and typologies should be examined for their level of abstraction or concreteness.

2: Social phenomena should be understood as being selected, interpreted, and explained within the framework of those particular principles and typologies employed in the study.

As we have noted, principles and typologies function at different levels of abstraction and for different purposes. Abstract principles describe and explain all social data and serve to generate middle-range concepts and typologies which become associated with their original, and generally polar, interpretation of the social world. That is, middle-range typologies are dependent upon higher-range parent principles or sets of principles which are linked with them. Typologies explain particular empirical data in terms of whether certain characteristics are visible or not. The typology selects certain characteristics to emphasize in analysis, but the theoretical principles with which it is associated have, at a higher level, "preselected" what the typologies will, in turn, select in more specific detail for examination. Since these selective features and levels of abstraction are so closely interwoven and difficult to distinguish in particular typologies, we need to examine particular cases to illustrate the problems to be solved.

The Parsons-Shils typology of pattern variables should serve as one example because of its complexity in moving between levels of abstration, and because of the tendency for some researchers to interpret the social phenomena outside the framework for which it was designed. The pattern variables are defined in this way:

A *pattern variable* is a dichotomy, one side of which must be chosen by an actor before the meaning of a situation is determinant for him, and thus before he can act with respect to that situation. We maintain that there are only five *basic* pattern variables (*i.e.,* pattern variables deriving directly from the frame of reference of the theory of action) and that, in the sense that they are *all* of the pattern variables which so derive, they constitute a system.[19]

The problem to be clarified here lies first with the kind of principles which guide the typology. The theoretical system generating the typology is heavily in the Durkheimian tradition, for its "theory of action" stresses terminology and a viewpoint associated with nineteenth-century naturalism. Human beings are referred to as "objects" of an actor's orientation system, in much the same sense, as we noted earlier, that Durkheim ruled that all social phenomena were to be analyzed. The problem which the typology is set to explain involves human choice and a "definition of the situation," a theoretical problem which would normally develop from a personal or inner perspective. However, the terminology of the theory would explain these choices almost wholly in physical terms. Even the distinctions which action theory makes between internal and external actions, seemingly a concept parallel to the inner and outer perspectives as we have discussed them, are actually both considered from the outer perspective. That is, such terms as *unit, inputs* and *outputs, magnitudes, consumatory-instrumental,* etc., are representative of how action theory explains the inner world in terms of the outer. Individual or group decision-making, it is assumed, can be accounted for in terms of the "internalization" of "cultural objects," as though people were swallowing ideas like food and the scientist must then trace the digestion in the mind. Clearly, the consistent use of such analytical terms, unless placed in perspective, leads to a conception which differs markedly from inner reality. The principles of action theory "preselect" the kind of phenomena to be studied.

There is also a special level of scientific abstraction involved in this analysis. The pattern variable typology provides insight into decision-making within the set of action theory principles, but does not exhaust the possibilities of explaining decision-making from other sets of principles. A misconception which often arises from the application of the typology is that a phenomenological or personal perspective is being employed in clarifying varieties of choice, or in describing the actual ways in which people "define situations." This, however, is not wholly the case for several reasons.

One is the use of abstract terms to describe what would actually be personal experiences of people who make choices. For example, the category of the "self-collective orientation" is not based upon decisions people might actually have to make between self-interest and group-interest, a decision

---

[19] Talcott Parsons and Edward Shils, eds., *Toward a General Theory of Action* (Cambridge, Mass.: Harvard University Press, 1952), p. 77.

which is understandable in personal terms. Pattern variable categories are described as "cultural expectations" of what is designed for particular role-sets in social institutions. This is a level of abstraction a step above the actual decision-making process, even though this level is constructed to refer back to what may take place. That is, there are additional meanings imputed at this level which are not contained in the real situation, but are imposed upon it to explain it in terms not directly consonant with the cases themselves. People do not make decisions which take into account whether these decisions are "universal" or "particular," "specific" or "diffuse," as the terms of typology would suggest.

People do not generally define personal decisions in impersonal, abstract terms. For example, firemen do not decide to "maximize their immediate gratifications" when they refuse to enter a burning building. These are terms which need have no symbolic significance to people in actual situations. Therefore, from one viewpoint, whether these theoretical types are actual choices is open to question. In fact, Don Martindale labels the pattern variables as a case of "surrealism."[20]

If a researcher explains a situation from a phenomenological viewpoint, and seeks to use pattern variables to do so, then an accusation of surrealism is understandable and meaningful. This would be a case of interpreting one type of social universe in terms of another, or, as we say, expecting one polar principle to completely explain the facts of another. The social universe of discourse in the phenomenology of everyday affairs is symbolically different in meaning than pattern variable analysis would suggest. Yet, it is possible and important to explain human interaction on this abstract basis (pattern variables) as well as it is possible and important to explain it on the concrete basis of the symbolic language of daily interactions. In the latter case, the observer must move within that framework of people who are the subjects of study, and then develop a vocabulary which begins within their perspective, subsequently moving on to points beyond, but linked to it. This is the approach implicit in the methodology of participant observation.

Illustrations of such kinds of explanations may be found in studies which utilize the method of participant observation. Field studies of anthropologists are replete with examples of how they have sought to explain the original meanings of primitive expressions, and sociological studies involving participant observation also give evidence of this kind of explanation. For example, a study of the processes of social change interpreted on this basis may be found in the monograph *Communities in Action,* a field study of how people took action to change local social conditions they deemed

---

20 Martindale, *The Nature and Types of Sociological Theory,* p. 497.

undesirable.[21] The study was directed especially at how change took place within the symbolic lives of the people who were involved. To accomplish this end, the observer had to enter into the process itself, and interpret it as it appeared to the people engaged. At some points, the observer and the subjects had to work in concert to obtain an adequate explanation, formulating appropriate, descriptive terms and phrasings to explain the change dynamically and personally as it was felt by the people, in terms which had meaning for them as well as for the observer. In other words, the terms employed to explain the process of social change were not rationally drawn from the perspectives of biology or physics, but came from the symbolic life of the people who were involved.

Such a personal, concrete explanation even though it is widely applicable, is not wholly sufficient in itself for the purposes of social science any more than is the impersonal abstract type of analysis, traditional to the physical sciences. Each is sufficient for certain levels of understanding, but cannot serve as a model for all of social theory. By themselves these approaches illustrate different principles and levels of inquiry, selecting what is important for study. Together, these approaches help explain the human perspective; separately, they are sufficient only unto themselves, and to each other, may appear to be unreal, even surrealistic.

3: Theoretical principles and typologies should be studied for their explanatory potential and autonomy, as well as for their boundary lines, beyond which their application is unwarranted.

The history of social theory has clearly demonstrated the disadvantages of exploring a polar principle all the way to its logical limits, as if it were the sole or primary principle of social analysis. But this history has also demonstrated that logical exploration of "limits" has a definite value, for exploration is the only way that the potentialities of each theoretical principle can be discovered. Some of the potentialities for explaining the nature of social phenomena by way of organic and physical principles have already been demonstrated; their power to generate new useful conceptions of the social world still seem endless. The great sociological openings produced through the seminal syntheses of Comte and Spencer have not yet ceased to provide insight into the nature of society, and the development of functionalism as an institutionalized part of the modern sociological enterprise is a major indication of the remaining potential which still lies in the organic perspective.

The work of George Lundberg, while in many ways valuable to social research and theory, reveals the logical limits of the physical principle ap-

---

[21] Severyn T. Bruyn, *Communities in Action: Pattern and Process* (New Haven: College and University Press Service, Inc., 1963).

plied to society. The works of Schäffle, Spengler, and other organicists, again providing useful insights, nevertheless reveal the limits of the organic principle when explored to its logical ends.

Drawing boundaries or limits to the application of major principles to explain social data is in the interest of curbing that human tendency to overstate a case or misconceive a situation where a principle is actually inapplicable. And, as we have previously stated, the models of analysis which are current in sociological theory have not provided an adequate basis for interpreting much that still must be explained in the symbolic, cultural life of people living in society. For example, theorists must face the question as to whether such concepts as *dysfunction* and *dystructure* are adequate to explain the full power, poignancy, and meaning of human crisis. Theorists need to determine whether their *normative theories* of social action are sufficient to explain the growth and significance of organized power within society; and whether such terms as *optimization of gratification* and *cathectic* are adequate to explain the deep spiritual craving and striving of man and its objective manifestation in the religious life of modern society. Theorists must conclude that while the concepts of *cause* and *function* are fundamental principles for explaining human behavior in their own right, neither is sufficient for explaining the "purposes" of man. Such concepts explain the reality of another order, an order which underlies man's consciousness in society.

Early theorists were not reluctant to include such concepts as part of their explanation of society, but their scientific orientation was often secondary to their reform orientation. Herbert Spencer, for example, explained in detail the stages of social evolution and then stated that man was motivated to pass through these stages because of his search for happiness. Emile Durkheim severely criticized Spencer's explanation on the basis that Spencer was explaining a collective phenomenon from a psychological orientation, and further, that purposive origins were not a proper subject for study by the social scientist. In his book *The Rules of Sociological Method,* Durkheim recommended the explanatory concept of function in place of purpose and the search for social origins. While Durkheim's criticism is well-taken in important respects, the viewpoint he supported completely ended serious interest among many sociologists in pursuing the meaning of man's purposes in society. While it is true that in the United States some reform-oriented sociology textbooks utilized the concept of purpose after the turn of the twentieth century, these approaches, as we have noted, were soon conceived to be incompatible with the interests of science. They took the form of ideologies.

Ideologies are composed of what men believe to be man's purposes. These ideologies differ from what we would term *theories of human science* in several ways. First, they purport to define what man's purposes ought to be, as well as what they are, whereas theories define only the latter. Second, ideologies are not set up to be empirically tested, but are believed absolutely to be true; they function at the level of social myth. Social theory, on the other hand, works in the spirit of the hypothesis; the theorist stands ready to challenge his own propositions with factual research. Third, ideology has, in the past, usually defined its opposite as evil or as something to be eradicated, and has thus missed major truths which may be found in the polarity that develops within it. *Social theory, we may now conclude, is at a point where it takes into account its opposites as a fundamental part of the methodological process of discovering truth.*

We can identify particular ideologies by the unguided effects of the polarizing tendency from which they have suffered. The adherents of these ideologies (*e.g.,* certain formulations of capitalism and communism) often ignore the boundary lines of the polar principles the ideologies express best (*e.g.,* individual vs. community) and distort the truth to be found in their opposites. Since much of ideology is based upon moral grounds, the true believer must seek converts and final commitments to his position. And since sociological theory is based on factual grounds, no firm commitments can be made until the theory becomes linked with reliable sources of verification.

While ideologies involving the purposes of man have often functioned in the past in an extreme polarizing posture, hostilely approaching their opposites as evils to be eradicated, ideologies of the future may take on more of the intellectual quality of scientific theory. Some statesmen, educators, and theologians already place less demand on their respective constituents to give full personal commitment to unverifiable beliefs and even counsel to wait for confirmation of ideas through experimentation and study of the facts. The values of scientific pragmatism contained in some sociological theories are finding common ground with American ideologies. For example, the interest in judging the veracity of propositions about the effectiveness of social organization in the light of social consequences of that organization in action over time not only exists in common with certain religious, educational, and political beliefs today, but also is allied with the scientific functionalism of many sociologists. While there is today some meeting between social science and ideology on these prevailing pragmatic grounds, these grounds are not firm. Sociological theory will likely be most productive in its capacity to explain the changing relationships between social organization and cultural beliefs without being dominated by the prevailing beliefs themselves.

In certain stages of explanation, sociological theory must necessarily be out of step with popular beliefs, exposing their social origins or revealing their limitations, much in the manner of the debunking motif which Peter Berger says characterizes sociological theory. This need be the case, however, only if this third guideline (exploring the autonomy and limits of poles) is followed and no further steps are taken. Indeed, the limits of poles have been misinterpreted frequently in sociological theory, leading to the debunking motif. But the debunking motif has been only a stage of theory in the past, and thus more of a fault than the virtue Berger would seem to imply. The initial inclination to identify the real by what is newly discovered and to interpret all else as appearance or epiphenomena, or to depend upon a narrow method for drawing conclusions about data, is not in the larger interests of social science. If conclusions are finalized at this polar stage of interpretation, the definition of the subject matter approaches the character of ideology.

Kenneth Burke has referred to this "debunking" tendency in social research and perceptively comments on it:

> I think that the typical debunker is involved in a strategy of this sort: He discerns an evil. He wants to eradicate this evil. And he wants to do a thorough job of it. Hence, in order to be sure that he is *thorough enough,* he becomes *too thorough.* In order to knock the underpinnings from beneath the arguments of his opponents, he perfects a mode of argument that would, if carried out consistently, also knock the underpinnings from beneath his own argument. But at this important juncture he simply "pulls his punch," refusing to apply as a test of his own position the arguments by which he has dissolved his opponent's position. If anyone is to say *"tu quoque,"* he leaves it to his opponents to do so. And he makes the application of the *"tu quoque"* test more difficult for his opponents by unconscious subterfuges on his part, involving ambiguities that are hard to discover.[22]

The debunking tendency results only in setting in motion the unguided processes of the ideational dialectic. The dialectic is, of course, what we began to set in motion in Chapter 2 by polarizing the methodological processes of research. Our purpose here, however, is not to debunk past approaches or to set forth the "real" approach to human studies; rather, our purpose is to set forth the complementary insights of each approach for revealing the nature of social data.

In certain cases, the polarizing method is a necessary first stage to reveal the nature of things, a stage which is part of a larger process of seeing "the truth in the whole." The next stage here, then, is no less important than the exploration of polar autonomies, potentials, and boundaries; it is that of exploring the interrelationships and mutual involvement that major principles have with one another.

4: Each major principle should be examined in terms of its mutual involvement with its polar principle.

As we have previously indicated, among the major theoretical problems which are still in the throes of resolution in sociological theory is that

---

22 Kenneth Burke, *The Philosophy of Literary Form* (New York: Vintage Books, Inc., 1957), p. 147.

problem which exists in the irreconcilability of the conflict and consensus theories of society. These two terms, consensus and conflict, are theoretical principles which refer to two modern trends in social theory, which actually may be traced historically to major differences between the original theories of Auguste Comte and Karl Marx. The Comtean perspective, sometimes referred to as the *consensual* viewpoint, is represented in modern form in *structural-functionalism,* or may be described as the *theory of social action.*[23] This perspective maintains a heavy influence in American social thought, standing in polar contrast to dialecticism or conflict theory, which is derived from the Marxian perspective which has been given greater attention and support on the European continent.

The mutual involvement and interdependence of these major principles in guiding modern theory have yet to be fully explored, but a significant beginning has been made by Pierre L. van den Berghe, who examines the *mutual involvement* and overlap of these two contradictory principles in the explanation of society, which is, we would contend, an important step in eliminating the false images contained in the polarity. The following excerpt is taken from his description. It illustrates how our fourth methodological rule should be followed, so we quote him in some detail:

> A second major overlap concerns the dual role of both conflict and consensus. Whereas functionalism regards consensus as a major focus of stability and integration, the dialectic views conflict as the source of disintegration and revolutionary change; each of those factors can have the opposite effect. Several authors, notably Coser, have stressed the integrative and stabilizing effects of conflict. For example, interdependent conflict groups and the crisscrossing of conflict lines can "sew the social system together" by canceling each other out and preventing disintegration along one primary line of cleavage. Furthermore, in a number of societies, conflict is institutionalized and ritualized in ways that seem conducive to integration. Gluckman goes so far as to argue that ritualized conflict evidences the absence of dissension. . . .
>
> Not only can conflict contribute to integration. Reciprocally, consensus can prevent adaptation to change and lead to maladjustive inertia, or precipitate the disintegration of a group. The high degree of consensus typical of "utopian" or "other-worldly" reform movements is related to their ephemeral character. Strict adherence to "impractical" norms (*e.g.*, celibacy, or the destruction of means of subsistence in expectation of the coming of the messiah) can obviously be disastrous. . . . In a different way, consensus on such norms as extreme competition and individualistic laissez faire, or suspiciousness and treachery as reported of the Dobu, or malevolence and resort to witchcraft is hardly conducive to social solidarity and integration.[24]

---

[23] Talcott Parsons, Edward Shils, Kaspar D. Naegele, and Jesse R. Pitts, *Theories of Society: Foundations of Modern Sociological Theory* (New York: Free Press of Glencoe, Inc., 1961), Vol. II, p. 1440.

[24] Pierre L. van den Berghe, "Dialectic and Functionalism: Toward a Theoretical Synthesis," *American Sociological Review,* **28**, No. 5 (October 1963), 702–3. Reprinted by permission of the American Sociological Association.

Van den Berghe goes on to say that if these two central concepts, dialectism and structural-functionalism, play roles opposite to those assigned to them by their respective adherents, then they are clearly complementary in character, rather than incompatibly separate, and some of the analytic concepts generated by each major principle are applicable in both approaches to the study of society.

There are some points, of course, which are not fully treated in van den Berghe's analysis. The dialectic was derived from a study of human history that categorized whole epochs, while functionalism was derived from a study of society relatively in its present state. This would make close comparison of the principles not altogether appropriate. Nevertheless, the analysis indicates the kind of procedure that is necessary to deal with the apparent polarities that continually emerge in modern social thought.

While the polar problem to be resolved in sociological theory in the immediate future appears to lie within and between the consensus and conflict theories, its most problematic dilemma has not yet been revealed. We can say that the conflict-consensus dilemma is now being recognized by some theorists as a "both-and" proposition within sociological theory, rather than an "either-or" proposition; the present task for these theorists is to explicate more systematically how these two basic formulations may be integrated. There is, however, a more serious subject-matter division in sociology, and the problem here goes to the roots of the history of sociology as a discipline: the history of sociological theory has been largely social in nature, and as such, cannot propose to deal with society in some of its most crucial dimensions, for cultural theories that deal with the place of historical configurations and personal realities of value, belief, and myth in a general theory of man in society have not yet been developed.

The beginnings of social theory lie in a fusion of physical and organic images of society; the social interpretations of these guiding images have pervaded most of sociological thought ever since. The root term defining sociology and the social sciences is *social,* and the basic terms generating from this principle have been *social structure, social function, social action,* and *social process.* The key terms of progenitors Durkheim, Simmel, Tonnies, and Pareto, for example, are terms of social structure such as *division of labor, anomie, sociation, Gesellschaft, systems of equilibrium,* and many others of the same genre; they are not formulated in terms of the primacy of cultural value or belief.

While it is true that sociologists do not deal wholly in the singular terms of social structure and process, but do make reference to cultural terms (admittedly, social science is a cultural phenomenon), the analytical emphasis is clearly social. If Simmel dealt with what might be deemed a cultural category, such as custom or coquetry, he dealt with it in social terms. Custom is a function of social class and estate, and coquetry is a form of social relationship. Any beliefs and purposes associated with these social forms would constitute cultural content, which for Simmel would be scientifically unanalyzable. When Durkheim dealt with a social problem such as suicide (which definitely has cultural dimensions), he analyzed it in terms of the breakdown of social relations and the collective social order.

Modern theories of conflict also have a social and structural orientation, and Marxism is no exception. To place Marxian theory in a class with American theories of social action and functionalism would seem, perhaps, the height of intellectual misjudgment, and yet this is the case where both give priority to social analysis. Karl Marx was a social structuralist of the first order, for he saw all of culture as a secondary outcome, an epiphenomenon of social structure.

We have yet to recognize that the modern-day categories of social structure and culture carry the dialectical problems which existed between Marx and Hegel, and which have not yet been fully defined in sociological theory. The problem cannot begin to be defined until the Hegelian tradition becomes part of the background for producing newly conceived theories of culture, just as Marx has been in the background of newly conceived theories of the conflict process.

Social theories have had several typological developments.[25] One type we will call the *formal theories of structure,* which have their antecedents in variations of Comte, Simmel, and von Wiese, and most recently have been expressed in the structural-functionalism of Merton and Parsons. Another development we will call social *dynamics,* which had its antecedents in variations of Marx and Spencer, and recently has been expressed in the work of C. Wright Mills. A third general category we will call *theories of social process,* which has had its antecedents in variations of Mead and Cooley, and most recently has been expressed in the symbolic interactionism of Blumer and Rose. The theories in each of the categories provide a link to developing theories of culture in sociology.

Theories of culture do not have such classical traditions in sociology. These traditions exist in other fields of inquiry, such as anthropology, history, and philosophy. It behooves the sociologist to look to these fields for data

---

[25] The reader should understand that such classifications as this are immensely oversimplified to call attention to the points about these theories that are relevant to the discussion. The reader should know, for example, that while Auguste Comte found consensus to be a basic requirement for the existence of society, he also was concerned with dynamics. In fact, Comte originally divided the subject matter of sociology into two divisions—social statics and dynamics. The works of Talcott Parsons, Robert Merton, and others included are individually much more complicated and ramified than our references to them would seem to suggest. Social theory, as it has developed within sociology, cannot be treated adequately in a few pages; that has not been our purpose. The significance of such summary statements lies in the perspective they provide. Our perspective here is the overriding emphasis on the social aspects of society in sociological theory in contrast with the cultural and historical aspects of society.

and ideas, and then to shape these data and ideas by following the requirements of scientific inquiry. Let us briefly consider the possibilities of developments in this direction.

There are several conceivable schools of thought for cultural theory that
parallel the several schools roughly visible in social theory. One school
might be termed *formal* in the sense that it would stress classical categories
such as justice and liberty. This school would conceivably have much in
common with social philosophy, except that formalists would study classical
ideas in the context of structural and empirical realities in which the
ideas were conceived. Although scholars who are considered by some
sociological histories to be sociologists, such as L. T. Hobhouse, have treated
classic subjects such as social justice, their treatment of these subjects is
generally in the older tradition of social philosophy. Hobhouse, for example,
was interested in applying ethical principles, rather than studying them
objectively as they have been culturally constituted in society.[26]

What is possible in sociology today is a realignment of the cultural viewpoint. What is conceived to be the "good" can be studied by the social
scientist as an "object" of analysis. Values have an objective dimension,
as well as a subjective dimension, which can be treated as part of the total
context of society. It is in this sense that Max Weber studied religious
patterns in society. Students of culture may take some cues from Weber
on how to make use of historical data, and how to develop the necessary
distance from their subject to view it objectively. The problem of how to
use history and develop distance would likely be one of the first methodological problems of the formal school of cultural studies.

Another school of cultural studies might conceivably treat the "dynamics"
of ideology within the context of society. Theorists of ideology would study
how the great classical concepts become translated into particular creeds
and codes of ethics within national histories, how such creeds function with
respect to the great cultural ideas that thread themselves through a whole
civilization; and what are the meanings of such heavily western beliefs as
social equality, progress, and efficiency, which have had a historical impact
on the structure of western society. Most likely, such theorists would hold
that creeds and ideologies shape and transform the structures of society,
for sociologists have yet to seriously and systematically follow the tradition
laid down by Max Weber and formulate essential historical configurations
(in the sense that the Protestant Ethic was formulated) to explain the
movement of society toward a new social structure.

Obviously, there are new levels of study to be reckoned with here. First,
we have said that the classical meanings of, for example, truth, goodness,

---

26 Cf. L. T. Hobhouse, *The Elements of Social Justice* (London: George Allen &
Unwin, 1922).

beauty, and justice are philosophically traceable to Plato and Aristotle. Second, the institutionalized and nationalized formulations of justice or beauty, in particular times and places in the history of society, become relevant to a theory of society. The dynamics of ideology must be understood in relation to the dynamics of social organization. Third, local and regional meanings can be found in the speech and thoughts of people in everyday settings; in this case the field studies of participant observers can be very important. Commonsense realities need to be clarified and validated, and their relation drawn to official professions of belief and creed. There were very likely some important, explorable differences between the goodness officially contained in the Calvinistic creed and what was actually practiced and thought about at the local level which participant observers might well have documented during its introduction into European society.

Another school of thought involves theories of value which are concerned with modes of human interest and objects which occupy people in the institutional life of society. (At this point, a link can be made to the social theories of symbolic interactionism and functionalism. Talcott Parsons' functional treatment of symbolism is here relevant. Parsons feels that all cultural objects have both cognitive and expressive meanings, and he suggests that social interaction requires a "language of the emotions" as well as a "language of ideas."[27]) Adherents of this school of thought in cultural theory would seek to determine the methods of inquiry into the nature of symbolic values. Here again the method of research in participant observation becomes important, for to understand values one must know them personally and participate in those activities designed to express them.

The priority which the social sciences have given so far to the social dimension distorts man's true nature. In fact, the alienation which man has sensed and expressed in modern ilterature—the separation between his own consciousness of values and the social organization of his existence—is closely allied with the disparity within the social and cultural frameworks of human studies. Clearly, the modern problem of social science involves determining how cultural categories (e.g., of value and belief) can be studied in relation to social categories (e.g., of organization and class).

Social and cultural categories are clearly polar to one another, generating concepts and typologies on their own, and yet reflecting each other in reality and being interbound. (The concept of *competition* is both a social process and a cultural value.) These categories are interdependent, and yet, as polar principles, one cannot fully explain the other because their natures are fundamentally different.

The process of finding how these principles conjoin in reality, separate into different vocabularies, and then explain different aspects of this reality

---

[27] Parsons *et al.*, *Working Papers in the Theory of Action*, p. 38.

may be a slow one, a kind of intellectual evolution rather than a revolution, because the change is massive and involves a new language of research methodology and theory. It is true that there are other major polarities which need careful study (*e.g.*, atomism-holism, individual-collective, being-becoming, etc.), but the social-cultural polarity involves the very nature of social science itself as conceived in the sociocultural studies of man. Calling these sciences "social" indicates how deeply the problem is embedded in language itself. Therefore, it is of some importance that the study of social and cultural categories should proceed with considerable professional support in order to indicate the boundaries of use and the potential of these categories for explaining the nature of society.[28] When some degree of understanding is reached, then another methodological step will be in order.

5: The major principles (and terms which these principles generate) should be examined for their relationship to the larger whole, a holistic perspective broad enough to take them into account and to explain their relationships to one another.

This final guide represents an everpresent, deeply human interest in unity of thought, an interest which has been a part of man's search for truth

---

[28] The meanings of the terms we use to identify central issues today in sociological theory cannot be given in detail here, for they are too complex for our purposes. We are simply pointing to key methodological principles which lead to the discovery of these meanings. Nevertheless, it may be important to indicate a few rudimentary distinctions. The term *social* traditionally has referred to forms of interpersonal *relationships* and the term *cultural* to forms of human *expression*. Analytical terms frequently classed as social have been kinds of human groups, processes, organizations, classes, and norms. Terms frequently contained in the cultural category have included ideas, values, ideologies, beliefs, and scientific knowledge—in short, "designs for living." At some points the categories appear to overlap, as, for example, with the term *norms* which sometimes appears under both the cultural and social categories. In other cases, they are distinctly different, as when material objects are included under *culture*, whereas such objects are never included under *social*.

The term social has more often been used to refer to those forms of human relations which go beyond the particular meanings that people who hold those relations share. The process of, say, "competition," Georg Simmel would contend, has its own character, regardless of the beliefs of particular unions and managements who are struggling with one another. The term social, it should be noted further, has been broadly defined to include institutional relations (*e.g.,* economic and political) as as subcategories. Therefore, many American sociologists would consider the economic system simply a subdivision of the social system, along with other institutional structures, thus indicating their theoretical differences with Karl Marx, who elevated the economic system to an importance which many contemporary theorists would not accept.

The term culture appears to be used more frequently in other scholarly traditions as a more inclusive concept covering even the forms of social relationships of man. Even these forms, it would seem, are cultural expressions of man. The essential character of culture, however, is not generally represented in texts as interpersonal from the very beginning of civilization. Any approach toward this end is cautioned by the fact that an "integrating perspective" will only end in yielding still another polar opposite. Such may well be the case in any particular attempt to do so, but we can only conclude that the field of sociological theory must be better for it, since new forms of knowledge and understanding inevitably arise from the process.

The possibility of having some measure of success in developing a larger perspective is both sobered and enlightened by reviewing certain points. First, not all forms of knowledge emerge in the form of polarities. Many different ideas can co-exist with a single, larger idea, yet not be in opposition to a more embracing idea. Second, not all theories can be systematically integrated into a larger scheme. Theories, like the societies they seek to explain, are continually evolving. Third, to seek a systematic formulation on the basis of polarities alone will likely lead to a misconception of the nature of that being studied, as happened with other theories. Marx, for example, could not validly divide the world into only two economic classes, for class structure is much more complicated than his analytical frame would fully admit.

Both the history of ideas and the history of events are much too complex to be seen solely in dualistic terms. While ideational opposites may be formulated for special purposes—*i.e.*, to open up new perspectives that would

---

relations, but rather as the connotative meanings of man, which may be anything from hobo mythology to Handel's *Messiah*. The category of culture thus reveals a historical character in its usage, and in this sense, frustrates the American social scientist who seeks to follow the older traditions of Kantian science. The scientist has always yearned to transcend history, to move beyond the unique and specific content of events. He has sought the underlying, timeless structure and relations of objects. The square of the hypotenuse of a right triangle is equal to the sum of the squares of its sides no matter in what society it is found or what time of year it happens to be. And yet mathematical conclusions such as this are themselves expressions of culture, which would suggest that the category of culture cannot be restricted to national and folk histories relatively specific in time and place.

Moreover, many cultural expressions, which are filled with historicity and value, vary in their capacity to transcend time and place. Such nonscientific cultural expressions as the following have different degrees of universality and temporality: urban renewal, Protestantism, democracy, and affection. These terms increase in their capacity to refer beyond time and place respectively. That is, urban renewal is an idea, a program, and a value which is restricted to modern American society, while affection, at the other end of the continuum, is an idea and a value which (depending upon the definition employed) can be understood by people in every society through history. Similarly, democracy has more widespread meaning in countries of the world today than Protestantism, and some of its meanings can be traced back to the early Greeks. This is to say, culture is a complex phenomenon with all the characteristics of man, including his scientific traditions; its systematic study should reveal more of the methodological requirements of the science which studies it as part of its subject matter.

The term *structure* is used here in connection with the social category only because of the historic association of the terms in the scientific development of sociology. Structure refers to fixed relationships maintained between items of observation, and

otherwise be denied to social inquiry—it is still true that these opposites, rather than being in strict opposition, may instead be made complementary to one another within a larger perspective without loss of their essential meanings. The recognition of this fact is enlightening and hopefully will encourage future theorists, whose future task will be to set into mutual relationship and logical order a number of theoretical dimensions which have strong professional traditions and bipartisan identities. The task is a sobering one, indeed.

There will always be some developing areas of sociological inquiry that cannot be fully integrated with current efforts to systematize theory, but these areas do not lie outside the domain of professional interest or even outside the general sociological perspective which provides the framework for research. However, an overall theme must be found which is broad enough and central enough to the concerns of the sociological enterprise to contain the range of studies developing in the field. This theme is implicit in the methodology of all human studies, and broadly speaking, we may refer to it as the human perspective. While traditional elements of the strictly scientific perspective have seemed at times to be hostile to this theme, we can say that the human perspective contains no basis for rejecting the traditions of science, in fact, considering them fundamental to the pursuit of knowledge about man.

Edward Shils has commented upon this point of human interest as being central to the sociological enterprise. His reference to "humanistic," however, should not be confused with the *ethic* of humanism:

> Sociology is humanistic because it attempts to understand whatever man does, in categories that acknowledge his humanity: his need for cognitive orientation; his capacity for rational judgment and action, for affectionate attachment, for esthetic expression and response, for moral decision. Naturally, there is not a complete consensus among sociologists in this respect. There are sociologists who deny or disregard it, just as there are philologists and archeologists and historians who lose sight of the connections between the objects they hold in their hands or before their minds and the humanity of the creators, recipients, and users of these objects. The great traditions of sociology are humanistic; and the general sociological theory and the sociological orientation that represent the present phase of those traditions continue and make more articulate their humanism. Behaviorism and experimentalism, although they have not been without a follow-

---

in this sense is applicable to the study of culture. When analytically considered, these fixed relationships need not be socially based, but rather, culturally based. For example, an ideology has a structure in the sense that it has fixed relationships between the ideas, beliefs, and norms which compose it. These relationships may compare with other forms of ideology emerging in other times and places. In such instances, the uniqueness of a culture, as well as its universality, must be considered. For these any many other reasons, the study of culture should lead to a deeper understanding of the role of social science in society today.

ing and have contributed valuably to sociological theory and research, have not moved to the center of sociology. The fact that sociology attempts to observe precisely, and to express with precision, events that by their nature have imprecise boundaries, does not diminish the essentially humanistic orientation of sociology.[29]

The human perspective, as we would term the basic theme of the sociological orientation, is that viewpoint which seeks valid, reliable knowledge about man living in society for the sake of making man more intelligible to man. Most research in this perspective pursues facts and knowledge in human terms—*i.e.*, on levels that have meaning and human significance. The pursuit of facts may, of course, be made without any special practical interests in mind, but it is difficult to conceive of human studies conducted without any human interest. The term *human* is central here because it represents a dimension of understanding which suggests that the main theme of the sociological orientation centers on man as man, without reducing him simply to organic or inorganic levels. Yet man is conceivably organic as well as inorganic, and thus these characteristics must be considered to be part of the human perspective. The point here is that these characteristics (organic and inorganic) do not control the orientation; rather, they become part of the larger human perspective.

It is true that the term human sets forth certain assumptions about the nature of man. For example, it connotes man's natural limitations and his vulnerability to social forces; yet, at the same time, the term also connotes man's capacity to exercise responsibility and to know what freedom means. Human connotes a capacity to act on the basis of one's sentiments, as well as on the basis of instincts, senses, or rational powers. The human perspective does not take these assumptions for granted; it expects them to be explored for their human meaning and for whatever objective forms they take as man lives within society. The human perspective requires that man be studied as he is, in his full complement as a human being.

Such a perspective must necessarily generate special concepts and typologies which integrate research dualities, but it also generates special problems. Central to the problems to be solved are: How can a truly scientific rationale be retained when guided by a theme having subjective dimensions such as those in the human perspective? What objective standards can be developed to research the human themes expressed in the life of society? In answering these questions we would raise still another: What can the social scientists learn from the humanities in their efforts to study human society?

Our polarizing instinct leads us to explore the boundaries and involvements of science with its forbidden world, the subjective world of man. We

---

[29] Parsons *et al.*, *Theories of Society*, p. 1417.

find that world expressed through man's culture, already lit by disciplines in the humanities. It is time we turned to these "disciplines of culture," for they bear directly upon our scientific interest in opening more doors to the human perspective.

4

Toward
a Human Perspective

The Procedure

In Chapter 3 we surveyed the field of sociology as having derived its method of knowing from the Kantian synthesis of rationalism and empiricism, and its original perspective of society from the Comtean synthesis of the physical and organic models of the outer world. Now we want to explore further the nature and boundaries of what may be called the human perspective in the social sciences. We shall take the humanities as our major point of reference, instead of the customary model of the physical sciences.

This exploration can only be suggestive, for the main task of carving out the human theme that runs through the social sciences of man must be accomplished gradually and creatively by researchers and theorists who continually encounter the dualities implicit in these two great cultural streams—the sciences and the humanities. Therefore, the main problem is to develop the basis wherein both the outer and the inner worlds of man, with their conceptual systems and special vocabularies, can be viewed from a human standpoint.

First, we shall recapitulate what constitutes the dualities in the two research orientations to begin to define the general scope of the human perspective and to clarify what requires theoretical integration. Second, we want to examine the general boundaries which the social sciences have with the humanities. And third, we want to consider nonscientific approaches to knowledge (*i.e.*, literary, historical, existential, etc.), in order to better understand these boundaries, and at the same time, to indicate how these different types of human inquiry are interrelated. Our assumption is that the social sciences are part of a still larger pursuit of knowledge of man living in society.

84

The Scope of Human Inquiry in Social Science:
The Dualities

As we have indicated, the mainstream of social research and theory has followed the path of the physical sciences, and as a consequence, the human orientation we call the *inner perspective* has been avoided, or at best, approached with considerable ambivalence. When the subjective element did enter into social research or theory, it entered as a secondary source of knowledge (*Verstehen*), and never became very clearly defined methodologically. Where subjective realities of individual or collective life entered into theoretical formulations, they were treated as objects of the physical world rather than objects of the human world. Since social researchers initially drew their concepts from the physical sciences, they did not have the vocabulary to describe certain phases of human experience, such as those which occur in the subtle reality of crowd feeling and are a result of the personal effect which political power has upon people living in different social systems. The symbolic meanings of terms such as *faith* and *commitment* in the sociology of religion, or the personal meaning of terms such as *community, compassion,* or *tenderness* in human culture could not be contained accurately under the rubric of "emotion" or "gratification," as though they all belonged to the order of animal behavior. The vocabulary that did develop to explain the sentiments and cultural capacities of man, such as *superego, patterns of orientation, relational systems, cathetic attachment,* and *high-energy systems* left unexamined (or distorted) much of what was true about the nature of man. In other words, these vocabularies which were formed to explain the inner perspective of man failed to discriminate among the symbolic meanings that actually exist in the rather complicated structure of man's sentiments; they failed to distinguish among the qualities of human experience and to explain the refinements, as well as the coarseness, of culture. In general, social scientists have insisted upon treating all phenomena as objects and knowing them only as such, rather than treating them as subjects also, and knowing them as subjects.

We have said that as a whole, the social sciences have considered "causation" to be their primary explanatory principle and have avoided the concept of "purpose," some purists eliminating "purpose" from their subject matter entirely, and others ignoring its technical role in the explanatory process. We have said that the sciences have maintained a deterministic stance, and have sought to avoid entanglement with the concept of freedom, or else have denied the reality of freedom, other than as a myth of man. In sum, the social sciences have sought to avoid the entire personal dimension insofar as possible, and have developed their own set of myths for explaining man in society. Yet much of the work which has been going on in research has indicated that the social scientist cannot do this and still accurately portray and explain man as he truly manifests himself in society.

If social scientists were today to follow the corollary of Emile Durkheim and "eliminate all preconceptions," taking a subject as it is given, they would find that man has a personal dimension which requires study from within as well as without. The preconceptions or myths which modern theorists must today abandon are not drawn from the beliefs of medieval theology about which Durkheim was concerned, but from the beliefs of natural science which are no longer applicable for studying human society.

Partly by way of participant observation, scientific social research has been showing that it is possible to assume a human perspective of man and study his personal dimensions without violating the basic standards of research as conceived in the propositions of what we may call *modern naturalism*. That is, the social scientist can study man's purposes without identifying with them or normatively prescribing them. He can study the nature of freedom without judging it from some normative standard of his own, and can study the nature of man as a subject—*i.e.*, from a subject's own viewpoint—as part of his research data. And so, a new order of study has been arising from the older scientific traditions, revealing a human orientation to the study of man in society.

Human studies in fields such as anthropology, economics, political science, psychology, and sociology, as well as similarly organized approaches developing within such fields as human geography, human ecology, and linguistics have a common heritage and reveal a common methodology. They stand apart from what is usually considered to be the "humanities" in the following ways. First, they are all systematic in their approach to knowledge, for they seek to generate conceptual systems or theories about the nature of human phenomena. Second, they all conduct field experiments or studies which consist of placing certain controls on observation methods to collect data about the subject with which they deal.

History, we should say, stands between these social or behavioral sciences and the humanities in the American scheme of studies. History has been traditionally more concerned with verifying the true character and meaning of concrete human events than with the development of conceptual systems, which are a fundamental part of the systematic disciplines or sciences. Individual historians have ranged in their productions between the arts and the sciences, from biographical portraits which are actually artistic creations to historical studies aimed at revealing generalizations about the "invariant" course of civilizations over the epochs of recorded time. History, then, serves the double function of informing both the social sciences and the humanities about the nature of man in society.

This general methodology of the human sciences can be described from the common features of the separate research approaches which these disciplines have taken in the past. Briefly, we can say, first, that these disciplines all consider verifiable human experience to be central to their points of inquiry—*i.e.*, what can be humanly experienced and cognitively understood becomes the knowable, legitimate starting point for study. Second, the human event, whether it be a controlled experiment, a professional exchange of ideas, or a political act, becomes the context within which data are gathered. It is through the experience of human events and social acts, which include man's rational powers, that the inner and the outer worlds of man conjoin to create human fields of knowledge; that is, both the physical reality of, say, a landscape and the spiritual reality of a legend or a myth find their mutual relationship and their symbolic meaning through a human reality. Third, we find that concrete interpretations and logical inferences are made on the basis of what is both experienced and objectively observed in an event; these are the researcher's opening tools of investigation. Fourth, inductions or deductions are made on the basis of the analytical framework of a particular field of study. That is, the human ecologist builds deductively or inductively on the basis of his assumptions about man's dependence upon the physical environment; the semanticist builds generalizations upon his assumptions about the nature and derivation of words, and so on. Fifth, interpretations, inferences and generalizations are subjected to critical review and validation among professional students of the subject. Validation is based upon various professional standards such as statistical adequacy, logical consistency, the sensitively accurate reporting of field experiences, and the "fit" of new information or data with past knowledge which has been tested and found true.

A more technical statement of what distinguishes the social sciences from the humanities and from the physical sciences would carry us into discussion of the place of mathematical symbols, the philosophy of science, musical theory, etc., which is not relevant to our immediate purpose—to learn from the humanities. We want to know what the humanities can tell us about the human perspective, while keeping in mind the possibilities of scientific research through participant observation. To achieve this purpose, as social scientists we must look to fields in the humanities as legitimate approaches to knowledge about the nature of man, and initiate an interchange of ideas with professional people in these fields. We will begin by discussing the ideas of people who have not functioned within the naturalistic traditions of science, but have been interested in the pursuit of human knowledge and the advancement of culture.

Robert Redfield was a strong advocate of this interchange. Not long ago he suggested social scientists should talk more with their neighbors in the humanities. He said, "What shall they find to talk about? What have they in common? The answer is simple. They have humanity in common."[1]

---

[1] Robert Redfield, *Human Nature and the Study of Society* (Chicago: University of Chicago Press, 1962), Vol. I, pp. 46–47.

The Humanities: General Boundaries

We will begin by tracing boundaries, noting that certain forms of knowledge and methods of knowing are embraced by fields in the humanities, but are not acceptable to the human sciences. Fields of study in the humanities, for example, are interested in the general, universal forms of knowledge, as are the social sciences, but they are also interested in the unique and the particular as ends in themselves only, which is not the case for the social sciences. While fields of inquiry in the humanities are interested in what can be definitively formulated from human experience, as are the sciences, certain fields are also interested in what cannot be formulated, about which science has nothing to say.

Fields in the humanities are interested in methods of inquiry by which formless, "pure" experiences (*e.g.*, certain spiritual or mystical states of being) can be cultivated, as ends in themselves or as states instrumental to literary or philosophical purposes. Certain approaches to the humanities, such as art and poetry, are interested in devising ways of cultivating the purely spiritual or esthetic dimensions of experience as means toward creating new forms or symbols in human experience. Whether one can create symbols without any meaning for anyone other than the creator remains an open question in poetry, modern art, or dance, whereas in the social sciences, clear communication of meaning is essential.

Other approaches in the humanities develop fields of knowledge which are clearly out of bounds for the social sciences. For example, a field such as theology is interested in discovering *metahuman knowledge—i.e.*, knowledge given man by nonhuman sources. As a major case in point, theology simply stands on different assumptions about the nature of human experience than do the sciences, which can only assume a human framework for the interpretation of experience and events. This has traditionally included sets of assumptions about the physical, organic, social, and cultural being of man.

Furthermore, certain fields in the humanities are interested in nonlinguistic symbolic forms, such as in music and art, whereas the social sciences are anchored in a linguistic base. Some of the symbolic forms in art may have a special meaning which is significant to participants in the arts, but as we shall point out later, these forms have a different or added significance in the social sciences. Finally, certain fields of the humanities are interested in normative knowledge in the prescriptive sense,—*i.e.*, in formulating ethical imperatives—whereas the social sciences are restricted to factual knowledge.

Therefore, the human sciences are interested in the particular or unique, in the expectation that they may yield the general or universal, instead of serving only as ends in themselves. The human sciences are not interested in the pure, unformed spirit of man, or in private knowledge unless this knowledge affects others, or better, unless it develops some symbolic meaning in interhuman relations. The sciences are not interested in normative judgments or supernatural beliefs, except as these judgments may be a part of the cultural world to be understood in factual terms. Explanations of metahuman reality, as in theology, are taken by the social scientist to be studied objectively only, without reference to their metahuman authenticity, but their authenticity may be judged in terms of their meaning and significance in the lives of the people who do make supernatural judgments. The polar problem that exists between the natural assumptions of the human scientist and the divine or supernatural assumptions of the theologian cannot be resolved within the social sciences, but, rather, becomes the problem of the philosopher. Metaphysical judgment of theological assumptions is clearly outside the province of the social scientist.

In sum, it is within given symbolic forms of human experience that the social sciences must work, and it is within and through these forms that a scientific, yet human perspective can continue to be forged. It is through the convergence of the inner and outer conditions of living through human events, as interpreted through controlled, verifiable experiences of social researchers, that the human perspective is developed. The humanly oriented social sciences assume that the inner perspective can be conceived to be part of the natural world, with its own distinctive character, and that the outer perspective can be understood from a human standpoint without violating the scientific meaning of the terms developed within it.

These observations should begin to delineate the area which the social sciences are coming to embrace, and at the same time, to specify what they cannot admit to be part of their legitimate domain of study.

Fields in the Humanities:
An Interlocution of Science and Nonscience

The domain of the humanities, as we have designated it, is shared with the social sciences. For this reason, fields in the humanities contain suggestions for theoretical formulation and contain methodological tools which may be refined for their use within the social sciences. With these assumptions in mind, we shall examine relevant aspects of phenomenology, existentialism, literature, philosophy, and history for what insights we can gain from the methods and perspectives they assume in studying man.

Phenomenology

Originally, the distinctive feature of the phenomenological movement lay in its claim to seek knowledge directly through immediate, intuitive apprehension of human experience, free from the impurities of scientific conceptualization. This method of seeking original knowledge involves the "bracketing" of preconceptions, as Edmund Husserl would put it, or the "reduction" of concepts to a point where the observer can obtain a pure apprehension of reality. Husserl's types of reduction have been cogently summarized by James Jarrett and Sterling McMurrin as follows:

> (1) *Eidetic reduction,* which considers the object as essence or form, in terms of the characteristics that define it as what it is rather than the particular circumstances that make it unique and specific, [and] (2) *Transcendental reduction,* a suspension of judgment that eliminates or "brackets" the objects of all existence judgments, leaving the stream of consciousness dissociated from its natural connections.[2]

Phenomenology represents a species of knowledge and a method of knowing that are not within the naturalistic traditions of science. And yet a phase of the phenomenological movement entered the United States through the field of psychology. Phenomenology serves as the rationale behind efforts to understand individuals by entering into their field of perception in order to see life as these individuals see it. A psychiatrist describes rather clearly the attitude of the phenomenologist who seeks this kind of perceptual knowledge:

> Planning to write a treatise on swimming, he will first go and swim; only he who knows the sea, the river, the brook and the lake personally, *i.e.,* with his body, will be able to say something about swimming.[3]

This position is paralleled by the method expressed by Florian Znaniecki in his *Method of Sociology:*

> When I wish to ascertain at first hand what a certain activity is, just as when I wish to obtain first-hand information about a certain object, I try to experience it. There is only one way of experiencing an object: it is to "observe" it personally. There is only one way of experiencing an activity: it is to perform it personally. Practical men insist on this; they will tell you that you cannot fully realize what they are doing until you do it yourself. Scientists have come to recognize this. . . .[4]

The position expressed by Znaniecki came to fruition in sociology through the fieldwork of the participant observer who sought to observe and experience the cultural life of the people he observed. The interests of the phe-

---

[2] James L. Jarrett and Sterling M. McMurrin, *Contemporary Philosophy* (New York: Holt, Rinehart & Winston, Inc., 1954), p. 442.

[3] J. H. van den Berg, *The Phenomenological Approach to Psychiatry* (Springfield, Ill.: Charles C. Thomas, Publisher, 1955), pp. 62–63.

[4] Florian Znaniecki, *The Method of Sociology* (New York: Holt, Rinehart & Winston, Inc., 1934), p. 49.

nomenologist and the participant observer are remarkably similar, although phenomenology never developed in the United States as it did in Europe.

A phenomenological branch of sociological theory developed in the context of European social thought in the writings of such theorists as Alfred Vierkandt, Max Scheler, and Georges Gurvitch. Some illustrations of their work should be included here so that we may interpret the role which phenomenology has in contributing to the human perspective in American social science.

Through the analysis of personal experience, Vierkandt sought to discover certain basic social dispositions of man in society. This personal-social dimension, he contends, adds important knowledge about man which the empirical approach could not possibly apprehend. For example, Vierkandt states that the personal experience of "shame" is much different from other forms of experience closely associated with it, such as "fear of undesirable consequences." Yet if one were to examine only the external character of behavior, one would never be able to interpret such qualitative distinctions. For Vierkandt, society must be understood in terms of the inwardly felt social bonds, the sense of community, and the personal demands of reciprocity, which exist among people living together. He would hold that the human group cannot be understood by a description of its outer manifestations, for it possesses a spirit of its own which can only be comprehended through participation in that spirit. What unites and divides human groups can be found in the meaningful social forms (essences) that underlie society, such as inwardly felt trust, sympathy, hostility, or sociability, which are all basic conditions of human society.

Max Scheler, a student of Dilthey and Simmel, taught at the University of Cologne where Leopold von Wiese was his colleague. His major influence on American studies has been in the sociology of knowledge. We can summarize Scheler's general position by saying that it is an attempt to study the world of values or essences in contrast with the world of empirical facts. Scheler believed that the empirical world changed rapidly, while the world of values was timeless.

Although Scheler's theories are too extensive to review in detail, we will comment on his study of sympathy as a primitive concept of human relationships, for this bears directly on the method of participant observation.

In his study of sympathy, Scheler distinguishes four different kinds of personal relationships. First, there is the "community of feeling," in which people share a certain type of common feeling. Scheler illustrates this by saying:

> Two parents stand beside the dead body of a beloved child. They feel in common the "same" sorrow, the "same" anguish. It is not that *A* feels this sorrow and *B* feels it also, and that they both know they are feeling it. No, it is a *feeling-in-common*. *A*'s sorrow is in no way an "external" matter for *B* here, as

it is, *e.g.,* for their friend *C,* who joins them, and commiserates "with them" or "upon their sorrow." On the contrary, they feel it together, in the sense that they feel and experience in common, not only the self-same value-situations, but also the same keenness of emotion in regard to it. . . .5

Second, there is "fellow-feeling," in which one or more persons commiserate with others. In such a case, the outsider's sorrow is not derived from the original motivating cause, but he nevertheless participates personally in the sorrow of another. This state must be distinguished from other similar types of human feeling which are often confused with it. One can be informed, for example, of another's suffering and know of this fact without "participating in it." One can also say, "I can visualize your feelings," (as the novelist or historian must do) without actually sharing the feelings. Scheler says that in that feeling which is intentionally reproduced (as in imitation), we sense the quality of another's sorrow or joy without suffering or rejoicing with him. We cannot simply imitate a gesture of fear or joy and achieve fellow-feeling, nor can we merely infer feelings by observing another's physical actions. Neither imitation of behavior nor rational influence produces "true fellow-feeling." Scheler stresses the fact that the relation between the feeling experience of the subject and that which the observer comes to know can only be mediated symbolically.

Third, there is "emotional infection" in which there is no community of feeling, nor true fellow-feeling at all, although these two types of feeling are frequently confused with it. Scheler illustrates this type by describing the cheerful atmosphere at a party, which may "infect" newcomers who become swept up in the gaiety. When someone wants "to see cheerful faces around him," it is clear, states Scheler, that he does not mean to rejoice with others, but is simply hoping for infection as a means to his *own* pleasure, therefore distinguishing emotional infection as a form of sympathy from true fellow-feeling.

Fourth, there is "emotional identification," in which people identify themselves with others. Such is the case of the absorbed spectator at a circus who identifies himself with the acrobat performer, and simulates his acrobatic movements in himself, or the movie-goer who comes out of the movies acting in ways similar to the hero. There are two kinds of identification to distinguish within this fourth variety, which are of longer duration than these examples would suggest. One type Scheler calls *idiopathic* and the other *heteropathic*:

> Thus identification can come about in *one* way through the total eclipse and absorption of another self by one's own, it being thus, as it were, completely dispossessed and deprived of all rights in its conscious existence and character.

---

5 Max Scheler, *The Nature of Sympathy,* trans. Peter Heath (London: Routledge & Kegan Paul, Ltd., 1954), pp. 12–13.

It can also come about the other way, where "I" (the formal subject) am so overwhelmed and hypnotically bound and fettered by the other "I" (the concrete individual), that my formal status as a subject is usurped by the other's personality, with all *its* characteristic aspects; in such a case, I live not in "myself," but entirely in "him," the other person—(in and through him, as it were).[6]

In the former case, Scheler notes that there is an "all inclusive" propensity to identify, and in the latter, a complete and total identification to the point where a complete loss of individuality occurs. Scheler illustrates these types in a number of cases which would be fruitful for a participant observer to examine in detail.

Georges Gurvitch is a European phenomenologist whose work is probably the most recent that has been done in this area. Concentrating on the study of the "noetic mind" or the human spirit as his subject, Gurvitch recognizes his debt to Bergson's "method of inversion" and Husserl's "phenomenology of reduction." He also recognizes his debt to Emile Durkheim, who directed attention to the study of collective symbols, values, consciousness, and representations which are irreducible to individual consciousness.

Durkheim's theoretical emphasis was placed clearly upon the external manifestations of the collective consciousness of man, as we have indicated, yet his studies of religious life and suicide led him to confront a subject matter that was heavily subjective in nature. Durkheim referred to the systematic study of collective symbols and institutions as "social physiology," a metaphor which reflects his interest in maintaining the natural scientific perspective. However, in building upon Durkheim's work, Gurvitch shifts perspectives, stating, for example, that this "classificatory reference" (social physiology) was an unhappy phrase. Gurvitch suggests that the field of study could be better termed the "sociology of the human spirit," since it is basically the study of human values.

In an analysis which follows Durkheim's reasoning, but gains descriptively in a phenomenological emphasis, Gurvitch explains eight levels of study in this area. He concludes by saying:

> Our description of the levels of depth of social reality enables us, I believe, to define clearly the aim of the sociology of the human spirit or of the noetic mind: *It is the study of cultural patterns, social symbols, and collective spiritual values and ideas, in their functional relations with social structures and concrete historical situations of society.*[7]

There is yet much to be done to define and clarify the conceptual approach of the phenomenologist, but this approach, as it now presents itself,

---

6 *Ibid.,* pp. 18–19.
7 Georges Gurvitch, *Sociology of Law* (New York: Philosophical Library and Alliance Book Corp., 1942), pp. 43–47. Eight levels of study are summarized here.

may provide the basis for building a systematic viewpoint which would embrace the factual realities revealed in the work of the participant observer. The link between American and European thought that could enable theorists to produce a "fitting" of the two schools may lie here as well as in the work of Max Weber, who has nourished theoretical minds on both continents.

A conceptual contribution which European phenomenology may make to American field studies lies in the term *essence*. While the research world is already beleaguered with concepts which still lack sufficient clarity of definition, the concept of essence should be added, we would argue, and its meaning threshed out. The concept will likely be destined for abuse and will be misunderstood (as has been the case for ideal type), but over time the concept of essence could achieve a useful place in research literature.

While we cannot take time to explore the meaning of essence in full detail, we must consider some background facts. First, it should be noted that Husserl's interest in this concept was considerably different from both Aristotelianism, which dominated late medieval thought, and science, which dominated modern thought. Essence, Husserl felt, was not a buried quality in the nature of things that was destined to reveal itself like the oak from the acorn. At the same time, essence was not empirical in that it was temporal and particular, for although essence was embodied in empirical fact, its real form had persistence beyond time and space. For example, the perception of a red table is an empirical fact observed by the senses, but the perception of "redness" is an essence which had to be intuited to be understood. Husserl's many examples of essences were largely categories of philosophy, for example "unity, multiplicity, identity,"[8] etc., so the work of the social phenomenologist becomes one of interpreting anew the meaning of essence in social theory.

Essence suggests a quality of social or cultural life which underlies and basically defines the particular phenomenon being studied. It suggests a quality which is permanent and necessary to the existence of the phenomenon, a quality which is intrinsic and primary to its being. The term may be applied to such concepts as primary group, social institutions, values, society, religion, beauty, morality, or whatever sociological phenomenon might be studied. It changes the traditional empirical perspective on concepts and issues when it is applied. We might ask, for example, what is the essence of society? We then might also ask, what is the essence of social consensus and conflict and other related concepts? The phenomenological

---

8 E. Parl Welch, *The Philosophy of Edmund Husserl* (New York: Columbia University Press, 1941), p. 179; see also Edmund Husserl, *Ideas,* trans. W. R. Boyce Gibson (London: George Allen & Unwin, 1931).

inquiry into the nature of social phenomena refocuses our interest and deepens our answer, moving behind surface realities to discover that inner quality of form which gives the phenomenon its being.

In a few cases, the essences of sociological concepts have been consciously sought by theorists. Ellsworth Faris, for example, was concerned with determining the essence of the "primary group." He found it not in "face-to-face" relations (which he deemed an "accident" feature), but rather in the "intimate" relations of people. Even though sociologists have developed no rules for determining essences, and have not considered them to be an important part of scientific inquiry, it is very likely true that many sociologists have unconsciously had essence in mind when seeking definitions of terms.

It makes a difference whether a term whose essence is being sought is a sociological construct or a social belief. If it is a social belief, it should not be determined by the scientist's own theoretical musings, but rather by what is inherent in the minds of those who hold it. The social scientist cannot ascertain the essence of religious ideas such as the Sermon on the Mount, or political ideas like "Americanism," except as they are constituted in the expressed meanings of believers.

Essence stands in contrast with the ideal type, which discloses the more formal features of historical phenomena. Max Weber was uneasy about essences in ideal types, and feared the value judgments implied in them, as we shall indicate later in this chapter. However, we may work with values implied in essences as long as we know whose values they are and as long as the concept of essence is used methodologically in the interests of scientific and human understanding.

The most difficult level at which an essence may be determined is the level of an entire historical epoch (*Zeitgeist*). This type of analysis, however, requires more historical and sociological instruments of study than the field technique of participant observation can offer, even though the *principles* underlying the method are involved in the analysis.

At a more concrete level, essence could be interpreted as an underlying quality of social life that is inherent in a particular cultural setting which the participant observer is studying. An essence can be expressed in a concrete concept—such as Scheler's fellow-feeling, a quality which may be recognized as such by all those in the situation—and it can be understood symbolically by a nonparticipant through references to his own personal experiences which are the same or similar to that situation.

The process by which one arrives at the essence of a phenomenon is synthetic, involving bringing disparate elements of experience together intelligently and intuitively. Intuitively, this process requires empathic participation with the cultural symbols in the social life of the people being studied. It is a process, however, which should also be made intelligible by explicit references and illustrations which allow it to be understood and confirmed by others in their study of the same phenomenon.

It was on the subject of essence that students of phenomenology and existentialism found themselves frequently in conflict, as these two intellectual trends emerged on the European continent. Otherwise, the intellectual interests and spirit of these two trends are so closely akin to one another that there is every reason for their merging or combining into one movement. In fact, of late there are significant indications of the development of a new field called existential phenomenology.

Existentialism

Phenomenology and existentialism grew up together, paralleling and interpenetrating one another as fields of human inquiry which sought to place man philosophically back at the center of the knowing process. They have jointly criticized the traditional assumption of science that man as a knower is a reflector and recorder of an objective truth which is given to him as it really exists in the outside world; instead, they insist that knowledge is created by man, that the kind of knowledge of the world which is revealed to the knower has everything to do with his own "stance" or relationship to that which he comes to know. As man's stance changes, so do the facts he gleans about the world.

The existentialist's method for knowing the world begins with understanding man's existence. The aim is to understand his "being-in-the-world" (*Dasein*), the nature of his becoming, as it is presented directly to his consciousness. In so doing, the existentialist seeks to abolish essence and move directly to a consciousness of man's *particular* existence. To the existentialist, essence is represented by any form of abstraction, and thus the traditions of philosophy and the social sciences appear to be in fundamental opposition to the original interests of the existentialist. "Existence" cannot be described. It simply is. Essence emerges from existence. The sciences, the existentialist has pointed out, have placed such a strong emphasis upon abstracting truths about the world of man that they have lost original meanings. Scientists have come to believe much that is purely mythical about man, and the more the scientist tries to describe man, the existentialist argues, the more the real man escapes him. The more theoretical systems are constructed ("edifice complexes," as the existential psychologists call them), the farther man becomes separated from reality. As Rollo May has put it:

> Kierkegaard, Nietzsche, and those who followed them accurately foresaw this growing split between truth and reality in Western culture, and they endeavored to call Western man back from the delusion that reality can be comprehended in an abstracted, detached way. But though they protested vehemently against arid intellectualism, they were by no means simple activists. Nor were they

antirational. Anti-intellectualism and other movements in our day which make thinking subordinate to acting must not at all be confused with existentialism. Either alternative—making man subject or object—results in losing the living, existing person. Kierkegaard and the existential thinkers appealed to a reality *underlying both subjectivity and objectivity*. We must not only study a person's experience as such, they held, but even more we must study the man to whom the experience is happening, the one who is doing the experiencing. They insist, as Tillich puts it, that "Reality or Being is not the object of cognitive experience, but is rather 'existence,' is Reality as immediately experienced, with the accent on the inner, personal character of man's immediate experience."[9]

Existentialism, then, may be seen as a movement away from the perspective of man in terms of abstractions, that is, in terms of "id," "ego," "social patterns," and "pattern variables." The existential approach seeks to move to the original nature of man as he is before ontology, that is, as he may be perceived directly by man's consciousness.

One of the earliest and most challenging assertions about the nature and origins of knowledge comes from the existentialist writings of Soren Kierkegaard. From his deep personal struggle with rationalism as the path to knowledge, Kierkegaard concluded that reason was not sufficient for knowing the meaning of life, and that knowledge was to be acquired, instead, through personal commitment in faith. The fact that this personal discovery of Kierkegaard's should have anything to do with social science would seem at first, perhaps, the ultimate in absurdity. Yet we can find meaning, both for the development of a human perspective and for social research. Like all human sentiments and spiritual feelings, personal commitment and faith have their existent character as well as their normative, imperative character. In this existent sense they become part of the subject matter of research and the human perspective.

This is the link which social science has with existentialism, which otherwise is in utter opposition to all that for which the social sciences stand. Both are concerned with what exists in human terms, so that although it is true that they have each emphasized different aspects of human existence, it is not true that they need represent fundamentally opposed positions. The social scientist need not elevate the realities he discovers through his theoretical world to a point of greater importance than the personal and immediate realities of life, for these personal realities are actually a part of the culture he studies. Cultural life includes the dimension of faith, and the social scientist must know of faith and be able to explain it by understanding both the outward symbolic expressions and the personal or inward meaning of these symbols in his own life. A social researcher cannot understand the deeply felt religious beliefs of people or those political beliefs that bring

---

[9] Rollo May, Ernest Angel, and Henri Ellenberger, eds., *Existence* (New York: Basic Books, Inc., Publishers, 1958), p. 14.

people to the point of sacrificing their lives until he has understood the symbolic forms (theoretical, empirical, and personal) which identify these beliefs from each perspective. This is surely what C. Wright Mills had in mind when he went to Cuba to observe directly and to document the personal realities shaping the course of action in the Cuban revolution (*Listen Yankee*). The typically abstract treatment of government in political science textbooks is insufficient for these purposes.

It is only through personal knowledge of the religious faith or the political loyalty of a people that the observer can formulate adequately the concepts explaining this reality. The concrete concepts which he formulates must have a real referent to the inner meaning of symbols, just as do the rules guiding empirical research require real referents in the outer, visible world.

We are not concerned here with how existentialism arose out of the breakdown of the European social structure during the last century; nor are we concerned about the relationship of existentialism to other modes of expression such as art or social therapy. While certain existentialists have become associated with certain religious or political ideologies (*e.g.*, Kierkegaard with Christianity, and Sartre with a form of socialism), existentialism remains basically a nonrational (some existentialists would say nonethical) approach to knowledge of man's being. While existentialism's interests are clearly different from those of social science, nevertheless the writings of its adherents continue to throw light upon the nature of research when guided by a human perspective. Our primary interest here is with the application of existential principles to research, and particularly to the role of the participant observer as he relates to his field of study.

The participant observer finds personal commitment to particulars occurs at every stage of his work. He cannot avoid this, but he must not allow this commitment to totally destroy his objectivity. Commitment exists on many personal levels, all of which may interfere with or contribute toward objectivity, depending upon the kind of commitment which is established. If the social scientist is so committed to special theoretical concepts that he insists upon applying them where they are inapplicable, this commitment may interfere with his accuracy. If he values his personal commitments to the people he studies over his findings, to the extent that he distorts them to place the culture in a better light, he loses both his scientific objectivity and his commitment to truth.

On the other hand, as he becomes personally involved with and committed to the people he studies, he may get to know them better, accepting them as human beings like himself, persons who are capable of learning, growing, changing, or of being stubborn. As the social scientist becomes committed to the people he studies as persons, he no longer sees them as *objects,* but as *subjects,* thus becoming aware of certain features of their social life.

This commitment to the people studied may be very deep without inter-
fering with the social scientist's objectivity if he does not project his personal attributes upon subjects which are not really there; his study must
record what actually exists in the framework of that culture. If faith is
fundamental to the inward character of a culture, he must learn what
this means through his own participation in culturally given procedures for
knowing the nature of that faith. But, we must add, hate or hostility may
also be fundamental to a culture. Therefore, it is the responsibility of the
participant observer to comprehend whatever emotional and symbolic patterns may comprise the culture he studies. The extent to which he should
become involved in particular instances must be further examined, but
the necessity for the participant observer to comprehend particular sentiments with both involvement and detachment is fundamental to his role in
research.

The writings of Martin Buber, a Jewish theologian in the existential
tradition, are particularly valuable for illuminating the nature of participant
observer research. In his original work, *Ich und Du*,[10] Buber makes distinction between two existential attitudes contained in what he calls the *I-It*
and the *I-Thou* relations, which human beings assume in their encounter
with the world. The I-It world of experience is a world of detachment,
causal relations, objects to be manipulated. The I-Thou world is a world
of relations with nature and with man, as well as with other spiritual beings.
The knowledge of the I can only be gained through its relationship with the
Thou, which is the Other, but not God. Meaning is to be found in the
subject-to-subject personal encounter of man to man. It is here that we
find a major source of theory for participant observation.

Buber makes the distinction between these two worlds to be essentially
one of detachment (I-It) and one of involvement (I-Thou), ideas which
are quite relevant to our interest in participant observation. In social research we know that all conceptual activity is based to some extent upon
reflection, and therefore is in the I-It category, but we also have indicated
that reflection need not lead us to think of people as objects to be manipulated or as subject only to causal relations. In this sense, the category seems
too inclusively drawn to be applicable to our use. Yet if we stay with Buber's
original definitions, we must conclude that whenever we reflect upon objects
in our experience with interest and without thinking of them as instruments
or means toward some end, we are involved, and the I-Thou relation holds.
Rational reflection as such is then diminished. As soon as the participant
observer thinks of the people he studies as means toward some end, instead
of understanding them for their own sake as unique individuals in his ex-

---

[10] Martin Buber, *I and Thou,* trans. Ronald Smith (New York: Charles Scribner's
Sons, 1958).

perience, he loses hold of the I-Thou relation and enters the I-It relation. Thus we must place the social researcher largely, but not exclusively, in the I-It category. As we have noted previously, the observer cannot come to know his culture without personal participation in it, without becoming so involved that at some points he does not reflect upon his activities. To the extent that this takes place, Buber's I-Thou relationship enters into the method of participant observation.

The researcher, Buber's writings seem to tell us, must see himself as a whole person whose many parts become significantly related in his work. In his book *Between Man and Man,* Buber describes these relationships in still greater detail, which becomes relevant for our purposes. There are three basic ways, Buber states, in which people perceive other people who enter their field of awareness and experience. First, there is the "observer," whom Buber notes is one who immediately depicts or describes what he sees. Second, there is the "onlooker," who relates to the other in an uncategorizing openness. Third, there is that type of interhuman relation in which one person finds himself affected by another person in such a way that he cannot describe it. Buber describes two of these types:

> The *observer* is wholly intent on fixing the observed man in his mind, on "noting" him.... He probes him and writes him up. That is, he is diligent to write up as many "traits" as possible. He lies in wait for them, that none may escape him. The object consists of traits, and it is known what lies behind each of them. Knowledge of the human system of expression constantly incorporates in the instant the newly appearing individual variations, and remains applicable. A face is nothing but physiognomy, movements nothing but gestures of expression.
>
> The *onlooker* is not at all intent. He takes up the position which lets him see the object freely, and undisturbed awaits what will be presented to him. Only at the beginning may he be ruled by purpose, everything beyond that is involuntary. He does not go around taking notes indiscriminately, he lets himself go, he is not in the least afraid of forgetting something ("Forgetting is good," he says). He gives his memory no tasks, he trusts its organic work which preserves what is worth preserving. He does not lead in the grass as green fodder, as the observer does; he turns it and lets the sun shine on it. He pays no attention to traits ("Traits lead astray," he says). What stands out for him from the object is what is not "character" and not "expression" ("The interesting is not important," he says). All great artists have been onlookers.[11]

The participant observer who is at all sensitive to the elements that enter into his field of perception must realize that these differences are part of his own experience. In a very real sense, these ways of perceiving the interhuman world may be conceived to be phases in the process of knowing.

------

[11] Martin Buber, *Between Man and Man,* trans. Ronald Smith (Boston: Beacon Press, 1955), pp. 8–9.

Martin Buber has made a consistent transition from his existential stance to a philosophic conceptualization of the world, but his existentialism has shaped his conceptualization. For example, Buber's concept of *community* as a result of his existentialism is in considerable contrast to the usual sociological concept, and the difference is illuminating. The sociologist will define community according to the analytical purposes he has in mind, but he typically defines the term as consisting of a territory and a common set of sentiments or attitudes of people living in the area. He may select an area for community research by its visible physical features, but he usually stresses the importance of determining boundaries by the local "definition of the situation." This definition is considered measurable, so the sociologist may empirically determine it by conducting a social survey of attitudes held by the local population of a community. In any event, Buber's definition would go much beyond the usual sociological approach. He would insist, for example, that the concept community cannot be understood simply as a set of attitudes, since it is more fundamental than attitudes and quite beyond social measurement. Furthermore, community cannot be understood as an abstract concept—a conclusion which, of course, would be nearly impossible for a social scientist to comprehend within his present interpretive framework. In Buber's words:

> Community should not be made into a principle; it too, should always satisfy a situation rather than an abstraction. The realization of community, like the realization of any idea, cannot occur once and for all time; always it must be the moment's answer to the moment's question, and nothing more. . . .
>
> In the interests of its vital meaning, therefore, the idea of community must be guarded against all contamination by sentimentality and emotionalism. Community is never a mere attitude of mind, and if it is a feeling, it is an inner disposition which is felt. Community is the inner disposition which knows and embraces in itself hard "calculation," adverse "chance," the sudden access of "anxiety." It is community of tribulation, and only because of that is it community of spirit; it is community of toil, and only because of that is it community of salvation.[12]

The existentialist, we must conclude, typically seeks a level of meaning well below that typically sought by the social scientist. That is, by comparison the social scientist works principally with surface realities. *The scientist has been a topographer in the field of human studies; the existentialist has been a miner, searching the depths of human meaning.*

Furthermore, we must conclude that the faith and commitment about which Sören Kierkegaard was speaking cannot be considered a cultural phenomenon in the fullest sense, because Kierkegaard intended it to be

---

12 Will Herberg, ed., *The Writings of Martin Buber* (New York: Meridian Books, Inc., 1956), p. 128.

individualized. That is, the kind of faith which Kierkegaard explains in *Purity of Heart*, to which each person is called upon to will or yield himself totally for a purpose beyond himself, is an act which the reader should discover individually. In general, we may say that existentialists would seek to emphasize man's individual and unique experience in the world. If we accept this interpretation, then, existentialism is a noncultural expression of man, yet paradoxically, it is also an expression which is common to man and belongs to the history of man as he has manifested himself individually. In this sense, existentialism is not peculiar to a particular period of time in Europe when it became a philosophic trend of thought, but it is an expression of man as he appears continually and inimitably down through the ages.

Nevertheless, it is only through culture that the existentialist may come to make his unique decision or act of faith at the level of meaning he seeks. Every individual, the existentialist must come to recognize, is at once both within and outside culture. If this is not recognized, and the existentialist stands alone with his special view of the world, as indeed many have professed to do, he would risk the penalities of developing stark caricatures of truth not unlike the extreme views of scientism which he would especially deplore. The challenge which social science presents to existentialism is that man is more than simply a unique individual, for he is known and understood through his experience of community and through a common set of meanings mutually arrived at. The challenge which existentialism presents to sociology is that man is much more than an abstract, impersonal mechanism; he is a personal human being with inner dispositions which lie beyond usual measurements, and he must be understood in this light. Perhaps through a common recognition of man's humanness and propensity to misrepresent himself in sociologisms and existentialisms, man may regain the unique stature and dignity which is manifestly his to enjoy as a member of society.

Literary Perspectives

The problem of an observer's personal commitment and emotional involvement has long been the subject of literary criticism and history. While it is not in the tradition of those who create literature to develop consistent conceptual systems to explain these works, theory is nevertheless an implicit part of both literary history and criticism. Its conceptual and attitudinal forms must be considered for the methodological tools which lead us toward the human perspective in the sciences. In other words, the methodology of poetry is in many ways instructive to the methodology of social research.

We have said that the emotion which arises out of the personal context of the work of the participant observer is part of his own necessary experience, both as subject and object, and must be understood for the proper place it has in his work. But emotion or feeling can be disruptive, and as such may destroy the interpretation of the objective content of, say, the type of sentiment expressed in an event which the researcher observes. In confronting this dilemma, the participant observer is not unlike the poet who also seeks a certain truth apart from disruptive emotion. William Wordsworth, for example, was quite cognizant of the fact that his poetry was derived from emotion; nevertheless he cautioned against its overwhelming effects:

> I have said that poetry is the spontaneous overflow of powerful feelings; it takes its origin from emotion recollected in tranquillity; the emotion is contemplated till, by a species of reaction, the tranquillity gradually disappears, and an emotion, kindred to that which was before the subject of contemplation, is gradually produced and does itself actually exist in the mind.[13]

When and how should an experienced emotion be recorded? Here is a basic question of reporting procedure about which little is known in the sciences, but which is part of the classic wisdom of literature. Until there is evidence to the contrary, we will assume that the participant observer examines his experience more clearly in that period of "recollected tranquillity" than in the passion of the moment.

The participant observer must also learn how to view his subjects and to interpret the life contained in their beliefs so that his work is not designed simply to persuade the reader and himself of the ultimate veracity of their beliefs. Here, too, the participant observer may take cognizance of the elements that compose the classic forms of literature. T.S. Eliot, for example, once said of Dante's *Divine Comedy* that a great value of the writing was that one could feel what Dante felt about Christianity without necessarily believing what he believed:

> My point is that you cannot afford to *ignore* Dante's philosophical beliefs, or to skip the passages which express them most clearly; but that on the other hand you are not called upon to believe them yourself. It is wrong to think that there are parts of the *Divine Comedy* which are of interest only to Catholics or to medievalists. For there is a difference (which here I hardly do more than assert) between philosophical *belief* and poetic *assent*.... In reading Dante you must enter the world of thirteenth-century Catholicism, which is not the world of modern Catholicism, as his world of physics is not the world of modern physics. You are not called upon to believe what Dante believed, for your belief will not give you a groat's worth more of understanding and appreciation; but you are called upon more and more to understand it.[14]

---

13 Nelson Bushnell, Paul Fulcher, and Warner Taylor, eds., *Literary Masters of England* (New York: Holt, Rinehart & Winston, Inc., 1936), p. 702.

14 Thomas S. Eliot, *Selected Essays: 1917–32* (New York: Harcourt, Brace & World, Inc., 1932), pp. 218–19.

With something more than a scientific hypothesis, yet less than total commitment, the researcher must find a basis for his personal understanding of the cultural beliefs of the people he studies. And, in like manner (almost as would a poet), he must seek to convey these beliefs in his ethnographic report so that the reader may understand, yet not feel compelled to believe.

Similar to Eliot's description, Samuel Coleridge once described how he found it necessary to create a "willing suspension of disbelief" when writing realistically about "characters supernatural":

> In this idea originated the plan of the Lyrical Ballads; in which it was agreed that my endeavors should be directed to persons and characters supernatural, or at least romantic; yet so as to transfer from our inward nature a human interest and a semblance of truth sufficient to procure for these shadows of imagination that willing suspension of disbelief for the moment, which constitutes poetic faith.[15]

To the methodology of participant observation, in terms of a concrete example, this poetic faith means that the social scientist who is a committed Protestant seeking to understand the culture of the Catholic world, or the Catholic sociologist who seeks to understand the Protestant world, must, as a social scientist, be willing to "suspend disbelief." The participant observer who seeks to understand the world of the schizophrenic must be willing to suspend his disbelief in the hallucinations and delusions he comes to know, if he wants to understand the schizophrenic, and, in addition, learn to record this same process in his writing.

Therefore, in various ways the methodological rules of poetry may have important application to human social research. In addition to its "tools" of study, however, literary theory has more direct applications to the development of a human perspective in the social sciences.

The task of being personally involved in the world of values and yet detached in what Buber has described as the I-It world of experience is more complex than we are perhaps willing to admit. In fact, it is nearly impossible for any scientist to accomplish the task successfully, for he is bound to fail at some point along the way. However, the meaning which must be drawn from this tension, which is built into the separate poles of detachment and involvement, runs deeper than the action of any single fieldworker, even though we can see the problem expressed there. The problem involves the basic relations between science and society, as science performs its tasks in the context of a society heavily affected by its observations and findings. When the effects of the involvement pass unnoticed by the "detached" scientist, the result, from a larger viewpoint, can have tragic implications. We may be able to understand something of the nature of

---

15 Samuel T. Coleridge, *Biographia Literaria* (London: J. M. Dent & Sons, Ltd.; New York: E. P. Dutton & Co., Inc., 1906), p. 161.

the human dilemma by examining Edmund Cherbonnier's explanation of the nature of tragedy in literature.

In witnessing Greek tragedy, Cherbonnier contends, the spectators must be able to take the roles of both observer and participant to understand it. In their role as observers, in contrast with that of the participant, they must assume something close to the Hegelian version of reality—*i.e.,* that ultimately "the truth is in the whole." This implies, as Cherbonnier has stated it:

> ...that an adequate philosophy of life must not only include everything but affirm everything. It must not suppress any aspect of reality simply because some particular moral code finds it offensive or ignoble; it must not disparage any human emotion or action simply because some find it unpleasant or shocking. Conversely, it must not prefer other aspects of life simply because they are accounted "beautiful" or "good." This would unduly elevate a mere part at the expense of the whole. In short, if the truth is in the whole, then reality is neutral, not partisan.[16]

Continuing with Cherbonnier's explanation of Greek tragedy, we see that it consists of two shifting backdrops, both of which the audience must perceive. First, there is the ultimate perspective of the observer in which all differences cancel themselves out. The observer looks at the characters objectively: he knows the general process of the play and the roles the actors must take in the irresolvable dilemma which the characters must confront, so he senses little or no discord within himself. Yet at the same time, the observing audience must become participants and become involved as they empathize with the finite participants who must make the choices which lead them into strife and contradiction. Cherbonnier notes that the hero, with whom the audience particularly comes to empathize, either treats some segment of reality as though it were the whole ("absolutizes the relative") or strives to introduce some absolute perfection into what is a relative world, which finally cannot stand the perfection, and which responds by exacting the ultimate penalty of death. (In Greek tragedy it is generally *hubris,* sometimes translated *human pride,* which is the element upsetting the equilibrium in nature, leading man to his doom.)

Therefore, Cherbonnier concludes, in order to fully understand the nature of tragedy, the audience must maintain not just one perspective, but both that of the ultimate (detachment) and that of the finite (involvement). If one or the other role is selected by the spectator and maintained through the play, the tragic vision is lost. Cherbonnier describes the choice of positions which the spectator may take and their consequences in understanding the nature of the play:

---

16 Edmund Cherbonnier, "Biblical Faith and the Idea of Tragedy," in *The Tragic Vision and the Christian Faith,* ed. Nathan A. Scott, Jr. (New York: Association Press, 1957), p. 26.

...If he adopts the finite perspective to the exclusion of the ultimate, tragedy becomes either a morality play or a picture of unrelieved frustration. If he relinquishes the finite in favor of the ultimate...tragedy is thus converted at a stroke into comedy, and the drama becomes a farce.[17]

The tragic vision applied to the drama of modern civilization may be understood by the fact that the two great players, science and society, are cast in a finite struggle, which is interpreted by many to be a morality play, in which a particular society may use science for its own ends, which are finite and polar to the ends of other societies, or where within a society, science may manipulate and control portions of that society for its own finite ends. While the ultimate perspective is never fully available to human experience, and therefore we are to that extent doomed to live through "unrelieved frustration," it must nevertheless be recognized that a complete separation of the two perspectives, which is attempted by some spectators of the drama, cannot be realistically maintained. Only by seeing the tragedy built into the structure of the human drama can there be any real understanding of how the potentially tragic relations between science and society may be creatively encountered.

The Greek play, it must be recognized, was based upon the Greek conception of the world, derived from a culture with its own understanding of reality. The tragic drama was based upon the interplay of polar opposites which inevitably clashed with one another and ended in the doom of the participants. While this is still true of cultural reality today (for example, the inevitable clash of two seemingly complete independent realities, life and death), man has shown his capacity to creatively encounter and thus transcend the daily clashes of opposites which enter into his world of experience. It is in this sense that the human perspective gains still further meaning in the work of the finite participant observer.

To some degree, the participant observer must encounter a normal play of opposites functioning in the culture he studies. If he is to creatively encounter these opposites, he cannot do it with a total disinterest or unconcern representative of his role as an observer; in fact, it is through his concern and interest that he comes to understand and creatively respond to the play of opposites.

It is not always possible to do this, of course, particularly in a crisis situation, but it is always possible and important to record a failure, so that it becomes part of the data and our understanding of the nature of human conflict. William Whyte, for example, records his failure to creatively encounter the political situation in which he found himself in *Street Corner Society:*

---

[17] *Ibid.,* pp. 35–36.

Here I violated a cardinal rule of participant observation. I sought actively to influence events. In a close and confused contest such as this, it is quite likely that my endorsement of Tony's position was a decisive factor [in his winning the contest].

Ironically enough, my effort to win favor with Tony was a complete failure. . . .

As I thought over this event later, I came to the conclusion that my action had not only been unwise from a practical research standpoint; it had also been a violation of professional ethics. It is not fair to the people who accept the participant observer for him to seek to manipulate them to their possible disadvantage simply in order to seek to strengthen his social position in one area of participation. Furthermore, while the researcher may consciously and explicitly engage in influencing action with the full knowledge of the people with whom he is participating, it is certainly a highly questionable procedure for the researcher to establish his social position on the assumption that he is not seeking to lead anyone anywhere and then suddenly throw his weight to one side in a conflict situation. [18]

As a rule of method, the participant observer does not encourage conflict, but neither does he avoid it if it is an important part of the cultural life of the people he studies. However, any encounter with a conflict must ideally be a creative one, because the participant observer must come to understand the nature of the conflict and yet not destroy his function as a participant observer through his actions.

Other kinds of experiences have been recorded in which minute, but significant events occur in the research experience which point to the observer's necessity and opportunity to move creatively through the point where the conflict destroys his role as an adequate observer. John Dollard, for example, records how his initial contacts with white Southerners in his study *Caste and Class in a Southern Town* were unrewarding. He found himself labeled a northern Yankee, and his research termed useless by white Southerners with whom he came into contact. This attitude was understandable, but what he did not initially understand were his own attitudes, which affected his research. He felt initially, he tells us, that the information which he received from white Southerners could not be considered valid. The latent conflict which he felt between himself and the white Southerners therefore manifested itself in the fact that they could not consider his work valid and he could not consider their information valid. Something did not seem right, and yet, he recalls, at first he did not understand the problem. His concern, however, led him to review the diary notes which he had taken during his early contacts with the Southerners. He found the following recorded:

---

18 William F. Whyte, *Street Corner Society* (2nd ed.) (Chicago: University of Chicago Press, 1955), p. 336.

These white people down here are very charming and really exert themselves to do friendly things once you are accepted, but they seem very much like the psychotics one sometimes meets in a mental hospital. They are sane and charming except on one point, and on this point they are quite unreliable. One has exactly the sense of a whole society with a psychotic spot, an irrational, heavily protected sore through which all manner of venomous hatreds and irrational lusts may pour, and—you are eternally striking against this spot.[19]

It was with a new perspective that he looked at his notes this time and he was "shocked," he said, when he saw the "invidious comparison" he had made between Southerners and psychotics during his first contacts. He had come to the community, he states, believing that he had acquired a scientific detachment in his training for field studies. Yet he was still unaware of the deepseated bias which he had unconsciously acquired in his Northern upbringing. This recognition was a creative breakthrough which led him to search for the extent to which the great American tragedy, the cleft between the North and the South wrought by the Civil War, had entered into his own mind and affected his perceptions and understanding of Southern people. Following the recognition of his own biases, Dollard states that he found it important to give as much serious consideration to what Southern white people told him about the interracial situation as he did the Southern Negro. *The result was that he began to obtain indispensable information from Southern whites that otherwise would have been barred from him.*

Obviously, there will be a conflict of interests at certain stages with which the researcher cannot creatively deal. This is the moral dilemma of the scientist today in studying society. It is in these small ways, in the recorded incidents in the life of the researcher, that the problems that exist between science and society can be seen "writ large." It is a polarity which contains moral, comic, and tragic dimensions, and behooves the social scientist to examine it carefully not only as a part of his research, but also as a part of the human perspective that is necessary to the formation of social theory.

Social Philosophy

Social philosophy directs our attention to the assumptions underlying science as an approach to the study of society, and in this sense, it has something important to contribute to our understanding of the human perspective and method of participant observation which is helping forge it.

We stated earlier that the human sciences do not prescribe what ought to be, but describe and explain what actually is. However, this difference

---

[19] John Dollard, *Caste and Class in a Southern Town* (Garden City, N.Y.: Doubleday Anchor Books, 1949), p. 33.

between what may be termed normative theory and factual theory is more complicated than it would seem at first, and the adequacy of the human perspective is dependent upon how well the social sciences cope with this problem. Normative and factual theory are actually two highly interdependent, mutually involved poles of knowledge, and it behooves us to examine the nature of this involvement.

Philosopher F. S. C. Northrop discusses the assumptions which underlie both the factual and the normative perspectives in what he calls the "logic of the humanities" and the sciences. Both perspectives are actually derived, according to Northrop, from the same "primitive," original assumptions about the character of man:

> The philosophy defining a particular normative social theory has the two apparently paradoxical properties of designating both an "ought" for culture which introduced choices, moral values and ideals, and an "is" for nature which permits verification. This combination of the "ought" and the "is" occurs because it is impossible to formulate any philosophy without at the same time making assertions about the nature of the natural man and of the physical universe of which he is a part and a manifestation.[20]

If we identify the primitive postulates behind the specific normative prescriptions about what man ought to do in society, and compare them with those postulates made by the natural and social sciences, we can ascertain, Northrop contends, whether the normative theory rests on sound grounds. In this way we can verify normative theory by reference to scientific theory.

While Northrop's point suggests one method of testing the adequacy of normative theory, more important for our purposes is the fact that the same conditions for testing the adequacy of factual theory may be placed in reverse. Northrop rightly recognizes that the most adequate social theory of society is one which "can take care of the widest range of facts concerning nature and natural man." This is as true of social theory, Northrop notes, as it was of Einstein's theory of mechanics, which is today generally regarded to be more adequate than Newton's, since it accounts for Newton's facts as well as those for which Newton could not account. The problem in sociological theory today is that it is Newtonian; it is hardly adequate to account for all the facts of society.

What Northrop challenges us to see is that factual theory can and should check its adequacy against the assumptions of normative theory. This is important for determining factual theory's capacity to express and explain the normative order of society. Scientific (factual) theory must account

---

[20] F. S. C. Northrop, *The Logic of the Sciences and the Humanities* (New York: The Macmillan Company, 1947), pp. 338–40.

for normative ideals as facts of society. The scientist observes how these ideals function as part of the natural order of society.

The social scientist observes, for example, that ideal standards fail to "actualize" themselves, and social problems subsequently arise. The difference between "social standards" and "actuality" constitutes the area of social problem theory.[21] A sociological theory whose primitive postulates fail to take note of the primitive postulates behind ideal standards of, say, freedom or justice, can hardly explain the disparity between those standards and actuality. Studying the actuality of freedom in Russia today, for example, would require standards that we have not yet acquired in social science. The standards the scientist uses should include Russian standards, but they should also be properly descriptive crossculturally as they are drawn from studies of cultural beliefs of the East and the West.[22] The values contained in these beliefs must be seen as facts of society.

Fact and value are separate in the social sciences, but are two sides of the same coin, for each is reflected in every dimension of human reality. Democracy and Christianity, for example, are each both a fact and a value of modern society, and the social scientist must interpret them accurately in each capacity. The social scientist is interested in the validity of both fact and value as they are expressed in the meanings of a culture.

It is the indivisible element of *meaning* that is the basic unit of analysis, bridging the differences between fact and values. It is the social scientist's task to treat them together in meanings as value-infused facts of society. (See diagram.)

Facts tend to be associated with observable social patterns, as in social organization, and values with expressive symbols. Yet particular expressive symbols can be viewed as *facts* of society and patterns of organization can be observed to express *values*. Fact and value are polar principles of analysis and both have been the subject of inquiry in sociology through the study of meaning complexes such as democracy and Christianity.

Robert MacIver's classic study of democracy, *The Web of Government*,

---

21 Robert Merton and Robert A. Nisbet, eds., *Contemporary Social Problems* (New York: Harcourt, Brace & World, Inc., 1961), pp. 697ff.

22 An article in an issue of *Social Research* reports of a study on the problem of freedom in Russia, as it was evidenced in opportunities for occupational choice. As a basis for judging how standards of freedom were being met, the author looked for definitions of freedom in the history of philosophical thought in Europe. Obviously, any such study has its limitations, but in this case, knowledge of the question has advanced beyond what is known through propaganda mediums. Had the author taken a solely deterministic position, the reality of freedom could not have been understood at all, except possibly as a figment of Russian imagination, without support in actual social life. The conclusion of the deterministic scientist in such a case would not be too far from the conclusions of radically conservative political opinion in the United States. Joan Fiss, "Freedom and Occupational Choice in the Soviet Union," *Social Research*, 30, No. 1 (Spring 1963), 53–76.

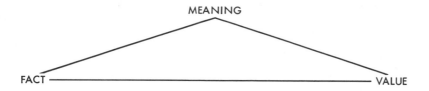

presents a factual consideration of governmental types of organization in society. MacIver builds a typology from the original Aristotelian formulation of governmental forms, and adds conceptually to it to include the new facts of political organization, at the same time carefully tracing the expressive meaning of democracy as it is evidenced in the social and political culture of western man. In Seymour Lipset's study *The New Nation,* the reader will find a typological consideration of essential values guiding selected western democracies analyzed within the framework of action theory and pattern variables. In both cases, sociologists are working at a theoretical level which requires research of both fact and value through participant observation.

When we view a value-infused culture complex such as Christianity (or one of its historical phases such as the Protestant Ethic) as a fact of society, we must take into account the expression of beliefs not only through an analysis of its documents, but also through participant observation. It is by following the procedures of participant observation that certain accuracies are obtained in reporting subjective beliefs that could not be obtained otherwise, since the scientific definition of Christianity should not arise solely from the scientist's own special formulation, but through his study of its natural formulation in society. This definition emerges through a careful study of the rationality of creedal documents and the personal meanings put to them by believers. Creedal and personal definitions, once ascertained, are then viewed within the context of objective interdenominational and international studies. Only by comparing institutional expressions of value-complexes such as Christianity in one society with those in other societies, can value-infused religious facts about societies in general emerge.

When the scientist studies crosscultural meanings of religious values as facts, and develops generalizations about them, he creates new cultural values and meanings in the process. These new values are included in the meanings of a category or typology designed to account for individual facts in separate societies. For example, when sociologists of religion such as Max Weber describe *ascetic* and *mystical* religious traditions, or theodicies of *immanence* and *transcendence,* these terms would at first seem merely classificatory, containing no religious value. Indeed, they are of classificatory use, but these terms also express religious values, since they are terms derived from the religious culture. This is as it should be if scientific knowledge is to be accurately related to reality.

A normative perspective is thus visible in scientific categories, such as those of Max Weber, aside from the normative perspective of science itself. This can be observed in a number of ways as social science interlocks its categories with the culture studied. First, the normative perspective of the culture studied guides the scientist's attention to that which is important to observe. In certain religious cultures, for example, the immanence and transcendence of deities are significant, and so the category normatively guides the scientific observer to examine such phenomena.

Second, the scientific category can create an enlarged perspective previously not comprehended nor valued. For example, Max Weber points out the similarity among religious groups who exhibit a common "distinctive content of salvation" involving "mystic illumination." This kind of group believes that ". . . God can speak within one's soul only when the creaturely element is altogether silent. In agreement with this notion, if not with these very words, is all contemplative mysticism from Lao Tzu and the Buddha up to Tauler."[23] In this way Weber identifies common elements underlying a number of otherwise different religious traditions (from Buddhism to Quakerism). The category necessarily produces a basis for unity between basically different peoples as well as a basis for generality in science, and a vision of community is created almost unavoidably in the process of categorizing value-infused facts.

In this case, the perspective of man is enlarged to include people societally different from one another. The new image of man has personal meaning as well as objective meaning, for it contains religious values in scientific categories. A common foundation (mystic illumination) underlying differing religious orientations is exposed by the scientist, rather than the prophet of religion. This process is unavoidable if we take Weber's stipulation seriously—i.e., that we understand these beliefs sociologically as "systems of meaning" (Sinnzusammenhänge) which must be interpreted subjectively. These interpretations, drawn from the religious orientations of separate peoples, are within the normative traditions of social science as long as the categories prove to be valid generalizations.

A third way in which a normative perspective is visible within a sociological category is, as we have already suggested, the inclusion of the category as a representative part of a culture. In this case, immanence and transcendence contain the values of the religious culture from which they were derived. These are examples of concrete concepts in the sense that expressions such as "God is immanent" or "The Lord has transcended this

---

[23] Max Weber, *The Sociology of Religion*, trans. Ephraim Fischoff (Boston. Beacon Press, 1963), p. 168.

world" carry spiritual meaning and emotive impact within the framework of a particular religious event. These terms become sensitizing concepts as the sociologist observes and describes the common elements that exist in the content of the otherwise diverse dogmatic expressions, and then typifies them in a category of analysis. The original values expressed through immanence and transcendence, however, are not entirely lost, but are appropriately retained in the use of the words (instead of creating a new biophysical name for the belief-phenomenon), and so continue to express something of the cultural meaning within the scientific perspective.

In these ways, the student of society observes culture as meaning-complexes with both fact and value.

History

The perspective of man as viewed by the historian yields many features of the human perspective that are of scientific value. The historian has dealt with both substantive and methodological problems very similar to those of the social scientist, some of which we shall discuss here.

In modern times, historians have reacted strongly against applying philosophic generalization in their interpretation of man (especially since Leopold von Ranke). The colorful writing of Gibbon and Macaulay seems to have been replaced by simple reporting of "hard facts." Nevertheless, as a group, historians must admit that facts are selected from a frame of reference guided by values, and that some degree of higher generalization is necessary to report history with any significance. What these values should be and what level of generalization is appropriate are questions closely related to the methodological problems of social science. We will examine the viewpoint of three historians who were all very much concerned with both generalizations and value interpretations, but found three different solutions: Heinrich Rickert, Wilhelm Dilthey, and Max Weber.

Heinrich Rickert (1863–1936) was a neo-Kantian, and as such considered the fields of science and history to be fundamentally different. Science, for Rickert, deals with facts to be explained by causation and Kantian categories of thought. History is not a science, rather, it deals with many unique, individual realities of men, and reflects values in its subject matter. The historian must select the data with which he works on the basis of the essential values he finds universal to the cultural epoch that he studies. In this way individual events of history gain significance from the "universal" values which are widely prevalent in a historical epoch. As Rickert puts it:

> The individual elements of history can be combined into a higher unity only by referring to a universal value.... If we would distinguish the essential from the nonessential in the world of experience, in a way which is universally valid, we must have a criterion of selection, an ideal norm which will enable us to

eliminate everything which is not of importance to the attainment of that universal end, and to arrange the most important moments of historical development in a hierarchical scale of values.[24]

Wilhelm Dilthey (1833–1911) held a position contrary to that of Rickert. He felt that the social sciences were closely allied with history; the qualitative distinction was to be drawn between the natural sciences and the social sciences. The subject matter of history and social science together was "meanings," and the meaningful configuration of events in history was important to the study of society. Let us look at Dilthey's work in more detail, since it reflects much that interests the participant observer in making field studies. It has further significance in that Dilthey's work was of some influence in framing Existential thought, as evidenced in the writings of Martin Heidegger, and some influence in the development of sociological theory, as evidenced in the writings of Max Weber.

Dilthey stresses the fact that the difference between human studies or social sciences (*Geisteswissenschaften*, within which he includes history) and the natural sciences (*Naturwissenschaften*) is that in the former, the inner world of culture must be understood and explained as well as the outer empirical world, whereas for the latter, only the outer world need be researched. The historian, as well as other students of human culture, must come to terms with the relation between the inner and the outer worlds of experience.[25] Significance, for Dilthey, can be found through the observer's disciplined awareness of the inner life of man as experienced in its immediately apprehended form. It is through this sensitivity to life that the formation of concepts explaining the human enterprise takes place:

> In the historical and social studies conceptualization, too, is constantly determined by life itself. I am referring to the connection which constantly leads from life and from the forming of concepts about the purposes of existence, destiny, character, passions, and values to history as a science. . . .
>
> Thus, the starting point from life and the constant connection with it forms the first fundamental feature in the structure of the human studies; for they rest on experience, understanding, and knowledge of life. This direct relationship in which life and the human studies stand to each other leads, in the latter, to a conflict between the tendencies of life and the scientific goals of the human studies. . . .
>
> Life and experience of it are the ever freshly flowing sources of the understanding of the social-historical world; starting from life, understanding

---

24 Quoted in Frederick J. Teggart, *Theory and Processes of History* (Berkeley, Calif.: University of California Press, 1960), pp. 65–66. The distinctions between these historians were first brought to my attention by: Don Martindale, "Sociological Theory and the Ideal Type," in *Symposium on Sociological Theory*, ed. Llewellyn Gross (New York: Harper & Row, Publishers, 1959), pp. 57–91.

25 H. P. Rickman, ed., *Meaning in History: W. Dilthey's Thoughts on History and Society* (London: George Allen & Unwin, 1961), pp. 124–25.

penetrates into ever new depths; only in reacting on life and society do the human studies achieve their highest significance and this is constantly growing.[26]

Dilthey had something to say about "significance" in human studies in his discussion of concept construction. He pointed out the importance of those scientific terms which have both an inner and an outer point of reference, that is, terms which can be understood both personally and objectively:

> In the natural sciences, power is a hypothetical concept. Where its validity is assumed it is determined by the principle of causality. In the human studies, power is the expression, in the form of a category, of something that can be experienced. It originates when we turn towards the future, which appears in different ways; in dreams of future happiness, in the play of the imagination with possibilities, in hesitation and in fear.[27]

In some ways, Dilthey can be conceived to be a neo-Kantian, but in other ways he cannot. He is therefore distinguished from certain excesses in the neo-Kantian tradition. Hodges, in his perceptive study of Dilthey's work, sums up this difference:

> Thus it is not into a neo-Kantian heaven of rational meaning complexes that understanding takes us, but into the heart of the time-process, the dynamic system of historical life. It shows us men caught in historical situations and summoning their powers to deal with them, feeling the impact of one another's thoughts and deeds, influencing and being influenced; it shows us the fruitful marriage of kindred minds, and the unresolved clash of opposing standpoints. All the many-sided splendour of human history comes thus to be reflected in our consciousness as we watch and understand and sympathize, and, in Dilthey's phrase, "life embraces life."
>
> The neo-Kantian philosophy, he says, goes the wrong way about explaining how we can understand one another. Instead of finding the ground of understanding in experience as we actually live it, neo-Kantianism argues to "a super-empirical subject which manifests itself in the individual consciousness. ... The creation of this transcendental method is the death of history, because the alleged realities are such that we cannot dig ourselves into them by fruitful historical concepts. ... We must move out of the pure, fine air of the Kantian critique of reason, in order to do justice to the wholly different nature of historical objects." That which really lies behind historical phenomena, and is the object of historical study, is not the transcendental self, but man, with his complex mind-body structure and his bundle of instincts; and we can make him an object of study because we are ourselves men.[28]

---

26 *Ibid.*, pp. 80–81.
27 *Ibid.*, p. 109.
28 H. A. Hodges, *The Philosophy of Wilhelm Dilthey* (London: Routledge & Kegan Paul, Ltd., 1952), pp. 152–53.

Wilhelm Dilthey had professional and theoretical interests which are basically different from those of other historians, including Rickert and Weber. We will comment on this shortly.

Max Weber (1864–1920) referred to history in his essays in *The Methodology of the Social Sciences* as the "science of reality" (*Wirklichkeitswissenschaft*), and further concluded that this is the point at which social science begins its inquiry.

> The social-scientific interest has its point of departure, of course, in the *real*, *i.e.*, concrete, individually structured configuration of our cultural life in its universal relationships, which are themselves no less individually structured, and in its development out of other social cultural conditions, which themselves are obviously likewise individually structured.[29]

Reality, we would say, is that which the observer finds important to record, and this, in turn, is shaped by what he believes is important to see. Rickert saw essential values as most important; Dilthey saw the inner personal life of man as most important. Again we have the basic problem of interpreting reality that we described earlier, which exists between phenomenology and existentialism. Is reality a matter of essences of value, or is it a matter of existence, of life itself? Weber was unique in seeing the importance of both interpretations, but he added still another factor to make interpretations scientifically adequate.

In addition to the expression of life and its essential values, Weber saw the importance of adding the generalizing (nomological) laws of science in his interpretation of man in society. His methodology captures the dialectical interests of existential phenomenology and science. In Weber's definition of meaning we find two important factors: the logical-mathematical factor and the personal factor:

> All interpretation of meaning, like all scientific observation, strives for clarity and verifiable accuracy of insight and comprehension (*Evidenz*). The basis for certainty in understanding can be either rational, which can be further subdivided into logical and mathematical, or it can be of an emotional empathic or artistically appreciative quality.... Empathic or appreciative accuracy is attained when, through sympathetic participation, we can adequately grasp the emotional context in which the action took place.[30]

Meaning, for Weber, has both an objective and a subjective dimension. Weber clearly considers empathic accuracy important to the process of gathering materials for the formation of an ideal type, but the type itself

---

[29] Max Weber, *The Methodology of the Social Sciences,* trans., eds. Edward Shils and Henry A. Finch (New York: Free Press of Glencoe, Inc., 1949), p. 74.

[30] Max Weber, *The Theory of Social and Economic Organization,* trans. A. M. Henderson and Talcott Parsons (New York: Free Press of Glencoe, Inc., 1947), pp. 90–91.

emphasizes the objective dimensions of meaning. The ideal type is distinctively different from the methodological interests of either Dilthey or Rickert.

Weber stated that two factors were necessary to form the ideal type. It must be (1) "objectively possible" and (2) "nomologically adequate." The requirement of "objectively possible" roughly means that the ideal type is not a total dream, a figment of the theorist's imagination, but rather a collection of traits that have some reference to historical reality. "Nomologically adequate" roughly means that this type should have some basis in the generalizing, causal principles of science.

The social scientist, therefore, describes phenomena as a participant, on the one hand, and as an observer, on the other. It is important that his interpretations of both subjective meanings in the history of the culture studied and objective meanings in the normative rules of science be adequate.

Max Weber was essentially studying society in what is often called "middle-range theory." He was conscious of the higher values guiding the selections of individual configurations in history, but did not reckon with them methodologically as he did with the ideal type. In the ideal type he was concerned with the course of people's conduct within special sectors of society, particularly within social institutions. Heinrich Rickert, on the other hand, was apparently functioning still more directly in the area of values, an area more occupationally hazardous, one in which he was less likely to be accurate in his interpretations. Let us examine this area for a moment, and then apply Weber's insights and cautions in order to see the place of this area in the methodology of human studies.

If a historian were to look for the essence of Christianity in Europe and then explain a course of human events in terms of this essence, he would very likely sacrifice his general interests in an objective account of history. He would be writing church history instead of general history. He could retain his general interests, however, and contribute toward scientific interests if he followed the procedures implicit in Weberian analysis. First, he would have to see the relativity of his configuration and stay within its effective limits, and second, he would have to use the configuration for comparative purposes. If he studied the essence of Christianity as it revealed its power and its limits in affecting European events, and if the historian compared this Christian belief to other beliefs in Europe, or perhaps, to another religious belief affecting the course of events in the Orient, let us say, he would be working with data in a way useful to both history and sociology. Note Weber's comments on this approach:

> All expositions, for example, of the "essence" of Christianity are ideal types enjoying only a necessarily very relative and problematic validity, when they are intended to be regarded as the historical portrayal of empirically existing

facts. On the other hand, such presentations are of great value for research and of high systematic value for expository purposes when they are used as conceptual instruments for *comparison* with and the *measurement* of reality. They are indispensable for this purpose.[31]

Weber continues in his discussion of essence types to exclude (from the purposes of the ideal type) the value judgment often contained in it. This value judgment is "always close at hand whenever the descriptive historian begins to develop his 'conception' of a personality or epoch." The ideal type is derived partly from the subject matter itself and partly from the logical judgments of the historian interested in comparative analysis.

Rickert's special approach to the interpretation of history on the basis of a central value of subject matter must be recognized as legitimate. This approach is visibly reflected in Weber's work. The central value of *rationality* threads its way through many Weberian constructs, and in effect, tells us what Weber found to be a central force of the modern era. Weber never developed this point in any grand-scale theory of society, and so he never encountered the methodological problems of interpretation at that level, but he did encounter them at middle range. Here he stayed effectively within the scientific tradition; he was just as interested in observing how cultural life deviated from rationality (as in charisma) as he was in observing how modern society was following the rational pattern.

The sociologist can study value-essences in field studies, and it is here that participant observation becomes methodologically important. In fact,

---

[31] Weber, *The Methodology of the Social Sciences,* p. 97. Weber then states that the scientific interpretation is initially a "value interpretation" rather than a "value judgment." What is suggested "in the course of analysis are rather possible *relationships of the objects to values.*" This is, indeed, the core of the methodological problem in cultural studies. What lies ahead in cultural theory is the explication of classes of relationships which objects have to values.

Weber examines some of the different modes of value interpretation in relation to historical study. He notes how our study of such varied objects of interest as Rousseau's *Confessions,* the ceiling of the Sistine Chapel, the experiences of St. Theresa, the Sermon on the Mount, Goethe's letters to Frau von Stein, Marx's *Das Kapital,* and others have multiple modes of interpretation legitimate to human inquiry. *Das Kapital,* for example, may be treated scientifically according to the "logical 'correctness' of Marxian forms of thought," but this need not bear at all upon other forms of value interpretation—linguistic, psychological, and esthetic— which are relevant to the examination of cultural objects for their own purposes. The student of esthetics, for example, is interested in appreciating the intrinsic nature of an object, and this, in one important sense, has nothing to do with the place of the object in historical events. Yet, Weber also demonstrates how historical study is intrinsically bound up with such modes of interpretation (*i.e.,* esthetic, literary, etc.) which are important if they aid in preparing accurate historical concepts, if they indicate the relationship of an object to the causal nexus of events, etc. It would be fruitful to carry further this kind of Weberian analysis of historical interpretation into a discussion of how social scientific interpretation relates to value interpretations in other fields of the humanities. Our discussion in this chapter is intended to be suggestive on this point in the Weberian tradition.

values very likely can be handled more discriminately by participant observers dealing in specific situations, than by historians and grand theorists, who have, in the past, dealt with values guiding historical epochs. Field studies in industrial sociology, crime and delinquency, stratification, race relations, and collective behavior contain many possibilities for value analysis. Let us take one example.

The civil rights movement of recent times has been motivated by a configuration of values centered on the meaning of *nonviolence*. This is a concrete concept which has played an important role in bringing about changes in attitudes which are currently affecting the organization of American institutions. Nonviolence is a concrete experience (as well as an important value) that is felt to be universal among those civil rights workers who aspire to it, and seek to live it together. It is in the scientific interest of sociology to study this formative value in modern society, and in so doing, we will see how the special approaches to historical reality of Dilthey, Rickert, and Weber combine to describe this phenomenon in its different dimensions.

Dilthey, we have said, was interested in re-creating the dramatic event itself, in reliving the historical experience of the people involved so that he could formulate adequate descriptive concepts.[32] The concrete value inherent in recurrent social situations involving nonviolence is derived from the life-experience of people involved. The method of participant observation is a fundamental part of the interpretation of these situations.

---

[32] Examples of how historical configurations of value (in the tradition of Rickert and Weber) can be used instrumentally as ideal models in research may be found in studies of community action programs. Examples of how the dramatization of life experiences can reveal the concrete reality of these values (in the tradition of Dilthey) can also be found in these studies. In this author's study of four Illinois communities, two ideal models ("community organization" and "community development") were selected for typological study. In this case, the ideal model was a truly valued ideal in the eyes of citizens, and at the same time was of typological value for the researcher who studied its consequences in action. In one community studied, the term "community development process" had acquired personal meaning to local leaders who were guiding the action program. This, then, became a concrete concept which was socially communicated and "dramatically relived" in town meetings. The term *process* was a dramatic concept which motivated citizens, and at the same time, functioned to clarify and explain their purposes in the action program. The term process, of course, has an objective meaning to community sociologists, but for citizens, to whom it was conveyed by way of a community consultant, it took on a motivational meaning. The study of this process in research was actually depicting what it meant to citizens; this involved a symbolic and historical re-enactment of the events which led to the formation of this meaning in their minds. Cf. Severyn T. Bruyn, *Communities in Action: Pattern and Process* (New Haven: College and University Press Services, Inc., 1963); Chistopher Sower, John Holland, Kenneth Tiedke, and Walter Freeman, *Community Involvement* (New York: Free Press of Glencoe, Inc., 1937); and Floyd Hunter, Ruth Shaffer, and Cecil Sheps, *Community Organization: Action and Inaction* (Chapel Hill, N. C.: University of North Carolina Press, 1956).

While such a concrete interpretation is important for verifying the nature of the phenomenon, we must examine how it becomes an idea and a value which contacts and engages other ideas and values effecting changes within a historical period. We have here moved to Rickert's interest in determining the essence of an entire culture complex which explains, in turn, the specific events which take place within it. We could say that the procedure for determining historical essences could begin with a survey of a culture's history, but Dilthey would insist that the meanings ferreted out from such a study must then be returned for verification to the concrete level which he emphasized. In this sense, the different emphases of Dilthey and Rickert on historical interpretation are interdependent in the scheme of social science, which must take account of the historical world.

If the configuration of values of nonviolence were to take on more of the empirical realities emphasized in the structure of social action (*e.g.,* its institutionalization in society), then its conceptual depiction would look more like the formal type. It would likely contain the rationality which Weber stressed as typical of the trends of modern society. If the values of nonviolence proceed toward institutionalization, functioning within large organizational realities, the character and meaning of nonviolence may change. Nevertheless, a formal typology of organizational characteristics cannot ignore the subjective meaning which nonviolence would acquire in the structure which the formal type depicts. This was a Weberian requirement for the social scientist—to keep in perspective his point of departure in historical reality.

Concepts of historical reality have traditionally been called *real*, and scientific concepts have traditionally been called *nominal*.[33] The nominal concept functions in a purely utilitarian fashion; it refers to the name that an observable phenomenon is arbitrarily given in the interest of scientific investigation. The phenomenon is studied and measured, and the reality which exists behind the arbitrary name is thus discovered experimentally. An example which we discussed in Chapter 2 is the operational concept IQ. A real concept, on the other hand, is designed to represent reality as it exists. An example we have discussed previously is the concept of being free, or the ones having historical significance to which we have just referred. These concepts are concrete and sensitizing, and refer to the reality of man's experience in history.[34]

---

[33] For an illuminating and thoroughly intriguing discussion of these two meanings, see Robert Bierstedt, "Nominal and Real Definitions in Sociological Theory," in Gross, *Symposium on Sociological Theory,* pp. 121–44.

[34] The function of the concept (nominal or real) depends upon the purposes of the observer in studying the phenomenon. Sociological concepts have served both purposes in both social and cultural dimensions of analysis. Let us consider social concepts first.

The more socially oriented concepts such as primary group, competition, conflict, and class can be considered to be either nominal or real, as the social scientist

The physical sciences emphasize nominal concepts in their vocabulary, while the humanities emphasize the real. Modern social research and theory include both nominal and real concepts, for social scientists are between the separate worlds of the sciences and the humanities, or what C. P. Snow has described as the "two cultures" of man. The traditional scientist's nominal world of measurement and the humanist's real world of culture are both finding their place in the social sciences. In the process, the study of history will continue to play a central role.

The Humanities in Summary

The humanities tell us what man is like outside the framework of traditional science; they also tell us how to know man in a human sense. Existentialism and phenomenology developed historically primarily for this purpose.

What existentialism has told us is that we must see people "in particular" to really see them at all. Martin Buber insisted that man is not a mere concept or essence; in fact, man is not like anything else in this world. In observing man, Buber has told us, we must see particular persons as ends in themselves, not as merely means to some manipulative or impersonal

---

intends. Methods for determining social class, for example, have been nominally expressed in the use of different approaches to the study of that phenomenon. The *reputational, subjective,* and *objective* types of approach each reveal a different class structure in studies of local communities. The existence of social classes in each case is determined respectively by "judges," "the people themselves," or by "objective indexes" such as income or educational level. Cf. Leonard Broom and Philip Selznick, *Sociology* (New York: Harper & Row, Publishers, 1963), pp. 182–89. Even though each approach reveals a different formation of classes (not wholly "real"), they each have their own utility in understanding and predicting social behavior. Objective indexes (*e.g.,* categories of income defined by the census) have reality for the scientist, but little immediate reality for the people studied except as they are reflected in local meanings. At the same time, "social class" is a substantively real concept reflecting what actually exists in community life. That is, it is real in the sense that the term *class* has meaning in the culture of the community itself, and affects the way people behave toward one another. It is true that the meaning of the term has been sharpened somewhat in sociological parlance as a sensitizing concept (and in special cases "operationalized"), but this is not to deny its reality and its usage in everyday life.

Cultural concepts such as justice, goodness, or liberty are also open to serving nominal or real functions in scientific usage. They may be nominally used in the sense that Max Weber used the Protestant Ethic for comparative purposes. Calvinism is a model of goodness in history which was a methodological device defined by Weber to analyze the changing institutional scene. At the same time, it was real for that particular time in history in the creedal expressions and the social conduct of people who held to veracity of this model. Similarly, justice likewise has its rules of fairness, whether in the lives of primitives or in the constitutions and supreme court judgments of modern peoples, which may be utilized as models for comparative analysis. In this way, the historian provides basic materials which the sociologist uses in studying the reality of man in society.

purpose of natural science. Immanuel Kant, we would add, also commented on this problem by saying that when we enter the moral world of action or reflect on it, we should be guided by the self-imposed law "to treat humanity in every case as an end, never as a means only."

From the existentialist's viewpoint, the scientific concept can freeze and distort reality. The scientist's interest in manipulation, prediction, and control can obscure man's individuality and freedom, and thus cancel the value of science to human society.

The century-long cry of the existentialist seems to be authentic. The impact of science and its special values on the world at large is indeed an important ethical problem today. But we must conclude that the distortion of concepts is an inevitable part of the discovery of full truth about man. Truth, we must assume, is a constantly growing reality in the consciousness of man, toward which science is a major contributor.

Martin Buber did not disparage the *It* world in itself; he criticized only its application to human relations without a *Thou* relation. Kant is similarly restrained, for he would treat cases "never as a means only." The importance of this moral imperative for its application to scientific research, however, need not be argued solely on moral or ethical grounds. It has strong grounds for supporting its application in research from within the purposes of social science itself.

The social scientist cannot understand people scientifically in any adequate sense unless he understands them in particular, and for their own sake. This is part of the human perspective which now must be understood as part of the scientific culture of man. It is a "participant requirement" for the researcher who seeks to know his subjects adequately. There is another requirement, however, for the researcher to fulfill. The culture and organization of people in society should be subjected to objective analysis. This is an "observer requirement." *And this is done as part of the purpose of understanding people in particular and valuing their individual existence.*

The literary perspective provides us with further insight into concrete human reality, in both its particular and universal forms. It gives us substantive concepts in literary works and criticism, and methodological tools in its variety of rhetorical forms. We shall discuss these rhetorical forms in detail in the next chapter.

We previously discussed one substantive concept of man in Cherbonnier's theory of *tragedy*. The meaning of tragedy grows out of the life-world of people as they communicate with one another, a world the participant observer studies. This meaning is not derived from the observation of behavioral acts interpreted solely by logical inference. The crucial elements of tragedy are symbolic and are found in day-to-day realities, as well as in the grander theories of literature. Tragedy must be conceptualized as part of the data which is revealed in the scientific observer's cultural studies. In this case, literary theory may be more useful than the concepts of the prevailing social scientific theories of man.

The philosophical perspective gave us insight into how to treat data of this kind. The philosopher looks at the world in its total being and its abstract form through the study of axiology, metaphysics, and epistemology, and in so doing, he sees the importance of finding connections between these forms. We have suggested from this perspective that the fundamental assumptions of scientific theory may be broadened and strengthened by examining the assumptions underlying the norms and ideals of society, and relating them to scientific assumptions. In so doing, *the social scientist is able to study culture on its own terms.*

The historian tells us how to move between the particular and the general. The two fields of social science and history meet, Max Weber tells us, in the ideal type or, more broadly, the "historical configuration." This configuration contains the generalized or universalized features of a given set of historical events which aid the intellectual understanding of history. Weber tells us the conditions under which the existential, the essential, and the rational interpretations of reality become important to the purposes of history and sociology. The purposes of the disciplines, he states, are to acquire adequacy in both the subjective and objective forms of knowledge. The forms of knowledge emphasized by Dilthey and Rickert indicate possible variations in interpreting reality, but the guiding rule of the social scientist is to combine both the subject and the object forms in the construction of his concepts. In so doing, we would add, he creates a basis for scientific work from a human perspective.

The term *human* may be understood to be a symbol which has both an inner and an outer reference, and is therefore of special value as a guide for developing theories of society. Its outer reference is objective, its inner reference, personal. The challenging, central task of the social sciences, as we have said, is to bring these two references together in a consistent design or image of man. The human symbol is complex because man himself is complex. Yet in the human concept lies a basic organizing theme for the social-cultural theorist who would bring together the congeries and contradictions of reality. The human perspective should guide the theorist in finding a human meaning in the special vocabularies of research; or as Cassirer would put it philosophically, it should guide the scientist in judging how the various "symbolic forms" come to fulfill one another in the larger whole. The positivist theories of man and the language of the statistician have an important place in the explanation of the realities of man, but they should be seen in perspective. The human perspective is designed to encourage logic and mathematics as fundamental symbol systems that explore and study man; but this perspective says, in effect, that man is larger than these systems alone, for these systems require human guidance. Furthermore, it is important to encourage other types of study and exploration as well.

The human perspective encourages new and meaningful images of the culture of man. It provides the methodological basis for man to deepen his understanding of the cultural histories of political, religious, educational, and economic life. In this way, the designs produced by theorists come of age social-scientifically because they become humanly relevant to man, and enrich his knowledge of the varied manifestations of the society in which he lives.

The social sciences constitute a major field of inquiry which cannot be deemed the same as the natural sciences or the humanities; they are interlocutors between the two extremes. While certain methods of study and certain substantive forms of man's knowledge interconnect and inter-penetrate with the other two fields, the social sciences have a rich heritage of their own to perpetuate and develop. Social scientists will develop this heritage through new research and logical systems, and, humanly motivated, should continue to contribute to man's larger pursuit of knowledge.

5

The Rhetoric
of Sociology

Language is the foundation of the sciences and the humanities—the link between participant and observer, subject and object, man and man. Language has the capacity to produce both continuities and discontinuities in man's attempt to gain knowledge of himself and his collective world. For these reasons alone, language should be studied systematically for its potential to yield answers to the riddles created by the science of man, which has posed problems that are different from the science of things.

The language of any society of men, including the society of social scientists, develops a power and a reality of its own which can easily move out of the control of its creators. Language, if left unstudied and unsupervised, may even come to control its creators. The social scientist may well become like the sorceror's apprentice; he can weave a magic and a spell with his words about society which can take the shape of myths having a force on the minds of men not unlike the myths of ancient times. Scientific language, then, must be studied not only for its own sake, as in linguistics, but also for other reasons, including the necessity of reducing the magical power that comes with use and misuse of language in social and political life.

A systematic study of social scientific language could accomplish a number of purposes. First, it could provide the means for a more accurate and sensitive *interpretation* of the concrete forms of society. This has been of vital importance in the fieldwork of the participant observer. What Edward Sapir and Benjamin Whorf have demonstrated in their studies—how language shapes and limits man's perception and understanding of the world—could well be applied to the language of science. The social scientist's ability to interpret societies in their many cultural shapes, depths, heights, colors, moods, and patterns is confined to the range of his scientific vocabulary. Second, such a study could provide the sociologist—or the social scientist, as we are more broadly referring to him here—with improved instruments for critical *analysis* of societal phenomena. With rhetorical instruments at his disposal to complement his mathematics and logic, he could conceptualize phenomena in analytical ways he has not done before by using traditional instruments. Third, such a study could provide the social scientist with increased consciousness of the role of rhetorical forms in his theories and of the power these forms exercise in shaping his *explanations* of society. Rhetorical forms which are contained in social scientific theories have a way of expressing meanings in unanticipated ways. As the social scientist becomes more conscious of how these rhetorical forms function in his work, he should increase his capacity to anticipate their effects and to exercise controls over them with greater foresight and wisdom.

We will select certain aspects of a few rhetorical forms and devices for discussion in this chapter, but it is clear that a systematic study that recognizes rhetoric as a basic strategy underlying social research and theory is in order. Today the social scientist must study rhetoric and incorporate it as part of his methodology just as seriously as he has studied and incorporated the traditional instruments of inquiry—statistical indexes, random and quota samples, and the proper use of dependent and independent variables.

Rhetoric is usually defined in the classic way of Aristotle and Cicero as constituting the principles which guide and explain the effective use of language. While this usage is still prevalent today, rhetoric has increasingly come to refer to the study of linguistic forms which structure a language. It is to this latter usage involving the study of the structure of a language which communicates meaning among men that we direct our attention, granting, of course, that the two usages are highly interdependent.

Some of the rhetorical forms which have been studied as a part of language are: metaphor, simile, analogy, allegory, irony, satire, caricature, metonymy, synecdoche, understatement, overstatement, paradox, allusion, personification, parable, epigram, epithet, oxymoron, catechresis, kennings, periphrasis, sign, symbol, image, etc.[1] These forms are so fundamental to social research that each should be examined independently and extensively both as subject matter and as part of the methodology of social science. Let us begin with signs and symbols which have generally been considered to be a basic part of the subject matter of social science, but which, we

---

1 These devices are explained in standard English texts. References used by the writer are: Laurence Perrine, *Sound and Sense: An Introduction to Poetry* (New York: Harcourt, Brace & World, Inc., 1956); Harold C. Martin, *The Logic and Rhetoric of Exposition* (New York: Holt, Rinehart & Winston, Inc., 1959); Herbert Read, *English Prose Style* (Boston: Beacon Press, 1952); Wallace L. Anderson and Norman C. Stageberg, *Introductory Readings on Language* (New York: Holt, Rinehart & Winston, Inc., 1962); Wayne C. Booth, *The Rhetoric of Fiction* (Chicago: University of Chicago Press, 1961); and Norman Knox, *The Word Irony and Its Context: 1500–1755* (Durham, N. C.: Duke University Press, 1961).

would stress, cannot be separated from the methodologies designed to study them.

Signs and Symbols[2]

The sign and the symbol are irreducible elements of language structure, and therefore should logically constitute the beginning of our examination of rhetorical forms. All culture consists of symbols and symbolic patterns, and as such, they are data of social and cultural research. A brief analysis of some basic types of signs and symbols should lead to a better understanding of the nature of cultural data and allow us to see more clearly how the role of the participant observer is so crucial to the study of culture. We begin our study with the sign, the basis upon which language and culture originally develop, and then move on to more complex symbols.

Signs[3]

George H. Mead, Ernst Cassirer, Suzanne Langer, Talcott Parsons, Leslie White, and many others in various fields have made an important distinction between sign and symbol which marks the beginning of culture. A *sign* is any individual's expression to another individual that communicates a message in a particular situation. Examples would be the gesture to wave goodbye, or to verbalize "go" or "come here," or to cry for help. The sign is an early development in communication expressed (as Mead illustrates) in the bark of the wolf to the pack or the cluck of a hen to her chickens.[4] The language of man begins with the sign, a form of communication he holds in common with animals. The development of human language has been traced anthropologically from the original "cry" of an organism (a sign of need) to a "call" (a sign expressed to specific individuals) to the "word" or the symbol, and finally to the differentiation of symbol com-

---

2 Gertrude Jaeger and Philip Selznick treat the subject of symbols differently than here, and their treatment is worthy of the reader's attention. The symbol, as they define it, is restricted to connotative meanings, those meanings which indicate a "not-too-fully specified set of suggestions and overtones, such as authority, knowledge, wisdom, etc." In this way the authors seek to show some relationship between the scientist's conception of culture and the humanist's conception, an important step in the development of a sociology of culture. (Gertrude Jaeger and Philip Selznick, "A Normative Theory of Culture." *American Sociological Review,* **29,** No. 5 (October 1964), 653–69.)

3 Pp. 127–32 adapted from Severyn T. Bruyn, "The Methodology of Participant Observation," *Human Organization,* **22,** No. 3 (Ithaca, N.Y.: Society for Applied Anthropology, Fall 1963), 227–29.

4 Anselm Strauss, ed., *The Social Psychology of George Herbert Mead* (Chicago: University of Chicago Press, 1956), p. 213.

plexes or sentence structures.[5] The external or graphic expression of language can also be traced in a similar fashion anthropologically, beginning with *pictographs* (illustrations of a specific event or thing) to *ideograms* (pictorial symbols of an idea) to *phonetic* expressions (symbols representing speech sounds).

Symbols

A *symbol* is anything that stands for something else. In contrast to the sign, the symbol requires that one abstract and recall that for which the symbol stands. That entity for which it stands can be removed from the immediate environment in which the symbol is communicated without hindering understanding of the symbol's referent. Most *words* can be understood as symbols in the sense that they stand for objects, images, or meanings which require people to understand them apart from the particular situation in which they originally were formed. The printed word "table," or its sound waves, may be considered to be a representation of an actual physical object or an image which can be pictured with the "mind's eye" or a meaning which has no object or visual image, such as the abstract notion of a table of numbers.

We shall now consider some basic types of word symbols, which should indicate the challenge this kind of data presents to the social researcher. In this sense, Charles Cooley once described how our language has already given us the basic data of research by the mere fact that man has already recorded and classified his states of being in the word:

> Under the leading of words we interpret our observation, both external and introspective, according to patterns that have been found helpful by our predecessors. When we have come to use understandingly such words as "kindly," "resolute," "proud," "humble," "fearful," "lonesome," "sad," and the like, words recalling motions of the mind as well as the body, it shows that we have not only kept a record of our inner life, but have worked up the data into definite conceptions which we can pass on to others by the aid of the common symbol.[6]

Denotative Symbols

The *denotative symbol* begins where the sign leaves off. Initially, such symbols are signs that direct attention to particular objects such as a tree,

---

[5] Géza Révész, *The Origins and Prehistory of Language* (New York: David McKay Co., Inc., 1930).

[6] Charles Cooley, *Sociological Theory and Social Research* (New York: Holt, Rinehart & Winston, Inc., 1930), p. 299.

the moon, or a table, each of which has some particular meaning in an immediate situation. But soon a broader image is necessary to communicate not simply the uniqueness and immediate necessity of knowing a particular object, but to communicate the meaning of different objects of a similar nature. At this point the elementary processes of abstraction begin to form through special linguistic devices such as the metaphor, a form we shall discuss later in more detail.

The process of learning the denotative symbol is somewhat complex. To know the idea of a table—*i.e.*, to form an image of the generic form of "table" and retain it—requires a considerable amount of empirical experience. The learner must acquire a sense of surface, an impression of solidarity, a notion of dimension, etc., before the elements comprising the generic image can come together in his mind. The image of table normally develops a central figuration which is conditioned by the learner's accidental acquaintance with certain table shapes along with secondary elements which are imagined possibilities of shape. That is, an essential requirement of table for an individual may be that it have a smooth top, but this table may not have to have legs to fit the image of a table.

This process must be understood since denotative symbols constitute the data to which the traditional empiricist confines his work. What is important to note is that while the empiricist seeks precision and clarity in his experiments, there is considerably more complexity and ambiguity in his concepts than most technicians would admit. In fact, the precision which he claims exists at this level is no greater, we would suggest, than that which may be reached in the study of the emotive symbol, a type of symbol about which we will have something to say shortly, but which the traditional empiricist will not include in his data.

The simple denotative reference to a piece of furniture—*e.g.*, a "sofa"—is fraught with such diverse images and meanings as are reflected in our language: davenport, settee, couch, divan, dais, ottoman, daybed, etc. These various denotative symbols stand for similar images in the mind's eye which overlap to some extent and are different to some extent. But such diversity in denotative symbolic references does not seriously interfere with the productivity of the empiricist; he achieves a certain verbal consensus on what he seeks and finds, and thus achieves his ends. However, the fact that he depends upon symbolic consensus for determining the meaning of the words he employs is significant for our purposes. Consensus in symbolic meaning, as we will point out later, is a basic criterion for assessing the validity and reliability for the participant observer's findings in his study of nonempirical symbols. Therefore, the terms of both the traditional empiricist and the participant observer must have clear referents which are commonly understood by the people involved in the study.

Abstract Symbols

As degrees of generality continue to be built in the mind of the learner, there are no more physical objects or images to which symbols may refer. The referents of symbols are no longer physical objects; rather, other meanings are symbolically removed from denotative reference. In other words, a symbolic *fundamentum* is gradually built from the common experiences of people. This foundation of symbolic concepts itself begins serving as the basis of reference, instead of a visual image of outer objects. For example, the word "society" is a highly abstract symbol around which is focused much sociological theory. Its level of generality is clearly higher than any of its constituent symbolic parts such as "institution." The word "institution," though, is still more abstractly removed than its symbolic part called "primary group," which is yet one more level above the denotative symbol "The Norton Gang." Such is the complex symbolic foundation of the social theorist. Nevertheless, the theorist must assume, like the operationalist, that there is something so common and understandable about most of this symbolic construction that he can work effectively by assuming agreement at certain levels. With a mass of assumptions behind him, the theorist feels that he can continue to contribute knowledge about man at the level of inquiry at which he is operating.

Levy-Bruhl once claimed that primitives could not be abstract, that they were prelogical beings who participated personally in the objects about them without being able to abstract themselves from the inanimate world. Such a perspective of primitive mentality must be qualified by recognizing at least an elementary logic in all human culture. The primitive does distinguish between subject and object, but as Radin wisely adds, he refuses to believe that "all reality lies in our external perception of it. There is an internal side and there are effects, constraints, from subject to object and from object to subject."[7] The primitive's failure to develop a language of logic, to deny the existence of spiritual beings in inanimate objects, has been a major basis for modern man to distinguish himself as civilized. However, we would say that in "civilized" man's efforts to overcome the primitive's crude anthropomorphisms, he has become subject to the alternate extreme, that of explaining his inner life primarily on the basis of logical symbolism.

Philosopher Filmer Northrop makes the distinction between the theoretic component, which is highly developed in western civilization, and the esthetic component, developed more extensively in the eastern world. It is difficult, he says, for Occidental man to understand Oriental culture be-

---

[7] Paul Radin, *The World of Primitive Man* (New York: Abelard-Schuman, Limited, 1953), p. 49.

cause of his linguistic habit of abstracting everything from experience. It is becoming rhetorically impossible for Occidental man to appreciate and know a person for what he is, to know him personally, to understand him empathically, and to consider this an end in itself.[8] As we indicated previously, there is a difference between knowledge *about* people and knowledge *of* people; the western scientist is quite capable of developing the former, which is based on abstract symbolism, but is less prepared to understand the latter, a kind of knowledge which the participant observer must come to understand.

Emotive Symbols

Like denotative symbols, we can say that *emotive symbols* may begin as signs. Their reference, however, is directly to inner needs and feelings, rather than outer visible objects. Expressions of pain or surprise, or a child's call of hunger, are examples of emotive signs.

In secondary levels of learning, these signs—the cry, or the call—become emotional states of being which are understood without reference to specific persons in a particularized situation. Just as the image of the table persists through time in the mind of the individual, similarly, the emotion of pride or anger takes on a persistence, is talked about, is conveyed to others, and has a life of its own independent of the original stimulus. It may be evoked by an outside reference or another symbol; just as the sight of a chair may evoke the denotative image of one, so the sight of an enemy or a reference to him may evoke the latent emotive condition of fear or anger, but the inner condition develops an independence of its own which is transmitted among participants and is retained by them over a period of time.

At the collective level we may witness a tribe developing a feeling of "loyalty" to the band. The loyalty may be reinforced from time to time by outside threats to the tribal band or evoked by tribal symbols of a physical sort, but the word loyalty is a symbol which refers to a persistent, collective emotion of man living in society and must be understood for its own nature. Other collective emotions emerge in other spheres of collective life. For example, ceremonial dancers cultivate a religious devotion to a particular secret cult, as described by A.P. Elkin in an account of Australian aborigines.[9] Devotion may not be an appropriate term for the description of that state of being which exists in the life of the aborigine, but it serves as a basic word symbol for which modern man has some understanding, and

---

8 Filmer Stuart Cuckow Northrop, *The Meeting of East and West* (New York: The Macmillan Company, 1946).

9 A. P. Elkin, *The Australian Aborigines* (Garden City, N.Y.: Doubleday Anchor Books, 1964).

thus aids the researcher in distinguishing the nature of its equivalent in the life of the primitive. Such subtle emotive distinctions must be the conscious concern of the participant observer in exploring the character of the cultural life of people in any society.

Spiritual Symbols

Emotive symbols move into another stage of development in which (like abstract symbols) they do not refer to an immediate external or internal cause. Such a stage of development involves what may be called *spiritual symbols* and symbols of sentiment representing the spirit of man, which has become more deeply set in experience, less moved by immediate stimuli. These symbols have their own level and pace of development. Examples of word symbols of modern man which indicate such states of being are "suffering," "joy," and "ontological anxiety." They are not altogether unknown to primitive man, but like abstract symbols, these symbols are less developed culturally and encountered less frequently.[10]

The primitive's emotional experiences are more particular with reference to "pain" or "pleasure," and generally have some connection to a cause which he identifies outside himself. "Pain," however, represents a different level than "suffering," and "pleasure," a different level than "joy." The symbolic level which we are now considering is not emotive, but is reflected in such symbolic expressions as "creative suffering"—perceived as an end in itself, or the Buddhistic state of "Nirvana," or the "Angst" of modern mobile man in mass society. These spiritual symbols are complex and cannot be researched or defined in empirical, denotative terms any more than "society" can be so researched and defined. These symbols refer to inner conditions which persist through the daily changes occurring outside the individual. They exist on a distinctly different level of experience than do emotive symbols, and, like abstract symbols, spiritual symbols grow more from their association with similar symbols of their own level than from the emotive or denotative symbols to which they are ultimately related. The way in which denotative and abstract symbols function and the way emotive and spiritual symbols function are different, however, and will be discussed in our description of allegories.

Other Symbols

This brief review of some types of symbols can only be suggestive of the kind of approach that can be fruitful in the study of language. There are many other types of symbols than word symbols, and other ways of ap-

---

10 An example of primitive suffering which seems to exist at this level of symbolization may be found in Knud Rasmussen, *Observations on the Intellectual Culture of the Caribou Eskimo* (Copenhagen: Gyldendalske, 1930), pp. 52–55, quoted in Radin, *The World of Primitive Man,* pp. 76–78.

proaching symbols analytically. There are, for example, ideological symbols such as "communism" or "Christianity." There are physical symbols with references to ideologies such as the flag or the cross. There are accidental symbols, universal symbols, mathematical symbols, literary symbols, and so on, which, if studied altogether systematically, would prove to make a very constructive contribution to the study of man in society. But for our immediate purposes, there are other structuring elements of language which must be considered here. One of the most important is the metaphor.

Metaphors, Models, and Myths

Metaphors[11]

A *metaphor* is an implied comparison between things essentially unlike one another. It is so much a part of language we hardly notice it, for example, the "leg" of a table, or the "face" of a clock. One image is superimposed upon another in order to provide a better perspective and understanding of the subject at hand. The metaphor, like other forms closely associated with it, is a device for seeing one thing in terms of something else.

The metaphor has been a major building block in the construction of sociological theory as well as a basic part of the growth of language. The major metaphors in the social sciences have been drawn from the physical and organic worlds. Social and psychological analysis of human behavior are replete with terms borrowed from the physical world such as structure, forces, system, etc., and terms borrowed from the organic world such as evolution, differentiation, integration, etc.

Sigmund Freud made extensive use of the metaphor. As Harvey Nash points out, Freud not only illustrated by metaphor, he conceived in metaphor; it was a major instrument in his study of personality. Nash notes the frequent use of the military metaphor as one example:

> Reference to military actions—stimulated no doubt by Freud's World War I experiences—often served to illustrate the strengthening, and especially the weakening of the ego. A temporary blockage of development was compared to an army held up for weeks by enemy resistance, on a stretch of country crossed quite rapidly in peace time. Regression was likened to troops giving ground in the face of enemy attack. Psychotherapy, on the other hand, was compared to the intervention of a foreign ally in a civil way: The therapist comes to the aid of the ego, which is under siege by the id.[12]

---

11 Pp. 133–35 adapted from Severyn T. Bruyn, "Rhetorical Devices in Sociological Analysis," 5, No. 2 (Spring 1964), pp. 101–4. Reprinted by permission of *The Sociological Quarterly*.

12 Harvey Nash, "Freud and Metaphor," *Archives of General Psychiatry*, 7 (July 1962), 25–26.

Freud frequently used metaphors of different varieties, some simple, some complex, some clear, some ambiguous. His varied use of the metaphor stands in contrast to another psychologist, William McDougall, who, Nash points out, concentrated his efforts primarily on a single image: fluid flow. All human striving, according to McDougall, was like the flow of a stream; instinctual tendencies were like wellsprings, attitudes toward the self were like the river bed which eroded to carry the flow from tributaries, but social character was more permanent, like the entire river basin.[13]

The metaphor is a device which can be misused by making it the sole focus of analysis, but the line defining the difference between its proper use and its abuse is hard to draw. We know that its proper use must be evaluated in the total context of the work of any theorist or researcher. If a single metaphor is relied upon too heavily, the real complexity of the phenomena eludes the analyst. This is true whether it be the classic metaphor of organism, or modern usages of, say, "mass society," or the singular use of the military "juggernaut" to probe the character of modern society. However, at this point we must restrict our analysis to the way in which the metaphor functions in social analysis.

Actually, there seems to be no limit to the variety of constructive uses of metaphors within any single study, as long as the function of these metaphors is clear. In fact, the richness of the use of metaphor has much to do with the quality and value of a study. George Homans, in his study *The Human Group*,[14] mixes such metaphors as a set of bedsprings, a gasoline engine, the vector between forces, as in physics, and an electrical circuit, along with the standard metaphors of the theater, such as role, actor, and scene. In such a context the reader is led implicitly to understand the heuristic or experimental way in which most metaphors are applied. This is important. Of equal importance is that the variety be used consistently within the study as a whole. This adds depth to the work and lessens the possibility of misconceiving the subject.

The essays of Daniel Bell in *The End of Ideology* are filled with metaphors, which, along with those works we have already cited, may lead us further into a discussion of their function in the social sciences. First, we see that Bell's use of metaphors fulfills the function of economy in writing. Like all good pictures, these metaphors are presented to the reader as flash images which say a great deal in a few words. They enable him to pack more ideas and meanings into a single essay than would otherwise be possible. Second, these metaphors reflect perspectives important to Bell's analysis

---

[13] *Ibid.*, p. 26.
[14] George Homans, *The Human Group* (New York: Harcourt, Brace & World, Inc., 1945).

of American society, functioning, at times, very much like ideal types. They select for emphasis certain features of a multifeatured subject and set the basis for analysis. For example, in discussing American ideologies, Bell suggests that the decisive fact about United States political structure is the two-party system:

> Each party is like some huge bazaar, with hundreds of hucksters clamoring for attention. Life within the bazaars flows freely and licenses are easy to obtain; but all trading has to be conducted within the tents; the ones who hawk their wares outside are doomed to few sales.[15]

The image created by this metaphor (stated in the form of a *simile*) introduces Bell's analysis of how this kind of political structure reduces the necessity (and opportunity) for social movements to transform themselves into political parties. The metaphor thus reveals the key traits of the political system which Bell has selected to guide his analysis. This appears as a manifest function. The latent function may be to give the reader some objective distance from the structure in which he may otherwise be personally involved. At the same time, the reader's interest can be stimulated to pursue the metaphor with regard to social reality, as would behoove the social scientist in his task of social research.

The metaphor has played an important role in the development of all scientific theory. In the physical sciences, for example, the metaphor has led theorists toward improved conceptions of their subject matter. Thus, electricity has been compared to a fluid; molecules and atoms have been likened to spheres or balls; light has been compared to waves when explaining one form of its complex behavior, and particles when explaining another. The metaphoric beginnings of light theory or atomic theory have been replaced today by mathematical formulas. The symbolic levels at which the chemist or the physicist today operates are quite beyond the informing value of metaphoric imagery. This leads to the question of whether the metaphor in social science will ultimately be replaced by the mathematical formula.

The answer must be no. The metaphor functions in a more complex way in social theory than in physical theory; it illuminates the nature of the subject matter of the social scientist so that it has end values as well as instrumental values. A purpose of the social sciences is to understand phenomena through the predictive power of mathematical formulas, but not entirely through them; within this purpose the metaphor clarifies the nature of

---

15 Daniel Bell, *The End of Ideology* (New York: Free Press of Glencoe, Inc., 1960), p. 94.

man with imagery that cannot be replaced by mathematics. The metaphor communicates new meanings of man's social world, and in this way carries terminal values for the discipline.

There is still another crucial difference in the use of the metaphor in physical science and social science. In both, the application of the metaphor involves a shift in perspective on the subject being studied, yet in the social sciences this shift is more than solely rational. Through the comparison of unlike qualities, there generally occurs a shift in attitude as well as a shift in imagery. When social theorists first introduced the metaphors from physics and biology, they simultaneously changed the attitudes which accompanied the study of, let us say, earth gravity or air compression or blood circulation, to the study of society. There were attitudes in this shift by metaphor which we usually refer to as "impersonal" and "objective."

The metaphor, then, functions to select both visible *traits* and *attitudes* which are considered important to the task at hand. The selective or screening process of both factors cannot be ignored by the social scientist. The gain and the loss in attitudes are as important for the social scientist to consider in his work as are the gain and loss in visible traits which describe the phenomena. The role of attitudes toward social data is especially important to consider, for attitudes shape the data, and consequently, the kind of theory which arises from the data. This screening effect in social theory is aptly illustrated by Colin Turbayne in a study of the metaphor. He says:

> The chess metaphor, for example, used to illustrate war, emphasizes the game-of-skill features while it suppresses the grimmer ones. A good metaphor produces thereby "shifts in attitudes."
>
> The attitude-shifts produced by an effective metaphor point to a later stage in its life. A story often told—like advertising and propaganda—comes to be believed more seriously. Those details stressed tend to stay stressed while those suppressed tend to stay suppressed until another effective metaphor restores them.... The tomato re-allocated to the fruit class changes its taste history. A dry-martini health drink loses its flavor.[16]

It is a mistake in social science, therefore, to represent a fact of one sort in the idioms of another without awareness of the total shift of perspective that takes place. This awareness can make the difference between the development of a theoretical model or a social myth.

Myths

Students of language such as Colin Turbayne are aware of stages in the life of the metaphor. The first stage involves giving a name to something

---

[16] Colin Turbayne, *The Myth of Metaphor* (New Haven: Yale University Press, 1962), pp. 21–22.

that belongs to something else. Initially, this is generally thought to be inappropriate or "going against the ordinary language." Examples would be Newton's calling sounds "vibrations," or we would imagine, Comte calling enduring social relationships "structure." The second stage is when the inappropriate name becomes appropriate, or in effect, a true metaphor. Other people besides the creator of the comparison acquiesce in the make-believe, yet still understand it to be only a comparison, not a complete identity. The third stage is when the metaphor is used so often that the difference is forgotten. The term then, as Turbayne would say, has moved from a "live" metaphor to a "dead" one. The identity is accepted. The user no longer compares the "leg" of a table, let us say, to the leg of a person. The word "comprehension," formed originally from the similarity perceived between the physical act of grasping (*prehendere*) and the inwardly sensed act of thought (*i.e.*, to grasp with the mind) is no longer recognizable in its ordinary usage. Thousands of such metaphors have died in the growth of language and are in constant use in our language today, a fact of which most people are unaware. New meanings are established and identities accepted without recurrent reflection.

When we deal with root metaphors—*i.e.*, those metaphors which are so basic that they generate the great ideas controlling or guiding the thoughts and actions of men in society—we work at the level of the *myth*. In the myth there is no recognition of difference or comparison; the identity is complete. When root metaphors function steadily in the language of any people, including social scientists, they become accepted without question as having their own reality. When metaphors of science become large and compelling and are viewed in this way, the metaphor functions as a myth.

The close relationship that seems to suggest itself between the metaphor, generally thought of as a minor rhetorical device, and the myth, generally seen to be a large-scale belief, is too close to dismiss lightly, even at the risk of oversimplifying the relationship. The social significance of this relationship can be illustrated in the changing structure of the German language which took place during the Nazi regime and the resultant political myths that then took shape. During these years the Nazis gradually and intentionally introduced new words into the German language which were designed to explain the new social order. The new terms produced a new climate of opinion, a new emotional atmosphere which set the stage for a new mythology. The formation of this myth as it came into being by way of these linguistic devices is described by Ernst Cassirer in *The Myth of the State:*

> I understand from the *Glossary* that in recent German usage there was a sharp difference between the two terms *Siegfriede* and *Siegerfriede*. Even for a German ear it will not be easy to grasp this difference. The two words sound exactly alike, and seem to denote the same thing. *Sieg* means victory. *Friede* means

peace; how can the combination of the two words produce entirely different meanings? Nevertheless we are told that, in modern German usage, there is all the difference in the world between the two terms. For a *Siegfriede* is a peace through German victory; whereas a *Siegerfriede* means the very opposite; it is used to denote a peace which would be dictated by the allied conquerors. It is the same with other terms. The men who coined these terms were masters of their art of political propaganda. They attained their end, the stirring up of violent political passions, by the simplest means. A word, or even the change of a syllable in a word, was often good enough to serve this purpose. If we hear these new words we feel in them the whole gamut of human emotions—of hatred, anger, fury, haughtiness, contempt, arrogance, and disdain.[17]

The development of the myth cannot be understood solely on the basis of small-scale changes in the structure of the language; it is much more complex than that. The myth grows out of popular literature, out of the effects of war, out of the whole history of a nation.[18] In other writings, Cassirer himself has noted this complexity, especially in that the myth is incommensurate with all our conceptions of empirical and scientific truth. It therefore eludes social scientific analysis:

> To be sure, all attempts to intellectualize myth—to explain it as an allegorical expression of a theoretical or moral truth—have completely failed. They ignored the fundamental facts of mythical experience. The real substratum of myth is not a substratum of thought but of feeling. Myth and primitive religion are by no means entirely incoherent, they are not bereft of sense or reason. But their coherence depends much more upon unity of feeling than upon logical rules. This unity is one of the strongest and most profound impulses of primitive thought. If scientific thought wishes to describe and explain reality it is bound to use its general method, which is that of classification and systematization. Life is divided into separate provinces that are sharply distinguished from each other. The boundaries between the kingdoms of plants, of animals, of man—the differences between species, families, genera—are fundamental and ineffaceable. But the primitive mind ignores and rejects them all. Its view of life is a synthetic, not an analytical one.[19]

Although the primitive mind cannot fathom the scientific method of understanding, Cassirer asserts critically, the scientific mind cannot fathom the myth. In his effort to understand the myth from the standpoint of impersonal categories, the scientist deludes himself into thinking he has explained the myth and thus done away with it. But the myth somehow

---

17 Ernst Cassirer, *The Myth of the State* (New Haven: Yale University Press, 1946), p. 284.

18 For a summary of some of the factors leading to the Nazi myth, see Henry Hatfield, "The Myth of Nazism," in *Myth and Mythmaking,* ed. Henry Murray (New York: George Braziller, Inc., 1960).

19 Ernst Cassirer, *An Essay on Man* (New Haven: Yale University Press, 1944), p. 81.

rises like a specter again and again to haunt even the scientists' own formulations. Those scientists who would recognize more of its reality as a great power in society misconceive its function in the scientific enterprise. This can perhaps best be illustrated in the field of political science.

While the myth is generally thought to be an emergent phenomenon—*i.e.*, a belief that gradually develops, as William Sumner would say, without purpose or wit—the political myth is increasingly being brought into being by rational design. For example, although the early myth of the divine right of kings was undoubtedly an "emergent," an archetype perhaps, the political myths of later years cannot be understood in the same category. Thomas Hobbes was one of the first modern destroyers and creators of political myths. While he helped break down the myth of divine kingship, he substituted his root metaphor "The Leviathan." Hobbes' concept of man contracting to protect himself from his own brute savagery took on its own mythical character. What Jean Jacques Rousseau later symbolized as the "Noble Savage" (devised in opposition to the Hobbesian image) took its place as the central political myth of western man. Rousseau's theoretical explanation of the political order in terms of the "general will," which conceived of society as functioning metaphorically as an individual, represents still another shift in political myth-making which had a significant effect in the shaping of political life. Still later, as science increasingly became the public medium of truth and the myth was recognized more for what it was, Georg Sorel combined the two (science and myth) in his "scientific" analysis of socialism in the modern world:

> To proceed scientifically means, first of all, to know what forces exist in the world, and then to take measures whereby we may utilize them, by reasoning from experience. That is why I say that, by accepting the idea of the general strike, although we know that it is a myth, we are proceeding exactly as a modern physicist does who has complete confidence in his science, although he knows that the future will look upon it as antiquated. It is we who really possess the scientific spirit, while our critics have lost touch both with modern philosophy and having proved this, we are quite easy in our minds.[20]

In society today, the political theory of democracy moves toward the shape of a myth insofar as it captures the passions and devotion of people who identify society or themselves with it, or believe that their particular type of democracy is right for all people for all time. The more intensely the conception is held, the less it becomes a theoretical model, and the more it takes on the true character of the myth.

Our reason for examining the myth as it enters into the structure of

---

[20] Georg Sorel, *Reflections on Violence*, trans. T. E. Hulme with an introduction by Edward Shils (New York: Free Press of Glencoe, Inc., 1950); quoted in Murray, *Myth and Mythmaking*, p. 364.

political theory lies in the significant position science has taken in the structure of modern society. Increasingly, science has moved into the position of secular authority that once was held by other institutions, notably the church, and more recently the state. Elliott and McDonald explain the transition of the myth from religious to secular authority in modern political theory:

> It is characteristic of all these approaches to the problem of authority under the social contract theory that they derive from assumptions about human nature that are treated as articles of faith, though each pretends to a scientific (which is more often like a theological) rationalization.[21]

In the social sciences we find many metaphors which have been so often used as the instruments of analysis that they are no longer creatively alive. They have become, as the rhetorician would say, dead metaphors, and yet they live on as though they were the only real and valid means of explaining phenomena. The organic and physical root metaphors in sociology and their offspring of space, mechanism, and fluids, the military metaphor of the id and the superego in psychology, the naturalistically conceived "market mechanism" in economics, etc., are, for different reasons, no longer fully applicable; yet they can be counted among the major myths of the scientific man today.

The myths of social science are not unlike the myths of theology, myths which were created for a purpose and provided insight at a particular place and period, but which today are no longer fully applicable. The dead metaphors of social theory function in embarrassingly similar ways to the myths of a religion such as Christianity. It is of particular interest, in this regard, that Christian myths have been undergoing considerable study and re-examination in recent years under the influence of Rudolf Bultmann and others following his lead. Bultmann is of the view theologically that what was once conceived and spoken at the time of the spiritual founding of Christianity had special meaning in the society in which it was formulated, but today is repeated ritualistically out of context. While some early Christian myths retain their meaning in the modern world, Bultmann contends, Christianity as a whole needs to be "de-mythologized."[22] Modern theology should direct itself, Bultmann continues, toward that original spirit (*Kerygma*) out of which the spoken word first came, and should now create a language which is relevant to modern times.

The parallel is striking. Science as an institution is subject to the same kind of rigor mortis, or better, death and rebirth. The old concepts or beliefs appear at first to be dead, but new concepts break through; later the old

---

21 William Elliott and Neil McDonald, *Western Political Heritage* (Englewood Cliffs, N.J.: Prentice-Hall, Inc., 1950), p. 9.
22 Rudolf Bultmann *et al.*, *Kerygma and Myth* (New York: Harper & Row, Publishers, 1961).

concepts find their place in the new scheme of things. The creative concepts of a Euclid or a Newton are inapplicable to the explorations of the complex world of the modern scientist, but they still retain their validity in a limited range.

The concepts of the physical scientist, however, do not take on the character of "myth" in quite the way of social scientific concepts. The social scientist is so uniquely linked to man's personal interests that he cannot avoid the reality of myth in the construction of his concepts. Therefore, a principal task of the social theorist in the years ahead may well be compared to that of the de-mythologizing activity of theology.

The theologian's purpose, however, is not to substitute fact and theory in place of old myths. Rather, he sees the truths that exist in the mythical explanations of man and would welcome new formations. The position of the social scientist is neither in the camp of the theologian or the physical scientist, but rather complexly between. Clearly he is not interested in creating myths which command attention to that which is deemed holy; nor is he interested in creating symbols designed to foster the spiritual life of man. And yet he must not be misled by the physical sciences into believing that he can create master metaphors and symbols without at the same time fostering a myth. The social scientist who believes he can substitute the scientific model as a "pure theoretical abstraction" in place of the myth—without experiencing the effects of the myth—misconceives the nature of the society he studies.

If we pursue this question carefully, we will find that all social theory must have some central, guiding imagery, and will produce symbolism which unites the separate parts of theory, and at the same time unites the sentiments and human interests of men. In this sense, the social scientist must struggle with the developing form of a myth in the construction of his theories of man. Whenever a basic idea about man in society becomes a part of the personal lives of people, it takes on the symbolic attributes of a myth.

The overall, guiding myth which we would propose as basic and true to the behavioral sciences lies in the human perspective. The root "metaphor" is human; it includes the ultimate image of the social sciences within which one finds many major and minor metaphors which contribute to the explanation of man. In the *human* metaphor there is true identity rather than implied comparison, and in this sense it is not a true metaphor, but rather a believable myth.

Like all metaphors and myths, the human perspective contains a shift in attitudes different from those which have been expressed in the mechanical-organic metaphors. The new attitudes are human; they are not consistently impersonal to all data. The human perspective includes impersonality when appropriate, but it is a much more broadly based perspective than previous master concepts, and therefore includes the possibilities of involvement and creative insight that go with involvement.

Within this enlarged perspective, there are many metaphors and models to explain man. Metaphors create new vision and a new spirit of understanding by illuminating a subject and leading to new understanding at the rational level. *Models* also function at the rational level and are designed for criticism and empirical study. The term model has been used frequently by scientists to refer to a range of heuristic forms from mathematical formulas to large-scale theories, but in any case, the model is designed to explain empirical reality or a scientific problem. Models, therefore, like scientific metaphors, are intentional devices to explain reality. Myths, unlike models and metaphors, emerge more slowly; they grow out of the feelings and beliefs of man, and become real as they are collectively shared. In this sense, then, the myth of the social sciences—the human perspective—can only develop gradually from the many creative productions of researchers and theorists who study man in a human framework.

The human perspective is a myth in that it draws upon the personal interests and touches upon the personal beliefs of scientists who would study man. It is a myth in that all social scientific concepts owe some ultimate allegiance to it. It is a myth especially from the perspective of the theologian (emphasizing a divine reality) and the philosopher (emphasizing other non-human realities), who claim that a single focus and interest in man alone simply elevates a part for the whole and misconceives the true nature of the world. But if this be true, it must be the limited and perhaps tragic commitment of single profession—not of man himself.

This tragic character is diminished to the extent that members of the profession do not have a sole, final commitment to their subject, and also to the extent that the symbols which are the focus of study find their relationship to the humanities as well as to the physical sciences. It is diminished to the extent that the myth of the human perspective is subjected to intellectual scrutiny to reduce the intensity of whatever devious sentiments scientific man associates with the systematic study of himself. Human sentiments will remain, of course, but only as they are subjected to the scrutiny of scientific investigation. Certain human sentiments have already shown their persistent qualities, their ability to co-exist with the demands of objectivity and intellectual study. And so the human myth should stand, creatively inspiring and guiding the many research programs through which man will learn more about himself in the years to come.

Analogies, Allegories, and Archetypes

Man's individual and collective life has a spiritual reality, which is represented and explained to him through myths, folktales, folksongs, fables, dreams, lyrical ballads, epics, parables, epilogues, allegories, and many other literary and artistic forms. These forms have emerged as an explanation of man's spiritual world, his personal world, in terms that make it comprehensible and meaningful to him. They derive from man's universal need to explain such matters as the origin of the world, the all-too-evident existence of pain and suffering, the reality of what he defines as good and evil, and his relation to the power or powers beyond himself. These matters, which have concerned man in every society in history, are felt and are answered in symbolic terms which are personal in nature.

These literary and artistic forms are part of the subject matter of social scientists who seek to understand man in his human dimension. In order to introduce these forms and explain how they function in the cultural life of man, we will use the analogy and the allegory as models.

Analogies are extended *similes,* which, in turn, are metaphors made explicit in sentences by the word "like" or "as," which is added to a comparison between unlike objects. An example of a simile would be: "Society is like an organism." The analogy extends the brief comparative reference of a simile into a broader theoretical comparison.[23] The use of the analogy between society and the organism was intentional for most Social Darwinists of the last century. Herbert Spencer, for example, was careful to point out the differences as well as the similarities between the two compared phenomena. He defended his comparison from critics on grounds that his analogy was only a "scaffolding" by which he built his theory of society; if the scaffolding were removed, the insights and propositions, he said, would hold firm. The analogy, then, is a very close relative of the metaphor, and like the metaphor, it is so fundamental that it enters into the explanation of all human thought and feeling.

Allegories are on the same order as analogies, but are a much more complicated kind of literary form within which the analogy, as well as irony, metonymy, satire, and other literary devices, may be found to operate as

---

[23] For example, extending our simile, Herbert Spencer visualized the following parallelisms between the organism and society: (1) Social and organic aggregates both grow and expand from small to large masses, and in the process their units become more numerous. (2) Both the organism and society advance from simplicity to complexity in an evolutionary movement. (3) In the advancement toward complexity there is a division of labor among the units (cells and institutions) of the aggregate. (4) The organism has a circulatory system like society has "arteries" of trade and commerce; the organism has a regulatory nervous system like society has a government and police regulatory system; the organism has specialized organs functioning on behalf of the whole like society has its "organs" in political, ecclesiastical, professional, and industrial institutions, etc. (5) Like evolving aggregates in general, Spencer said, societies show evidence of "integration," "coherence," and "definiteness" as they move from "homogeneity" to "heterogeneity." Cf. Herbert Spencer, *First Principles of a New System of Philosophy* (New York: DeWitt Revolving Fund, 1958); *The Study of Sociology* (New York: Appleton-Century-Crofts, 1929).

structural parts. An allegory sets forth a central idea, doctrine, or thesis of some kind by converting it into a fictional narrative in which the imaginary agents in an imaginary setting correspond to real people in real settings. While the correspondence between the fictional and the literal is ideally one to one, it is usually obscured by the writer for various reasons and not always followed in perfect fashion. In some allegories the correspondence is clear and direct, as in John Bunyan's *Pilgrim's Progress.* In this narrative, Bunyan allegorizes the Puritan doctrine of salvation by telling the story of how Christian, warned by Evangelist, flees from the City of Destruction and makes his suffering way to the Celestial City. On the way he meets such people as Faithful, Hopeful, Giant Despair, and triumphs through settings such as the Slough of Despond, the Valley of the Shadow of Death, and Vanity Fair.

The allegory need not be conceived as a rhetorical instrument expressing moral or ideological doctrine purely for persuasion. The social analyst may well study it for the insight it provides into the nature of man's relations to man. In a scholarly review of the use of allegory in modern literature, Edwin Honig summarizes its instrumental character:

> In one of its aspects allegory is a rhetorical instrument used by strategists of all sorts in their struggle to gain power or to maintain a system of beliefs. (Such usage and the motives lurking behind it have recently had the close study of critics as part of the semantic problem of symbolic action.) In addition to serving the expression of ideological aims, allegory is a fundamental device of hypothetical construction. In this broad way allegory is part of the creative process, observable in all literature generally where the formulation of vital beliefs seems essential to maximum creativeness.
>
> The literary allegory does not oppose a realistic account of the universe. Its very power lies in its giving proof to the physical and ethical realities of life objectively conceived.[24]

Allegories reflect the political and moral life of people in societies at different periods of history, and in this way may provide the student of society with considerable insight into the nature of that particular society. The society of the fourteenth century, during which Dante wrote the *Divine Comedy,* or the society of the seventeenth century of *Pilgrim's Progress* was very much different from the society of the twentieth century during which Franz Kafka produced *The Castle.* Both the *Divine Comedy* and *The Castle* have allegories in them which center about similar themes, yet each work is a totally different expression of those themes.[25] One common

---

24 Edwin Honig, *Dark Conceit* (Cambridge, Mass.: Walker-de Berry, Inc., 1959), pp. 179–80.

25 For a literary comparison of these two works of Dante and Kafka, see Donald Pearce, "The Castle: Kafka's Divine Comedy," in Angel Flores and Homer Swander, *Franz Kafka Today* (Madison, Wis.: University of Wisconsin Press, 1958).

theme is man's quest for absolute knowledge and his individual salvation from suffering. In Dante's world there were guides and charts which were taken from a theology integrated with a total world view. The *Divine Comedy* reflects that precision, order, and simple faith that existed in the society of the fourteenth century. Kafka's world, however, is full of ambiguity, disorder, and doubt. In Kafka's allegories it is virtually impossible to find any intelligible relation between men, and particularly between his leading figures and people in authority. Unlike Dante's concept of heaven, Kafka's is ambiguous and is subject to devilish devices leaving man in a perpetual state of uncertainty.

Although allegories which are proposed by the more articulate members of a society cannot explain the differences between cultures by themselves, they can be an aid in this direction. Fables, myths, and folksongs complement these allegories, since they emerge from the conversational life of the common people at different strata of the society. The *fable,* for example, is a story which is generally told and retold among ordinary people in a simple mode of imagery which speaks directly to the less critical, less trained mind. The fable typically personifies animals, vegetables, and inanimate objects to convey moral truths to people who can project themselves into the imaginary characters and events. The fable is a type of allegory which functions on a different plane than literary productions, and thus complements them as part of the evidence providing insight into the structure of the culture of a particular society.

The stories of Kafka are not rational or orderly in the usual sense of a fable or an allegory, and this lack of clear correspondence with a literal reality at some points limits their being classified as true allegories. In some of his works, Kafka's figures seem to move in a special world separated from sensory reality, appearing as dreams or approaching poetry. This poetry may seem to be somewhat distorted, but like most poetry and dreams, it reflects the nature of a spiritual world unconnected with the laws of sense. The symbols of this world, however, may still be socially derived and conditioned even though they function at a different level than what we have referred to as the level of denotative and abstract symbols. Thus, they present a challenge to the social scientist whose basis of interpretation is drawn from Kantian laws of causality: space, time, and number.

The symbolic world of the allegory is shaped by both the laws of the sensory world and the laws of the spiritual world of man. In other words, the allegory stands midway between the empiric world of sense and what we may call, alternatively, the world of feeling or spirit. It represents both worlds as a literary device and seeks correspondence between them. To understand the allegory, the social scientist must grasp the explanatory principles associated with the nonempirical world as well as the empirical. This nonempirical world of feelings, as we call it (as represented in dreams and poetry), may function without reference to explanatory principles of time, space, or causal relations. Instead, such symbols must be interpreted on the basis of other principles such as identity, intensity, and telic relations.

The principle of *identity* may be vividly expressed in a poem or a dream. The poetry of Walt Whitman is replete with symbolic expressions of his personal identity with the growth of American society, and with the world of objects and persons with which he came into contact. This principle, however, can perhaps be most directly and meaningfully conveyed in the dreams which most people have had in which they identify themselves with another person, object, institution, beast, angel, or whatever. In the reality of that dream, the dreamer *is* the figure with which he identifies. At the spiritual level of reality, then, traditional scientific principles such as the laws of space and time are not applicable.

How such identities are formed becomes a subject in itself. For our purposes, the rhetorical device through which identity is made is the metaphor. In poetry, the metaphor functions in its fullest and perhaps truest capacity, bringing together two essentially unlike entities. At this point we should note how the metaphor serves as a kind of linguistic keystone between the two symbolic worlds of feeling and reason.

In addition to the principle of identity, there exists the principle of *intensity,* which Erich Fromm discusses in his book *The Forgotten Language.*[26] The principle of intensity is illustrated by Fromm through the story of Jonah, which may be considered to be a religious allegory. The story of Jonah is told in the Bible as though it were true. The sequence of events is as follows:

> Jonah hears God telling him to go to Nineveh to preach to its inhabitants to rid themselves of their evil ways. Jonah is reluctant to take on the responsibility and tries to run away from God's commandment. He finds a ship which should take him to Tarshish. On the way a storm arises. While others are fearful of the storm Jonah goes into the bottom of the ship and falls into a deep sleep. The sailors awaken him because they believe that God must be punishing them and may require a sacrifice to appease him. Jonah convinces them he is the one who should be sacrificed and they toss him overboard whereupon he is swallowed by a big fish. He stays in the belly of the fish for three days and nights. He finds the conditions unbearable and prays to God to release him. God makes the fish throw him up upon dry land and Jonah then goes to Nineveh to fulfill the commandment and save the inhabitants of the city from destruction.[27]

---

[26] Erich Fromm, *The Forgotten Language* (New York: Grove Press, Inc., 1951). Fromm discusses what we have called the identity principle as the principle of association.

[27] The summary of the Jonah story is drawn from Fromm's description (*ibid.,* pp. 21–22).

The story makes some sense in terms of time and space. The sequence of events has causal meaning as Fromm indicates, in the sense that Jonah took to the seas *because* he wanted to flee from his responsibility to God, he falls asleep *because* he is tired, etc. But some parts of the story are not sensible, such as living inside a fish's belly for three days and nights. Other principles than those of logic and sense must be utilized to understand the story and explain its meaning. The symbolic explanation must be based upon the principle of intensity as Fromm points out, and, we would add, on the basis of purpose.

The events clearly follow one another symbolically in increasing degrees of personal intensity. That is, Jonah's efforts to escape are seen first in his boarding the ship, then going into the ship's belly, then falling asleep, then being thrown into the sea at his own request, and finally being swallowed by the fish. Each event represents an increasingly regressive search for security that increasingly leads to the very opposite of security, to the point where Jonah is intensely insecure and in a frightful state of imprisonment in the belly of a fish. Thus, the events cannot be explained on the basis of their causal relationships to each other; rather, each succeeding event indicates the increasing personal intensity of Jonah's efforts to escape responsibility.

There is a universal as well as a relative truth about man's purposive life that is expressed in this allegory. A modern allegory might express the same or a similar theme, but with different symbols and in more indirect ways. In a modern allegory, we would imagine, there would not be a direct commandment from God, since in modern society there is less compelling and widespread belief in such direct communication from supernatural powers, but the message would likely remain in substantially the same form, since it expresses a fundamental truth about the nature of man in society. The message is a paradox, for it says, among other things, that it is only through obedience that man may find freedom. While the converse may also be true— *i.e.*, that man may find freedom through disobedience, this message still stands as a moral fact about an invariable relation between personal order and freedom in a purposive world. Even the man who is disobedient, if he is to find freedom, must be obedient to some order. The kind of obedience which is demanded or expected by people at different times in different societies is, of course, a matter which becomes relative to the culture, but the fundamental interdependence between obedience to some kind of order and freedom is a universal fact about man in society.

It is in such allegories and in the fables and myths of mankind that cross-cultural universals or *archetypes* may be found. The archetype is, of course, much different from the allegory, and it leads us back into the theoretical dimension of social science in much the same way that the metaphor led us to the discussion of the model. The archetype may be tentatively formulated on the basis of interpreting a limited number of cases of human behavior (*e.g.*, as with Sigmund Freud and Carl Jung), but they must eventually be verified by careful systematic study of hundreds of empirical studies from around the world. Efforts have already been begun in this direction by G. P. Murdock, Clyde Kluckhohn, and others to document the intuitive leadings of clinical theorists. The archetype, unlike the allegory, is a rational construction of what is believed to be a recurrent theme in the culture of man. It is therefore subject to rational and empirical criticism. For example, how universal the Oedipus myth actually is depends upon what elements should theoretically be allowed to enter into its description. Present anthropological studies indicate that if all the elements which have been found to be important in psychoanalytic theory are included in the definition of the Oedipus myth, this myth may be found in very few cultures, but if the definition is broadened or made more highly abstract, it can be found in the allegories of folktales and myths of many cultures. Studies have shown the widespread existence of similar allegorical content in other myths, such as in the stories of creation, of world flood, of sibling rivalry, of incest, and other types of myths which Clyde Kluckhohn has recently summarized.[28] The archetype, then, functions in the world of sense and abstraction. It is a rational image of many stories with allegorical quality (fables, myths, folktales) in diverse cultures. In this way, the archetype produces a different, yet no less important, kind of sociological truth than the allegory which functions more as an expressive truth of man's moral life.

There are interesting parallels that might be drawn between the literary allegory and modern methods of scientific analysis. For example, the scientist, like the allegorist, weaves a series of fictions (theories) which are intended to account for a literal (empirical) truth. He intends to provide a one-to-one correspondence between his scientific fabrication of symbols and the actual reality. He does not succeed too well in every respect. The symbol H_2O in chemistry does not represent the reality of water very well as it is perceived by the senses. In fact, modern scientific theories, like modern allegories, have become more complicated and indirect in their references to the literal world than in earlier years. Mathematical symbols are no longer symbols of things but of abstract relations; literary symbols, too, express less the reality of things than the reality of complex relationships. Modern scientific theories, like modern allegories, can be simplified, of course, for the uninitiated. For example, atomic theories have their popular descriptions, but this does not do justice to the original theories, and one who understands the

---

[28] Clyde Kluckhohn, "Recurrent Themes in Myths and Mythmaking," in Murray, *Myth and Mythmaking,* pp. 46–60.

simplified version cannot honestly say that he fully understands the meaning of the symbolism. Similarly, a modern allegory can be simplified by saying, for example, that Kafka's castle represents heaven and the village represents the earth, but this kind of explanation does not convey the complexity of these symbols, and a full understanding of them will elude the observer. In these ways, interesting parallels may be observed between the scientific and the literary devices of the two separate cultures, the sciences and the humanities.

Imagery and Irony

Imagery

The concept of *image* is a rather complex one. In a recent book called *The Image*,[29] Kenneth Boulding has called for a whole new science to be formulated about the concept. We may say that an image is that form which is created by rhetorical devices such as those of the metaphor family: the simile, analogy, allegory, fable, parable, and myth. In its simplest form, the image is the visual picture of sensory experiences which develops in the mind as an aftermath of such experiences. In its more complex form, image may be used to refer to the meanings which are produced by more complex symbolism. In any case, the image is very close to the symbol in meaning, since it represents or stands for an entity rather than being an entity itself.

Insofar as it represents an actual entity, an image must necessarily be removed and different from the entity. Therefore, the social scientist can study subjective phenomena such as the passions and sentiments of man while retaining some degree of objectivity. Passions and sentiments are the materials of the novelist and the dramatist, as well as the social scientist, but we must conclude that neither the literary nor the scientific workshops contain the original entities. In a memorable phrase, Shakespeare had Hamlet say of the player that his purpose was to hold "as t'were, the mirror up to nature; to show virtue her own feature, scorn her own image, and the very age and body of the time his form and pressure." In commenting upon this conception of the dramatist's role Cassirer aptly adds:

> But the image of a passion is not the passion itself. The poet who represents a passion does not infect us with this passion. At a Shakespearean play we are

---

29 Kenneth Boulding, *The Image* (Ann Arbor, Mich.: University of Michigan Press, 1956).

not infected with the ambition of Macbeth, with the cruelty of Richard III, or with the jealousy of Othello. We are not at the mercy of these emotions; we look through them; we seem to penetrate into their very nature and essence.[30]

This is not to suggest that imagery does not have its own emotional effects, but these effects are a matter for the social scientist to study in his own works. In so doing, we might add, he may learn techniques of rhetorical criticism from studies in literature which bear directly upon his problems. An excellent guide to critical studies of the emotional effects of imagery is Caroline Spurgeon's work on the substructure of Shakespeare's tragedies. In this seminal study she has shown how the reader is led unwittingly to conclusions based upon the accumulated effects of Shakespearean imagery:

> By recurrent imagery I mean the repetition of an idea or picture in the images used in any one play. Thus in *Romeo and Juliet* the dominating image is light with its background of darkness, while in *Hamlet* there hovers all through the play in both words and word pictures the conception of disease, especially of a hidden corruption infecting and destroying wholesome body.[31]

Spurgeon's analysis of *Hamlet* demonstrates that the recurrent images of disease, that is, the effects of recurrent analogies of ulcer, cancer, etc., lead the reader to conclude that Prince Hamlet was not really to blame for the demise of the ruling lineage of Denmark, but rather that the whole state of Denmark was diseased. A similar study of the rhetorical imagery in some sociological studies might prove quite enlightening.

Imagery is produced by devices other than those of the metaphor family. Irony is another major rhetorical form which deserves our careful attention for its place in sociological studies.

Irony[32]

Irony is a rhetorical device which has taken many shapes, for it is probably one of the most complicated of all devices. Therefore, its full meaning cannot be traced here. In order to examine irony as a device in sociological research and analysis, we must consider its usage in other forms of literature, its presence and function in contemporary sociological studies, and its metaphysical implications in the methodology of social science.

---

[30] Cassirer, *An Essay on Man,* p. 147.

[31] Caroline Spurgeon, *Shakespeare's Imagery* (New York: The Macmillan Company, 1936), p. 213.

[32] Pp. 150–57 adapted from Severyn T. Bruyn, "Rhetorical Devices in Sociological Analysis," *The Sociological Quarterly.* 5, No. 2 (Spring 1964), 105–12. Reprinted by permission of *The Sociological Quarterly.*

Two examples from literature may illustrate the nature of irony. In O. Henry's short story, "The Gift of the Magi," a poor young husband pawns his most prized possession, a gold watch, in order to buy his wife a set of combs for her hair for Christmas, and his wife sells her most prized possession, her long brown hair, in order to buy a chain for her husband's watch. The situation is ironical. When King Midas, in the famous fable, is granted his fondest wish, that anything he touches will turn to gold, this, too, is ironic, because even his daughter turned to gold. In both cases, the power of nature, its fortuity (and inevitability) is stronger than the best or worst motives in man.

Irony was a prominent part of Greek thought as it was manifested through the Greeks' conception of the struggle between man's finite purposes and the laws of nature. Irony reveals how the reality of nature (both intrinsic and extrinsic to man) has a greater power than man's most prideful or even altruistic purposes. Irony is seen in a depiction of human action the consequences of which are opposite to what is intended by the participants. Irony exists when empathy is created by a dramatic description of man's finite limitations. The original Greek conception of irony is so deeply embedded in western culture that any penetrating analysis of modern society can hardly avoid becoming involved with its effects.

Irony exists in sociological analysis, but is seldom recognized. If it is recognized, it is not generally considered legitimate to the scientific enterprise. It has failed to obtain legitimacy partly because it is commonly known in its simpler or cruder forms where it is expressed either as *sarcasm* (sometimes called *verbal irony*) or in critical attacks against some aspect of the social order, as in *satire*. However, in a technical sense, irony is neither cruel nor kind. It need not be used for purposes of reform nor solely to create the emotional effects of criticism. It is simply an instrument, like the surgeon's scalpel, which the writer may use in performing his analytical work, for its true purpose is to illuminate. Irony is used most effectively in research as part of a larger analytical framework, within which it functions to add the human coefficient. In order to really clarify this function in applied research, we must first review some of the ways in which irony has entered into sociological analysis.

Examples

Two ways in which irony has been a basic part of past sociological studies are first, as it is actually produced by the analyst in the content of the study and second, as an unavoidable effect upon readers of such studies, with or without the author's intention.

Numerous writers have produced irony in the content of an analysis. Actually, the effect of irony is built into the theoretical pattern of functionalism; it is created in functional research when the social scientist seeks to uncover the unintended consequences of social action. Alvin Gouldner's analysis of industrial bureaucracy is a case in point. There is considerable irony produced in his analysis of the latent dysfunctions (ineffectiveness) of rules in the industrial plant which was the site of his research.[33]

Irony in sociological analysis appears to be more generalized and less direct than irony in any other form of literature. Gouldner's study, for example, could have been designed simply as a critical attack against the foibles of the plant administration. However, the focus of his analysis was on the hypotheses and generalizations that could be made about the workings of bureaucracy in modern society. The errors of management are all clearly revealed in what Gouldner calls punishment-centered bureaucracy, but the fault is found to lie in types of bureaucratic structures, rather than in the particular plant management. The generalized focus makes it more possible for a particular management to accept the finding without feeling blame. Nevertheless, irony is still revealed in the evidence Gouldner accumulates, for the unanticipated consequences of the two ineffective types of bureaucratic structures he describes are a mockery of the original organizational intentions.

Another example of irony clearly evidenced in research is found in Vidich and Bensman's *Small Town in Mass Society*. Here irony is bluntly produced in a description of local efforts of citizens to maintain the appearance of a small town in spite of the fact that the community has come to reflect the characteristics of mass society. The metaphors which the researchers employ reveal the ironic mold in which they are cast. Certain features of military, economic, chemical, and medical imagery are selected to describe the social changes which have taken place: "jurisdictional *surrender*," "cultural *importation*," "*atomization* of personality," and "political *paralysis*."[34]

Another way in which irony may be produced in sociological analysis is by juxtaposing different sets of facts to reveal their incongruities. Maurice Stein has noted how irony is effectively employed by the Lynds through the continual use of contrasting images. In portraying the business and middle classes of "Middletown," the Lynds revealed the irrationalities present in the two perspectives without allowing the values of one to be the criteria for judging the other, and without allowing their own judgments to enter into the analysis. The incongruities were revealed by the juxtaposition of the two classes in the descriptive text without destroying the integrity existing in either of the two perspectives. Similarly, Stein notes how the first study, *Middletown,* was contrasted with *Middletown in Transition*. Here the care-

[33] Alvin Gouldner, *Patterns of Industrial Bureaucracy* (New York: Free Press of Glencoe, Inc., 1954).

[34] Arthur J. Vidich and Joseph Bensman, *Small Town in Mass Society* (Garden City, N.Y.: Doubleday Anchor Books, 1958). [Italics mine—Au.]

ful reader can see how "intrinsic meanings" became sacrificed in the pursuit of market commodities and the ever-rising standard of living.[35]

In the field of criminology, E. H. Sutherland has presented a striking analysis of white-collar crime which has considerable irony.[36] In his study, Sutherland makes a perfectly objective comparison of the subculture of the upper status businessman with the subculture of the professional thief. He found that the criminality of the corporate businessman was persistent and much more extensive than prosecution would indicate, just as was true of the common thief. He found that the businessman did not lose status in his own company for wrong-doing; in fact, he felt and expressed contempt for the law, just as did the thief. Sutherland found that the man of distinction carefully organized his crimes through a network of informal agreements with his associates, just like the professional thief. The only real difference between the two was the public's conception of them, for the businessman was held in esteem, and the thief in disfavor.

In his scientific role as a taxonomist of social phenomena, the sociologist classifies his subjects on the basis of those objective similarities which he finds important in his work, but which would not necessarily be perceived in everyday affairs. So it becomes ironic (whether intentional or not) that Sutherland should classify the businessman and the professional thief on the same level. Similarly, when Lloyd Warner described Memorial Day in America in the same terms as he would describe a primitive ritual, "a cult of the dead," there is irony in the comparison.[37] There is a leveling or equalizing effect that occurs as science arbitrarily considers separate phenomena together.

This effect may be explained by the fact that the Greek concepts of justice and equality are so much a part of western culture that as the social scientist goes about classifying social unequals, he reveals discrepancies between appearance and reality; he seems to express inexorable laws of the social universe—laws which are beyond everyone's ability to do anything but merely witness events. Thus, the social scientist becomes a modern counterpart to the Greek Oracle, making predictions, stating the natural laws of the world, against which man has pitted his finite will. The scientist becomes the impersonal agent of nature, expressing indisputable truths about the world to which men and their institutions must find some kind of adjustment.

Irony, then, is unavoidable in some cases. Even the purely statistical

---

[35] Maurice Stein, *The Eclipse of Community* (Princeton, N.J.: Princeton University Press, 1960), p. 312.

[36] Edwin Sutherland, *White Collar Crime* (New York: Dryden Press, Inc., 1949).

[37] W. Lloyd Warner, *American Life: Dream and Reality* (Chicago: University of Chicago Press, 1953), pp. 1–26.

analysis of the Kinsey report has ironic overtones as the facts become juxtaposed against the appearances of American morality.

Metaphysical Implications

The scientific quality of works in sociological analysis is diminished when they contain value judgments which place the analyst in an ethical position superior to his subjects. The basic question here is: Does irony require such value judgments? The answer is that value judgments are implied in any analysis, but they need not become the dominant characteristic of the analysis; nor does the work need to express any ethical superiority of the analyst. In the story of King Midas there was clearly an ethical judgment about the folly of the monarch. But in the story of the Magi there is no such ethical judgment about the motives of the participants, aside from O. Henry's intent to demonstrate how his characters were subject to fateful circumstance.

While value judgments are elusive and often hidden, they cannot be ignored in sociological analysis. Irony can be subtle—even in the Magi story an implicit judgment is made that nature is more powerful than the purest motives of man, for man's actions are his own undoing. Functional analysis is no less subject to implicit or explicit value judgments. A case study of bureaucracy in a functional framework may range from a sympathetic account of participants who are subject to fateful circumstance to a description of the folly of administrators. Wherever the audience is allowed to participate or empathize with the actors, and where the consequences of the characters' actions contradict their intentions, there are both irony and some value judgments. Irony, as the controlling rhetorical device of sociological analysis, is consistent with neither the relativism nor the naturalism which together have been central themes in the philosophy of science.

The philosophy of naturalistic idealism[38] is the social scientist's main

---

[38] By naturalistic idealism we mean only to suggest a viewpoint which would integrate opposition principles in these two philosophic traditions. This viewpoint would consider the mind to be a natural phenomenon (as it *is* in its own being), but without studying it as though it were *only* a biophysical mechanism. It would view culture with its values and ideals as being of its own kind, having a distinctive character to be investigated openly in the spirit of the natural scientist.

The two rhetorical devices, irony and paradox, are excellent tools for revealing the character of this culture to the observer. Irony is the more dramatically effective of the two, and because of its critical power, it cauterizes painfully through to the truth. Clearly, confronting social realities can be painful. The paradox is normally used simply to disclose the nature of things by giving the observer higher, or more subtle clues to reality. It generally appeals to the cooler reaches of the intellect, without utilizing satire or criticism. Together, irony and paradox have rhetorical powers that function remarkably well in revealing man to himself.

guide into the realm of research and theory; it is his original and master value judgment, the foundation upon which the superstructure of sociological theory is built. The rhetorical device which is consistent with idealism is irony, but the rhetorical device consistent with naturalism is the paradox.

Paradox

The *paradox* is an apparent contradiction between two equally valid ideas or principles, which is nevertheless found to be true. The paradox is explained generally by revealing how the two principles are interdependent through some third principle. In form, the paradox is closely related to irony; sometimes it is difficult to determine when one becomes the other. Yet the proper use of these two devices represents one of the knottiest problems in scientific methodology.

How researchers have approached the study of bureaucracy is a good illustration of the use of irony and paradox. Certain studies have clearly revealed the irony inherent in the efforts of bureaucrats to produce efficiency by the elaborate use of rules and procedures which actually result in inefficiency, the opposite intention. However, a truly naturalistic explanation would restate the problem as a paradox in which each contrary fact is dependent upon the other through some unseen factor. With regard to bureaucracy, the social analyst seeks to answer the objective question of why much human effort and activity should result in little production. The human interest and personal ideals of the participants are omitted or deemphasized. The natural laws of bureaucracy in modern society are revealed and the audience (and the researcher) has no sense of personal involvement and no sense of irony embedded in the situation.

More simply, as a problem in methodology, the position of the social scientist in relation to his research objectives can be viewed as both ironic and paradoxical. The social analyst intends to avoid the prejudices and feelings that inhere in social situations in order to understand people better and more objectively. The irony is that although the scientist's aim is to understand human relations, the more impersonal his research and the less sympathetic his attitude toward the personal interests and values of his subject, the more likely the scientist will fail to understand them.

The paradox is: How *do* these two contrary principles co-exist in the framework of the social scientist? Restating the paradox as a question in correct methodology: How *can* the social scientist sympathize with the private worlds of the participants and still retain his objectivity and the naturalistic perspective? The answer is in the balanced use of both irony and paradox in sociological analysis, where irony is employed in research to capture the personal reality and paradox employed to objectively explain the contradiction as a natural phenomenon.

This unique combination is visible, at least at its suggestive beginnings, in Lloyd Warner's approach to community studies. Irony is revealed in the poignant portraits, the case studies, which are set in the larger framework of objective analysis of class structure. Warner allows the reader to empathize, to enter into the human context. We can see how it feels to be taught equality in school and to face social exclusion in the community. Then, in his theory of community studies, Warner transforms the antithetical principles (social equality vs. class structure) into a paradox by explaining that both have been essential to the continued functioning of society.[39]

Social science is in the process of shaping irony to fit its own purposes and its own methodology. Examples of how irony has taken form in non-scientific literature can throw light on its place in sociological studies. Kenneth Burke denies any Pharasaic quality in true irony. He describes the transformation of irony in modern literature:

> True irony, however, irony that really does justify the attribute "humility," is not "superior" to the enemy .... (Eliot's problem in religion has resided precisely in his attempt to convert romantic irony to classic irony, really to replace a state of "superiority" by a state of "humility"—and *Murder in the Cathedral* is a ritual aimed at precisely such purification of motives.) True irony, humble irony, is based upon a sense of fundamental kinship with the enemy, as one *needs* him within, being consubstantial with him. This is the irony of Flaubert, when he recognizes that Madame Bovary is himself. One sees it in Thomas

---

[39] The value judgment contained in the paradox as Warner explains it, however, is unnecessary. If Warner had stated only that social inequality has been historically necessary (*i.e.,* as a theory of social origins rather than as the "proper" function of contemporary society, implying that class inequality is basically good for society), he would have been closer to the scientific facts and would have remained within the naturalistic framework, Warner conceives class structure to be a kind of incentive system that draws and sorts talented individuals into higher positions and achievements. Warner's critics claim that this is a special case of the market mechanism model of classical economics which cannot be accurately applied to the study of class structure in general. While class structure does contribute functionally to the maintenance of modern societies, its dysfunctional role (*e.g.,* destroying incentives) has yet to be fully examined. W. Lloyd Warner's observations were as follows:

"I wish to affirm, that paradoxical as it may seem, both these antithetical principles when properly balanced, are necessary for the proper functioning of contemporary American democracy....

"The principle of equality is necessary to provide all men with a sense of respect and to establish the secular essentials of the Christian belief in brotherhood....

"The principle of rank and status is necessary to provide men with the motives to excel by striving for positions of higher prestige and power for themselves and their families.... I do not believe that the American system could operate, that the present method of carrying on human affairs could continue, if Americans did not possess the kind of status system which it has been their good fortune to develop." (Warner, *American Life,* pp. 104–5.)

On the complexity of this interpretation and others like it, see Dennis Wrong, "The Functional Theory of Stratification: Some Neglected Considerations," *American Journal of Sociology,* 24, No. 6 (December 1959), 772–82.

Mann—and in what he once called, when applying the term to another, "Judas psychology." And there was, if not the humility of strength, at least a humility of gentle surrender, in Anatole France.[40]

Such irony is visible in the development of applied research when analysts reveal unexpected truths that contradict the interests of the institution in which they participate—where researchers reveal how they have contributed to actions contrary to their own and their institution's interests. This kind of irony may occur in the "academic marketplace" as well as in industrial studies, and may be what Burke has in mind.

Paradox and irony, then, are both important rhetorical devices in socio-logical analysis. The overuse of irony in applied research results in crude criticism; the overuse of the paradox omits what may be most important to understand in the situation—the sense of values, the human meanings which have their own place in explaining human actions.

Synecdoche and Metonymy

The rhetorical devices of *synecdoche* and *metonymy* are closely associated in meaning and have been used interchangeably by some writers to mean the same thing. Metonymy is generally understood to be the substitution of the name of one thing for the name of another thing or person. The newscaster who says "The White House has just announced..." does not really mean that a house has spoken, but rather that the President has spoken.

In the substitution of one name for another, it is generally the case that a simpler image is selected to represent a more complex one. Kenneth Burke has described this feature of metonymic devices (what social scientists would call "reductionism") in the construction of words. He illustrates how the complex word "emotion" is derived semantically from the material-istic conception of "motion," and how we still refer to the heart (a physical phenomenon) when speaking of emotional states.[41] The language of soci-ology functions in similar way. The concepts which have been forged from physical and organic images represent society in oversimplified terms. To a great extent this is unavoidable, for this is largely how language is built and therefore how sociological theory has been built.

In other words, new or complex phenomena normally must be understood initially in terms of one's past experiences. Generally, varied metonymic metaphors are applied to a complex subject such as society or culture until it acquires a substantive meaning of its own. The complex phenomenon

---

[40] Kenneth Burke, *A Grammar of Motives* (Englewood Cliffs, N.J.: Prentice-Hall, Inc., 1945), p. 514.

[41] *Ibid.*, p. 506.

eventually develops an image of its own, which then becomes established for those who frequently refer to it. Subsequently, this image then becomes the source for describing still more complex phenomena.

There seems to be no absolute necessity, however, to explain social phenomena in terms of physical or organic imagery, even though this apparently simplifies the task of communicating the meaning of the phenomena. In fact, higher level comparisons would be much more revealing and productive than those of space, fluidity, and function. There is no reason why, in explaining the nature of social institutions, for example, that one institution and its components might not be the basis for comparing another institution. The structure of the political institution compared with the economic, or the religious compared with the economic, would prove very interesting indeed. There is no reason why what we think of as physical theory need employ solely physical metaphors. It might prove fruitful for physicists or biologists to see their data in terms of social phenomena, thus reversing the metaphoric procedures normally employed in science. In his recent study of the metaphor, Colin Turbayne examines the theory of optics in terms of the structure of language, instead of the geometric figure by which it is generally conceived. After a rather thorough analysis, he concludes that of the structures of two figures—geometry and language—the structure of language is the more fruitful and realistic metaphor to employ as a basis for a theory of optics.[42]

Synecdoche embodies much of what we witness in the nature of social analysis. Synecdoche is a figure of speech in which the part is used for the whole, or the whole for the part; the cause for the effect, or the effect for the cause; the species for the genus, or the genus for the species. The statistical index is an example of synecdoche insofar as it is a part which represents the whole. In examining various figures of speech, Kenneth Burke concludes that synecdoche has much to say analytically about the structure of human relations:

> The more I examine both the structure of poetry and the structure of human relations outside of poetry, the more I become convinced that this [synecdoche] is the "basic" figure of speech, and that it occurs in many modes besides that of the formal trope. I feel it to be no mere accident of language that we use the same word for sensory, artistic, and political representation.... In theories of politics prevailing at different periods in history, there have been quarrels as to the precise vessel of authority that is to be considered "representative" of the society as a whole (chief, nobles, monarch, churchmen, parliamentary delegates, poet, leader, the majority, the average, the propertied, or the propertyless, etc.), but all agree in assuming that there is *some* part representative of the whole, hence fit to stand for it.

---

[42] Turbayne, *The Myth of Metaphor,* Chaps. vi–viii.

A "fetish" usually thought of as belonging in a totally different category, is thus seen likewise to be an aspect of the synecdochic function, as when the beloved's shoe is proxy for the beloved. The "scapegoat" becomes another kind of "representative," in serving as the symbolic vessel of certain burdens, which are ritualistically delegated to it.[43]

Synecdoche, as a figure of speech that indicates "some part representative of the whole," reflects a protean idea in culture. It is the mirror of diverse social patterns ranging from *fetishes* and *scapegoating* to the sophisticated philosophy of modern democracy. Rhetorical forms have this summative character, for they capture the most basically different forms of social relations in one idea, and are thus employable as instruments of social analysis.

In summary, we would say that we may find much about the nature of man in the structure of language and literary genre. If man is represented only by biophysical metaphors, we lose sight of his intrinsic worth as a human being and violate his dignity. There is, in fact, something of Burke's irony to be seen in the scientist's persistent efforts to debase himself in "reductionisms," for whether the scientist admits it or not, he is a direct contributor to the cultural life which he valuates in his descriptions.

The social scientist has inadvertently been bringing a new rhetoric to the life-world of the layman, new concepts which have influenced the social, economic, and political life of society. This rhetoric can function in society like the Greek Oracle or Marx's communism to control, in one way or another, the destinies of whole nations and perhaps a civilization. The social scientist must see the phenomenon of the myth as it functions within the traditional canons of science. He must see it as outside the explanatory awareness of sense and logic, as Ernst Cassirer has noted, and study it as it exists in the subjective lives of people. If methods for studying the inner life of society are seriously considered and carefully developed, the social scientist may anticipate the consequences of his work with more wisdom, and he may contribute even more significantly toward that knowledge which guides the hearts as well as the minds of men in society.

---

[43] Kenneth Burke, *The Philosophy of Literary Form* (New York: Vintage Books, Inc., 1957), pp. 23–24.

6

Methodological Assumptions

In the coming years, the method of participant observation must be carefully examined in terms of: (1) assumptions about the *nature of man* which guide research; (2) assumptions about the *process of knowing* research data in the mind of the observer; and (3) assumptions about the *method of verifying* the data acquired. These are matters which we will now consider in an exploratory manner.

The Nature of Man

Sociocultural Data

The research data with which the participant observer works consist basically of human meanings interpreted through the observer's communication with his subjects. The term "meaning" is used here instead of value, norm, regulatory pattern, or some other term because it applies most specifically to what the participant observer studies.

In other words, the observer seeks to discover and explain the nature of the particular sociocultural reality, the shared human reality, of his subjects. He seeks to determine what the interactive world of his subjects means to them. Subjective meanings become verified through the observer's work, then serving as the basis for drawing inferences about values, norms, regulatory patterns, and other constructs which are the scientist's own meanings, if you will, of those meanings he observes.

While "meaning" can be a theoretical construct, it also functions as a term directly connected with the commonsense realities which the observer seeks to explore, and for that reason, meaning most aptly expresses the nature of the subject matter. The observer, therefore, can more readily ask, "What do you mean?" than he can ask, "What are your norms?" Meaning is a root term in the language of human research which best expresses what the researcher seeks to know.

The methodological importance of participant observation in gathering data of this kind is indicated by George Herbert Mead's conception of what constitutes the nature of meaning:

> There are two characters which belong to that which we term "meanings"; one is participation and the other is communicability. Meaning can arise only insofar as some phase of the act which the individual is arousing in the other can be aroused in himself. There is always to this extent participation. And the result of this participation is communicability, *i.e.,* the individual can indicate to himself what he indicates to others.[1]

This is the initial and perhaps most fundamental methodological assumption underlying the work of the participant observer: the participant can communicate a message to another participant and have it understood as he intended it. The assumption is that people can arouse in others that which is aroused in themselves, or as Mead puts it, "the individual can indicate to himself what he indicates to others."

The meanings which people share do not always coincide with precision; this is why the observer must have checks for verification. Nevertheless, there is enough truth underlying this proposition, that is, enough probability that the meanings can be close enough to be functional, that the observer can act methodologically. Actually, this assumption lies profoundly at the base of all human communication—it is the essential ground for the emergence of society. Without the truth contained in this assumption we could have no culture, since the alternative would be to assume that life consisted of a series of falsehoods. In fact, truth itself could not exist. Therefore, this premise is fundamental to the nature of man.

Bronislaw Malinowski once contended that the aims and methods of modern science originated from primitive magic rituals, in which early man sought to control the world about him. Similarly, it is from a simple human act of knowing by way of mutually aroused symbolic action that the participant observer takes human meanings as his data, and proceeds to refine his methods of verification and discovery.

If sociocultural meanings are to be understood as the data of the observer, as definitions of the reality of man, then we must conclude that the theoretical task of interpreting this data is an ontological one—forming postulates about the nature of man's being-in-the-world. *Ontology* is a term not nor-

---

[1] Anselm Strauss, ed., *The Social Psychology of George Herbert Mead* (Chicago: University of Chicago Press, Phoenix Books, 1956), p. 183.

mally employed by the social theorist, and yet we feel it is applicable to the foundations of the phenomena which the participant observer studies. The concept of ontology reinforces social theorists' interpretation of the nature of man's being, when human realities are interpreted at the level of meaning. Social theory does not replace its formulations with those of phenomenology, existentialism, theology, or some other field carrying ontological formulations. Quite clearly, however, the present emphasis of concepts in the theory of social system (*e.g.,* structure and function) has yet to be balanced by concepts in a theory of culture which clarify the imagery and historical configurations of value that control and guide the lives of men in society. Researchers must concentrate on the actual historical realities as the basis for developing the conceptual landmarks and bridges between the cultures of societies which can provide the basis for a general cultural theory comparable to social system analysis. Only then can a more comprehensive theory develop which is guided by a synthesis of social and cultural concepts explaining the structure of life in the society of man. Such an integral theory should be capable of expressing and accounting for the divergent dimensions of knowledge we have stressed as significant so far—the interpretive forms of symbolic and historical knowledge, the factual correlates of traditional study, and the analytical knowledge of the structural-functionalist.

Ontological Assumptions : The Problem of Reality

The ontological problem of the theorist is how to establish the nature of human reality—*i.e.,* that which people see as basic in their world. The researcher looks for the meaning of reality in the culture he studies, and is therefore concerned with discovering and verifying the existence of a certain reality through human meanings. The theorist, however, must bring these meanings together into some larger whole; in so doing, he creates a certain reality for himself. The theorist must formulate basic definitions and postulates inclusive enough to encompass sociocultural realities of man wherever they may be found in social research. He is creatively adding to human reality when he does so. The theorist must also formulate models of middle range which deal with these realities, models upon which the researcher may draw to make interpretations of what he finds in the culture he studies.

We have suggested that, in addition to the present-day theory of structural-functionalism which explicates research findings in the positivist and behaviorist traditions, there is now a need for a theory of cultural life to explicate the findings of participant observers. However, it would be a mistake to stress too strongly the schism between the major forms of social and cultural theory. Our own basic assumption is that man is a "whole being." We assume he is often in conflict, but he is not basically fragmented at the core, and he must be understood in this holistic sense in the final analysis. We assume, further, that "structure" and "function" are aspects of man's "being." The distinction is made here only to stress that this problem in contemporary thought must be recognized before it can be treated systematically as a new theory.

We have already seen how certain realities of man's being are revealed by the participant observer in different terms than those defined by positivistic organicism. If we can accept these differences and admit that they are authentic at the level which we are describing, we then can begin to offer some basis for our assumptions about the nature of man. We have suggested that the realities by which men live include primitive assumptions that men are both free and determined; that their lives are linked purposely and causally in space and time; that they are both individuals and collective beings; that their lives have comic dimensions as well as tragic dimensions; that they can transcend conflict, live through it, or not live through it in their human world; and that their lives are guided by sentiments, common sense, and many other factors to which we could refer if we were treating this problem systematically. We would say, further, that socialized man finds himself living collectively in a moral framework, and that he has a sense of beauty and ugliness, a sense of justice, and so forth. This social scientific perspective implies a human reality which has yet to be treated in a more systematic fashion.

The realities of tragedy, comedy, purpose, freedom, transcendence, and justice are all part of the data of participant observation, and thus become the working materials of the theorist. While it is true that such realities contain ethical imperatives, the social researcher must simply report and verify them, and the theorist must only interpret these realities as existent entities. Neither the researcher nor the theorist need subscribe to them in their roles as scientists. It becomes the task of the theorist, we would say, to translate the normative imperatives of such realities into existent meanings which can be the basis for analyzing man's social and cultural being in society. If pursued systematically, this should lead to theories of man with greater objectivity than has previously been the case where theories claim neutrality while explaining society on a mechanistic or organismic basis.

To be more objective about man in society, social science today must become more subjectively adequate. The theoretical basis for analyzing man must be assessed for adequacy both subjectively and objectively. To be objective about man, paradoxical as it would seem, we must understand the subjective world of meanings. And although some men have sought to do this and have failed to achieve full objectivity, this indicates only that objectivity is an ideal never fully achieved.[2] While we admit it is humanly

---

2 The works of such men as Robert MacIver in sociology, Loren Eiseley in anthropology, and Henry Commager in history, which take subjective interpretations into

impossible to escape man's own limited frame of values entirely, we must insist that only through these values is it possible to achieve greater objectivity. Objectivity, then, can be attained through accurate subjective interpretations of reality which broaden the theoretical basis of analysis.

A theory of sociocultural being assumes that man is a creative as well as a destructive creature, individually and collectively. It assumes that the world of man's personal experience is an authentic world even though it allows for critical observation of particular forms of that world. It assumes that it is in man's everyday world of meanings that we can understand him in an essential part of his nature. This kind of theoretical development is most evident in European social phenomenology. In the words of Alfred Schutz:

> The primary goal of the social sciences is to obtain organized knowledge of social reality. By the term "social reality" I wish to be understood the sum total of objects and occurences within the social cultural world as experienced by the commonsense thinking of men living their daily lives among their fellow-men, connected with them in manifold relations of interaction. It is the world of cultural objects and social institutions into which we are all born, within which we have to find our bearings, and with which we have to come to terms. From the outset, we, the actors on the social scene, experience the world we live in as a world both of nature and of culture, not as a private but as an inter-subjective one, that is, as a world common to all of us, either actually given or potentially accessible to everyone; and this involves intercommunication and language.[3]

A viewpoint which is a dimension apart from the structural-functionalism prevalent in the United States is emerging in the work of Schutz and other European social theorists such as Gurvitch, Scheler, and Vierkandt. While at the present time these theories would appear to thrive on fundamentally different assumptions of man's nature and how he can be studied, it is possible to conceive of both these theories as part of the human perspective. If man is at the creative center of the knowing process, we can assume he is as capable of finding the relationship between such theories as he was capable of producing them separately in the first place.

It is clear that man's nature cannot be understood solely by the tradition of positivistic organicism or even its residual form controlling the rhetoric of social action theory. The human factors which combine to make political revolutions, the vandalistic acts of juvenile gangs, the turbulence of a race

---

account and fail to be fully objective, have yet yielded fuller measures of objective truth than positivists and empiricists who profess to interpret society objectively without reference to subjective meanings. Man is the subject as well as the object of himself.

[3] Alfred Schutz, *The Problem of Social Reality: Collected Papers I* (The Hague: Martinus Nijhoff, 1962), p. 53.

riot, the spiritual discoveries of a religious renaissance, or the social impact of science in modern society cannot be comprehended fully by those methodologies which rely solely upon sense data, logic, and ontologies of mechanism. Our purpose now is to examine further the assumptions underlying the methodology of knowing these realities.

The Process of Knowing

Kant's Sources of Knowledge

Historically, scientific research has utilized two major sources of knowing: the senses and reason. These two modes, procedurally refined as empiricism and rationalism, were originally separate, debatable methods of conducting valid inquiries, but toward the end of the eighteenth century were uniquely combined in the systematic philosophy of Immanuel Kant. Since that time they have served together as the foundation of the scientific method.

Kant believed that the original nature of the outer, empirical world ("*noumena*") could not be known. What becomes known to the mind as a "phenomenon" is that which is perceived, which is in turn the result of constructive activity of the mind. The form of that activity is contained "a priori" (inherent in the mind itself) in the structure of the intellect, and it imposes a certain order and meaning upon what is given to the senses from the outside world. Inherent in the structure of the mind, claimed Kant, are the "forms of intuition" such as "time" and "space," and "categories of the understanding" such as "quantity" and "quality" which are not derived from the outside world. These a priori forms and categories give order and meaning to an otherwise structureless array of sense stimuli encountered by the observer. Both reason and sense observation are necessary to the scientific method of knowing. In Kant's own well-known phrase: concepts without percepts are empty and percepts without concepts are blind.

The social sciences were barely emerging when Kant was writing, and he was therefore not in a position to examine the relation of his philosophy of science to the systematic study of man in society. Kant believed that the natural sciences should deal solely with the spatio-temporal world of fact, which he distinguished from the world of value and morality. He made a synthesis of the scientific methods of inquiry in his major work, *Critique of Pure Reason,* and then dealt with ethics and morality in a second major work, *Critique of Practical Reason.* By separating these two works, Kant reflected the schism that had developed at that time between the natural sciences, which dealt with the mechanical world, and moral philosophy, which dealt with the world of values. As the social sciences continued to emerge, their methodology was built on Kant's synthesis of rationalism and empiricism, applying Kant's scientific terms of space and number to the study of man. Social science has ever since struggled with the problem created by this separation of fact and value and the separate methods devised to study them. It is to Kant, however, that we owe a great debt for placing man back at the center of the knowing process; he constructed a human perspective of man in his study of morality, for he saw man as something more than a spatial entity that was to be studied as a natural object.

Reflecting momentarily, we may say that Durkheim applied Kant's scientific perspective, examining man as an object, and Znaniecki applied Kant's moral perspective of man as a personal being, seeking to study man's values as found in the letters and documents of the Polish peasant. Our position is that man must be viewed both ways in the social sciences, but the methodology for understanding man as a person as part of a moral order of society is only now developing. We may say, too, that Max Weber's concept of *Verstehen* was an early expression of that method necessary to understand man in this human dimension. The relatively undefined, yet significant, concept of Weber's has yet to be more adequately elaborated, both as a philosophy of social science and as a procedure for knowing man subjectively. For this purpose, we must add another source of knowing for the observer besides sense and reason.

Intuition

Intuition has been frequently used throughout the history of social thought. Kant himself used it to distinguish the rationally "self-evident" properties of the mind as distinct from the empirical content given to it. Kant held that we intuit time and space, rather than discover them as forms in the world about us. But what Kant meant here was an immediate apprehension of what appears self-evident in the structure of reason, a meaning different from our usage here as well as other past usages of the term. There is a familiar ring to Kant's definition, however, which was known through medieval and early periods of its interpretation as that mode of knowing which involves simply becoming *immediately aware* of something. The medieval "something" was not forms of "sensibility," however, as with Kant, but images of a God who presumably transcended man and provided an extrahuman or divine object of knowing. While the social sciences cannot deny the possibility of such a divine source, they are not structured to assume anything more than what is defined as human.

Another closely allied use of the term has been to describe that kind of knowledge which one gains mystically in a communion with a state of being which is ineffable, incapable of being communicated. Still another more recent use of the term has been to refer to that knowledge which appears to be unconscious in its origins or on the periphery of consciousness.

By intuitive knowledge we do not mean that kind of knowledge which cannot be communicated, nor that kind of knowledge which presumably stems from supernatural origins, nor that which is vaguely understood to be outside the frame of consciousness. What we do mean is that knowledge which is derived from the feelings, sentiments, and manifest human spirit which has acquired some measure of independence from the senses and the logical powers of man. *As we conceive it, intuition is the capacity to apprehend personal meanings which inhere in a social context.* It is a human capacity which, like logic or sense, can be disciplined, and a set of procedures may be developed around it for purposes of gaining knowledgeable access to this portion of man's nature. This is the kind of knowledge which social researchers must understand, for it is man's feeling as well as his reason that cause him to join a radical political movement, become a criminal, or more commonly, to get married, raise a family, or support a local Community Chest drive.

There would be nothing especially challenging or debatable about this point if we were not proposing that it be considered a legitimate, authentic source of knowledge in its own right within the social sciences. The authenticity of intuition as an original source of truth has been questioned in western society ever since the Greeks started man on the road to reason.

It is true that there have been periods of disappointment with reason as the sole source of truth. The Age of Reason or Enlightenment, for example, during which Kant was writing, was soon followed by the Romantic movement, and the rise of science was followed by the emergence of existentialism as a nonrational expression of man's search for truth. Nevertheless, the weight of Occidental tradition must lie with reason (the exceptions revealing the rule), in contrast to eastern or Oriental traditions which have given greater weight to the nonrational mediums of determining truth. At a time not far removed from the classical heights of Greek thought, Buddha was saying significantly in the East that reason was a two-edged sword; it could be used in whatever way one wanted to use it, and unless the "spirit" was disciplined, man could not find real truth.

In the West, the development of science and its fruitful consequences has given added weight to disciplined reason and sense procedures as the mediums through which truth is realized. The social scientist, in following the methods of the physical scientist, has continued the tradition of finding in reason the highest form of truth. But there is a system of values which belies these methods and which must be understood if movements such as existentialism are to be understood.

The social scientist who values reason as the highest form of truth has tended to misconceive or misinterpret the other values of man. Through this mode of knowing alone, he cannot understand personal or social meanings that exist in culture. When the social scientist studies the nonrational portion of man's life, he tends to interpret it without the sensitivity and discipline necessary to understand its true character. He has even defined it as a kind of "disorganized" behavior, failing to see its significant role in creating organized behavior or in laying the basis for reason and sense to function clearly. While many scientists such as Vilfredo Pareto have seen the vital importance of sentiments in guiding man's thought and action, the tradition of science has demanded that sentiments be given a positivistic meaning.

Those who have judged this intuitive faculty of man as important to providing valid knowledge from its own resources have been rare indeed. Pitirim Sorokin is one such rare individual, but his approach on this point has never been systematically developed in American sociology. The eastern world's conceptions of intuition as a source of truth and harmony as a basic verificatory criterion, have been misunderstood or deemed unacceptable by western standards of truth. For this reason, we must treat the epistemologial assumptions which lie behind intuitive knowledge before we can proceed to outline the methodological principles associated with this form of scientific inquiry.

Epistemology : Identities, Dichotomies, and Continuities

Two basic ways of knowing which have been defined as problem areas of epistemology are *monism* and *dualism*. The monistic theory of knowledge assumes that what an individual knows is identical with that which the individual seeks to know outside himself. The dualistic theory assumes that what an individual knows is different from or representative of that which he seeks to know outside himself. All scientific knowledge has been based upon this latter theory, while some poetic, esthetic, or mystical forms of knowledge in the humanities have been based upon the former theory. The problem presented here is similar to our previous discussion of the relation of social scientific knowledge to Martin Buber's existential philosophy, and our conclusion now must be of the same order. In spite of much philosophic opinion to the contrary, knowledge in the social sciences cannot be cataloged as solely dualistic. To understand human values, ideals, and myths, the social scientist must know them monistically—*i.e.*, by personal identity.

We can easily see that the wave theory of light in physics is different from the light itself, as a phenomenon perceived outside the mind. The wave theory stands for the light and partially explains it, but in no way is it thought to be the same as the light itself. This is what we mean by dualistic knowledge. The same condition would hold true in the social sciences for those logical-empirical constructs which are designed to represent a reality visibly perceived outside the mind. Such human constructs are defined only to represent an outer reality, not to express that reality directly as it is in its original nature. The same theory does not hold, however, for that kind of knowing which seeks, as Weber would say, to reproduce through sympathetic participation in ourselves the motives and purposes of other persons. In this case, we have knowledge by identity, or at least a demonstrable sameness which approaches identity.

Actually, any social meaning, even at the theoretical level, has this characteristic of sameness in the experience of people who communicate. While two social scientists may use the concept "culture" and think of the term dualistically as representing human artifacts or behavior patterns that are visible outside the mind, at the same time they assume that what they mean by the concept is the same, that their minds are in accord on its meaning. If any differences exist, they are routed out and discussed to the point where the two professional people have nearly identical interpretations. But still more significantly for our purposes, the expression of the word "culture" is an original expression of what is indicated by the term itself; it is a direct example of what it represents. The sign and its referent are one. This is an example of the monistic knowledge which is fundamental to the social sciences. It is a process of knowing through unity or identity, rather than through separation or representation, as is the case of dualistic knowledge.

There are three basic experiential processes of knowing: *unity, separation,* and *continuity*. Much could be said in terms of how these three processes enter into the making of all knowledge through the three capacities: intuition, sense, and reason. We can say that sense observation, for example, tends to locate separate items which appear in one's awareness as either existent or nonexistent in the outer world. As we noted in our discussion of polar typologies, the empirical referents are intended to be defined so as to be discrete, discontinuous, visible items in the observer's awareness. Then, it is through logic that we tend to see the continuities because reason can draw abstractions which connect and relate the seemingly dichotomous, separate items of one's awareness of the outside world. And finally, it is through intuition that we find some unity in what we observe so that we can personally identify with items which appear in human experience, or know them through immediate apprehension. A reciprocity of perspectives takes place in the field experience of the participant observer who must know cultures symbolically both by unity and by separation; in developing some continuity within this experience he produces a species of knowledge containing, if you will, an intersubjective logic of culture.

The participant observer's search for an accurate interpretation of the personal qualities of the social meanings with which he works must go beyond the theorist's purely rational apprehension, to include the attitudes and sentiments which are expressed in the culture. The participant observer must know *attitudinally*—i.e., personally—the values of those people he studies. Then, having some certitude about knowing them, he must be able to express these attitudes so that their genuine nature is retained even though they are placed within an objective context which allows the form to be examined analytically. Before we proceed to explore the latter problem, let us refer briefly to the matter of personal identity with the values of the culture studied.

Knowing by Personal Identity

It was knowing by personal identity that Auguste Comte claimed was the most primitive form of knowledge. Primitive man, Comte concluded, identified himself with the world about him—the trees, stars, and rocks—and was never able to abstract himself from this mystical union between himself and nature. It would seem the height of heresy to suggest that social scientific knowledge should return to such a primitive form of knowledge if it is to understand man in a civilized fashion. And yet this is what is implied in the participant phase of participant observation, for we must find a unity between subject and object. The participant observer, as observer, must know by "separation," but what has not been thoroughly examined in social research is his alternative role as participant, which means becoming identified with the lives of the subjects he studies.

The participant observer thinks imaginatively about the culture he studies, as does the traditional researcher who observes artifacts and behavior, but the observer also moves toward his subjects personally and becomes as one with them. There are two qualifications on this point which we should bear in mind. First, while the observer moves toward some unity with his subject, he must do so by principles of indirection, a matter which we shall discuss later. Second, the participant observer moves only partly toward unity. This is the key to understanding the role of the participant observer as we have indicated up to now; he is partly involved and partly detached.

This capacity to function in a role in which one is both involved and detached may sound, at first, to be impossible.[4] It is a reality, however, for

---

4 In order to indicate to the reader that the role which we are describing is not an impossible fiction, but a rather normal role for many people in society, we will suggest that there are many parallel cases in nonscientific, yet public roles in which these requirements exist. Robin Williams' description of two kinds of American patriotism is one example. (Cf. Robin Williams, *American Society*, (2nd ed.) (New York: Alfred A. Knopf, Inc., 1960).) One kind of patriotism is exemplified by those who sympathize completely with the House Un-American Activities Committee, giving their uncritical stamp of approval on all the investigations. Such citizens are totally identified and involved in what they believe to be Americanism. A second kind of patriotism is exemplified by those who identify with their country and have loyalty to it, and yet, in a detached way, criticize its policies quite strongly. The difference between these two types is dramatized by the latter group, which calls the House Un-American Activities Committee, "un-American." People learn both involvement and detachment in the process of becoming socialized into the family, the church, or the modern state in order to survive as individuals. It is a normal socialization process which can be refined in a formal educational program in the interests of social research.

the field researcher. In fact, he believes it is a process which may be learned through a program of training and discipline. The observer, as participant, must learn to move in and make his home, so to speak, in the culture of the observed, and yet, as he studies and reports his findings, he must move out of the culture and find his home again in the culture of his professional world. The personal knowledge which he gains in his field research must connect with the theoretical and empirical knowledge which also develops around his subject, and it must connect without losing its essential character. Other professionals must come to know the sentiments, attitudes, and feelings of people in the culture studied. These essential elements constitute the personal knowledge of the researcher and his subjects, but it must be conveyed to other nonparticipants through language, and more explicitly, through metaphors, analogies, parables, fables, simple stories, and concrete illustrations, which are part of the common background of all those involved. In other words, the nonparticipant professional observers who seek the same knowledge may do so in most cases through symbolic involvement and identity with those social meanings common to the cultures of both the nonparticipants and those being studied.

Let us look momentarily at recent studies in the etiology of juvenile delinquency. The field studies of participant observers are replete with illustrations of what gang members have said and what happens under certain conditions that lead to their breaking the law. The following quotation is an authentic expression of what Clifford Shaw found to be characteristic among the gangs his staff studied—stimulation and excitement gained through play. One of the gang members expresses what happened at an early stage of his delinquency:

> When we were shoplifting we always made a game of it. For example, we might gamble on who could steal the most caps in a day or who could steal in the presence of a detective and then get away. We were always daring each other that way and thinking up new schemes. This was the best part of the game. I would go into a store to steal a cap, by trying on one and then when the clerk was not watching walk out of the store, leaving the old cap. With the new cap on my head I would go into another store, do the thing as in the other store, getting a new hat and leave the one I had taken from the other place. I might do this all day and have one hat at night. It was fun I wanted, not the hat. I kept this up for months and then began to sell the things to a man on the west side. It was at this time that I began to steal for gain.[5]

On the basis of other research, we know that this kind of developmental experience does not occur for all delinquent gangs, but for this particular type of gang and this period of growth it is true, and it is by means of

---

[5] Chicago Area Project, *Juvenile Delinquency: A Monograph* (Chicago, 1948), p. 5. (Revised from Clifford R. Shaw, "Juvenile Delinquency: A Group Tradition," Bulletin of the State University of Iowa, No. 23, N.S. No. 700 (1933), p. 5.)

this concrete illustration, as raw data of the participant observer, that we can better understand experientially what constitutes the movement of boys into delinquency. We understand it at the personal level because the elements of excitement, daring challenges, pleasure, and chance that enter into the game are universal and can be reproduced experientially in the mind of the professional observer. There are variations in the kinds of attitudes which become associated with different games, of course, but we do not need to break down these meanings any further to understand what the boy has told us. Most people have learned that set of attitudes and personal dispositions which is associated with the games of early childhood; at this stage the adult first begins to play "peek-a-boo," and thus begins to stimulate those primary sentiments which later develop into more complex forms and become a basic part of the patterns of living in society.

In this portion of the record of the delinquent, we not only get to know the factors experientially (through the analogy of the game), which are part of becoming a delinquent, but we also see a purpose in the delinquent's actions. If we were to pursue Shaw's data still further, we would see that the boy would obtain a sense of freedom in this experience. The participant observer, then, must understand vicariously the purposes involved and the phases which the delinquent experiences while carrying out his activities. The observer reproduces in himself those same symbols which concretely universalize the experience, and thus convey meanings with which he can personally identify to some degree.

Three Forms of Knowledge

The etiology of delinquency can be viewed in three ways. At the *theoretical* level, delinquency is generally understood to be systems of relationships ("subcultures") which arise from disorganized slum areas in the form of conflict or retreatist gangs, or from well-organized slums in the form of criminal gangs which are a product of the web of politics and rackets.[6] Such theories have been aided by both empirical studies and studies made by participant observers. Empirical studies, however, represent another way of knowing delinquency in terms of *statistical* categories operationally defined as "urban dwellers," "young working-class males," etc. The third way of knowing is through participant observation, which is knowing at the level of *personal* meanings, such as the one to which we have just referred. These latter sets of meanings inform the theorist about the inner life of the delinquent. This inner life involves the delinquent's personal knowledge of the

---

[6] Richard Cloward and Lloyd Ohlin, *Delinquency and Opportunity: A Theory of Delinquent Gangs* (New York: Free Press of Glencoe, Inc., 1960); and Lewis Yablonski, *The Violent Gang* (New York: The Macmillan Company, 1962).

world about him, including his own feelings and attitudes toward that world.

The term "personal knowledge" often connotes a privately held knowledge. The number of people who may hold this "private" knowledge, however, is relative to the case in point. Many people may have a personal knowledge of baseball in the United States. The term personal directs attention to that which is experienced by the individual, although the basic elements of that knowledge can be shared by others. People in a large nation can develop a personal knowledge of that nation that is widely shared because of mass communication systems; the members of a sizable ethnic group can have a personal knowledge of suffering from discrimination which they feel collectively and personally. The term personal simply emphasizes that the experience is an individual one.

The term "social knowledge" may include personal elements in it (*e.g.*, individually felt attitudes and sentiments), but it emphasizes an interactive awareness of shared expectations in a human group. It is a consciousness of the positions and roles taken by people in the organization of a group. Social knowledge, we should add, is different from sociological knowledge. The latter implies a more theoretical and structural understanding of human groups, while the former refers to a personal acquaintance with human groups.

These three forms of knowledge—theoretical, empirical-statistical, and personal-social—constitute basic categories of knowledge necessary for understanding man scientifically in the context of society. The term sociological includes all three forms of knowledge (in addition to others such as historical and cultural), even though its own particular emphasis is upon an intellectual understanding of man in society. We can assume that one's sociological understanding cannot be adequate without some close acquaintance with these other forms of knowledge.

The more participant-observer research adds to sociological knowledge, the more the human meanings which define society as it exists in the daily affairs of people will influence theoretical interpretations. The phenomenon of delinquency, for example, like the phenomenon of society, is conceived at the research level by the theoretician as a "system." The popular concept of system, a dominant motif of theory, takes certain social meanings out of the observer's data and substitutes the impersonal, manipulative world of the scientist. A "system" does indeed exist in some delinquent subcultures, but it does not have all the intellectual meaning that the theoretician ascribes to it. It is ironic that whatever factors may be found to co-exist in the two separate cultures of scientist and delinquent (*e.g.*, impersonality) may be the very factors contributing to the delinquent reaction. In other words, to define society or the delinquent world as a system is to screen out personal concern, care, purpose, and that sense of freedom which does exist in human beings, including delinquents. Such meanings exist (with causal power) except for the scientist's own definition of the situation.

To say metaphorically that delinquency is a game, would, of course, be no more accurate, even though this statement contains personal meanings which are clearly evident in certain early stages. (To say that the game is a developmental experience for this type of gang and to understand it on this basis is accurate and meaningful.) The central motif for explaining delinquency is one that must be developed out of the convergence of these three different forms of scientific inquiry. The work of the participant observer is a fundamental part of this inquiry. Only when we know by re-enacting symbolically in our own minds the feelings as well as the thoughts of others we know socially and personally will we acquire a legitimate, authentic, important kind of knowledge which enriches and contributes significantly to the scientific enterprise.

Methods of Verification

At present, no method has been established to check the validity of the participant observer's findings, except for some criteria of empirical and logical models. And these criteria are not strictly valid, since systems for checking validity differ with respect to data and modes of knowing. The methodology of participant observation is no exception.

The criteria for determining the adequacy of *theory*, for example, are different from those which determine the adequacy of empirical *fact*, and both are different, we would say, from criteria determining the adequacy of expressive *meanings* found in the data of the participant observer. Each form of knowledge has a relative place in our total knowledge of man in society; furthermore, each form has a relative place in our sociological understanding of man. We will set this problem in relativity aside for the moment, for when we examine a framework of knowing, a methodology through which researchers may study man in society, it is important first to establish certain criteria for ascertaining the adequacy of findings within that framework regardless of the larger problem of the relative position of the framework. It should be said, however, that to the extent to which particular findings in each framework seem to support one another, much progress has been made toward removing the distortion of the truth found only partially in separate facts, theories, and meanings. Our point here is that given that the internal checks of each framework are different, we have yet to develop a set of criteria which may guide the participant observer in his work that is in any way comparable to that of the traditional empiricist or the theoretician.

The adequacy of a theory is determined in part by *coherence*, a term which signifies that a set of propositions follows the rules of logic. These rules have been gradually established down through the ages of philosophic inquiry. The adequacy of a fact, on the other hand, is determined in part by the degree of *consistency* which may be found between operationally defined concepts and their visibility to the senses. The adequacy of a social meaning, we would submit, is determined in part by social *consensus*, which is established by communication with the people who hold these meanings.

Coherence, consistency, and consensus are simply examples of how people determine that knowledge is orderly, enduring, and accurate. The central motives for the theorist, the empiricist, and the participant observer are certainty and knowing the nature of man as an end in itself. Beyond that, their motives differ in terms of determining adequacy. The theorist seeks coherence among the logical constructs he creates and their relation to empirical reality; the empiricist seeks consistency between sense constructs and outer reality; the participant observer seeks to establish true consensus of meanings among the people he studies. All three forms of knowledge are interdependent and serve as checks upon the accuracy of any interpretation made separately by one approach.

There are many ways that these approaches interdepend in the discovery of scientific knowledge, and we cannot explore them fully here. However, it is important to indicate some of these ways in order to clarify the importance of the role of participant observation in the accumulation of social scientific knowledge.

We know, for example, that theory guides the researcher in finding certain kinds of facts; in turn, facts functioning independently shape theory. Although in the past the major aim of science has been to verify what was imagined theoretically with what was evident to the senses as "fact," we must also say that the opposite is equally important. What is evident to the senses must be explainable conceptually, or it will not have firm status as fact. What underlies determining soundness of scientific knowledge in general is the relationship between orders of knowledge that are directed toward knowing what exists in the nature of things. Theory has illuminated fact and made it meaningful, and fact has illuminated theory.

The social scientist is now in a position to add another dimension of knowledge to provide an even sounder base for his field of study. This dimension lies in the personal realities and the symbolic meanings in the data of research, which can illuminate traditional dimensions of both fact and theory. The confirmation of these meanings in the framework of research problems is the significant contribution of the participant observer.

This dimension of knowledge has many more implications for the philosophy of social science than we can pursue here, but we should indicate its place particularly as it functions to complement the traditional approaches to knowledge. We may know, empirically, for example, that slum areas

and well-to-do areas of cities correlate statistically with high and low delinquency rates respectively, or, we may know that the change in certain economic beliefs correlate highly in time and place with a change in religious
beliefs. These facts are important. But without experiential data which goes
beyond the visible facts or even the theory proposed to explain the facts of
these correlations, we are in a bind to really understand the connection.
In addition to these facts, we must learn what experiential connection
relates them in people's lives. This must be done through participant
observation. The cause of delinquency cannot simply be attributed to deterio-
rated buildings or low-income indexes.

If we assume, with Edwin Sutherland in his classic text *Criminology,*
that the "social accompaniments" of the slums cause delinquency, not just
"poor housing," we still cannot find the link between what we might
theoretically imagine these accompaniments to be and those actual "causal-
meanings" which are so regularly found under these conditions. We must
know the personal meanings, the ways people interpret reality, which lead
them to crime. The accuracy of the participant observer in discovering and
conveying those meanings is limited by many factors, just as the statistical
correlation of the empiricist is limited by many intervening variables, but
the observer who works in such a setting can contribute a certain kind of
knowledge which leads significantly toward social scientific knowledge and
human understanding. The accuracy of both "interpretive" and statistical
knowledge is increasing as these skills are applied in the social scientific
enterprise. Max Weber saw the importance of relating both kinds of knowledge in order to be fully adequate in our understanding of man:

> We apply the term "adequacy on the level of meaning" to the subjective
> interpretation of a coherent course of conduct when and insofar as, according
> to our habitual modes of thought and feeling, its component parts taken in
> their mutual relation are recognized to constitute a "typical" complex of mean-
> ing. It is more common to say "correct." The interpetation of a sequence of
> events will on the other hand be called *causally* adequate insofar as, according
> to established generalizations from experience, there is a probability that it
> will always actually occur in the same way.... Thus causal explanation depends
> upon being able to determine that there is a probability, which in the rare
> ideal case can be numerically stated, but is always in some sense calculable,
> that a given observable event (overt or subjective) will be followed or accom-
> panied by another event.
>
> A correct causal interpretation of a concrete course of action is arrived at
> when the overt action and the motives have both been correctly apprehended and
> at the same time their relation has become meaningfully comprehensible.[7]

---

[7] Max Weber, *The Theory of Social and Economic Organization,* trans. A. M.
Henderson and Talcott Parsons (New York: Free Press of Glencoe, Inc., 1947),
p. 99.

Let us summarize these methodological assumptions about social scientific knowledge which we have discussed or implied up to this point:

1. There is a knowable, communicable sociocultural reality which can be described and explained through the constructs of social theory in conjunction with the findings of social research.
2. This reality has an objective and a subjective dimension, both of which must be understood by the social scientist to have an adequate understanding of it.
3. Theoretic coherence, empirical consistency, and experiential consensus are the generic terms of verification upon which the adequacy of social scientific knowledge is based.
4. Social scientific knowledge draws upon three sources of the mind—reason, sense, and intuition—for different types of understanding, yet all three function together in any single act of knowing.
5. A high degree of statistical probability and/or social anticipation of the future, along with understanding as an end in itself, is what can be expected through the verification of knowledge.
   a. Although propositional or mathematical statements can aim toward perfect correlations, they cannot necessarily achieve them.
   b. Although descriptive statements at the level of meaning can aim toward perfect identity of existent meanings, they cannot necessarily achieve them.
   c. In either case, an approximate statistical and/or personal understanding of the phenomenon is achieved; these two types of understanding may be considered together as complementary forms of research knowledge.

The implications of these statements have yet to be thoroughly examined. While we have stated that a verificatory index of the participant observer is a consensus, we must recognize that all the indexes of the objective dimension have emerged out of consensus. Social consensus is part of the human reality of living in society, of which scientists are one part. The indexes for verifying truth in the logic of theory and empirical studies emerged from the consensus of scientists and became gradually refined until they acquired a status relatively independent of the public at large. For example, the "law of contradiction," a logical criterion in social theory, is so established in the minds of many scientists today that they would hold to it regardless of an immediate, disagreeing consensus from other people. The statistical criterion called "correlation coefficient" is an empirical index that has achieved a similar independent status. These indexes point to fragments of the total picture of scientific knowledge, but increasingly their place in the larger whole is becoming understood. And so it must be for indexes of subjective reality; they must emerge from the consensus of scientists who find them valid and useful in their work, and be refined until they are an independent part of a much larger whole. Later we shall discuss criteria for verifying social meanings other than consensus, although at this point, it seems important to stress the central role consensus has had in the general process of verification.

Social consensus has an outer aspect which is visible in verbal agreements, but there also exists an inner aspect which is built from faith or confidence in the soundness of those signs or indexes of knowing truths. Man's faith has come a long way from being placed in those signs and forms of truth existent in the Medieval period to the signs and forms of truth in a scientifically oriented modern society. Man's faith has become firmly placed in the objective dimensions of reality as science has gradually become an institutional part of society.

What we are assuming here, however, is that the subjective reality of man has a character of its own which must be known and understood in its own right. It is independent of, and yet still interdependent with, the objective dimension. We assume that separate indexes which point to the subjective adequacy of social research may be developed here. By subjective adequacy we mean the extent to which the social analyst interprets accurately the meanings contained in the culture of the people he studies. It is toward the possibility of developing such a set of indexes that we now turn our attention, beginning with Max Weber's original formulation of the idea of *Verstehen* as part of scientific understanding.

Adequacy at the Level of Meaning

Max Weber discussed the importance of subjective adequacy for social research at the turn of the twentieth century. He stated that in order for any certainty to be contained in social scientific facts, they must be adequately verified at both the level of cause and at the level of meaning. The distinction he was making then is very similar to the distinction we are making between the work of the empiricist and the work of the participant observer.

Max Weber never discussed in detail how *Verstehen* should function in social research, aside from indicating that this concept involved reproducing imaginatively in the observer's mind the motives behind the subject's actions. Yet he considered *Verstehen* essential to scientific explanation. Significantly, in his own studies Weber sought to obtain "adequacy at the level of meaning." In *The Protestant Ethic and the Spirit of Capitalism* he explained not only how the two institutions changed simultaneously in time and place, but also how the values of Protestantism made possible the values of capitalism. Yet the exact processes of how such subjective interpretations were to be made in social research remained largely unrationalized. It was for this reason that Theodore Abel sought to explain further how *Verstehen* should function in social research. In a brief, clearly written article in the

American Journal of Sociology, Abel provides several examples of how this process takes place.

In one key example, Abel notes that competent statistical research has established a high correlation $(r = .93)$ between the annual rate of crop production and the rate of marriage in a given year. The statistical bases for determining adequacy at the level of causal correlation are clear, but the relationship between crop production and marriage is not understood without the operation of *Verstehen.* Abel continues:

> We use as items of information the fact that failure of crops (A) materially lowers the farmer's income (B) and the fact that one is making new commitments (C) when one marries (D). We then internalize B into "feeling of anxiety" (B') and C—since the behavior in question is "postponement of marriage" —into "fear of new commitments" (C'). We are now able to apply the behavior maxim: "People who experience anxiety will fear new commitments" $(B'-C')$. Since we can fit the fact of fewer marriages when crops fail into this rule, we say we "understand" the correlation.[8]

Abel notes that when we say we "understand" the correlation, we do no more than recognize the interpretation as a possible one. We cannot conclude that it is "probable" on the basis of the operation of *Verstehen.* Furthermore, Abel concludes, *Verstehen* is "not a method of verification," any "quality of crucial importance is not an attribute of the operation of *Verstehen,*" and finally, *Verstehen* is a "source of 'hunches' which help us in the formulation of hypotheses," but "the probability of a connection can be ascertained only by means of objective, experimental, and statistical tests."

It is, of course, true that such armchair imaginings of what takes place in people's minds are no basis for producing anything more than a "hunch." This kind of approach clearly could not serve as the basis for verification. But what we have been suggesting up to now is that *the method of participant observation is a research procedure which can provide the basis for establishing adequacy at the level of meaning.*

What is significant about Weber's work is that he recognized the crucial role of subjective understanding in determining the adequacy of sociological explanations of social phenomena. *Verstehen* is an essential element of the process of scientific verification. Beginning with Weber's unelaborate but highly significant concept, then, how can we build knowledge around the procedures of participant observation which will give us some assurance that what is being discovered is true?

---

8 Theodore Abel, "The Operation called *Verstehen," American Journal of Sociology,* **54,** (1948); article reprinted in: Herbert Feigl and May Brodbeck, eds., *Readings in the Philosophy of Science* (New York: Appleton-Century-Crofts, 1953), p. 681. For an alternative viewpoint, see Peter Munch, "Empirical Science and Max Weber's *Verstehende Soziologie,*" **22** (February 1957), 26–32.

Validity and Reliability

In some ways, the participant-observer approach has already been demonstrated to be more reliable than other formal empirical methods. Florence Kluckhohn has described how the direct interview and the questionnaire create special or unnatural situations. The subject may not know how to respond to formal situations, may unconsciously or intentionally err, or may have a faulty memory. In contrast, the participant observer is actually in the social setting about which the empirical interviewer may be seeking to discover knowledge, and has the opportunity to record what actually happens when the "experiment" or the formal questioning is over. In the subject's natural setting, the participant observer is in a unique position to evaluate any rationalizations which the subject may make in response to a questionnaire or formal interview.

Beyond these initial insights of some researchers on the value of participant observation in verifying and supporting empirical findings there exists a much broader problem—the "fit" of the method with the pragmatic heritage supporting western scientific thought. By pragmatic standards, the methodology, as it emerges, must be judged by the fruitfulness of its products and their long-range applicability. The workability of the method under varying conditions must be tested, and its ability to contribute practical knowledge which connects with the traditional empirical and theoretical approaches to knowledge must be examined. Finally, the reliability of the procedures and conclusions of particular researchers must be tested over the years. If a piece of research cannot be repeated there is no basis for considering a study valid or reliable or, consequently, scientific.

In the process of establishing participant observation as a methodology in its own right, there is great need for developing a system of signs or indexes which gauge the degree to which a researcher records fully and accurately that portion of the cultural life of a group which he seeks to study. We will therefore suggest certain general measures which may serve as a framework which can be studied and tested for its dependability to yield useful or enduring knowledge.

Six Indexes of Subjective Adequacy

We shall describe roughly in the spirit of hypotheses those factors which appear most clearly related to the problem of making adequate interpretations in community studies. Later we will describe these factors as procedures to guide the participant observer in scheduling a research program. They are affected by many other variables which we must hold constant for the moment, such as the size of the population studied, the delimitation of the research problem, and the depth and breadth of particular meanings to be studied. Aside from particulars, however, we may still be able to examine the relevance of such major factors as time, place, circumstance, language, intimacy, and consensus as important to any study in participant observation. (While these are deemed important when we consider the problem of determining subjective adequacy, objective adequacy is also involved when these conditions are met.) Our procedure now is simply to follow George Homan's well-phrased maxim for exploratory studies: state the obvious in its fullest generality.

Our criteria for adequacy revolve around the question of the extent to which the observer has had an opportunity to personally experience the culture which he seeks to know. We want to know whether he has been able to obtain complete understanding of it, that is, whether he has experienced all significant manifestations of what he seeks to know, which is generally affected, we assume, by the following conditions:

Our first conditioning index is *time*. Our hypothesis is that, other factors remaining equal, *the more time an individual spends with a group, the more likely it is that he will obtain an accurate interpretation of the social meanings its members live by.* If a person spends a very short time with the members of a group or a community he will not know them as well as if he spent a longer time with them. While it is true that his research design may limit him to interpreting only, say, the immediate aftereffects of a flood disaster on a community, and he will thus spend more time with a group beyond his research purposes, this will nevertheless not detract from the fact that the longer he has known these people, both before and after the disaster, the more thorough and accurate will be his understanding of their motives and reactions.

A person might spend a great deal of time studying a group of people, but still not know them well, if he were not in any direct contact with them. Our second conditioning index, then, is *place*. At one spatial extreme an observer will evaluate a group only through their writings or documents. If he assumes he knows his subjects personally, as he would in the context of a particular community, we should not accept his conclusions. (With other objectives, however, documentary studies have an important place in social research.) The participant observer typically lives and works near his subjects, in fact, as close to them as cultural limits and his own requirements allow, so that he has a better opportunity to observe his subjects personally in an environmental context. Thus, we submit the working hypothesis that, other factors remaining equal, *the closer the observer works geographically to the people he studies, the more accurate should be his interpretations.* The idea "geographically close" does not refer simply to spatial distance, but rather to type of physical setting and opportunities for actual observation of the subjects in their everyday lives.

The assumption underlying this hypothesis is that *Verstehen* depends upon the ability to witness in person the physical setting of the group. We assume that offices or neighborhoods as spatial settings have something to do with the motives and reactions of people who occupy them; they cannot be understood fully unless the same stimuli operate upon the observer. The danger of overidentification or disruption of relations because of geographical closeness is a real possibility; however, if we assume that the individual can function under these conditions normally, we must grant the importance of the spatial setting favorably conditioning experiential data of the participant observer.

We shall call our third index *social circumstance*. The number and variety of social circumstances which the observer encounters within the social structure of the community has much to do with the accuracy of his subjective interpretations. We assume that the social position of the observer shapes the kind of data he receives when he is in communication with his subjects. We also assume that the observer's subjects will often react differently to the same stimuli in different social situations (*e.g.,* in church meetings in contrast to business meetings), and unless the observer is able to observe his subjects within the daily round of their social lives, he cannot expect to interpret their way of life adequately.

Again, we should note that the research design may be limited in its objectives, but that would not detract from the fact that a full course of study should add more substantial knowledge of meanings in any single activity; nor does it detract from the fact that this is a crucial criterion of adequacy in any study of the social setting as a whole. Therefore, *the more varied the status opportunities within which the observer can relate to his subjects, and the more varied the activities he witnesses, the more likely the observer's interpretations will be true.*

Time, place, and variety of social circumstance would have no meaning if the observer were not thoroughly familiar with the language of the people he studies. *Language,* then, is our fourth conditioning index. The importance of language is most obvious where it is foreign to the observer. However, the language requirement applies equally to the study of people who appear to speak the same tongue as the observer. The observer should be sensitive enough to recognize different word connotations, phrasings, and sentence structures in daily use among the people he studies. If we assume he has adequately met the other requirements, we would hypothesize that *the more familiar the observer is with the language of his subjects, the more accurate should be his interpetations.* All other factors remaining equal, the converse should also be true—*i.e.,* that the less familiar the observer is with the language of his subjects, the less accurate will be his interpretations.

These requirements, crude as they may be, add some measure of reliability to a cultural study. But they are hardly sufficient. A person may meet all these requirements and still not know the people personally or become closely acquainted with those activities that really count in their lives. Our fifth conditioning index, then, is *intimacy* of encounter. We would hypothesize that, barring overinvolvement, *the greater degree of intimacy the observer achieves with his subjects, the more accurate his interpretations.* There are many signs which should indicate to the observer that this requirement is being fulfilled sufficiently. If the observer, for example, is invited to join in group activities or ceremonies which are generally considered private to the group, or if he is asked to discuss matters with his subjects that are discussed only among the members themselves and not with outsiders, such signs are indicative of the extent to which the observer is meeting this criterion.

As important as intimacy of association appears to be, it is not sufficient in itself or even in combination with our previous indicators of adequacy. The most dramatic illustration of the failure of these index requirements to function adequately is in marriage. Two people may live together for many years in what is generally considered the most intimate of associations, and yet fail to interpret each other's motives on questions important to both partners in a marital relationship.[9]

This should sharpen our search for indexes of subjective accuracy and direct our attention to the individual capacity of the researcher to empathize with his subjects. By "empathize" we mean the capacity of the individual to imaginatively take the role of another and accurately interpret attitudes and opinions. Empathy studies in experimental psychology can be of some aid in determining those personality traits most closely associated with this capacity. However, studies of empathy do not allow individuals to confirm predictions of others' opinions without experiments, for this would run counter to the purpose of the experiments—i.e., to measure the intuitive capacity of the individual to anticipate reactions of others without foreknowledge of what will actually be said. The participant observer, however, can often do just this. And so we will add a sixth conditioning index, social *consensus*.

By consensus we mean some form of verbal assent or confirmation that the meanings interpreted by the observer are correct. The observer may be able to confirm his interpretations directly with those he studies, but in some cases the exigencies of observing make it impossible for him to do so. Nevertheless, the observer can record the ways in which people confirm their meanings among themselves by indicating how assent is given to meanings directly in the conversations of people in their natural setting, or indirectly in ceremonies and general conduct. We will call this "confirmation in the context" of the community or cultural setting and consider it a vital part of any research of this kind. We will say, hypothetically, that *the more the observer confirms the expressive meanings of the community, either directly or indirectly, the more accurate will be his interpretations of them.*

---

[9] There is some empirical support for our assumption that the intimacy requirement is associated with accuracy. Glenn Vernon and Robert Stewart studied the abilities of college students to interpret the feelings their dates had about various phases of their dating experience together. Questionnaires were administered to 104 students at Central Michigan College about the time set for the date, feelings about the kind of date, the amount of money spent, the means of transportation used, etc. The degree of involvement or intimacy was measured along a continuum marked by such stages as: no dating, just dating, going steady or pinned, engaged, and married. The researchers found that accuracy of interpretation increased as involvement increased along this continuum. The statistical association between empathic ability and involvement was observed through chi square analysis to be significant beyond the .05 level. Two other variables were observed to be closely associated with involvement statistically: frequency of dating and the question of whether the individuals had dated each other previously. (Glenn M. Vernon and Robert L. Stewart, "Empathy as a Process in the Dating Situation," *American Sociological Review*, 22 (February 1957), 48–52.)

However, confirming meanings through consensus involves many problems. One obvious problem stems from the varying sizes of groups studied. If a group is extremely large, achieving consensus is difficult, or at least requires special means. The same problem occurs in statistical sampling. In a large group, a team of observers may function best; team members must locate and participate in those groups which play the most significant roles in answering the questions posed in the research design.

It would seem at first that consensus is the basic criterion upon which the observer may depend, and if it can be achieved, all other criteria may be ignored. As fundamental as consensus is, however, it too is subject to error. It is possible, for example, that the observer and the subject could give verbal assent to what the observer records, but because of a lack of understanding the *language*, a misinterpretation would be made. It is possible that a consensus could be drawn too hastily, that the observer and the subject might not have the *time* to establish that kind of rapport that leads to satisfactory confirmation. It is possible that the observer might not study the subject under enough varying *social circumstances* and in enough *places* to determine that what information he is obtaining is true under conditions other than those which are conventionally related to him. The subject himself may not even be aware of how different his beliefs and actions are when he relates with people other than the observer, or when he communicates under different circumstances. Some subjects, of course, may consciously lie to the observer and tell themselves or their *intimate* friends still another story. Therefore, the first five indexes to subjective adequacy must remain as checks on consensus. Our confidence in the observer's report increases as his ability to answer well to all of these requirements increases.

In addition to the indexes associated with the methodology of participant observation, a sociological study of any complete living unit such as a community requires special techniques of different kinds to achieve scientific adequacy. A community study, for example, requires an analysis of its institutional processes, its ecology, its vital statistics, its modes of production, distribution, and consumption of goods, its communication systems, etc. The methodology of participant observation is only one part of such a study. *It focuses its research upon the experience of people living together under these conditions.*

The time dimension gives the observer a sense of how *history* affects the experience of the people he studies, as well as his own experience. The place dimension gives the observer a knowledge of how the *physical world* is part of the experience of people. The varying circumstances under which the researcher observes his subjects gives him perception into how the *social organization* with its statuses and roles affects their experience. The requirement of intimate association provides him with a knowledge of how the *culture* is created and transmitted in the experience of the people studied. If we assume that a basic quality defining culture is values, and if we assume that the values of any people are acquired from personal association, then we may say that the researcher's knowledge of values must be acquired in the same way. Language has the task of providing a link between these different worlds of human experience, since it functions to mediate knowledge of each of them. The requirement of consensus or confirmation-in-the-context links the observer's own experience with the reality of the people he studies. It is through these six structures of experience that the observer acquires both subjective knowledge of what exists in the minds of those he studies, and a phenomenologically constituted knowledge that results from his special experiences in studying these subjects.

It is possible to achieve a verbal consensus and an accurate interpretation of the culture studied and still retain a sense of unreality about what has been observed. This sense of unreality should serve as a caution for the observer to follow certain procedures when conceptualizing his data for scientific purposes. It can be an indication that the observer is holding fast to an ontological perspective which by its superiority will lead him to value judgments with metaphysical conclusions about the culture studied. Judgments which are more than descriptive in research reports require some theoretical sophistication to handle adequately. Therefore, let us consider the problem of interpreting reality in particular cases.

Ontological Implications

Consensus, or confirmation of original meanings in the context of a culture, is important in establishing the validity of social meanings studied, but the participant observer takes on an additional task. He must also phrase the natural expressions of his subjects and their meanings in his own ways, and he must interpret these expressions in the light of theory. Although the observer may intend to express original meanings, he may be engaged in his own abstractions, which are not meaningful to those he has studied, and which do not coincide with his subjects' meanings. There are subtle differences which must be taken into account between that original level of meaning which is confirmed and the conceptual level of interpretation of the social scientist himself. At the level of original meaning, the scientist must seek confirmation in the cultural context; at the level of conceptualization he must seek indexes of another sort in order to be adequate in his analysis. One index concerns the consistency of concepts with the theoretical principles with which they are associated and the kind of generalizations the scientist draws from them. If these theoretical principles are polar in type and only one side of the polarity is emphasized, then the conclusions are bound to be biased unless these polar limits are expressly stated. Let us illustrate with a particular research report.

The Case of "Small Town"

Examples of these levels of interpretation—the original cultural expression, the researcher's reformulation of it, and finally the researcher's theoretical interpretation of it—are all conveniently illustrated in the very perceptive and worthwhile study, *Small Town in Mass Society*. The authors of this study sensitively record the existential meanings of people who live in a town they call Springdale. The meanings described are called *images*, a concept which has theoretical implications. Nevertheless, these town "images" are documented in the original expressions of townspeople. Self-images are recorded in such statements as "We're all equal" and "just plain folks." The expressions of self-images are then contrasted with expressions that townspeople have of the city, which are largely formulated in summary form by the author.[10]

Aside from the authors' summary descriptions, we have not yet considered any interpretations beyond the level of original interpretations of the context in which the observers were functioning. We are assuming that these interpretations are adequate, although all the information about the indexes we discussed are not present. In any case, the original expressions of the townspeople are not the subject of our interest so much as the theoretical interpretations of the authors, which are presumably "confirmed" by the data. Let us look at some of the problems raised by these findings.

First, it is important to note that the authors select local meanings that they call images as well as empirical facts which they place in juxtaposition with these images. (The juxtaposition of the subjective images and the objective facts produces, as we indicated in Chapter 5, a sense of irony in the study.) The image which Springdalers have of themselves, the authors report, is largely that of being independent of the outside world, being unaffected by it, and being that much better for it. The objective facts which the authors describe along with this image seem to contradict the validity of the meanings supporting the image, for they lead to the conclusion that the image is totally false, that the citizens are really living under a delusion. The authors point out that the town is, in truth, highly dependent upon the city and heavily affected culturally by it in every major area of life. A considerable portion of the research report is a description of how mass communication, university extension programs, urban business and commerce, and schools exercise considerable influence over local life. The authors indicate that the local people would probably not face up to this discrepancy, but would rather seek to stay in their dream world, building up

---

10 Arthur J. Vidich and Joseph Bensman, *Small Town in Mass Society* (Garden City, N.Y.: Doubleday Anchor Books, 1958). An example of the authors' own formulations of original expressions can be found in their summary, pp. 81–82.

unconscious rationalizations in order to live with this delusion. Here, consensus would seem nearly impossible, and not necessarily a requirement, for the problem is a theoretical one. Or, to use the term which most appropriately describes this theoretical perspective, the problem is an *ontological* one: Which meaning is really the true one—the subjective interpretation of the local citizenry, or the objective interpretation of the social scientist? The researchers consider themselves looking at the community "objectively," and from the researchers' perspective, the citizenry are subjectively setting up defenses against the facts of social life. The authors conclude:

> Objectively, the community members live in a world which they do not control. They come to this world, however, with a belief in their ability to shape their own destinies. In fact, in almost every sphere of their lives they find their inherited beliefs and traditions at odds with their institutions and social environment.
>
> But the people of Springdale are unwilling to recognize the defeat of their values, their personal impotence in the face of larger events and any failure in their way of life. By techniques of self-avoidance and self-deception they strive to avoid facing the issues which, if recognized, would threaten the total fabric of their personal and social existence. Instead of facing issues, they make compromises and modify their behavior in some cases, and reaffirm their traditional patterns in other cases. They do this, however, without any overt, conscious recognition of the basic problems.[11]

This interpretation leads us to a basic problem in cultural relativity and social reality. The fact that the community members "live in a world which they do not control" is certainly true from the perspective of structural determinism. However, since this perspective is only part of the total reality, a polar principle of analysis, we must conclude that it is not a fully objective basis for interpreting social reality. Indeed, it becomes largely subjective when carried to its limits as a basis for interpreting social life. While not formally subscribing to a determinist perspective, the authors nevertheless devote a large portion of their study focusing upon how the community was determined by forces outside itself, in contradiction to the image of independence citizens had. The study concludes that the true picture of reality is that of the authors, and the false picture is that of the citizenry.

If the authors had begun their study with stated assumptions about a framework of man's freedom, as well as their implicit assumptions about man in a deterministic framework, they would probably have drawn conclusions that were more complex and at the same time more objective. In other words, a model of how man conceives himself to be free becomes necessary in addition to the methodological model of determinism in order to accurately interpret this dimension of man's cultural life. If we can

---

[11] *Ibid.,* pp. 319–20.

validly assume that all men living in society have some degree of freedom, then we are guided in our research to examine methodically those ideal constructs of freedom which most appropriately apply to the case under study. An ideal construct of freedom must be considered only as a construct without positing any final validity to it, and it does not have to conform to a particular case in every detail for it to be useful to research. Rather, it functions as an ideal type to illuminate the data.

An ideal construct of freedom, however, functions logically from within a theory of cultural being, not within a theory of social system. The meaning of freedom cannot be assessed from the standpoint of social systems, for freedom has no meaning from a solely systematic viewpoint. If the researcher were to look for the explanation for such realities as originality, creativity, free will, personal independence, and freedom in his data, from the viewpoint of "system," he would not find it there. Systems can be related to these realities; certain kinds of social systems inhibit freedom, while other kinds increase it according to the cultural definition of freedom, but the definition itself is not derived from categories of system.

If the authors of *Small Town* had pursued the meaning of freedom ontologically, they could have transformed the controlling effects of their irony into a paradox. The paradox which remains unanswered in their research lies in the question of how an otherwise sane citizenry could genuinely derive such a myth about themselves without there being any real foundation. The authors seek to answer this question, but only on the basis of what they describe as negative defense reactions and superficial accommodations made by the citizenry in the face of their "impotency." According to the researchers, the Springdale culture had no originality (it was "spurious"), and citizens believed falsely that they were culturally and politically "independent." Let us examine theoretical alternatives to these interpretations.

We could look at the meaning of freedom that is implicit in the American concept of federal government, and then re-examine the town's image of itself in the light of existing alternative models of town-state-federal relations. American models are not cataloged by social scientists so that one can choose clearly among them for research, but are instead guided by a concept of federalism that would lead us to document the degree to which people see real gains as well as real losses in freedom because of their "surrender." The isolated fact of a town's establishing multiple external relationships may not necessarily mean a loss of freedom; to those who are participating in the relationship, it may mean a signfiicant gain in freedom. Giving up independence in certain areas of life may provide greater leisure time, greater physical safety, and greater social independence for people who are involved in the social arrangements. However, in making such an analysis, the social scientist cannot know whether people are more or less independent apart from the models (existent in the general culture) which define man's way of life. The social scientist can only examine the relationships that exist between ideal models of reality and that which is given in the context in which he works.

The social scientist has not yet focused at length upon crosscultural concepts of freedom to the extent that he can ascertain what universal elements or general types exist among models in different social contexts. In other words, to date he has no adequate socio-historical constructs of freedom which describe how the referent "freedom" is construed by people in different cultures. At best he must depend upon philosophers' idealistic constructs as given cultural definitions and examine the relations of these constructs to what he finds expressed in the culture he studies as a participant observer.

Ideal constructs of freedom appropriate to Springdale could also be found in the works of writers such as Arthur Morgan and Baker Brownell.[12] Both these writers have taken positions similar to those expressed by Springdalers, and yet they are aware of the realities of small town life that Springdalers denied. The first responsibility of the researchers in such a case would be to determine the extent to which such ideal conceptions are applicable to the *Lebenswelt* or "life-world," as Husserl would describe it, of the Springdalers. This could be as far as the researcher would want to go; that is, through his case study he may at best determine only the extent to which the local definitions of reality fit the philosophers' sophisticated definitions which take into account the changing structural realities of the small town.

This is not to ignore the evident disparity between the changing facts of social structure of the small town and the seeming lag in awareness of these facts at the local level. Some local beliefs that are dependent upon structural realities can be tested by empirical methods. For example, the Springdalers who say, "Everyone knows that most of the outstanding men in the country were raised in small towns" are expressing a belief in an empirical reality (rather than an idealistic reality) which can be tested by traditional empirical means.[13] But the closer the researcher comes to describing the idealistic, personal world of the townspeople, the more impossible becomes his task of defining the validity of local beliefs by these same means. For example, it is one thing to say that many townspeople have little knowledge of the decision-making processes of the higher political levels (which can be deter-

---

12 The most recent work among Arthur Morgan's many writings on the philosophy of the small community is: Arthur Morgan, *The Community of the Future* (Yellow Springs, Ohio: Community Service, Inc., 1957). See also Baker Brownell, *The Human Community* (New York: Harper & Row, Publishers, 1950).

13 An empirical study of 30 years ago would support the Springdaler's image on this point. See Wilson Gee, "Rural-Urban Origins of Leaders in Education," *Journal of Rural Sociology,* 2 (1937).

mined in part empirically), and another thing to conclude that the belief in "local independence and self-determination" is an "illusion." What is illusion and what is reality must be judged from theoretical or ontological constructs which purport to explain the difference from separate standpoints.

Even when supported by empirical facts, a theory of structure cannot serve as the sole basis for judging the validity (or the illusory quality) of the life-world of the Springdalers. Those commonsense realities, as Schutz would call them, which are exemplified in beliefs of independence and freedom must be studied not only structurally, but phenomenologically and ontologically as well. *They are studied phenomenologically in terms of how these beliefs are culturally constituted in the minds of local townspeople; they are studied ontologically in terms of how these beliefs fit the ideal constructs which are formulated at the theoretical level to explain them.*

Ideal constructs of "cultural being" can be understood in the same manner scientifically as ideal constructs of structure. The ideal features of Arthur Morgan's concept of the small community, for example, may be translated into a constructed type available for research, just as researchers have utilized Max Weber's construct of bureaucracy. The ontological construct, then, must be studied for its appropriateness to the commonsense realities of people as well as for its comparative value with constructs of a similar order. Human studies of this kind yield their own form of knowledge, which must ultimately connect with empirical knowledge, but such studies lie within the methodological framework of participant observation.

The social scientist who would study man in society cannot avoid the reality of freedom. If he tries to ignore it he will misinterpret the nature of man, but if he admits its reality, he at least has a chance of being accurate in his interpretations of freedom as data, for his interpretations will be enhanced by adequate theoretical supports. The theorist must examine the polarities and varieties of conceptual usages of terms—*i.e.*, personal, religious, political, and economic freedoms—which man has been creating in his civilized life so that appropriate models may be derived for research.

Of course, this is idealistic work for the social theorist in a number of ways. It is probably wiser to begin inductively, rather than deductively, on a large concept such as freedom. The theorist who begins deductively is bound to fail. Such cumbersome categories as "freedom," "justice," "love," or "community" cannot be embraced easily in any single sweep of theory. Rather, they should be approached in terms of hypothetical components which can be typologically considered. The large enduring concept will always challenge and draw the theorist toward it, but he may do well to study only that part which he can handle for his immediate purposes and let the findings accumulate within the research of his own discipline. Participant observers, then, need to test the fitness of middle-range ontological models of freedom to those meanings discovered in the cultures they study just as the empiricist would study middle-range models for their fitness to the observable facts of structure.

The social scientist's aim is not to eliminate relative perspectives of social reality, but rather to contain them authentically within a larger framework. Maurice Stein puts this point most clearly in his discussion of how "dramatic theory" provides the basis for community research:

> From a dramatic standpoint, the central problem of the community sociologist is to achieve an objective perspective that encompasses the partial perspectives held by various groups in the community in such a fashion as to call attention to hidden processes without losing sight of the meanings of the various partial perspectives. The playwright seeks to present his characters sympathetically without going so far as to allow the sympathy they evoke to swallow the larger meanings that emerge when they are viewed within the context of the entire plot and action of the play. The play suffers as much when the context is allowed to override full presentation of diverse characters. The playwright seeks a profound balance and it is similar to the balance sought by the community sociologist.
>
> Dramatic sensibility, then, consists of the capacity to encompass multiple interpretations of a social world within a larger context which distinguishes objective structures without obliterating subjective meanings.[14]

The true reality within which man lives can only be approximated in any epoch of man, but social scientists are a major group now involved in defining it. The nature of this task brings scientists close to those who are also defining reality in both the humanities and the physical sciences. Therefore, we must re-examine some of the conceptual similarities among these major divisions of knowledge, noting where their constructive activities run parallel at some points and converge at others, as each division sets its own course toward an adequate interpretation of man's world or reality.

Objectivity : The Containment of Relative Meanings

Social reality is relative to man's definition of it, and man's definition has been notoriously relative to his consensus in particular times, places, and social circumstances. Therefore, it is most important for us to consider further the relationship between the cultural concept of reality, which is found to be valid among the people studied, and the observer's own concept of reality, which he uses to interpret phenomena.

If sociological theorists take the dialectic method seriously and seek to broaden ontological theory by examining the symbolic and logical truth

---

14 Maurice R. Stein, *The Eclipse of Community* (Princeton, N.J.: Princeton University Press, 1960), p. 325.

which appears through the combination of opposites, it would seem plausible that we may move steadily toward an adequate definition of human reality. In so doing, we should move toward adequacy at both the level of subjective meaning and the level of objective meaning. Eventually we may be able to contain relative meanings within the special systems that exist within the broader framework, systems which are valid in their own contexts, but which when juxtaposed, appear to be in contradiction.

Systems of knowledge must be built from limited assumptions, and facts must be understood and validated within these frameworks, even though a larger, unified system of knowledge does exist. This is as true of physics as it is of the social sciences. The difference between physical theory and sociological theory with regard to relativity is that human irony and conflict can be produced when human systems of knowledge are juxtaposed within their own limited frameworks. Between different levels of analysis, that which is defined as *appearance* alternates with what is defined as *reality*. This is what we have seen in our discussion of determinism and freedom; yet we must move from one level to the other in making analyses of society within limited frameworks.

This shift in the social sciences from one reality to another is apparently paralleled in the physical sciences. In examining the outer appearance of matter such as tables and chairs, we find one "reality"; but when we move to the molecular structure or the atomic structure, we find different levels of analysis with appearance and reality alternating. That which is real becomes that which exists at the level of the observer's study of the phenomena. Molecular analysis is not the same as atomic analysis any more than the analysis of man's freedom is the same as the analysis of how man is determined by outside forces. While both molecular and atomic analysis are major principles around which analytical systems may revolve, the development of theories of freedom or justice within social science has been limited largely because these theories have been considered ethical or normative in type and inappropriate to the scientific study of man.[15] Therefore, we

---

[15] The reasons why social scientists have not been willing to consider political ideas of justice and injustice and religious ideas of good and evil as part of their theories of society are many and various. Most scientists would be concerned that any theory of justice conceived would be viewed as an ethical concept, instead of a scientific concept. Furthermore, even if such a theory were considered to be scientific, it could not be tested in the scientific tradition. A theory of justice would simply become a subjective idea as opposed to some other subjective idea, without any empirical foundation.   However, this line of reasoning is no longer valid in the light of the methodology of participant observation.

A theory of justice in the social sciences functions similarly to a theory of light in physics. A theory cannot express simply the scientist's own independent conception of what exists; it must meet the tests of reality. The social theorist is only idealizing (typifying) the reality of the culture he observes. His ideal type is then tested for its capacity to expressively describe a number of intersubjective realities of people with

should re-examine ethical theories and their close relationship, indeed their convergence at some points, with scientific theories of man.

The aim of ethical theory is to propose a system of rules or a way of life which prescribes what is right and wrong by virtue of some concept of "goodness" in man. Some segment of social reality is denied existence or some way of life is rejected as not being the way man ought to live. The framework of the sociocultural theorist differs insofar as he must take the position of the devil's advocate seriously, (but nonjudgmentally) as a given part of human reality. He must study a society's definition of goodness as a typological part of the human perspective of reality. The multifarious ways in which man defines himself as good or bad become the data of the social scientist and are studied as such through comparative analysis of meanings of both fact and value. This is part of what we must now examine briefly.

The first problem the scientist faces in comparative analysis is deciding which meanings to analyze and study. He makes his choice on the basis of both his own professional values and the primacy of values inherent in the human beliefs and ideologies which are part of his data. Values in human beliefs are many and various, but the researcher must discover these values with respect to their subjective character and build his studies around them. From these studies the theorist can acquire a factual knowledge about people from which he can make his own professional judgment of what is important to study among societies in general. The character of the scientist's own values is both analytic and particular; he assumes that through the analysis of particulars he can attain analytic generality, and through generalities he can understand the particular. This dualistic interest is not doubletalk, but simply one of the paradoxical aspects of social science in its studies of man.

In beginning a study of society, the interests of the scientist and those of his subjects are the same to some degree. The social scientist is interested in an adequate description of the reality of participants, for which he often needs their cooperation (which may involve following their rules); but he is also interested in an adequate comparison of this reality with other realities. In making this comparison, he must follow his own analytical rules which provide for ascertaining the "representativeness" of the reality de-

---

a cultural concept of justice, and express it through their social organizations. This scientific requirement of reality reference (in contrast to empirical reference) then eliminates the ideological commitments in which scientists in the past have feared they would involve themselves if they theorized on a subject such as freedom or justice. In this case, their theory is directed toward describing existent realities and must be tested by participant observers for its validity, not in terms of goodness or badness, but for its validity in expressing what people actually believe the theory is designed to explain in those cultures.

scribed and the correctness of the arrangement of values in the cultural description, among other requirements of logical and empirical analysis. Logical analysis includes examining the relation between value components of one system with those of another in terms of position and function within the belief systems (*e.g.*, relative positions of values compared in hierarchies). Empirical analysis includes accurate determination of the relation of beliefs to components of observable social organizations and their activities in different societies comparatively studied.

While the researcher discovers with subjective accuracy the nature of relative beliefs of people in different cultures, the theorist seeks nonrelative postulates with elements common to these beliefs as they are compared. Science is constantly seeking postulates to link relative postulates (one of which we shall term in the next chapter as "themes" of cultures observed by the researcher) associated with subsystems of social and cultural knowledge. In so doing, the scientist only refines and elaborates a natural process of social adjustment which man has made to his constantly expanding knowledge about the world. This adjustment is reflected in language as new words are created (or old words redefined) for qualities or phenomena that are newly perceived among people. These new perceptions are seen through words which contain nonrelative perspectives of relative parts. Let us illustrate this semantic process of adjustment with the word *culture.*

Culture is one word among many which have been adjusting to changes in the relative perspectives of man. Harry Levin discusses the "Semantics of Culture" in a recent article which we may take as our point of departure. He notes how the word culture had its semantic beginnings in association with the cultivation of the soil. Culture was introduced into English from the French as a synonym for tillage or husbandry. Levin notes that the word was so unambiguously associated with the idea of tillage after the fifteenth century that the clarifying prefix *agri*-culture did not need to be added for two hundred years:

> Meanwhile, English writers were not slow in extending a metaphorical application to the training of the intellect, which had been implicit from the original Latin in the Ciceronian *"cultura animi."*[16]

The term broadened over succeeding years to become relative in meaning not to the working of the soil but to the "cultivation" of artistic and intellectual life. The Germans borrowed the word from the French, and *Kultur* became identified by various German writers with Teutonic nationalism. Oswald Spengler then popularized the idea of culture in association with

---

16 Harry Levin, "Semantics of Culture," in *Daedalus: Journal of the American Academy of Arts and Sciences,* **94,** No. 1 (Winter 1965), 1.

an international perspective of nations in historical development. His *Kulturgesichte,* a history of the "vitalistic" cultures as opposed to the petrifying civilizations, was a step in the process of introducing the term culture into humanistic studies of man. The concept has since continued to be refined in this century as it has become part of the subject matter of the social sciences. It now refers to all the "ways of mankind," including agriculture, nationalistic beliefs, and the artistic and intellectual life of man. C.P. Snow's references to the realities of "two cultures" is a recent sign of the stresses through which the word is now passing in its most recent period of professional definition.

The theoretical task of the social scientist parallels what happens in the development of new words (or the redefinition of old words) to bridge the new spheres of knowledge with nonrelative concepts. The social theorist has the theoretical as well as the semantic task of formulating the basis for linking these relative perspectives through nonrelative postulates about the nature of man. Let us examine how some scientists have moved in their recent thinking to encompass some of the realities of the ethical world of man which (since Immanuel Kant) has resisted scientific foundations.

Let us take scientific theory in psychology and ethical theory in theology as an example of converging trends, since the theory or "logic" of each discipline has shifted in recent years toward conceptualizing man as he exists in his world of experience. The reasons for this include the impact of many traditions in science, including pragmatism, and in philosophy and theology, including existentialism. In any case, psychology and theology today both postulate conditions of man's being in the world rather than postulating solely the conditions of his behavior in the world.

Early psychological and psychiatric conceptions of man were violently in conflict with theological conceptions of man. To the psychologist, man was instinctual and mechanistic, and his behavior was best observed through experimental controls; to the theologian, man was divine and purposive, and his behavior was best observed through explicitly stated norms. Modern trends of thought have eliminated much of this basis for conflict. Although schools of thought such as behaviorism and experimentalism in psychology and orthodoxy and fundamentalism in theology still exist, new trends in both disciplines are converging. The self-actualization theory of Abraham Maslow in psychiatry, for example, is not too far removed in some ways from the existential position of Paul Tillich in theology. The basic drive of man existing in society, it is said commonly by some psychologists and theologians, is not sex or physical instincts. These are real but partial perspectives. The basic drive of man is to "actualize himself," to live in full command of his powers and in spontaneity of feeling and thought. Such a theory of man, shorn of most of its terminology in each field, represents the converging tendency taking place between scientific theories and theological theories of man.[17]

The social scientist and the theologian both seem to be taking more seriously the *human* nature of man. As the social scientist discards his supreme postulates about the reality of instincts and mechanisms, the theologian drops his emphasis upon the early beliefs of the singular divinity of a particular belief for explaining the spiritual realities of man. In fact, some theologians are departing from traditional conceptions and beginning to pursue fresh ontological questions about man's state of "being and becoming," and the scientist is beginning to do the same. Ontology is a current meeting-ground of the social sciences and the humanities. At this highly abstract, yet meaningful level of assessing the nature of man, theories are similar; but as one moves on to elaboration of primitive postulates, the two fields diverge quite radically.

The closer we come to reality, the less important are the distinctions between subjective and objective knowledge. When we are able to express reality meaningfully according to the common values within it, and at the same time describe reality factually in the postulates which explain it, then we will have achieved an ideal unity in our knowledge of man in society.

This is an ideal which is fulfilled in stages as knowledge advances, but which in any final sense would always seem to lie beyond us. However, the theologian and the scientist still have their separate tasks of creating norms for the pursuit of truth. The theologian is guided by what he considers to be the divine perspective, and he pursues that truth through mediums of ritual, revelation in mystical contemplation, confirmation of his faith, and the elaboration of ethical rules which meet the moral needs of man in the face of changing social realities.

---

17 It is important to note that as the meaning of the "self" concept is elaborated, it becomes a westernized, Judeo-Christian concept which has its modern origins in the philosophy of Renaissance individualism. If social scientists were to examine the crosscultural beliefs in self, and take them seriously as existential data, they would find that an opposite conception about the self prevails in the East. The beliefs of Buddhism, for example, a religious order that has maintained a long and honorable tradition in the Orient, exhort man to constantly eliminate the self and all the desires associated with it. Here is a self-concept almost the very opposite of the actualizing, self-fulfilling western idea of man. In pursuing the ontological nature of selfhood as conceived in the meaningful creations of man's culture, the social scientist must be willing to study the meanings that are given in cultures such as Buddhism. In so doing, the scientist is forced, first, to examine the different types of desires associated with the self in the Buddhistic concept and the different kinds of selves imagined in American life, and second, to examine the relation of a person to a cultural order which contains conceptions of immortality. This kind of examination raises new polar problems in cultural study. Nevertheless, it is only by honestly examining polar ideas that exist in human culture in this manner that the nonrelative postulates which explain man's relative manifestations of human existence can be developed.

The social scientist also pursues truth through an elaboration of rules, which for him reveal what exists meaningfully in the world from a human perspective. He must also perform rituals which allow him to discover knowledge about the changing social realities. In Chapter 7 we will discuss some of these rituals as procedural rules which are becoming a part of the method of participant observation in the social sciences.

7

Methodological
Procedures

Let us now formulate a set of methodological procedures for the participant observer which can be tested for its capacity to yield findings that are both meaningful and verifiable. We will necessarily build upon the assumptions of Chapter 6, trying to gather together those principles which will direct the social researcher toward a kind of truth which has eluded him, a truth embedded in the communicative life-world of people.

Participant observation and traditional empiricism can be seen as two distinct styles of social thought that are represented in the classic writings of scholars down through history. In our search for significant procedural principles we are tempted to look back to those classic writers, who have contributed so much to the conceptual advance of man, to determine whether their works might somehow reveal these methodological guides to us in our modern perspective. The principles of traditional empiricism, for example, are clearly visible in the works of Aristotle, the great cataloger of the sensory world. We could hope that some principles of participant observation could be discerned in rough outline in the works of other great writers who had the vision and the temperament for it. Plato, for example, is in certain respects an early exemplification of tendencies to work with dualities and synthetic principles, the conflicting and transcending features of human experience which can be associated with participant observation.[1]

Some of the most important advances in social science have been made

---

[1] This comparison cannot be drawn too sharply. Aristotle, for example would search for the "universal" embodied in the "particular," which is the position we have taken in our description of the method of participant observation, whereas Plato makes a separation of the two descriptive elements, a position closer to the pattern-variable typology of social action theory.

possible only by breaking away from empirical rules of evidence and pursuing what we would identify as the procedures of participant observation. Sigmund Freud's brilliant and far-reaching insights, for example, cannot be said to have been wrought from his exercising tight controls over experimental variables operationally defined in the tradition of empiricism; nor could we say that his conclusions were derived solely from the logic of his day. While in some ways he did follow the language and logic of science, especially in his use of spatial metaphors, we must conclude that in other important ways Freud functioned as a very perceptive participant observer.

Other writers such as Sören Kierkegaard and Franz Kafka, who are still farther from the orthodox scientific tradition, certainly followed no empirical or logical rules of evidence, but they can be said to have gone beyond even Freud in important ways to contribute to modern thought. The reality which they wrote about was not compromised by the pale cast of scientific theory; the evidence they presented of the modern dilemma of alienation was mercilessly direct and convincing. It is true that their work lacked categories and systems, but they have given us the raw data necessary for an important perspective of man. They functioned largely as participants in the process of living through individual phases of what Durkheim called collectively "anomie." While they functioned largely as participants, these writers were still detached enough to observe phenomena and report them in a form that has few equals in the annals of psychological science.

The brilliant insights of Alexis de Tocqueville, another familiar figure, have been of inestimable worth to social scientists. And yet we must draw the same conclusion in regard to his work. He gleaned the social complexities and trends of a modern democratic society very early as an untrained participant observer in nineteenth-century America. His interpretations are profoundly important today because their meanings are so widely relevant to societies of this kind developing around the world; the implications of his work are still grappled with and studied by modern political scientists.

Such students of man in society reveal certain methodological traits in common. They all observed, and at the same time participated in, the social processes of communication in their societies. They interpreted man not simply at the level of sense-data, but at the level of meaning evident in these processes, and were thus able to acquire a kind of interior vision which explained an inescapable and powerful reality of man living in society.

The unrecorded elements, the unwritten procedures which entered into the making of such significant interpretations of man, could be made explicit for others to follow in their own arenas of social research. In future years those principles of procedure which guided the masters of perception and articulation might gradually be made more clear to others; or as Max

Weber would say, in future years the special "charisma" of such intellectual leaders might come to be in part "routinized." Such may be the unintended outcome of the effects of these writers on succeeding generations of students, but any systematic study of their methods will likely remain undone, and the possibilities of learning a great deal from them are, therefore, limited.

There is still another alternative to the bureaucratization of individual genius which is available to us in our pursuit of valid, useful procedures for obtaining knowledge through participant observation—*i.e.*, analysis of the many small-scale, yet significant studies which participant observers have been conducting up to this time. These recorded activities and procedures are already contributing toward the outlines of a methodology. Eventually, this outline should develop further with greater clarity of form and principle as researchers continue to test procedures laid down in the past. Therefore, we will now consider some of the primitive principles and procedures that seem evident at this early stage of research development.

All social research contains elements of participant observation, and participant observation functions to a large extent within the tradition of empirical research. The two approaches are so inextricably intertwined at some points that it would seem they should not be separated. Yet the data of the participant observer are so manifestly different from those which have been traditionally accepted that we must distinguish between them. A separate systematic effort to describe the method is necessary.

Research Methods: Together and Separate

Objectives

The two research methodologies examined together have similar research aims insofar as they both seek to develop valid, reliable knowledge about man in society. Their aims differ, however, in defining the kind of knowledge which they are separately gathering. The traditional empiricist, we have said, seeks to locate variables he defines as existing outside himself, visible to his senses. Whether he finds what he seeks has much to do with his conclusions, but he is interested in going beyond the mere identification of visible descriptive traits. He wants to find the statistical correlation between his variables or between sets of variables, and eventually the inter-correlation of all those variables which he defines as significant to his research design.

The participant observer initially seeks to locate particular meanings which people share through communication. He is immediately concerned with whether what he identifies and describes as existent meanings really exist. Like the empiricist, the participant observer's accuracy of identification of what is really there with what he defines as being there has much to do with the validity of his work. Again, like the empiricist, he is not satisfied with this stage as an end to his work, but is ultimately concerned with the accurate description of the total configuration of meanings existing within his universe of study; this has really been the forte of participant-observer studies in the past. Like the empiricist, however, the participant observer is not satisfied with mere description, and thus he moves on to the level of "explanation." Here, both types of researchers function at the level of theory. The transition from one level to the next is difficult to trace and yet, as we have indicated so far, this difference can be crucial in drawing accurate conclusions about research findings.

Structure vs. Style

The natural scientist traditionally has followed a somewhat structured, carefully defined approach to experimental studies. Similarly, the social scientist has attempted the same so that his studies can be repeated by others to determine their reliability. The work of certain participant observers is marked by this same tradition, including concern for perfection of procedure and precision in terminology.

The work of other participant observers, however, is marked more by a style than by any careful procedures, more by the observer's own sensitivity to what he sees than by what he believes others will ordinarily see, more by the observer's special interests in studying the social scene than by purely scientific interests. We do not wish to evaluate these approaches by comparing them at the general level, for both approaches have, at times, proven to be productive, and at other times, have proven to be rather unproductive. The stylists—those who radically break with procedural tradition—can be as productive or even more productive than the researcher who rigidly structures his work. Therefore, it is important to indicate the special place of the stylist's work in the larger scheme of study. In so doing, we must clearly indicate the stylist's limitations, as well as his potential for contributing to that body of scientific knowledge which has been so well supported by the carefully structured study.

We shall discuss the stylists at a later point in this chapter. Now we shall set down what have been the more systematic procedures that guide the participant observer who believes that there is a great deal of value in producing a structured study.

Systematic Procedures

The methodology of participant observation is building its principles of procedure upon a scientific tradition which already has a well-established foundation of rules and procedures that are quite applicable to this kind of research. Most of these rules and procedures must be set aside for the moment since they are not germane to our task; they can be studied in any standard text on social scientific research. Nevertheless, it is still important to make some reference to general principles underlying all social research as they influence both the traditional empiricist and the participant observer.

The participant observer who structures his work like the traditional empiricist must first carefully define his research problem. The effectiveness of his work, he believes, depends a great deal upon the research he does prior to entering into the actual operations of his study. The participant observer, however, in contrast to the traditional empiricist, has shown a greater reluctance to follow certain matters of scientific design; for example, he has appeared to be more reluctant to exercise predetermined controls over his subjects and has shown less interest in setting up a series of hypotheses to be verified. We would say that this is because the participant observer's primary interest is in discovering the nature of the culture he studies as it is given; any manipulative activities could destroy or change the condition which he is studying. Nevertheless, careful research of this kind must formulate in a definitive way the purposes, hypotheses or anticipatory statements, and procedures used to gather the data, so that other researchers can pursue the reliability of the findings.

The initial rules of social research, then, are: first, to define the problem to be researched; second, to study the literature dealing with the subject; third; to design the major outline of the cultural study procedures; and fourth, to begin obtaining clearance for entering into the field situation as a natural part of the social setting. The "clearance" phase of the procedures of participant observation is a most crucial step which deserves special attention. How clearance is accomplished may be primarily responsible for the kind of data that is received, and may be the critical basis for judging the value of the study.

Clearance

It is not always necessary or even possible to obtain official or formal clearance to become a part of the life of the social group to be studied. The various ways in which an entrance can successfully be made into a new social context have yet to be classified or fully described. However, at this point we can describe some of the ways in which participant observers have already confronted particular problems that arise in association with clearance.

One problem in making a successful entrée is effectively defining the researcher's social role. In his work *Urban Villagers*,[2] Herbert Gans gives us some initial information on how he was able to solve this problem. He felt that he could not define his role as an "observer" who studied the everyday lives of those with whom he came in contact, for it would make people uncomfortable and end the spontaneity of his relationships with them. He felt he could not discuss all his purposes directly with his subjects, but he could discuss some of them and have them accepted. Gans therefore described his scientific role in terms of making a historical survey of the organizations and institutions of the area, a method that was both honest and inoffensive, for such a definition was understandable and of interest to those he studied and quite compatible with his aims. In this way, he was able to function as an official researcher without producing unnecessary anxieties. His research subject could always be deemed external to those he questioned, not purely personal.

This compatibility of the researcher's definition of his role with cultural standards and expectations of those he studies in part determines how well the observer can perform his tasks. However, regardless of how well the official definition fits the standards of the culture, it is most important that the researcher establishes a genuine human relationship with those he studies, one which is friendly, direct, and honest. Such characteristics as honesty and "sincerity in the relationship," which have been noted repeatedly in field notes of observers of delinquent gangs, are basic to the social survival of the observer.

During the initial period of contact, the subjects observed must judge whether the observer's role is compatible with their standards. In somes cases, the subjects must go through the process of eliminating certain stereotypes which they initially project upon the observer. Delinquents must determine that the observer is not a policeman, a social worker, a pool shark, a homosexual, a big brother, or some other rejected type in disguise before they can begin to accept him for what he is. But this is often determined by the personal relationship which the observer establishes with the group, if he is not one of the negative stereotypes which they have built up a tradition to reject. In one case, an observer of a delinquent gang told the older boys he was trying to "help the younger boys find jobs." This was partly true in this particular case and met the need for definition at the time the question was raised. Later, he expanded on what he was doing when they began to have more confidence in him. In another case, an observer told his young questioners he was a sociologist. The term "sociologist" was sufficient at the time, and as the observer related later, the gang members did not know what

---

2 Herbert J. Gans, *Urban Villagers* (New York: Free Press of Glencoe, Inc., 1962), pp. 344–45.

a sociologist was, but thought they should have known, and so did not inquire further. What was important to them was that "Bob," the observer, was a genuine "right guy" and could be trusted.

Establishing genuine human relationships as a matter of clearance would appear to have a crosscultural meaning. Gerald Berreman, for example, found a similar response among villagers of India when he sought to study them as a participant observer. One of them said to him perceptively: "You may be a foreigner and we only poor villagers, but when we get to know you we will judge you as a man among other men; not as a foreigner."[3]

The participant observer who studies a complex social organization must be aware of the fact that clearance at one level of organization does not insure clearance at another level. It is very important that the researcher takes into account the levels of power and decision-making extant in the group he studies before he makes his overture to become part of the group. Some of the complicated factors which must be accounted for are reported in the papers presented in *Human Organization Research*.[4]

Next Steps

The next phases of social research which are characteristic of both major methods of research may be summarized as follows: record, assemble, classify, and interpret data according to a clearly stated system of procedures. The participant observer must be explicit about how he assembles his data, and he must interpret this data just as must the traditional empiricist. A most useful description of how to proceed in the assembly and interpretation of data through participant observation is found in the research reports of Howard S. Becker and Blanche Geer. Referring particularly to their experience in a state medical hospital, Becker and Geer describe how the research team coded the data obtained through team members' separate experiences, and how they then proceeded to classify and interpret the expressed meanings.

In systematic ways, particular intersubjective meanings can be interpreted in the larger social context. In Becker's study, the larger setting was the culture of all the medical students in the social setting of a particular hospital. The researchers systematically checked such items as the *frequency* with which they found subjective interpretations by medical students, the varying *circumstances* under which they were expressed, the *collective character* of the expressed meanings, that is, the extent to which they were

---

[3] Gerald D. Berreman, *Behind Many Masks,* Monograph No. 4 (Ithaca, N.Y.: Cornell University Society for Applied Anthropology, 1962), p. 8.

[4] Richard Adams and Jack J. Preiss, eds., *Human Organization Research* (Homewood, Ill.: Richard D. Irwin, Inc., 1960).

shared and made "the proper and necessary way to act in this area."[5] This is how participant observers record verifying procedures essential for this kind of research.

The careful researcher will note how the principles underlying the two major methodologies converge and separate in actual practice. The more the researcher emphasizes recording visible behaviors and counting action patterns, the more his procedures will represent traditional empirical methods. In other words, the more emphasis that is given to the traditional approach, the less likely the observers will go beyond visible behavior to grasp essential meanings conveyed through communication, and the less chance an accurate estimation of the total configuration of meanings can be made. It is possible, of course, for an observer to utilize some techniques of both approaches and achieve something of the value of each. At the same time, the observer may sacrifice certain values in both. If accurate counting of typical social acts is strongly emphasized, then opportunities for accurate apprehension of subjective meanings can be restricted, and the total picture distorted; if actions are not recorded with numerical accuracy, statistical applications become impossible, and verification can be made difficult. The time and the kind of activity involved in each procedure differ in each case, and it is therefore important to indicate early in the research design just what are the basic purposes of the research.

The two methodologies—traditional empiricism and participant observation—may be roughly considered to be the two ways in which the social scientist establishes adequacy at objective and subjective levels respectively. In a general sense this appears to be true. Yet, the participant observer cannot ignore the problem of maintaining objectivity in his reports and investigations even though he seeks to make adequate subjective descriptions. In his role as a "participant" he must record and interpret subjective meanings accurately within an objective framework. This is not easily done. He records subjective meanings accurately because of his own involvement and identification with cultural symbols which surround the lives of the people he studies. At the same time, the "participant" cannot allow himself to become so involved he loses objectivity as an observer. Therefore, we must be equally concerned with setting down certain rules which safeguard the objective dimension of his work as well as the subjective dimension.

In listing rules of research for the structured study in participant observation, we must note how the researcher may be guided on both subjectivity and objectivity. The rules for maintaining adequacy at the subjective and objective levels together become a measure of the adequacy of the research report. Any further substantiation of findings, then, must be made

---

5 Howard S. Becker and Blanche Geer, "Participant Observation: The Analysis of Qualitative Field Data," in *ibid.*, p. 285.

by other researchers who follow the method and procedures recorded in the field journal and articles describing the research. The observer's ability to note the following rules of experiential evidence in his work then becomes a gauge of the accuracy of his findings.

The Structured Study

Guides to Adequate Subjectivity

Time

Record the different temporal phases of data-gathering which the observer experiences in becoming a natural part of the culture studied.

We have assumed that the longer the participant observer remains in the social setting, the more knowledgeable he becomes about the people. At different stages of observation, however, we know that his data changes by virtue of many factors, including the fact that as time goes by he is gradually given the opportunity to witness and participate in different social activities of the people he studies. Gerald Berreman, for example, notes how the time factor entered into his study of a local caste system in an Indian village:

> It was six months after my arrival before animal sacrifices and attendent rituals were performed in my presence although they had been performed in my absence or without my knowledge throughout my residence in the village.[6]

Time is a major variable for the researcher to consider in assessing the adequacy of his data. One sociologist, Robert Janes, who studied an Illinois community called Riverville on the basis of participant observation, has provided us with important information about how his data changed over the years of his contacts with the community.[7] Janes reports that his status in Riverville underwent progressive redefinition over the course of five sequential phases which he describes as: (1) newcomer, (2) provisional member, (3) categorical member, (4) personalized member (rapport), and (5) imminent migrant. The image which people have of the observer in each of these phases can largely determine the kind of information he obtains. By examining and reporting these time differentials carefully, the researcher may avoid gathering data which can be easily misinterpreted.

Misinterpretations are often made in trying to assess the durability of meanings expressed in cultures. Durability of meanings has long been diffi-

---

[6] Berreman, *Behind Many Masks,* p. 20.
[7] Robert W. Janes, "A Note on Phases of the Community Role of the Participant-Observer," *American Sociological Review,* 26 (June 1961), 446–50.

cult to estimate because people grow and change; their views of some issues change very quickly, although with regard to others, their views are retained over longer periods. The participant observer can contribute valuable information on this assessment of durability to the experimentalist or scheduled interviewer who enters the lives of people for only a short time. On the other hand, the participant observer can benefit from relevant empirical and theoretical knowledge which accumulates regarding different rates of cultural change in different spheres of society under certain conditions. These complementary forms of knowledge can add significantly to the objective adequacy of his report.

The element of time enters into the adequate assessment of many sociological problems besides durability. It is time which often tells us how deeply people feel about certain subjects. It is time that tells us how long it takes an outside influence to become a meaningful part of the lives of people in a culture. Those social meanings which really count in people's lives cannot be calculated by reference to the temporally limited, stimulus-response framework of the experimentalist. Cultural influences have an incubation period which takes time and close association to study.

This latter problem of assessing the meaningful effect of outside stimuli upon the lives of people can be illustrated by the Cambridge-Somerville study of delinquency prevention.[8] This study was conducted to observe the controlled influences of social casework on the lives of delinquent boys over a ten-year period. In this research, two sets of boys were equally matched for social background and abilities. One set was counseled by individual social workers and the other set was left to the normal patterns of their environment. After ten years the researchers concluded that the effect the social workers had upon the lives of the youths was not as strong as expected; in fact, the two sets of youths, both treatment and control groups, ended up with similar criminal records. It would seem perhaps minor to note that following the ten-year experimental period, when the authors were writing their text report on the relative ineffectiveness of the professional contacts, one of the boys wrote a letter to his counselor stating how then (ten years later), for the first time, he had begun to realize the meaning of the contacts he had with that counselor. However minor this incident seems, it reminds us that meanings are bred in human beings slowly through communicative association of a certain kind, and that human meanings grow and are nurtured through time in ways that have yet to be understood. Social meanings are of many kinds, but some have depth and character and therefore require the researcher's time and involvement to understand them adequately.

---

[8] Edwin Powers and Helen Witmer, *An Experiment in the Prevention of Delinquency* (New York: Columbia University Press, 1951), p. xiii.

Place

Record the experience which people have with their physical environment.

Whether or not everything that geographical determinists have to say is valid, enough evidence has been marshalled in their support for them to be taken seriously. Most social scientists today accept the principle that the physical environment can have much influence upon a culture, even if they would reject the extreme assumption that the relationship is fully determinant. Therefore, the personal relationships which people acquire in the context of their environment must be a basic part of the record of the participant observer. His task is to record as accurately as he can the experience which people have with their physical surroundings, documenting where possible the connection it has with their culture.

The observant accounts of Laurens Van der Post in his contacts with African Bushmen can perhaps best exemplify how this interdependence between culture and physical environment can be recorded. Social meanings such as this one reported by Van der Post are *experientially derived* out of the physical contact people have with their environment:

> One night round the fire, all of us obsessed with discharge of disquiet in our blood, Ben told us something which perhaps shows how deeply contained is the natural Bushman in the rhythm of the seasons, and how much he is part of their great plans. Ben told us that little man's womenfolk would become sterile during periods of drought and until the rains broke would cease to conceive. He knew this from his own experience and from that of great hunters before him. That was one reason why the Bushmen had such small families. Had we not noticed, he asked, that there were no pregnant women around? Where else in Africa would we see so many married and vigorous young women and not one in the family way? Yet this fear of drought went even deeper than that. If a woman had conceived in a fall of rain that was not maintained and bore a child in a period of drought which threatened the survival of all, immediately at birth the child was taken from her, before as Dabe confirmed, "it could cry in her heart," and was killed by the other women. The anguish and bitterness with which those who loved children performed this deed, Ben said, proved how necessary it was.[9]

There is an important difference between the observer's recordings of (1) the cultural experience of subjects with environment, (2) the experience of the observer himself, and (3) the conceptualization the observer makes of the cultural interpretation of the subjects' contacts with the physical world. The first type of recording is exemplified by Van der Post's account. The other two types of recordings can be illustrated most vividly in Robert Redfield's reflections on his work with the Mayan Indian villagers of Chan Kom, Mexico. Redfield describes three different types of conceptions he

---

[9] Laurens Van der Post, *The Lost World of the Kalahari* (New York: William Morrow and Co., Inc., 1958), p. 263.

formulated through his contact with the Mayan culture. We shall quote the second conception in some detail since it illustrates so well how Redfield's methodological openness and heightened awareness of the environment led him to conceive of the relationship between the physical world and the cultural world of the villagers:

A second development of the organized systems in terms of which I strove to understand occurred as I became more attendant to features of the natural environment which were involved in these practical activities. In short, I changed the system in my mind to make it include features of the land itself. When it came to considering more carefully the choice of the site of the cornfield, I learned the difference in soils, the indications by way of the kinds of trees growing there and other signs on the land which would enable the agriculturalist to choose tracts which might be more fertile than others. I came to understand the hazards and uncertainties attendant upon the first coming of the rainfall, and how this uncertainty affected the choice of the day on which the felled trees for the new cornfield were to be burned.

In short, I began to see that the activities of the Indians were in part reflections of the regularities and irregularities of nature; of the invariably changing seasons and of the variable weather. I became more attentive to the land and to the heaven above. Gradually I came to see that these Indians dwelt in a very simple landscape in which a few features, some natural and some manmade, limited and expressed the activities of the community. I saw four of these principal features. One, the bush, the thorny, low forest covering all of the flat limestone shelf on which the people lived. Two, the natural wells, called cenotes, places at which the limestone has fallen away to leave deep dark holes down to the ground water; these cenotes provide all the water for the people; there are in this land no rivers, streams, or lakes. These two features, forest and cenote, are nature's provisions. The cenote is a fresh, green punctuation in a dry monotony of thorny bush; only at cenotes may men make their settlements. Three and four of the major features of this land are manmade: the maize field or milpa, and the village itself. Man clears the forest to make the milpa; man goes to the cenote to build his house. One might almost state these relations as a proportion: the milpa is to the bush as the village is to the cenote.

In this consideration of these relationships a new form of thought for organizing particular facts into systems was beginning to grow in my mind. It would be possible to group much of the life of Chan Kom around the prominent pattern of the land itself and man's making-over of that land. Such a system would not be chainlike; it would take the form of a map. Around the bush, the cenote, milpa, and village one would group the activities of the people and the ideas the people have of their land and of their activities upon it. Such a system would be a topography of the people's doings and ideas.[10]

Redfield reveals in this description how the form in which he came to understand the Mayan culture came to be, as it were, phenomenologically

---

10 Robert Redfield, *The Little Community* (Chicago: University of Chicago Press, 1955), pp. 21–22. Reprinted by permission of The University of Chicago Press. Copyright 1955 by The University of Chicago Press.

constituted in his experience. It is important to note here, however, that Redfield is not simply reporting original meanings of the people, as was true in the Van der Post illustration; rather, he is describing his own experiences in conceptualizing the relationship between the physical environment and the organization of cultural life. The account illustrates how Redfield's own mind creatively contacted what he saw, and how he shaped this experience into a conception that could be developed theoretically and applied in studies of other villages. This account must be seen as an example of creative theory building based upon research experience, not simply conceptualization and reporting of meanings as conceived by the people. Theory can go beyond the interpretive experience of the people, but a test of adequacy of theory is measured not only by its "fit" with original meanings, but also by its internal coherence and its capacity to explain and connect with other related theories. In this case, if Redfield were to verify his topographical system as expressed meanings in the Mayan culture, he would have to pursue the question of the awareness of the Mayan villagers of their dependence and relationship to the cenote and milpa. However, this is a different methodological task. Redfield is explaining the stages of interpreting and conceptualizing *his own experience* with the environment in the context of the village.

It is true, of course, that useful historical studies have been made of people with whom the researcher never had any geographical, living contact. The scholarly works of the historian William Prescott, for example, which include *The Conquest of Peru* and *The Conquest of Mexico,* have taken their places in the halls of classic studies. Yet, we must say that in spite of all his efforts to document his accounts, Prescott was forced to depend entirely upon secondary resources (*i.e.,* reports of Spanish conquistadores and Catholic officials), which leaves the essential question of verifying the original interpretations largely unanswerable. Prescott's careful research involved endless checking and counterchecking of resource materials for consistency, and has been of inestimable worth in assessing the way of life of the Aztecs and the Incas, but it cannot remove doubts over meanings in the original cultures. In many historical and archeological studies of ancient societies there is no alternative, but the social scientist studying living societies cannot depend upon such documents. The methodology of participant observation, as distinct from purely documentary or library research, typically involves original, first-hand social contact which requires that the researcher live in the geographic setting of the people he studies.

Social circumstance

Record the experiences of people under contrasting social circumstances.

Inaccurate interpretations have been avoided and excellent insights added by researchers who have observed their subjects in contrasting social circumstances and environments. This provides for recording both social situations and the variety of social roles, or the generality of a single role, which the observer is able to undertake in his study of a culture.

Witnessing a variety of social circumstances that contrast the subject under study increases the observer's ability to accurately interpret that subject. We may illustrate again from Robert Redfield's perceptive account of the Mayan villagers, this time noting how he discovered the Mayans during a visit to the seacoast, an environment contrasting markedly with their normal one, and saw maize to be a major organizing, governing principle of the culture. Redfield reflects how other pieces of the puzzle of their culture could be brought together around this principle:

> When, later and after my first visits to the village, some Chan Kom people for the first time traveled to the swampy seacoast and gazed out upon the vast ocean, one of them remarked, "But how do people live here where is no maize?" For to them maize is life itself. The maize provides most of their food. It is sold to provide goods bought from outside. And it is central to the religious ideas and practices. The pagan deities are protectors of the maize; the important ceremonies addressed to the rain-gods and the earth-gods are prayers for rain and for good harvest of maize, and the Virgin is addressed in prayer as "the protector of the young maize plant"! The good man, the moral man, is he who grows maize and is reverent in doing so. . . .
>
> So I began to form another way of conceiving parts as related to one another in a system of activity and thought. This third system is neither chainlike nor maplike. It is radial: maize is a center and other things are grouped around it, connected to it in different ways, some by a series of useful activities, some by connections of symbolic significance. The mind goes out from maize to agriculture, from maize to social life, from maize to religion. Maize is always the center of things.[11]

The medical studies of Howard Becker and his associates also indicate the importance of observing subjects under contrasting social conditions. Becker reports observing medical students in conventional social settings with fellow students and separately in isolated settings with the observer, and finding different kinds of responses even though the subjects were the same:

> Thus, students in their clinical years may express deeply "idealistic" sentiments about medicine when alone with the observer, but behave and talk in a very "cynical" way when surrounded by fellow students. An alternative to judging one or the other of these situations as more reliable is to view each datum as valuable in itself, but with respect to different conclusions. In the example above, we might conclude that group norms may not sanction expression.[12]

---

11 Robert Redfield, *The Little Community* (Chicago: University of Chicago Press, 1955), p. 22. Reprinted by permission of The University of Chicago Press. Copyright 1955 by The University of Chicago Press.
12 Howard S. Becker, "Problems of Inference and Proof in Participant Observation," *American Sociological Review, 23* (December 1958), 655.

The way Becker has interpreted these two attitudes toward medicine, the idealistic and the cynical, is significant to understand in this kind of research. It calls for a basic interpretive principle about which all researchers must be mindful: the data which the observer obtains in his contact with his subjects are *always valid,* given the conditions under which the relationships are formed. It is only with generalizations about cultural data that difficulties arise. In other words, subjects may falsify their answers or respond differently to questions under different circumstances, but their answers are still valid for those circumstances. They contain at least part of the subjects' definition of the situation and are therefore phenomenologically valuable. However, for accurate generalizations of these data, the participant observer must see his subjects "in the round," in their normal as well as in their abnormal environments, before he can derive reliable conclusions about his own special contacts with the subjects.

It is crucial for the observer to record what social position he occupies in the culture he studies and what images others develop of him as he functions in this position. In most cases, a team approach becomes the best way to deal with the subtle problems of securing data on a large, complex social system, since the observer cannot assume all roles significant to his study simultaneously. However, it is possible in some cases to develop a generalized role which allows equal access to different portions of the population studied. I have observed some cases of street corner gang workers making an adequate entrée into the life of the gang and subsequently developing regular close contacts with legal officials under the sanction of both the gang and the officials. It normally takes a highly skilled worker many years to establish confidence on both sides, a task which is difficult to achieve at all, much less maintain for very long. The maintainence of a stable, general role between two conflicting groups is difficult enough to accomplish to warrant our concluding that two or more observers must collaborate to obtain adequate data under conditions which are socially conflicting or socially complex.

Language

Record the experience of learning the symbolic forms of language which bear upon the social meanings under study.

The term *language* is considered here in its broadest sense as representing all those forms of communication which enter significantly into the lives of the people studied. The observer is interested in the part language plays in forming the meanings under investigation. Language as we are considering it has many dimensions, as Edward Hall and William Whyte have noted:

> Man communicates not by words alone. His tone of voice, his facial expressions, his gestures all contribute to the infinitely varied calculus of meaning. But the

confusion of tongues is more than matched by the confusion of gesture and other culture cues. One man's nod is another man's negative. Each culture has its own rich array of meaningful signs, symbols, gestures, emotional connotations, historical references, traditional responses and—equally significant—pointed silences.[13]

As the participant observer becomes personally involved with the language of the culture he studies, his own behavior changes accordingly. It then becomes very important for him to record these changes as they influence understanding of the culture. William Whyte illustrates how such changes took place in himself during his fieldwork for *Street Corner Society*. He says, significantly, that the linguistic changes in his own behavior went unobserved until a friend came to visit him and noticed them for him:

> My behavior was nevertheless affected by street corner life. When John Howard first came down from Harvard to join me in the Cornerville study, he noticed at once that I talked in Cornerville in a manner far different from that which I used at Harvard. This was not a matter of the use of profanity or obscenity, nor did I affect the use of ungrammatical expressions. I talked in the way that seemed natural to me, but what was natural in Cornerville was different from what was natural at Harvard. In Cornerville, I found myself putting much more animation into my speech, dropping terminal g's, and using gestures much more actively. (There was also, of course, the difference in the vocabulary that I used.) When I was most deeply involved in Cornerville, I found myself rather tongue-tied in my visits to Harvard. I simply could not keep up with the discussions of international relations, of the nature of science, and so on, in which I had once been more or less at home.[14]

The observer should make a list of specific kinds of linguistic factors that bear upon the interpretation of his subjects. He may need to examine such matters as the length of sentences, the average number of syllables in words expressed, the words most often repeated, the favorite slang expressions, and so forth.

Language, as we stressed earlier, is the link between subject and object. In this case, the observer's recordings become objective, outward manifestations of an inner reality which becomes subjectively understood through the sheer expression of the language. In other words, language threads through subject and object, creating, expressing, and representing the life and character of the people studied.

Here we must reiterate the difference between expressed meaning as it is

---

13 Edward T. Hall and William F. Whyte, "Intercultural Communication: A Guide to Men of Action," *Human Organization*, **19**, No. 1 (Spring 1960), 7.

14 William F. Whyte, *Street Corner Society* (2nd ed.) (Chicago: University of Chicago Press, 1955), p. 304.

originally given in the culture and the observer's own special interpretations. The observer may note that through the repetition of certain phrases or linguistic expressions, for example, the subjects reinforce or develop certain feelings of anger, affection, pleasure, sympathy, or whatever. The repetition of a prayer ritual, let us say, produces a certain presumed state of mind in the participant. Whatever state of mind is presumed by the observer to exist for a subject, however, can only be a presumption and nothing more, unless the observer takes further steps to determine how the subject himself perceives it. The American researcher is so used to theorizing on the spot that he often conceptualizes meanings from his own standpoint without checking the meaning which actually exists from the viewpoint of the people he studies. To pursue this question with accuracy, he must make the following steps an important part of his design.

Intimacy

Record how the observer experienced and encountered social openings and barriers in seeking accurate interpretations of privately held social meanings.

Normally there are many sociological factors within any cultural setting which must be recognized for verification purposes. Structural social barriers generally arise between social classes, racial groups, ethnic groups, and religious and political organizations which censor information from the public or screen special interpretations of reality for public consumption. Certain cultural meanings cannot be understood without successful entrance into these private groups.

Every formal structure has both a private and public aspect. Erving Goffman describes some of the sociological features of formal structures as constituting "back regions" to which access is difficult for outsiders; officials in such structures are preoccupied with what Goffman calls "impression management," and consequently any invasion into what lies behind the scenes is hazardous:

> We often find a division into back region, where the performance of a routine is prepared, and front region, where the performance is presented. Access to these regions is controlled in order to prevent the audience from seeing backstage and to prevent outsiders from coming into a performance that is not addressed to them. Among members of the team we find that familiarity prevails, solidarity is likely to develop, and that secrets that could give the show away are shared and kept.[15]

---

[15] Erving Goffman, *The Presentation of Self in Everyday Life* (Garden City, N.Y.: Doubleday & Company, Inc., 1959), p. 238, quoted in Berreman, *Behind Many Masks,* p. 11.

This model of formal structures which Goffman describes was used by Gerald Berreman as a basis for analyzing the lives of peasants in a village in the lower Himalayas of North India, which he studied as a participant observer. Berreman's account is an important guide to other observers who would move into a highly stratified foreign culture such as this. Berreman's major problem was effectively establishing intimate contact with members of the various caste divisions. Within the same village great social barriers had been erected between castes:

> In a tightly closed and highly stratified society the difficulty of impression management is compounded. In a closed society the outsider may be prevented from viewing the activities of its members almost completely. The front region is small and admittance to any aspect of the performance is extremely difficult to obtain. Pronounced stratification makes for many teams, many performances, many back regions (one for each performance group as well as for each audience), and considerable anxiety lest one group be indiscreet in revealing the "secrets" its members know of the other groups.[16]

Berreman tells how he functioned as part of a team of participant observers, and how in this case it became important to have persons of different faiths (a Hindu and a Moslem) as members of the team. Each provided the necessary entrée into different castes:

> I had not anticipated the full implications for research of the differences in status of my associates, Sharma and Mohammed. For example, villagers had early determined that Sharma neither ate meat nor drank liquor. As a result we were barely aware that these things were done by the villagers. Not long after Mohammed's arrival villagers found that he indulged in both and that I could be induced to do so. Thereafter we became aware of frequent meat and liquor parties, often of an intercaste nature. We found that these were important occasions; occasions from which outsiders were usually rigidly excluded....
>
> Mohammed's age put him virtually above the suspicion which Sharma had had to overcome regarding possible interest in local women. Mohammed's association with me in my by then generally trusted status precluded undue suspicion of missionary intent or governmental affiliation. Probably his most important characteristic with regard to rapport was his religion. As a Muslim he was, like me, a ritually polluted individual, especially since he was suspect of having eaten beef. For most purposes he and I were untouchables, albeit respected for our presumed wealth and knowledge.[17]

Berreman states that until Mohammed became his interpreter he was identified as allied with the high-caste group, since he was seen most frequently with Sharma. In his later closer association with Mohammed, Berreman became identified with low-caste villagers, who then began to

---

16 Berreman, *Behind Many Masks*, p. 12.
17 *Ibid.*, p. 10.

speak frankly about village "secrets" and other topics about which they had previously feared high-caste detection. It becomes important, then, for the observer to record the objective barriers which he finds existing between group communication in the setting he studies and the different ways he was able or was not able to overcome them.

Finally, we would add, it is important to record how people *define the information* which lies behind these barriers. People may define information communicated in the "back regions" in various ways. In this regard, Buford Junker provides an objective guide for participant observers to follow initially, based upon the commonsense realities he has found through his own studies:

> *Public:* "What everybody knows and can talk about." One form of this is "the news," either as it appears in a newspaper or other public record or as it turns up in whatever people are interested in and "talk about openly." Fieldworkers sometimes call the information received at this level the "community norms," the "logics" or "ideologies," the "apologia," etc. (Even children may recognize it, as in satirizing "teacher talk.") But what may appear to be evaluated as "public" within a situation may also be regarded as "confidential" or "secret" vis-à-vis outsiders, and in that event the fieldworker's sensitivity to such a basic fact about the social organization under study will help him avoid blunders.
>
> *Confidential:* What is "told in confidence." One form of this is the statement made "not for attribution," which means that if it is ever used in a fieldworker's published report, it is to be so presented as to protect the giver's anonymity.
>
> *Secret:* What is known to members of an in-group who avoid letting it be known to any outsider, since its exclusive possession is important to the in-group's solidarity and continued existence. As such it cannot be reported by a social science fieldworker, but it can be imparted in a scientific communication as information received and reported, like information at the confidential level, in such a manner as to protect the anonymity not only of the giver but of the in-group itself. One form of this is information obtained in a secret society, or in the "inner fraternity" of a profession, or in a suppressed group presenting some opposition to authority (slaves, convicts, adolescents, etc.).
>
> *Private:* What is personal to an individual and can be told only with certain kinds of help from others (such as a psychotherapist, who receives private information in accounts of dreams, free associations, and other kinds of private symbolic behavior). One or another form of this is presented to the fieldworker continuously, instant by instant, as he goes about his fieldwork—the unconscious gesture, the "Freudian slip," the style of dress or room furnishing, the multitude of personal choices people make in everything they do.[18]

While sociological factors must be considered in obtaining accurate data of this kind, the observer must also be conscious of the psychological factors that impede or open human understanding.

---

[18] Buford H. Junker, *Field Work: An Introduction to the Social Sciences* (Chicago: University of Chicago Press, 1960), pp. 34–35. Reprinted by permission of The University of Chicago Press. Copyright 1960 by The University of Chicago Press.

Record how the observer encountered psychological barriers and openings in seeking accurate interpretations of social meanings.

We have said previously that the observer must assume *all data he receives to be valid* under the social circumstances in which he operates. Nevertheless, he must be alert to the psychological aspects of the special circumstances under which he obtains information. In this sense he must be alert to some of the factors which are known to influence data of the formal interviewer. William Whyte reviews some of these key factors:

1. *Ulterior motives* may affect the informant's reporting. On one occasion a foreman of a South American company expressed great interest in being interviewed. He went on to express enthusiasm about every aspect of the company. When the interview closed, he said, "I hope you will give me a good recommendation to the management."

2. The informant may *desire to please* the interviewer so that his opinions will be well received. An interviewer identified with better race relations might well find informants expressing opinions more favorable to minority groups than they would express among their own friends.

3. *Idiosyncratic factors* may cause the informant to express only one facet of his reactions to a subject. For example, in a follow-up interview an informant was told that she had changed her attitude toward Jews. She then recalled that just before the initial interview she had felt that a Jewish dealer had tried to cheat her. She recalled that she was still angry about this incident and had reacted in terms of it to the questions about Jews in the interview. A few days earlier or a few days later she would probably have expressed herself quite differently. Mood, wording of the question, individual peculiarities in the connotations of specific words, and extraneous factors, such as the baby crying, the telephone ringing, etc., all may influence an informant.[19]

Since the participant observer is normally in the social setting for longer periods and observes subjects under more varied circumstances than does the formal interviewer, many of the pitfalls generally associated with the formalities of interviewing can be avoided. Nevertheless, many psychological factors become paramount to consider. The researcher must become tuned to how meanings are communicated; he must note the figure and the ground, the gestalt of cultural expressions. He must be conscious of the social expectancies of the setting, the cooperativeness and motivation of the subjects, the extent to which subjects are free from social threats, and so on. Training in the subtleties that take place in the development of rapport and therapeutic relationships can be of great value to the participant observer. He should find it useful to understand the dynamics of transference, projection, repression, and other psychological mechanisms involved in the more intimate

19 William F. Whyte, "Interviewing in Field Research," in Adams and Preiss, eds., *Human Organization Research*, pp. 360–61.

contacts between persons if he is to understand adequately those meanings he seeks to understand in his research design.

Finally, we would say that if the participant observer studies psychological theories carefully, he should not take them too seriously in his fieldwork, for they also can interfere with understanding. The observer must be on guard constantly to distinguish between his own theoretical interpretations about what constitutes, say, "defense mechanisms" in his subjects, and the actual meanings presented in the cultural expressions which he receives. His first obligation, we repeat, is to report the data as given and verify them. It is only then that he may begin to interpret it on the basis of social scientific theory.

Consensus

Record how social meanings are confirmed in the context of the culture studied.

The verification of the observer's work is highly dependent upon how well he is able to confirm his interpretations of social meanings significant to his research design. Interpretations, we have repeatedly stressed, are often readily offered by researchers, but they tend to be theoretically oriented rather than seriously concerned with the original meanings in a culture. In order to successfully "confirm" original meanings, it is not always necessary for the observer to make his scientific interests known to those he studies, although such an effort can provide an important dimension to the verification of data. The observer must, however, indicate in his record those conditions under which he observes the meanings *expressed* and *shared* in the culture he studies, keeping in mind all previous rules as they may bear on this sharing of meanings in each context he observes. That is, the observer may find the meanings openly shared (mutually confirmed) among those he studies at different stages in *time*; he may find them shared in only special *physical* or *social* settings; they may be shared in different *forms of communication* at different times, either *privately* or *publicly*. These are matters which must be recorded by the observer who would document the subjects' own confirmations of meanings in the natural context of their culture.

Confirmation of general social meanings is achieved when the researcher can observe repeated instances of expressed meanings over a period of time in different settings. He may achieve a direct confirmation on specific meanings through consultation with those he studies. With regard to those meanings significant to his design, it is highly important for the researcher to: (1) document the specific circumstances under which the meanings were confirmed; (2) indicate the number of people who confirm them; (3) describe the way in which they were confirmed; and (4) record the period of time in which the observations were made.

It is possible for the observer to confirm meanings within a small group of people who, it is assumed, are representative of the larger group. The assumption the observer makes is that the meanings of the small group are held in the larger group, but such an assumption cannot be construed as an original confirmation. The observer may draw upon certain factual or theoretical knowledge to make a convincing stand that a particular group is truly representative, but he cannot generalize immediately from his small-group confirmation without added supports. These added supports may come from empirical studies which have shown that prestige groups and persons of high status in organizations "carry" the values which permeate the larger culture of which they are a part, but this is a different kind of knowledge which can aid in interpreting original data and cannot necessarily be verified in the data.

As the observer moves on in his interpretations to set the original and confirmed meanings of the culture within a larger theoretical and factual framework, his work tends to become more objective. But the observer must remain acutely sensitive to the authenticities of both the subjective and objective poles of knowledge, and seek to maintain the right connection between them. The problem of maintaining adequate objectivity is as subtle as the problem of adequate subjectivity, so we must alternately consider these problems in some detail.

Guides to Objectivity

Objectivity may be studied as part of both the character of knowledge and the conscious experience of the observer. We shall treat these two forms separately. We shall examine the first form, objectivity of *knowledge* in two ways: (1) in terms of the relationships the observer draws between his subjective data and other forms of scientific knowledge, and (2) in terms of the relationships the observer draws to the larger contexts of his subject. We shall examine the second form, objectivity of *consciousness,* in terms of the degree to which the observer remains open to viewpoints other than those he is involved in studying, and thus avoids becoming overinvolved in the context of his work. The guidelines for maintaining objectivity of consciousness are discussed in terms of: (1) the degree of distance the observer maintains from his subjects, and (2) the degree of distortion that appears in the record of his observations.

Knowledge

RELATING TYPES OF KNOWLEDGE.   George Lundberg's definition of objectivity is implied in much of what we have said so far and requires serious consideration here:

> By "objective" and "objectivity" we mean a way of responding to phenomena and reporting our responses so that other people can verify our reports. An objective report is a statement such that all qualified persons who observe the phenomenon agree with the statement.[20]

In other words, Lundberg defines objectivity on the basis of social consensus, an act of symbolic agreement. Since Lundberg represents the traditional empirical position, it is significant that his definition has relevance also for participant observation. There is a difference, however, in the categories of knowledge which would be considered admissible to scientific study. Lundberg would not admit any such terms as "will," "feeling," "motive," or "values" unless they could be defined operationally in physiological terms. On this point we have already indicated our departure from the traditional position. But even if we do not operationalize data on the reductionist basis, we must still come to terms with the subtle differences between these two forms of knowledge, the subjective and the objective.

For our purposes, these two forms of knowledge can be conceived to be at opposite ends of a continuum, or better, they are generic to a series of continua. Like all great words, ranging from "capitalism" to biological "races," the criteria defining these forms of knowledge are multiple and vary independently. Criteria for designating subjective knowledge, for example, have included that which is deemed personal or individual, private, unreflective, concrete, particular, and qualitative in type. Criteria for designating objective knowledge, on the other hand, have included that which is deemed impersonal, public or shareable, rational, general, universal, and quantitative in type. These terms and others designating the broadly conceived continuum between subjective and objective could be cast as separate continua (*e.g.*, particular-general), which altogether represent separate references of the protean concepts subjective-objective.

These two concepts of subjective-objective are clearly ambiguous in their commonsense usages and require some clarification. They are ambiguous for at least two reasons. First, different people place emphases upon different criteria for defining them. Therefore, when the concepts are employed in discussion without careful definition, confusion in meaning results. Second, several criteria are often implied simultaneously in the definition people give to these terms. These criteria operate independently of one another, making the terms difficult to apply in particular cases with accuracy. For example, certain scientific knowledge can be rational and impersonal (*e.g.*, the second law of thermodynamics), but it is not public (not widely shareable and

---

[20] George A. Lundberg, Clarence C. Schrag, and Otto H. Larsen, *Sociology* (New York: Harper & Row, Publishers, 1958), p. 43.

understandable in its technical meaning), and thus it functions as a relatively private idea in the minds of select scientists. Again, certain political knowledge (*e.g.*, social relations in the career of Richard Nixon) may be public, yet personal to the people involved, and at the same time quite rational. And so the conventional criteria function independently in particular cases to cause some difficulty in the clear application of these terms.

Our employment of the terms *subjective* and *objective* is simply exploratory and not intended to be definitive. We want to indicate only our general orientation to this problem.

For our immediate purposes of definition, we would suggest that at the very extreme subjective end of the subjective-objective continuum of knowledge there exists a state of pure, unreflective consciousness. Such a state may be characterized by a certain mood of being. Whether such a state can be described as "knowledge" is again a matter of definition. For our scientific purposes it is not. But as soon as consciousness finds an object the beginnings of objectivity are evident. There is some degree of objectivity, then, in all subjective knowledge. Since it is impossible to *observe* consciousness without an object, we must conclude that there is at least some objectivity in all data of participant observation.

If we look at the opposite end of the continuum, the objective end, we find a pattern of knowledge which relates sense to reason. This is science in its traditional form; scientific knowledge is the modern prototype of that which is "objective." Science is a patterning of mathematical and sense constructs with logical constructs. This patterning is thought to be an "objective" scheme of reality. But it would be equally difficult to think of any scientific knowledge of this objective sort without any subjectivity. Man is always in a special symbolic relationship to the world he studies. This special symbolism of science in general represents only a partial perspective of the total world symbolically understood by man. But, then, each scientist has his own niche in that scientific world, his own professional life-world, in which a special slice of that total world is cut out. The physicist may see all things as atomic, the biologist may see all living things as molecular or cellular, depending upon his speciality, the social scientist may see all human relationships as social in nature. The poet or the theologian, on the other hand, may see the whole world primarily in personal terms, that is, terms which have some feeling associated with them. If we search for that which is universal to man, we cannot say that the special symbols of the atomic scientist are more universal than the personalness that pervades the symbols of the poet or theologian. In fact, all men see major portions of their world (if not all of their world) in personal terms. Even the physicist develops a feeling for the abstract symbols with which he works. Symbols exist in great variety, but they find some common ground in being personal.

Our point here is that without a metaphysical scheme that masterfully takes into account the unity within the variety of man's life-world, the scientist must necessarily recognize that his methodological propositions subjectively bias the world he studies. Even though that world makes logical sense to him, and his data are therefore systematically observed and verified, all his observation and verification procedures take place within a partial perspective of the world.

It is true that the scientist periodically destroys his symbolic world and reconstructs it as we have previously indicated. At one time the molecular world was the most basic unit of all things, and Newton's laws were the most fundamental laws of the universe. But in his destructive act, the scientist also constructively rediscovers the place of these symbols in the larger perspective explaining the world. The old symbols simply lose their former bid for universality and finality. Yet within this process of creative destruction the scientist has traditionally functioned with only a partial perspective of the totality.

We mean by "objectivity" those systematic schemes of reality which involve constructs of logic and sense supported by symbols of measurement and mathematics. Now we can see something of the task ahead for sociology and the social sciences. The task involves relating the meanings found in the subjective forms of knowledge to these systematic schemes without destroying the truth to be found in either form. There is truth to be discovered (in its relative place) in the forms of subjective knowledge as well as in the objective forms of verified theory. Indeed, by discovering the most fundamental truths in each of these polar forms we discover syntheses which take away the differences between subjectivity and objectivity altogether. In the process of discovering descriptive relations between opposing forms of knowledge, each polar position gains in its values through the values of its opposite. For example, the social scientist gains objectivity in his theoretical constructs as he develops analytical relationships to subjective knowledge, that is, knowledge containing personal meanings and signifying particular historical objects. He gains objective values if by "objectivity" we mean the consensual discovery of nonrelative generalities which explain wider and deeper realities of man as a concrete being.

On the other hand, the social scientist gains values of subjectivity as he gains values of objectivity if personal and particular meanings are discovered within and through these generalities. When the youthful scientist first discovers the meaning of Newton's third law—*i.e.*, that all action produces an equal and opposite reaction—it is a personal experience. He blows up a balloon and observes it. (Later, he may measure the relationship.) In this detail of his human experience he personally incorporates the lawful meaning into his life-world. It is a personal experience in which the object and the subject find contact, and the scientist's orientation to the world he knows is expanded and thus objectified. The general law makes contact with the particular balloon in the *Lebenswelt* of the scientist.

In the social sciences the participant observer gains subjectively and objectively at the same time if he adequately performs his task. What we mean by gaining "subjectively" is *getting at the heart of human existence,* getting to what is most basically human in the context of research as well as to what exists in relative variety. Getting to what is basically human means finding out what is most personal and universal to man in the research context. If the researcher can discover this, he gains in both polar values—the subjective and the objective—if we realize that at the heart of our understanding of man's existence there is no difference between the highest generality about a culture and that which contains the deepest personal meaning for man. The differences between the terms *subjective* and *objective,* then, are no longer important. The differences must be understood only when we elaborate these primitive interpretations of man's existence in our explanation of the various classes of human experience which are a part of human reality.

A principle which lies at the heart of human existence is that of unity. This is one of the deepest expressions of man and one of the widest references in social reality. It is evidenced in Auguste Comte's postulate that all societies must be founded on social consensus if they were to exist at all as societies. But the meaning and implications of the unity principle as we conceive it here are greater than Comte imagined. The meaning is evidenced at both the personal and the abstract levels of man's symbolic world. It is also evidenced in symbolic expressions ranging from ceremonial communions and beliefs about monotheism in religion to the unified field theory of physics and ecological observations of human collectivities in the social sciences. In fact, the expression of the principle of unity in the symbolic interpretations of man's world is actually expressed in such wide variety that the principle easily demonstrates its power and depth in explaining the nature of man.

Such variety or diversity of symbolic expression would seem contradictory to the very nature of the unity principle. Indeed, it would if another affiliate principle were not in human existence, the principle of continuity, another deep and widely expressed principle evidenced universally among people living in cultures. The need for continuity in symbolic existence can be easily seen in the reactions of people to the possible loss of such continuity. The threats to continuity in political existence, for example, can be seen in the vivid descriptions of nations at war; the threats to continuity in religious and personal existence can be seen in the myths of death and immortality of both primitive and modern man. When the personal expressions of these basic principles of unity and continuity have been observed and recorded, it becomes important to look for their objective elaborations such as in the sociology of religion and the systems of conflict and defense in political theory. The social scientist's problem is to determine how these principles of unity and continuity express themselves, both in the personal realities of people living in society and the theoretical systems posited to explain them.

These are primitive postulates about the nature of man which lie at the common root of scientific theory and ethical theory. Fundamental axioms of unity and continuity and their complementary expressions of diversity and discontinuity illustrate the start of what F. S. C. Northrop called factual and normative theory. A fundamental understanding of the meaning of the discontinuity principle, for example, will lead the sociologist who is a statistician to recognize the meaning of dichotomous categories, or the social theorist to recognize the meaning of "anomie"; it will lead the modern theologian, on the other hand, to the meaning of "*Angst.*" These are primitive postulates which lie neutrally behind and within both scientific and ethical theories of man in society.

Both the sociologist and the theologian can recognize the expression of the diversity principle in the world, and in their common recognition of its importance they will find consensus and unity of interest. Thus, the principles which explain man's being in society are in a state of co-existence and interdependence. What Thomas Carlyle once said of beauty we would postulate applies also to other cultural expressions of man in society: unity exists within diversity. The sociologist can look for expressions of unity in his search for truth just as the theologian or the statesman must look for its expressions in their search for reconciliation or world peace.

The modern scientist whose subject matter is culture is unavoidably conditioned by the unity principle. Like other human beings, the cultural scientist looks for unity and continuity in his special world of symbols. He seeks continuity among such varieties of symbols as are found in mathematics, empirical studies, statistical correlates, myths, attitudes, and theories, all of which take on a certain continuous meaning for him as a cultural scientist. The scientist today, however, is threatened with discontinuity and diversity without the balancing principles of unity and continuity evident in his work. As a result, he seeks to narrow his methodological perspective to keep from being inundated with new symbols which have no meaning (or diverse meanings) in his scientific perspective. He does so, we believe, prematurely. The neo-positivist who shuts out subjective symbols (*e.g.*, symbols of goodness, beauty, or freedom) develops an understanding and a predictability about only a small part of the social world. Similarly, the new cultural scientist cannot limit his methodology, but must keep it open while affirming, at times, the loss of continuity in his overall perspective. He must be open to the human perspective within which only fragments of cultural reality can be codified and systematized at different times. While threatened with the loss of continuity, he recognizes that this is part of the human reality to be discovered and recorded as part of his study of society.

We have said that the data of the participant observer contains personal elements such as those in Clifford Shaw's report of a delinquent's story of stealing caps in a dime store, and in Van der Post's report of the Bushmen who believe they must kill their children when they are born in a drought. We have said that these elements must be understood personally if they are to be understood adequately. These accounts are subjective in type because they convey attitudinal knowledge through the rhetoric of their descriptions, and yet we are now stressing that as social meanings they must be tested within an objective framework. The very act of categorizing the Bushmen belief as a "myth," of course, is the first step toward creating an objective framework. Myth is a rational concept of broad meaning and wide reference to man's personal worlds of reality. A more systematic effort would involve relating the myth to contemporary theory.

The authentic sentiments which are conveyed in the rhetoric communicating this data to observers must be retained, but at the same time their rational counterparts must be found and related to empirical knowledge discovered through traditional methods. If the observer cannot find a way of creating this analytical relationship, the scientific adequacy of his work is open to question. The best that can be said is that the work is unfinished. The participant observer must find this objective relationship.

Relate the research findings to empirical facts and contemporary sociocultural theory.

If the theory of knowledge which we have so far proposed is correct, objectivity should increase as the knowledge of one order is brought to bear upon the knowledge of another order, and a perspective explaining and encompassing both forms is produced. We assume that complete objectivity is an ideal never fully achieved by social scientists, even though it is increased by expanding the knowledge of reality through ever-widening descriptive relationships among different orders of knowledge.

We have said that the social scientist relates three orders of knowledge in his study of human reality. We have called them, briefly, statistical, theoretical, and personal. Only as the social scientist is able to bring together these three orders as they are derived from sense perception, abstract conception, and personal-cultural meanings can he approach adequate objectivity in his work. We do not identify objectivity with precision alone, but see its larger dimensions and associate it with an adequate grasp of how the parts are related to the whole.

In addition to relating together the formal and personal aspects of knowledge to obtain objectivity, the researcher must also treat the social context of his research in such a way so as to permit a perspective of a concrete, historical reality related in space and time.

Relate the research findings to other social contexts.

In addition to connecting scientific forms of knowledge, the participant observer must expand his perspective from the delimited universe of his research design in order to make accurate references to other social complexes contingent upon or socially related to the culture studied. Research studies which have enlisted the method of participant observation have demonstrated the importance of finding these contextual relationships. William Whyte, for example, found it important to trace the gangs he was studying to their external connections with the political and racketeering organizations of Cornerville. Alvin Gouldner found it important to relate his industrial study of the Oscar Center Plant to the community setting and to the geographically removed and yet bureaucratically related centers of policy-making which affected the local plant. W. Lloyd Warner did the same in Yankee City. It was by examining the earlier stratified organization of craftsmen in the shoe factory that Warner could then interpret the meanings of the reactions to organizational changes in the new context, reactions which were produced as a result of the leveling of status among workers in the new production line. He did not simply focus upon the immediate context of striking workers, important as that context was, but linked his problem with outside events. The new local managers brought into the community to supervise the workers by distant top management in both Warner's and Gouldner's factory settings were different from those managers who grew up as part of the plant community.

As we look back upon these cultural studies we realize that our understanding of the gangs of Cornerville was enhanced and made more accurate by seeing them in the larger political context, and in Gouldner's and Warner's studies our understanding of what happened to the workers to motivate them to strike was strengthened by seeing the industrial firms in the context of an urbanizing society. New urban centers of power were removing local rights to power that had come to be valued at the local level. This contextual link gives a local study perspective which adds objectivity if the references to the larger context are accurate.[21]

In order to move adequately toward objectivity as well as toward sub-

---

[21] A recent study by Stephan Thernstrom shows that some of Warner's statements about Yankee City history are unsupported by actual historical evidence. This finding strengthens our point that accurate reference to historical contexts increases the objectivity of a study. (Stephan Thernstrom, " 'Yankee City' Revisited: The Perils of Historical Naiveté," *American Sociological Review,* **30,** No. 2 (April 1965), 234–42.)

jectivity, the observer must find relationships which exist between social contexts of a microscopic nature as well as those of a macroscopic nature. Our emphasis is on *broadening* the perspective accurately (seeing "man in society in history"), rather than on narrowing it to specific interpersonal relations, because the method of participant observation in the past has leaned toward the latter and has minimized the perspective of the former. We would assume here that objective knowledge may be found in the ever-widening context of human relations accurately interpreted.

Consciousness

DISTORTION. Distortion occurs when the observer either misinterprets the subjects' inner world of meanings or misinterprets the facts evident in the outer world of sense. A guidepost is needed for each pitfall.

Record those signs of distortion which appear to disrupt the process of neutrally interpreting social meanings.

We assume here that indexes to objectivity can be found in the observer's ability or inability to function within the naturalistic perspective. He must be able to describe phenomena without morally judging them. Morris and Charlotte Schwartz discuss the fact that "distortion" was evident in the reports of participant observers studying the cultural setting of a mental hospital. They indicate that some of the signs of distortion can be located in the emotional involvement of the observer:

> We noted some indexes of the distortion of data as a result of affective involvement. These included strong moral or evaluational reactions, such as judging staff's or patient's behavior as "good" or "bad." We found that such reactions as anger, resentment, disgust, condemnation, pity, and excessive worry or concern about a patient or her therapeutic progress were signs that the investigator was not functioning as an objective observer.[22]

Such "indexes" need to be studied for their capacity to distort data. Observer reactions such as anger, resentment, etc., must be understood in the context in which they appear; they cannot be deemed important by themselves without knowledge of the conditions under which they lead to distortion. Moralizing about the behavior of the subjects studied, however, is one indication of a lack of research objectivity.

Record those signs of distortion which appear in the process of interpreting human behavior and evaluate the data with reference to them.

The concept of distortion implies an "objective" standard by which data can be judged and by which the very act of knowing can be evaluated.

---

[22] Morris S. Schwartz and Charlotte G. Schwartz, "Problems in Participant Observation," *American Journal of Sociology,* **60** (January 1955), 347.

This would seem to introduce a kind of vicious circle for the researcher, who would take seriously the principle of the subjective dimension which holds that all truth is relative to the viewer. We have said, however, that another principle is functioning in the objective dimension. It is possible to bridge relative perspectives with a larger nonrelative perspective. This would seem at first glance to be asking the observer to accept a case of "double-think." But it is actually a commonplace phenomenon. While the social scientist slowly seeks to attain the larger unified field theory, the same process of bridging perspectives is continually taking place in the commonsense realities of everyday life. As we have indicated, the history of language is a story of how words have continually been forged to bridge individual and cultural differences in subjective perspectives to express the more commonly recognized factual realities. These newly forged terms cast a new perspective that is no longer relative to the previously separate viewpoints. It is on the basis of this principle of objectivity that the participant observer makes his judgments of distortion.

Distortion of sense realities is not necessarily a problem in the consciousness of the observer so much as it may be a problem to discern in his informants. William Whyte has stressed the importance of checking the "objectivity" of informants' reports on the basis of his experience in fieldwork. He lists some of the sources of distortion in first-hand accounts from informants which the observer must evaluate:

> The objectivity of an informant's report depends on how much distortion has been introduced and how this can be corrected. The major sources of distortion in first-hand reports are these:
>
> 1. The respondent did not observe what happened, or cannot recollect what he did observe, and reports instead what he supposes happened.
>
> 2. The respondent reports as accurately as he can, but, because his mental set has selectively perceived the situation, the data reported give a distorted impression of what has occurred. Awareness of the "true" facts might be so uncomfortable that the informant wants to protect himself against this awareness.
>
> 3. The informant quite consciously modifies the facts as he perceives them in order to convey a distorted impression of what occurred.
>
> Naturally, trained research workers are alert to detect distortion wherever it occurs. How can they do this? First of all, there is an important negative check— *implausibility*. . . . A second aid in detecting distortion is any knowledge of the *unreliability of the informant* as an accurate reporter. . . . A third aid is *knowledge of an informant's mental set* . . . and how it may influence his perception and interpretation of events. . . . Perhaps the major way to detect and correct distortion is by *comparing an informant's account with accurate accounts given by other informants.*[23]

---

23 Whyte, "Interviewing in Field Research," pp. 362–63.

The reality which is distorted in these cases is a sense reality often re-ferred to as the objective world. The data are to be confirmed in terms of overt observable *behavior*. For example, Whyte explains what he means by an "implausible" story given by an informant who lived near the campus of a coeducational college. The informant reported that she knew that a college girl had been raped in a classroom during hours of instruction by some male students. The story did not seem "plausible" to the researcher. In counterchecking this information, it was found that the incident had occurred, but at night, not involving college students, and not on campus. The informant's story, then, was a distortion of fact, a distortion in a record of behavior.

DISTANCE. Problems of objectivity arise when the observer achieves a relationship too close to the subjects studied. One problem lies in being "taken in" as a full member of the group in such a way as to bar any further inquiry into matters which are important to the research design. In some kinds of intimate or friendly relations the conditions are such that certain questions cannot be asked without disrupting the relationship to the point of losing all rapport. This is something referred to as "over-rapport." A second problem arises when the observer sympathizes so much with the interests of his subjects that he becomes strongly partisan in his reports and interpretations of the data. These two problems can be examined by follow-ing this guide.

Record the extent to which the observer's own personal needs and interests are the same as and different from the people who are being studied.

The observer can avoid the problems of over-rapport by distinguishing his own interests and values from those he studies and recording the differ-ences. The differences he distinguishes enable him to maintain a level of detachment from the group. Herbert Gans reports this occurring in his work:

> The dangers of overidentification are also reduced by the many differences between the researcher and the people he is studying. Since the researcher is an observer more often than he is a real participant, he is always conscious of value clashes when they occur during the field work. Thus, while the participant observer cannot argue with his informants and respondents as fully as he would like—because it might endanger his rapport—he is continually made aware of his own points of view on the subjects that come up in conversation. This not only produces insights useful to his research, but also keeps him detached from the people he is studying.[24]

---

[24] Gans, *Urban Villagers*, p. 343.

However, distance is not so easily achieved for all researchers. The problem of over-rapport appears in two forms. In one, the people studied identify themselves too closely with the observer, and in the other, the observer identifies himself too closely with the people he studies. The first is illustrated in an experience of S. M. Miller, who studied a problem in the field of union-management relationships:

> On the other hand, once I had developed a close relationship to the union leaders I was committed to continuing it, and some penetrating lines of inquiry had to be dropped. They had given me very significant and delicate information about the internal operation of the local; to question closely their basic attitudes would open up severe conflict areas. To continue close rapport and to pursue avenues of investigation which appeared antagonistic to the union leaders was impossible. To shift to a lower level of rapport would be difficult because such a change would induce considerable distance and distrust. It would reveal that the attitude of the participant observer to the leaders was not the same as the leaders' feelings of friendship for the observer. They accepted the observer as an individual, a friend, not as one playing a delimited social role. Friendship connotes an all-accepting attitude; to probe beneath the surface of long-believed values would break the friend-to-friend relationship.[25]

This study, Miller notes, continued toward completion but was without full data. The more extreme case of over-rapport, we would add however, is when the observer completely identifies with the people being studied. Robert Redfield tells of a student of the Zuñi Indians who became so personally identified that he became, in effect, an Indian himself, apparently being inducted as a Priest of the Bow of their religious order. After that ceremonial event, Redfield notes, he told outsiders nothing more about the Zuñi.[26]

Less severe than the problems of losing data or abandoning the study altogether through total identification is the problem of reporting one's findings in a partisan fashion because of human sympathy. In order to deal with this tendency and check its excessiveness, we set down the following guide.

Examine all contrasting or conflicting social roles and groups which are significant to the research design as they exist within their separate perspectives.

The fallacy of the partisan reporter lies in his assumption that the perspective of those he studies is valid in every significant respect; the result

---

25 S. M. Miller, "The Participant Observer and Over-Rapport," *American Sociological Review,* 17 (February 1952), 98.

26 Redfield, *The Little Community,* p. 82.

is that he overgeneralizes his conclusions. Some participant observers of delinquent subcultures, for example, have tended to sympathize with their subjects and then either romanticize the life of the delinquent or report his "plight" under a "severe" environment. In such cases, the observers who would examine the symbolic meaning of such words as "cop" or "turf" in the *Lebenswelt* of the young slum dweller may do so correctly and yet produce misleading or biased conclusions. We would say that the delinquent's stereotype of the "cop," while adequately interpreted by the researcher, may shut out the meaning of the word "brat," or "cop-killer," or "hood" for him in making interpretations; such words represent a perspective which must be understood separately by the researcher in studying the culture of the police officer. Police cultures are a significant part of the context in which gang cultures emerge, so that to study one without the other leaves a serious gap in understanding the total context. To avoid such partisan tendencies the researcher should study both the subject and object of those cultural perspectives significant to his research design. That is, he must study those people who are "significant *objects*" of the subjective world of the people he studies as "significant *subjects*" if he is to move toward his goal of objectivity. He must assess which social groups and social roles are most significant to one another in the social context of his work and study them in their polar positions from their original subjective viewpoint.

Howard Becker touches on this point briefly in his book *The Outsiders*. After he stresses the difficulty, indeed, the impossibility of presenting opposite viewpoints in full measure simultaneously, Becker states:

> We can describe the perspectives of one group and see how they mesh or fail to mesh with the perspectives of the other group: the perspectives of rule-breakers as they meet and conflict with the perspectives of those who enforce the rules, and vice versa. But we cannot understand the situation or process without giving full weight to the differences between the perspectives of the two groups involved.[27]

Thus, if the observer can carefully study the perspectives of two groups that are in conflict with one another as they exist separately in their own authentic worlds, we would say that the chance that the observer will have acquired the distance necessary to achieve adequate objectivity is strongly increased.

The problem of maintaining proper distance between the object of study and the observer is basic to other fields besides the social sciences. In the field of esthetics, for example, a similar kind of problem presents itself

---

[27] Howard S. Becker, *Outsiders* (New York: Free Press of Glencoe, Inc., 1963), p. 173.

wherein the art critic or the esthetic viewer of art must find the proper balance between personal identification with and distance from the art object. Art philosophers state that "distance" is necessary in order to fully appreciate and understand an art object as it is presented in its intentional form. There is a certain limited space, for example, within which the observer should place himself before a painting or a string quartet in order to obtain the full expression and intentional form of the artistry. The problem of distance in esthetics, however, goes beyond merely spatial distance to include a more complicated kind of "psychical distance," which is similar to what we have been discussing for the participant observer. The art critic must be capable of both personal "restraint" and what critics call "release" when esthetically viewing art forms.

Edward Bullough maintains that "psychical distance" is the essential feature of the esthetic attitude. If one is esthetically looking at a sea fog, for example, Bullough states, the observer must "abstract from the experience of the sea fog, for the moment, its danger and practical unpleasantness," and direct his "attention to the features 'objectively' constituting the phenomenon—the veil surrounding you with an opaqueness as of transparent milk, blurring the outline of things and distorting their shapes into weird grotesqueness." This "distance," Bullough continues, appears to lie between the "self" and the "affection," the latter term understood in the broadest sense as anything which affects a person's being, "bodily or spiritually, *e.g.*, as sensation, perception, emotional state or idea." Bullough describes how distance is acquired :

> Thus, in the fog, the transformation by distance is produced in the first instance by putting the phenomenon, so to speak, out of gear with our practical, actual self; by allowing it to stand outside the context of our personal needs and ends —in short, by looking at it "objectively," as it has often been called, by permitting only such reactions on our part as emphasize the "objective" features of the experience.[28]

The term "objectivity" is not to be equated with the term "impersonal," Bullough continues, although he says there are no adequate words to describe the "personal but 'distanced' relation" which the observer develops toward an art object. "Distance," according to Bullough, is a function of two variables, the "distancing-power of the individual" and "the character of the object." It is possible for the observer to "over-distance" or "under-distance" according to the condition of these two variables. Bullough describes the results of each extreme form of distancing:

---

[28] Melvin M. Rader, *A Modern Book of Esthetics* (New York: Holt, Rinehart & Winston, Inc., 1935), p. 317.

The consequence of a loss of Distance through one or [the] other cause is familiar: the verdict in the case of under-distancing is that the work is "crudely naturalistic," "harrowing," "repulsive in its realism." An excess of Distance produces the impression of improbability, artificiality, emptiness, or absurdity.[29]

The rhetorical consequence of extremes in "distance" for the participant observer are recognizable in his productions. Cultural studies are, at least in part, works of art.

The quality we have been describing as "distance" must yet be studied in more detail to be fully understood. It may be reduced to the form of a continuum and studied empirically; a scientific tradition for so doing lies in the social distance studies which began with Emory Bogardus.[30] However, the present need is for a classification of what types of relations constitute "under-distance" and "over-distance" and for illustrative examples which may guide the participant observer in future studies.

Rhetorical Guides

The problem of maintaining the proper "distance" in observing and reporting subjective meanings in an objective framework is associated with rhetorical form. We want to review rules suggesting how the observer may develop some rhetorical control over this problem. First, we will consider the importance of illustrativeness in reaching clarity of meaning through rhetorical devices, and second, we will consider the narrative viewpoint taken by the observer in his research report.

Illustrativeness

Illustrate studied cultural meanings with the variety and depth that expresses their intrinsic place in the culture as a whole.

We have said that the participant observer is interested in concrete universals, those meanings which are personally felt and shared among all members of the culture being studied. The observer must depict shared meanings as they are given, whether they be the meanings of a Christian cross to the members of a religious sect, or police-hating attitudes of a rebellious delinquent gang. The meaning is shared, is personally felt, and is rhetorically communicated among the participants of a particular culture.

Those meanings which the observer investigates, even those which are not part of his own culture or of his own experience, must be conveyed

---

[29] *Ibid.*, p. 324.
[30] Emory S. Bogardus, *Immigration and Race Attitudes* (Boston: D. C. Heath & Company, 1928).

through rhetorical devices, largely, we would say, through devices of the metaphor family. The following experience of an individual's discovery of her own self-identity illustrates how a person who has had what appears to be a "unique" experience seeks to convey its meaning to others by means of analogy. This woman reported having labored under the feeling of being rejected as an "illegitimate child," but then eventually accepted herself as a legitimate human being. She discovered her own worth and said: "Since I am, I have the right to be":

> What is this experience like? It is a primary feeling—it feels like receiving the deed to my house. It is the experience of my own aliveness not caring whether it turns out to be an ion or just a wave. It is like when a very young child I once reached the wonder of finding the inner seed, good to eat in its bitter sweetness. . . . It is like a sailboat in the harbor being given an anchor to sail, but always at times it can cast its anchor to weather the storm or rest a little. . . . It is my saying to Descartes, "I am, therefore, I think, I feel, I do."
>
> It is like an axiom in geometry—never experiencing it would be like going through a geometry course not knowing the first axiom. It is like going into my very own Garden of Eden where I am beyond good and evil and all other human concepts. . . . It is like the experience of the poets of the intuitive world. . . . It is like owning Cinderella's shoe and looking all over the world for the feet it will fit and realizing all of a sudden that one's own foot is the only one it will fit. It is a "Matter of Fact" in the etymological sense of the expression. It is like a child in grammar finding the subject of the verb in a sentence—in this case the sentence being one's own life span. It is ceasing to feel like a theory toward one's own self.[31]

While this account is a highly individualized experience, its richness in analogy is suggestive of the way in which the nonparticipant can be introduced to an understanding of another's experience. The reporter of the event experienced must search for elements held in common between what he as a reporter has experienced and what he knows his audience understands from their separate standpoint.

This same analogical device was used by a member of the committee of the *festas* (annual festivals of patron saints of the Catholic Church) in Cornerville to convey to William Whyte the meaning of the patron saint in the minds of the local participants:

> . . . Some ignorant people think that the saint can perform miracles. That is not true. The saint can only ask God to perform the miracles. God is a God of Mercy. If the sinner prays to the saint, the saint stands in right with God, and God takes pity upon the sinner and forgives him his sins. That is the spiritual world. It is the same way in the material world except that here we are dealing with material things. If you drive a car, and the policeman stops you for speed-

---

31 Rollo May, Ernest Angel, and Henri F. Ellenberger, eds., *Existence* (New York: Basic Books, Inc., Publishers, 1958), p. 43.

ing and gives you a ticket, you don't wait till you go before the judge. You go to the sergeant, the lieutenant, or the captain—some person of influence—and perhaps the captain knows your brother or some friend of yours. Out of friendship he will forgive you for what you did and let you go. If the captain won't listen to you, you talk to the sergeant or the lieutenant, and he will speak to the captain for you.[32]

The researcher must inquire at different times among people in his study for similes, analogies, allegories, or parables which may best explain the meaning of what he is studying. He cannot allow himself to improve on the original metaphoric expressions by introjecting his own without reporting his procedures. He may, of course, conceptualize by metaphor himself, and thus obtain a new and meaningful interpretation of his data, but that is another interpretive level that we shall discuss later.

The rhetorical style of the researcher in keeping a journal record of his experiences is no less important than his correct use of rhetorical devices. Let us turn momentarily to this problem of style setting forth a procedural rule which may guide researchers in making notations in their journals and in formulating their reports for publication.

Narrative viewpoint

Make use of that style which best expresses the viewpoint of the people involved in the study, avoiding the stylistic extremes.

How the observer writes and thinks through his daily journal and official reports makes a difference as to what he discovers in his field of observation. His observations are determined not only by his scientific objectives, but by his narrative style of thinking and writing. He may, for example, choose to write in the first person, second person, or third person, or he may choose what is known in modern rhetoric as the omniscient position. These positions and variations on them play an important role in shaping the data of the observer, and thus should be considered to be part of the study design. What we will say briefly about them is illustrated in more detail in any standard text on writing.[33]

The first person narrator can be subclassified in two forms. In one, the narrator is a direct nonreflective participant, personally involved, telling a story as if everything happened to him. In the second form, of writing in the first person, the narrator writes with the pronoun "I," but includes

32 Whyte, *Street Corner Society,* p. 271.

33 The description which follows is drawn from Jessie Rehder, *The Young Writer at Work* (New York: The Odyssey Press, Inc., 1962). Other useful texts are: Cleanth Brooks and Robert Penn Warren, *Modern Rhetoric* (New York: Harcourt, Brace & World, Inc., 1958); and R. W. Pence and Fred L. Bergmann, *Writing Craftsmanship* (New York: W. W. Norton & Company, Inc., 1956).

some of his own observations on what is happening around him. He is separated from others, but in a more limited way than in the first form. He is able to speak knowingly about the thoughts of others in the story and is able to comment objectively on what is happening to others.[34] *The second person "you"* is also used in narrative writing, although less often, since it is difficult to sustain the reader's belief in such a position throughout a story. This technique functions to involve the reader (not the observer-narrator) in what is happening in the story. The *third person position* can be subclassified into three stylistic forms. They are generally known as the limited narrator, the interpreter, and the effaced narrator. The third person *limited narrator* keeps the story focused upon a single actor in the story, showing only what this actor himself hears, sees, knows, or experiences. The third person *interpreter* describes what is happening to the main actors in the story and analyzes what is going on in their minds beyond what is immediately apparent in their actions. He can tune in, so to speak, on a number of actors at the same time. The *effaced narrator* writes like a newspaper reporter or scientific experimentalist, simply recording objectively what he sees has happened, never commenting, interpreting, or analyzing the actors' thoughts or including his own viewpoint as narrator.

Finally, the omniscient writer or narrator is fully in charge; he can tell the reader what all his characters are thinking, where they have been, and where they are going. In effect, he controls their destiny. Jessie Rehder says advisedly to fiction writers:

> This point of view is usually scorned by authors whose primary interest is the realm of feeling rather than the world of action. If you want to reproduce a mood, a feeling, or an instant of revelation in an inner world of a character, perhaps a subjective approach will suit you best. If, though, you wish instead to manipulate a world in which action is dominant, then the omniscient might well be best. Be careful to keep your limitations of time, place, and of the action itself in an organic pattern.
>
> The omniscient offers a sliding scale so that you can switch your attention from one character to another; you can show your people in a close-up shot or make them distant figures in a landscape. You can present them flatly or show them in depth, revealing their outer masks and inner conflicts. Time and space are at your disposal to use as you will. But again, be sure to observe time, space, and action limits that will draw your reader into the story. You will exclude him if you manipulate your fictional world so openly that it is obviously artificial.[35]

The extreme writing styles are similar to the extreme positions taken in social research. While effective for some purposes, the powers of observation

---

[34] This style of writing may be illustrated in Robert K. Bain, "The Researcher's Role: A Case Study," in Adams and Preiss, eds., *Human Organization Research,* pp. 140–52.

[35] Rehder, *The Young Writer at Work,* p. 111.

and description expressed in these extremes are nevertheless limited in their application. That is, the first person full participant (nonreflective) style clearly leads the observer into complete personal involvement with his own experience. On the other hand, the effaced third person (sometimes crudely called the fly-on-the-wall position) is just the opposite. The narrator is unable to say anything about what is happening inwardly to himself or to others; he only records impersonally their separate actions. The extreme stylistic positions of either involvement or impersonal observation cannot be the controlling form of observing and reporting in this kind of research. The kind of style which is most suitable we would call the "limited omniscient" position, in which the destiny of the actors is not fully known by the narrator; the inner world of the actors is described insofar as it is known, and yet the description can remain objective. It is possible to conceive the use of a variety of different styles within the general style of the limited omniscient as long as the occasional use of extremes is guided by the scientific purposes of the particular design of research.

These are matters which are particularly relevant to the researcher functioning in the field, reporting his experiences in his daily journal. What we must now consider are the steps he takes toward higher levels of interpretation.

Meanings, Themes, Configurations, and Theories

Indicate in the research report which descriptive level is being examined: original meanings, themes, configurations, or theories.

There are four levels of interpretation which can be roughly defined for the participant observer. The first level consists of explicating the original expressions and meanings which are observed in a culture in order to be descriptive of what exists, but in this process conceptual interpretations are often unavoidably involved. The translation of meanings from one language to another, for example, may involve some degree of conceptual interpretation—i.e., any meaning brought to the data which is based on terms outside the cultures from which the data is reported. The validation of original meanings without the observer's own conceptual interpretation is what we have been stressing to be of initial importance.

The difference between the first level of pure description in the terms of the original culture and the scientists' own conceptual level is one of gradation and is sometimes difficult to distinguish. The concept of the "theme" expresses a stage of conceptual interpretation. The theme is an explanatory principle postulated by the observer as a major motif visibly threading its way through important dimensions of a culture. In Morris Opler's definition, the theme is a postulate which may be openly declared by subjects in some instances and clearly implied by their behavior in others, but it is, in any case, a cultural value tacitly approved throughout a culture which controls and guides the activities of the members.[36]

Opler illustrates such themes in his study of the Chiricahua Apache culture. Among the Apache, Opler explains, it is explicitly clear that "long life and old age are important goals." This theme is evident in customs relating to childbirth, puberty rites, demands for respect given to the aged, and so forth. A theme is limited in its applicability, however, and cannot explain all the actions and thoughts of the Apaches; moreover, it is often counterbalanced and challenged by other themes. For example, Opler notes a second theme which he calls "validation by participation" that limits the full applicability of the first theme. In other words, the value of being older is limited by the requirement that those who are older must demonstrate that they actually have added wisdom through effective participation in social activities. If an older man cannot keep pace and participate responsibly in tribal activities, the normal social advantage of his years does not prevent his forced retirement. Opler identifies other themes of the Apaches, such as "Men are physically, mentally, and morally superior to women." He shows how themes of this kind pervade much of the Apache's cultural existence without one theme serving to explain the whole of the culture.[37] However, it is through witnessing the interplay of such themes that the total culture can be understood.

The researcher describes themes by illustrating how they are symbolically expressed in cultural activities. In this way, those who read his reports, who seek to understand or confirm his findings, may witness the same activities; through imaginative participation in the symbolic expressions, they may or may not be drawn to the same conclusions. The theme is an interpretation of behavior patterns and original meanings which is close enough to actual description in some cases for the observer to confirm his findings with the people he observes. A theme may or may not lie within the consciousness or self-awareness of the subjects themselves. It was undoubtedly for the purpose of exploring this point of self-awareness that William Whyte, in a late stage of his study, presented his findings on the gang structures and interpretive themes (which he had gathered over the three and one-half years of his contact with the gangs) to the gang members themselves. Their reactions are noteworthy:

---

[36] Morris E. Opler, "Some Recently Developed Concepts Relating to Culture," *Southwest Journal of Anthropology*, 4 (1948), 120. References to Opler's approach are drawn from the interpretation found in Ralph L. Beals and Harry Hoijer, *An Introduction to Anthropology* (New York: The Macmillan Company, 1959), pp. 238–53.

[37] Morris E. Opler, "Themes as Dynamic Forces in Culture," *American Journal of Sociology*, 51, No. 3 (November 1945), 192–206.

The corner boys do not explicitly recognize the structure of the gang, but it is implicit in all their actions. When, toward the end of my study, I discussed these matters with my informants, I made them conscious of the nature of their unreflective behavior. To that extent I changed the situation; the men talked to me about things that they have never formulated before. This did not mean that they were enabled to act more effectively. Doc, my chief informant, once told me:

"You've slowed me up plenty since you've been down here. Now when I do something, I have to think what Bill Whyte would want to know about it and how I can explain it. . . . Before I used to do these things by instinct."[38]

The third level of interpretation involves the total configuration of the culture. The aim of many participant observers is not only to discover themes, but to discover the configuration of themes in the culture which they study. Checking validity at this level of interpretation is that much more difficult and complex. If the observer is interested in arriving at a "gestalt of meanings," it becomes more important that he spend sufficient time in the culture to obtain adequate reports of the separate parts of that culture. The researcher's explanation of the total configuration of the culture is meant to be descriptive; that is, the researcher describes how the various separate meanings he confirms as existing within the culture together make the culture coherent. In so doing, however, he inevitably encounters both conceptual and theoretical levels of interpretation.

Conceptual interpretation by the researcher, we have suggested, occurs when the meanings of his expository terms are not a primary part of the culture itself. A conceptual interpretation of the observer is not an expression of the people, nor is it descriptive of the cultural reality the people experience. The researcher's concepts begin where the experience of his subjects ends. The distinction is not always a sharp one, as William Whyte has illustrated. Whyte's concepts of social structure were on the border of the gang members' consciousness. Such scientific concepts, however, have comparative and theoretical implications which should be elucidated in the study.

We will now illustrate a level of conceptual interpretation Ruth Benedict displays in her explanation of the character of two Indian cultures. She describes these cultures in terms of major themes which have theoretical implications, and her work also illustrates how a researcher approaches the descriptive level of the cultural configuration.

Ruth Benedict assumes that cultures are integrated on the basis of some underlying principle which sums up descriptively all the significant parts of the cultural life of a society. She describes the differences existing between the southwestern Indians (Pueblos) and northwestern Indians

---

[38] Whyte, *Street Corner Society,* p. x.

(Kwakiutls) on the basis of two principles described by Nietzsche in his studies of Greek tragedy. These two principles—Dionysian and Apollonian —represent two diametrically opposed ways of arriving at the values of existence. The Dionysian seeks to escape "the ordinary bounds of existence" by cultivating extreme or frenzied psychological states of being. The Apollonian distrusts extremes and stays in the middle of the road, moderating and controlling his behavior.

In seeking to demonstrate how the Dionysian principle is *not* operative among the Pueblos, Benedict proceeds to document the "moderateness" of these Indians in contrast to the "excessiveness" in ritual and belief which prevails among other Indians surrounding the Southwest:

> The Southwest is surrounded by peoples who seek the vision by fasting, by torture, by drugs and alcohol. But the Pueblos do not accept disruptive experiences and they do not derive supernatural power from them. If a Zuñi Indian has by chance a visual or auditory hallucination it is regarded as a sign of death. It is an experience to avoid, not one to seek by fasting. Supernatural power among the Pueblos comes from cult membership, a membership which has been bought and paid for and which involves the learning of a verbatim ritual. There is no occasion when they are expected to overpass the boundaries of sobriety either in preparation for membership, or in initiation, or in the subsequent rise, by payment, to the higher grades, or in the exercise of religious prerogatives. They do not seek or value excess. Nevertheless the elements out of which the widespread vision quest is built up are present: the seeking of dangerous places, the friendship with a bird or animal, fasting, the belief in special blessings from supernatural encounters. But they are no longer integrated as a Dionysian experience. There is complete reinterpretation. Among the Pueblos men go out at night to feared or sacred places and listen for a voice, not that they may break through to communication with the supernatural, but that they may take the omens of good luck and bad. It is regarded as a minor ordeal during which they are badly frightened, and the great tabu connected with it is that they must not look behind on the way home, no matter what seems to be following. The objective performance is much the same as in the vision quest; in each case, they go out during the preparation for a difficult undertaking—in the Southwest often a footrace—and make capital of the darkness, the solitariness, the appearance of animals. But the experience which is elsewhere conceived as Dionysian, among the Pueblos is a mechanical taking of omens.
>
> Fasting, the technique upon which the American Indian most depended in attaining a self-induced vision, has received the same sort of reinterpretation. It is no longer utilized to dredge up experiences that normally lie below the level of consciousness; among the Pueblos it is a requirement for ceremonial cleanness. Nothing could be more unexpected to a Pueblo than any theory of a connection between fasting and any sort of exaltation. Fasting is required during all priestly retreats, before participation in a dance, in a race, and on endless ceremonial occasions, but it is never followed by power-giving experience: it is never Dionysian.

The fate of the jimson-weed poisoning in the Southwest Pueblos is much like that of the technique of fasting. The practice is present, but its teeth are drawn. . . .

Peyote has had an even more drastic fate. . . . In their strict Apollonian *ethos,* the Pueblos distrust and reject those experiences which take the individual in any way out of bounds and forfeit his sobriety. . . .

The Pueblos do not understand self-torture. Every man's hand has its five fingers, and unless they have been tortured to secure a sorcery confession they are unscarred. There are no cicatrices upon their backs, no marks where strips of skin have been taken off. They have no rites in which they sacrifice their own blood, or use it for fertility. They used to hurt themselves to a certain extent in a few initiations at the moments of greatest excitement, but in such cases the whole matter was almost an affair of collegiate exuberance. In the Cactus Society, a warrior cult, they dashed about striking themselves and each other with cactus-blade whips; in the Fire Society they tossed fire about like confetti. Neither psychic danger nor abnormal experience is sought in either case. Certainly in the observed fire tricks of the Pueblos—as also in the fire tricks of the Plains—it is not self-torture that is sought. In the Fire Walk, whatever means employed, feet are not burned, and when the fire is taken into the mouth the tongue is not blistered.

The Pueblo practice of beating with stripes is likewise without intent to torture. The lash does not draw blood. Far from glorying in any such excesses, as the Plains Indians do, a Zuñi child, whipped at adolescence or earlier, at the tribal initiation, may cry out and even call for his mother when he is struck by the initiating masked gods. The adults repudiate with distress the idea that the whips might raise welts. Whipping is "to take off the bad happenings"; that is, it is the trusted rite of exorcism. The fact that it is the same act that is used elsewhere for self-torture has no bearing upon the use that is made of it in this culture.[39]

This is a portion of the richly detailed description of social meanings and types of conduct which illustrates how Ruth Benedict would demonstrate the efficacy of her summative concepts to explain the whole of the culture. If another observer were to check the validity of these references, he would have to determine the validity of such statements as: "A visual or auditory hallucination" is not regarded as "a sign of death"; it is "an experience to avoid, not one to seek by fasting"; fasting is never followed by a "power-giving experience"; and (behaviorally) there are "no rites in which they sacrifice their own blood."

The configurative pattern is analyzed not only on the basis of the relationships of elements within the culture, but also with regard to the relation of these elements with elements of other cultures. This comparative reference introduces conceptual interpretations which are not explicitly stated in the

---

[39] Ruth Benedict, *Patterns of Culture* (Boston: Houghton Mifflin Company, 1934), pp. 79–84.

study. In Benedict's study, the comparisons of Pueblo Indian culture were drawn to other neighboring Indian tribes who were more excessive in their beliefs and practices than the Pueblos. However, if the Pueblo Indians had been compared with other non-Indian cultures, they might be cataloged as Dionysian on the basis of their relative excesses. That is, the Pueblo Indians may not be judged as indulging in extreme excesses when they fast, take drugs, or whip-lash teenagers, when these practices are compared with neighboring tribes; however, these practices in themselves may be considered "excessive" when compared with other more modern cultures. Americans, for example, do not fast, or if they do, it is for very minor sacrifices such as not eating lunch to give benefits to a charity, or giving up for Lenten season what they may already consider an excessive practice such as smoking or drinking. If an American took drugs as part of a religious ritual and saw visions, he would be considered very odd or would be placed in a mental institution. Drugs which have excessive effects are outlawed in the United States. If parents whip-lashed their children they could very well be jailed for maltreatment. Ruth Benedict uses the term "torture" comparatively; in comparison with other Indian tribes the Pueblos do not indulge in torture, but from the relative standpoint of American culture, their practices seem torturous.[40]

The problem of determining how the configurative pattern can best be explained is a difficult one. Robert Redfield has given us some important clues. He states that the cultures must be understood in terms of "intuited wholes" as well as analyzed parts. Taking the study of the little community as an example, he points out how it can be conceived as having an ecological system, a particular social structure, a special outlook on life or cultural ethos, a distinct history, in summary, as constituting a whole with many parts. How these parts are to be related to one another, however, is still a controversial issue and depends upon one's theoretical viewpoint.

We do know some things about the relation between the parts and the whole. We know, for example, that not all cultural themes are dialectical and, in fact, to formulate them as such could misrepresent the configuration. We know, further, that all major parts are interdependent in various ways, but we also know that some parts are independent to the extent that they are internally unaffected by other parts. The game of chess, let us say, functions in many societies as an independent subcultural system having rules which remain unaffected by the special system of values existing where it is played. Less can be said for such complex subcultures as Christianity or capitalism. We can say further that a description of a culture based

---

[40] A recent debate among anthropologists on the problem of interpreting interpersonal relations in peasant societies presents issues similar to those we have been discussing. See esp. Julian Pitt-Rivers, "Interpersonal Relations in a Peasant Society: A Comment," *Human Organization,* **19,** No. 4 (Winter 1960–61), 180–83.

on a summative concept such as in the Benedict analysis can do some injustice to these parts, which may not be comprehended fully by this description. At the same time, we can say that this is one of the ways in which a culture may be interpreted in scientific research.

The social scientist must come to terms with the descriptive configuration and with the fact that discrete statistical units and historical "laws" are themselves insufficient to explain social reality. Max Weber goes to some extent to stress this point as we have indicated previously. He points out further how the configuration is important in advancing us beyond the limited power of quantitative analysis to explain social reality:

> The real reason is that the analysis of reality is concerned with the configuration into which those (hypothetical!) "factors" are arranged to form a cultural phenomenon which is historically significant to us. Furthermore, if we wish to "explain" this individual configuration "causally," we must invoke other equally individual configurations on the basis of which we will explain it with the aid of those (hypothetical!) laws.[41]

There are theoretical interests in Weber's emphasis just as there were theoretical interests in Ruth Benedict's analysis of the two Indian cultures. Benedict stressed the idealistic tradition (of the material-ideal polarity), a tradition in which Nietzsche existed, from whom she selected her explanatory concepts of ethos. The Indian culture itself did not require that she describe those details to verify an ethos, a *Weltanschauung* of the Indians; this was of her own choosing. The kind of knowledge which we have just been describing thus finds its European roots in idealism. At different times this idealistic tradition emphasized the particular, the historical, and the universal idea as important to cultural analysis. It deemphasized the empirical, the analytically general, the structural categories of the physical science tradition.

The fourth level of interpretation, then, about which the observer must be conscious, is the theoretical. In this case, it involves interpreting the cultural configuration in terms of general theory. At the present stage of social theory this is extremely difficult, and means finding the relationship of the culture configuration to the theory of social action, which is presently characterized by structural-functional categories. We have previously suggested that a general theory need not be controlled by such categories, even though they should remain as an important part of methodological and substantive considerations of man. At best, the cultural student can only study these structural categories of action to determine what manner of relationship is conceivable between the meanings basic to both traditions. An adequately conceived relationship may have to await a new general theory.

---

41 Max Weber, *The Methodology of the Social Sciences*, trans., eds. Edward Shils and Henry A. Finch (New York: Free Press of Glencoe, Inc., 1949), p. 75.

At this point, we will stress that the historical and configurational schools of thought constitute an important part of research, even though they cannot be deemed scientifically finished. They fulfill certain needs for understanding, but they must ultimately articulate with a general theory of man in society.

The Stylistic Study

We have said that scientific researchers "structure" their studies through systematic procedures which lead to certainty about the world. We shall now add that researchers actually examine the *character* of the world rather than its *personality*, to use metaphors which personify our subject for purposes of perspective within the idealistic tradition. The character of the world is reflected in the scientific process of knowing, which has form, system, and structure. The structured study thus mirrors itself in its findings. The process begins with the assumption that all phenomena can be understood in discrete categories or continua, and finds them as such. It proceeds with the assumption that all phenomena are patterned and predictable, and finds this to be true for the data that are accessible to pattern and prediction. Although the scientific process predicts what appears to be an unknown future, it does so within closed systems; and although it purports to study change in the world, it does so by abstracting laws or patterns of phenomena which are historically repeatable and are based upon the relatively permanent character or structure of the world. This is the reality discovered through the scientific tradition.

Social science, however, cannot ignore still other facets of reality in its studies. Therefore, another type of research has earned a place of special value within the field—that study which does not follow the systematic traditions of science, but rather has a particular style of its own. It functions to reveal new meanings in data as well as new meaningful possibilities in theory.

A particular style can belong to only one man. Students of society of recent times such as C. Wright Mills and Erving Goffman have their own styles which have contributed in distinct ways to the sociological enterprise. They are not empiricists in the older traditions, yet both have freely discovered new meanings in data they have observed that have affected the more systematic works.

A particular style can be a school of thought, a general way of proceeding in research activity which is characteristic of the times. (Science itself can be considered to be a style of observation.) We shall review styles of the more structured studies in participant observation which we will term the "categorically factual" and the "analytic." These are styles which are characteristic of some researchers who would normally be thought of as part of the systematic schools of social science. The other examples of styles we shall discuss briefly are selected only for illustrative purposes, and should in no way be considered systematically reviewed. We will simply comment on some of the values and limitations of the styles of participant observation.

Examples of Style

Studies in participant observation reveal a variety of research styles with regard to subject matter. Some researchers do not realize that what they discover is shaped by what they themselves are—their temperaments, perspectives, attitudes, and social and personal interests. They have often been unconscious of how these human elements affect their receptivity to the wealth of stimuli capable of reaching them in their research setting. They also have been largely unconscious of the effect upon their own perspectives of current professional styles. Yet these human influences must be understood as a methodological part of social research if the people who are studied are to be understood adequately.

Some of the styles which have been evident in past studies are: (1) romantic, (2) realistic, (3) poetic, (4) factual, (5) analytic, (6) satiric, (7) journalistic, and (8) existential.

The *romantic* response to the details of field experience is derived from the early traditions of British and American anthropology in which the researcher reveals his intellectual interest in the life of the "natives." Robert Redfield's study of Tepoztlan, Mexico, carries the mood and style of the romantic ethnographer, a mood which can be traced back to Rousseau's era, when the life of the savage was thought to be noble.[42] In Redfield's study, for example, Tepoztlan is introduced to the reader in a picturesque setting, hidden by a dense cluster of trees bearing edible fruits and showy flowers. The village itself is described first in terms of pre-Columbian and Spanish influences on the architecture of the houses. Subsequently, a picture is painted of the simple beauties of native life, but this picture disregards many realities. In fact, what is conspicuously absent is the language of the realist.

In this case, Redfield's language is such that he refers to food preparation in Tepoztlan as "cookery," that which is drunk during meals as "beverages," and that which is worn as everyday clothing as "costumes." The "cookery of Tepoztlan" is not really suggestive of the delicacies produced by a French chef; tortillas and beans are the main dish for villagers three times a day. If some of the "costumes" worn by villagers were worn in some urbanized setting they might be called "rags" by neighbors, but Redfield observes

---

42 Robert Redfield, *Tepoztlan: A Mexican Village* (Chicago: University of Chicago Press, 1930).

the dress as though he were witnessing it in the dramatic performance of a play. The "rags" interpretation is an example of the crude perspective against which the classic ethnographer reacts, for his unexpressed aim is to find some esthetic appreciation for his subjects, regardless of their seeming depravity. The ethnographer wants to create respect for the cultural varieties of man in society without the customary attitude of disdain that arises from class bias or ethnocentricity. In so doing, he creates his own world of "facts" which are not inherent in the linguistic lives of his subjects.

Redfield's choice of metaphors leads the reader away from the realities of "poverty" and the "hardships" placed upon people who lack technical progress to a vaulted image of "the culture." He speaks of *time* in the village as not being determined by the "clock in the tower of the Palacio Municipal which strikes the hours"; rather, the "metronome of human interests" (time) is measured by the seasons and the "waxing and the waning of the moon." It is through the "cadences of nature" and the "chronometers of sunset and sunrise" that the "simpler peoples" are more directly dependent.

Redfield discusses the "ritual of death" in terms of the villager's conduct during these times of crisis, rather than in an interpretation of their immediate agonies. What suffering Redfield does reveal is recorded in songs and poetry. Village folklore in song and poetry, of course, does translate the personal desolation which can be a human response to death into something beautiful and memorable, and thus more fitting to the romantic tradition.

Seventeen years later, Oscar Lewis went to Tepoztlan to restudy the community.[43] His result was a more thoroughgoing, complex analysis which contained interpretations opposite to those of Redfield. Lewis' study contained psychological *realism*. He came to the community armed with psychological techniques, in particular the Rorschach test, which was administered to the local inhabitants. The Rorschach test "validated" much of what Lewis and his associates had seen there: hostility, jealousy, suspicion, and deception in the lives of the inhabitants.

Upon reviewing Lewis' study of Tepoztlan, the extreme differences in conclusions led Redfield to conclude that each approached the community with different questions in mind. Redfield said he must have implicitly asked, "What do these people enjoy?" while Lewis must have asked himself, "What do these people suffer from?" How much the difference in perspectives was a matter of conscious choice, how much a matter of unconscious temperament, and how much a matter of the spirit of their separate generations is difficult to determine. It is especially noteworthy, however, that the

---

[43] Oscar Lewis, *Life in a Mexican Village: Tepoztlan Restudied* (Urbana, Ill.: University of Illinois Press, 1951).

differences between these two researchers continued to be revealed in their later studies of Mexican culture.

Lewis' later studies continued to emphasize the stark psychological realities of living in poverty. He sharpened his focus on family life and the dire effects of political and economic changes upon the lives of individuals by allowing the people to speak for themselves. And yet the personal relationship which both Lewis and Redfield had with the people they studied and the influence these researchers had over their selection of data was never discussed. This existential part of the ethnographic process was not emphasized until later by other participant observers.

Ruth Benedict's studies are in a class by themselves. It was her virtue to have *poetic* powers for observing and describing the deeper spiritual forces of the cultural life of man in society. The life forces of man were as evident to her in the lowly southwestern Pueblo as in Greek civilization. She grasped these life forces intuitively and sought to reveal them in prose. No amount of historicizing or factualizing her experience in categories could accomplish this task adequately, for it required special human contact, through words, between herself, her subjects, and her readers. Through her word we see the greatness in primitive man, his violence as well as his gentleness. Benedict opens the doors to intuitive perceptions for others to witness.

Research styles of this kind follow more closely in the tradition of the humanities than in the sciences. There is much poetic prose in the work of Laurens Van der Post in his writings of African Bushmen. There is poetry in Redfield's later writings; there is romanticism also, but it becomes less controlled by the proprieties and interests of classic ethnography. Social scientists usually shy away from poetry, and yet it remains a part of human reality to be seen and grasped and studied. Most field observers must suppress their esthetic and personal interests in their subjects to attain what they consider optimum objectivity. Others have written sensitively about their subjects, but have felt it necessary to write under a pseudonym to separate themselves from their professional interests.[44] The stylist is in a position to argue this point. He would likely say that while it is sometimes important to suppress feelings in the interest of objectivity, it is possible, with professional maturity, to report objectively and subjectively at the same time, to write from both the heart and the head, and in so doing, gain in accuracy and insight into the culture studied.

The tendency to be categorically *factual* throughout a research report is found in most American studies which purport to be more strictly systematic. In such studies, the aim of the researcher is to fit the details of his ex-

---

[44] Cf. Elenore Smith Bowen, *Return to Laughter* (Garden City, N.Y.: Doubleday Anchor Books, 1964).

perience into predetermined categories of social science which may later provide the basis for analysis and theorizing. Social scientific categories include the class system, the division of labor, social institutions, occupations, roles, and statuses. A particular researcher may spend time studying only one or two of these categories. For example, American community studies in the 1930's and 1940's emphasized the class system. A vast amount of data was accumulated to demonstrate the existence of class and how it functioned in the life of the community. In these research reports the author typically devoted a great deal of space to a description of his rating procedures, but very little or none of his own personal involvement in the community.

We should note, however, that a much greater amount of space was devoted in these stratification studies to the subjective realities of the people themselves than was the case of the more intellectually oriented works of archeologists, ancient historians, and classic ethnographers on whom the modern students of community had to depend for precedent. Throughout the studies of Yankee City, *Jonesville, Deep South, Elmtown's Youth,* and *Plainville,* are biographical notes of individuals and interpersonal recordings of the subjective feelings of townspeople. Still, the main lines of research were predetermined in terms of class description.

If the social scientific category did not control the selection of detail in the more formal studies of participant observers, the hypothesis did. In *Elmtown's Youth,* for example, Hollingshead oriented his observations around his search for evidence of a "functional relationship" between adolescent behavior and family status in the community.[45] In such cases, the researcher's attention must be focused upon certain behavioral responses which will validate or invalidate that which he is interested in studying, according to his scientific predilections.

The *analytic* studies follow closely in type on the heels of the categorically factual. Analytic theories which researchers have followed most closely have been structural-functionalism, psychoanalysis, and symbolic interactionism. In the analytic style, a formal theory is generally incorporated into the running commentary of facts reported in the field study. Through this style of research, the author can fulfill several goals. One is to create new meanings and a special understanding of data by means of a theoretical interpretation. Another is to add evidence to substantiate a theory and therefore indicate to the reader that the theory has validity as a system of thought. These are scientific interests, but an unintentional and human consequence of this style is the effect it has upon the researcher. One effect is to create social distance between the researcher and his subjects, leading him from understanding the immediate reality in the lives of his subjects. Another effect is to convince the researcher (through his selection and elaboration

---

[45] August B. Hollingshead, *Elmtown's Youth* (New York: John Wiley & Sons, Inc., 1949).

of these details which fit the theory) that his is the true way of understanding the data.

The studies of the British anthropologists have typically followed the method of structural-functional analysis. Anthropologists who have written in this tradition have been Radcliff-Brown, Levi-Strauss, Raymond Firth, and Evans Pritchard. Structural-functionalism is often mixed with the theories of psychoanalysis and symbolism, which are traceable to Sigmund Freud and Emile Durkheim respectively.

These theories have influenced researchers (widely divergent in place and time) such as Bronislaw Malinowski (*The Sexual Life of Savages*), John Seeley (*Crestwood Heights*), and W. Lloyd Warner (Yankee City). In Malinowski's case, for example, psychoanalysis is mixed with functionalism. Warner mixes psychoanalysis with a theory of symbolism. In Warner's latest volume on Yankee City (*The Living and the Dead*),[46] he describes Catholic religious rites in sexual metaphors. (One topic heading reads "Holy Coitus and Sacred Procreation.") Warner's intent is to show the power of man's sexual life in the rites of the modern church. The analysis is reminiscent of Freud, who was no less disinclined to analyze religious life in terms of what he believed to be the more basic reality of sex. While the symbolic relationship between religious life and sexual life may be theoretically proposed, the assumption that the sexual perspective is more "real" keeps the analyst from understanding what is believed to be genuine and primary in the lives of religious persons. Religious symbolism appears to the analyst as a kind of epiphenomenon of sex life. Actually, there is no scientific reason why the symbolic perspectives could not be reversed so that religious life and its symbols would become "real" and sex life would become the epiphenomenon. The value of the analytical style is its ability to cast a new light on the subject studied, but it cannot serve as a substitute reality. If the researcher aims to substitute a reality for that which he is studying, he transgresses the methodological rules of participant observation.[47]

---

[46] W. Lloyd Warner, *The Living and the Dead* (New Haven: Yale University Press, 1959).

[47] A cardinal rule in the method of participant observation is to accept the reality of the subjects as given, and study it as it is authentically constituted in the subjects' minds. The inauthentic must be judged, of course, but in this case (at the level of institutions) it seems wiser for the social scientist to describe the transition which realities are now undergoing in the context of modern society, rather than to judge these realities. It would seem more prudent to describe, rather than explain, in view of the fact that the scientific reality may be challenged and judged to be inauthentic in the future. The scientific profession has always considered the reality found in the physical or physiological aspects of man as primary in contrast with those aspects of man considered to be refined and spiritual. The economic system or sexual drive is a more basic reality than is religion or art; the social world is more basic than the cultural world. Until the realities observable within culture come under more careful study in sociological theory, it is wise for the social scientist to "bracket" his judgments, as the phenomenologists say, and study the differing institutional realities that co-exist in modern society, including the reality of science.

Warner's use of the image of the dead lamb to illustrate the various ways in which a single mental image may be analyzed symbolically can, in itself, be interpreted symbolically for our purposes here. The poignant meaning of the lamb symbol (innocence, simplicity, and vulnerability) which lies within the Judeo-Christian tradition is not understood through the scientific tradition of analysis. The lamb is killed. It is dead. In a purely analytical framework of study, the lamb remains an impersonal object without life and meaning, and the essence of the particular culture is lost.

The studies which are *satiric* are closely associated with the analytic emphasis, but this style is not really concerned with the systematics of analysis. Many of Erving Goffman's very provocative and extremely perceptive observations reflect this more informal satirical style. In Goffman's studies of "total institutions," for example, he describes the inmate world of prisons, mental hospitals, tuberculosis sanatoriums, monasteries, and the like.[48] His emphasis is upon the plight of the individual as he is subjected to the total forces and total control of the institution. The "self" of the new inmate undergoes a "process of mortification," wherein he first confronts a "civil death" (loss of civil rights) as he enters the institution, then undergoes "obedience tests" and "will-breaking contests," then suffers from a "personal defacement" (removal of clothing, combs, cosmetics) and a "personal disfigurement" (direct mutilation through beatings or surgery), at regular intervals confronts "physical indignities" (such as being forced to eat solely with a spoon or having to stand at attention when an officer approaches), and so on. These types of observations, accurate in their behavioral references, nevertheless are described metaphorically to evoke sympathy for the inmates and great anger towards all total institutions. Such sympathy and anger can be important toward stimulating social reforms, but the observer's focus is again selective for a purpose beyond the larger objective interests of study. Certain data are omitted to meet the interests of social criticism. There is no data from Goffman, for example, about the plight of the administrative officer—the indignities which he suffers at the hands of the inmates, the bureaucratic controls he must live with, and the bureaucratic traps into which he falls. Without the perspective which comes from the description of subjective opposites in an institutional setting, a study is bound to serve the interests of social criticism more than the interests of objective analysis. Furthermore, the terms of description in this case are not those of the participants themselves (inmates do not speak of "personal defacement"), but are those of the observer, who sympathizes with them and invents by metaphor what he believes will be per-

---

[48] Erving Goffman, *Asylums: Essays on the Social Situation of Mental Patients and Other Inmates* (Garden City, N.Y.: Doubleday Anchor Books, 1961).

sonally meaningful to the reader and hopefully will contribute to further critical analysis of total institutions. The scientific terms and perspective of the analysis make it a modern satire; it becomes the work of a Charles Dickens in the guise of modern science.

These kinds of studies are not far removed from scientific *journalism,* which aims to deal with current social problems. However, journalistic reporting shows no interest in the subtleties of satire which are evident in a study such as Goffman's, but it is nevertheless the same in its interest in commenting socially on affairs of everyday life. The Park Forest study of William Whyte, for example, was geared to reveal the extent of social conformity in the modern suburb. There was a personal selection of detail (from the welter of details that could have struck the researcher) in dealing with social conformity as a topic of social concern in the modern suburb. Anthropologists have shown a similar concern for current problems in their selection of detail from field experiences. For example, the studies of Margaret Mead show something of this special concern in reporting. She feels that the problem of war is not a biological necessity since certain primitive peoples (*e.g.,* the Eskimos and the California Mission Indians) do not know the meaning of group warfare. The social question this fact raises is whether modern warfare is inevitable. Similarly, the problem of whether masculine and feminine traits as conceived in western society are biologically determined is treated by reporting the traits exhibited by primitive men and women. Western traits are found by Margaret Mead to be reversed in the roles of men and women in tribes of New Guinea. This kind of selective reporting becomes extremely relevant to the times; it gives some sanction to those in modern society who would break traditional patterns associated with sex roles. Other modern problems are treated similarly. The problems of whether infants should continue to be breast-fed rather than bottle-fed and whether adolescents should have some kind of rite of passage into adulthood in order to prevent them from becoming delinquent are treated through reports about primitive societies. These reports bear directly upon modern problems and suggest indirectly what ought to be done about them. This is not to say that such studies have no scientific interest beyond these social interests; however, sometimes the items are selected and described by the fieldworker in the light of his own social interests in treating these problems.

Authors of research studies have recently begun to report their own *existential* orientation, that is, their own personal interests and relationships with their subjects. The very open, honest account of William F. Whyte ("On the Evolution of *Street Corner Society*") is a poststudy reflection along this line. It is an attempt to unveil the author and what lay behind the formal aspects of his research to outside observers and critics. Other researchers have done the same. In a recently edited collection of essays

(*Reflections on Community Studies*),[49] Stanley Diamond, John Seeley, Kurt Wolff, Art Gallaher, Morris Schwartz, and others have written of their own subjective concerns in the process of research.

The existential insights of Morris Schwartz, derived from personal reflections on his study of a mental hospital, are particularly significant for future researchers to follow in conducting their own studies. He raises basic questions about himself as an observer:

> Who was doing the observing? Why was I there? What stance should I take? Where shall I look, and what shall I look for? With what am I looking? How shall I describe what I see?[50]

These are the existential questions which each researcher may do well to ask himself, for his own answers reveal what will strongly influence the outcome of his study.

Summary

The stylist ideally finds his home more in the cultural world of man than in the structural world. He assumes that the phenomena he studies have quality and are rich in meaning. He assumes that what he studies contains innumerable possibilities for interpretation, of which his is only one. He assumes that man's nature is of infinite variety and that man is to be explored in this light.

The stylist is the bane of the structuralist, who would see only one view. The structuralist who builds his theory from the tradition of empiricism functions with an "either-or" outlook; the stylist often functions with a "both-and" outlook. Paradoxically, both can be correct because they involve different worlds. The traditional empiricist studies the world of sense, and the stylist, the world of meaning. Although participant observers may generate styles as they study society, the methodology of participant observation is broad enough to account for the nature of the "system." The participant observer can make his study systematic and come close to paralleling a study in experimental behavior, or he can stylize it in accordance with the cultural world he studies. He need not concentrate his observation primarily in the world of sense, however, in order to be systematic in his work and obtain verifiable data.

The participant observer must tell the truth about what he studies, but this truth is so complex that he cannot tell it all at once. The best he can do is to choose a perspective consonant with his ends. Then he should

---

[49] Maurice Stein *et al.*, eds., *Reflections on Community Studies* (New York: John Wiley & Sons, Inc., 1964).

[50] Morris S. Schwartz, "The Mental Hospital: The Research Person in the Disturbed Ward," in *ibid.*, pp. 85–117.

exercise some control over the descriptive language of his research, rather than having his language control him and deceive him as to what really exists.

The observer should exercise this control, paradoxically, by releasing it, by allowing himself, his viewpoint, and even his language to be influenced by his subjects. He must be able to "surrender," as Kurt Wolff has so aptly put it.[51] He should have some control over his perspective, but he cannot control the perspective of his subjects or remain uninfluenced by them, and still understand them. It is through this encounter between observer and participants—wherein the viewpoint of the observer is modified by contact with the reality of the subjects—that the observer discovers a greater truth about the nature of himself and his subjects. If the observer can accept this principle, he can then act more openly toward his subjects and allow them to influence him more freely without being concerned about maintaining great distance. He need not defend his perspective by distance if he realizes that all perspectives, including his own, are partial. Cultural life can be conceived to be romantic, realistic, factual, poetic, lyric, satiric, tragic, or existential, but these are partial perspectives of man which function as part of the human perspective.

One viewpoint can be technically more advantageous than another to the social scientist, however, and this is important to note. The viewpoint with the advantage is that one which can reveal in full measure the perspective of those being studied, and yet still observe it clearly from a more basic standpoint. This is no easy task. There must be within the observer's own perspective the ability to *maximize the value* found within the perspective of his subjects *from their viewpoint*. If the subject's perspective is romantic, let us say, the observer's perspective must allow this perspective full measure of expression, and the observer must still be able to present what may be his more realistic "facts" in conjunction with it. The style which can reveal the subjects as they see themselves, and yet still comment—tragically, humorously, or realistically—upon their culture without demeaning or destroying it, has the greater power. For a cultural perspective to contribute further to scientific purposes, however, the order that lies within it must be studied for its place in general theory.

The requirements of participant observation are rigorous. What we have said is tantamount to saying that the participant observer must remain a scientist with the insights of a Shakespearean dramatist. No one can expect perfection in such a demanding role, but one can expect researchers to be aware of the professional ideals surrounding it and to guide their work as closely as possible by these ideals.

---

[51] Kurt Wolff, "Surrender and Community Study: The Study of Loma," in *ibid.*, pp. 233–63.

All sociocultural perspectives eventually rest in the human perspective. The human perspective at its best would maximize the value of its component viewpoints, while generating a basis for productive contact with these viewpoints. If the researcher and the theorist can realize the human aspects of their work, they may find some creative ground upon which to combine their viewpoints to reveal the nature of man in society.

The researcher literally creates his facts as he brings his personal interests and his special perspective into contact with his immediate experience in a culture. Determining what is fact and what is not fact has, in the past, been dependent upon whether a scientific assertion is based upon sense stimuli which are reproducible for other observers. Now the participant observer has been finding that facts are relative to one's perspective and that assertions about non-sense stimuli are meaningful within the special perspective that creates them. One researcher can validate the social insight of another researcher if he can assume the same perspective and then observe how that insight is linked to the symbolic life of his subjects.

The larger truth will appear in the judicious combination of those partial perspectives which, on the one hand, can predict the behavior of man, and on the other hand, can enlighten his world of choice by disclosing its variety, thus increasing his freedom of action. Man is truly a paradox steeped in irony. He is predictable and he is unpredictable. He is unique and he is general. He is individual and he is communal. He is, indeed, richly endowed.

These claims about the nature of man demand that we accept the condition that not all of the process of research is reproducible, for some parts of it are unique, individual, and unpredictable. But that which *is* reproducible should be accepted as a methodological part of the scientific enterprise, even though it may be unorthodox.

The scientist makes his discoveries uniquely as an individual, but also socially within a community. The scientific enterprise itself is basically communal. What lies ahead in research, then, is the further delineation of those procedures and perspectives—the further clarification of that culture of knowledge—which leads social scientists more directly to the discovery of truth as it exists in the society of man.

Verification
Procedures

Participant observers who are interested in defining their procedures must ultimately face the problem of verification. Verification is generally dependent upon checking two factors—the reliability and the validity of a work.

Reliability is based upon two assumptions. The first is that the study can be repeated. Other investigators must be able to follow exactly the same steps of the original investigator. This means using the same categories of study, the same procedures, the same criteria of correctness, and the same perspective that was used originally. The second assumption is that it is possible for two or more people to perceive the same meanings by using these categories and procedures.

Validity is based upon human intent and reality. In order for the researcher's work to have validity, his conclusions and his subjects' intentions in their original meanings must be the same. What the researcher says is reality in the minds of those he studies must be reality in the same way that they conceive it.

Another researcher may want to follow different procedures and use different categories from those of the original study to determine validity. This produces healthy complications. A second researcher may discover that the objects of study can be known only through the special categories and procedures established by the original researcher. This raises questions, in turn, about the authenticity (or usefulness) of the theory underlying the procedures. Validity, then, is determined not only by what exists in the subjects' minds, but also by what categories of investigation exist in the mind of the observer.

We have previously mentioned four levels of interpretation which become related to the categories of investigation and which are necessary to study in meeting the large problem of truthfulness of the study. These four levels are: original meanings, themes, configurations, and theories. Each higher level intends to be descriptive of the level below it, but in so doing, synthetic judgments are made about the data. That is, the observer necessarily adds new elements to the data he studies which create a higher (or different) order of understanding. The new elements are conceptual and are derived from the observer's experience with the comparative data he gathers. The observer's conceptualization gives added meaning to the terms in the lower level, meaning that has to do with the order and relationships of the data under the conditions of observation. Since the observer is in a special position to record his data under conditions we have elaborated as time, place, social circumstance, cultural intimacy, language, and consensus, he adds meanings to his data by virtue of how they relate under such conditions. While his basis for adding meaning may be philosophically constituted (Kant would specify the forms of intuition and understanding), we would emphasize values and facts derived symbolically by the observer from his social and personal experiences in the culture studied. This basis, in any case, is made clear in the researcher's account of his findings.

Each level of interpretation contains a certain degree of subjectivity as well as objectivity, as we have previously suggested. Each level contains a picture of reality which contains values and is relative to the viewpoint of the observer who holds it. This makes it somewhat subjective. At the same time, each level contains objects shared in the consciousness of people. This makes it to some extent objective. One would normally expect objectivity to increase as levels of interpretation broaden toward theory. Our point here, however, is that these levels of interpretation should gain both in subjectivity and objectivity. In the process of moving from one level to the next, judgments must be made to re-order the values and facts contained in the more specific level. This is what creates the new level of interpretation. The function of the new level is to be descriptively expressive of the values, as well as explanatory of the facts, contained in the more specific level.

The elements found in common among the realities described at the more specific levels are of two kinds—general facts and universal values. The observer generalizes about those elements (facts) he observes in common among the various classes of data at specific levels (*e.g.,* original meanings); these generalizations constitute the basis for higher-level interpretations (*e.g.,* themes). Those elements (values) found to be universal among the cultural data studied are also expressively contained in higher-level interpretations. A theme, for example, should be both accurately expressive of original values studied and accurately descriptive of the facts about them. When expression and description are combined in the theme, the researcher takes his first step toward an explanation of the culture, since a perspective is added in the process which is not solely in the original meanings. A configuration, in turn, should be both expressive and descriptive of the different themes which it proposes to explain through its added meanings of order and relationship. A theory, finally, should be both expressive and descriptive of the different configurations of reality which it proposes to explain through its added meanings of order and relationship.

Any one of these levels can be tested for its adequacy, and thus for its degree of validity, by relating it to another level next to it. The final validity of any single level, then, cannot be determined merely by the examination of itself since it is interdependent with other parts which are in continuous adjustment with each other in the larger whole. Validity can be established with sufficient certainty, however, within the limits of any study that seeks to do so between levels. Original meanings that are described by the researcher are studied for their correct relationship with the culture of the people studied; themes are studied for their correct relationship with original meanings; configurations are studied for their correct relationship with themes; middle-range theory (including typologies) and higher principles of theory are studied for their correct relationship with each other and with configurations.

The correct relationship of one level with another is determined by the answers to a number of questions, including the following: Does the broader level disclose the actual nature of the terms in the more specific level by concepts that take into account how the more specific terms are originally expressed? Does the broader level clarify how the meanings in the more specific level exist within the broader, ordered picture of reality? Criteria for judging whether affirmative answers can be given to such questions may involve linguistic and esthetic, as well as logical, standards which should be made explicit in any verificatory study.

What we are asking is: To what extent are the original terms in the more specific level individuated, differentiated, and integrated into the larger whole? By *individuated* we mean how these terms retain their individual character. (It is as important to retain original or existential meanings as it is to apply theoretical meanings, for both are basic and interdependent in judging validity.) By *differentiated* we mean how these meanings become separately distinguished and clarified in relation to each other. By *integrated* we mean how the relationships among these meanings are systematically brought together; this includes how a new conceptual order is created by adding elements synthetically which did not exist previously in the data.

In order to fully validate a study, an observer must know what level he is validating, for each level has its own kind of problems. Our primary interest here is the validation of original meanings, and we have led up to a discussion of levels of interpretation simply to indicate the extent of the validation problem. In a structured study theory enters into the elaboration of procedures and the formulation of categories of study. Validation of original meanings, then, is highly interdependent with existing theory, and the researcher must judge the capacity of his theory to illuminate the procedures which will lead to an accurate accounting of original meanings.

Whether one can begin research totally free of previous assumptions or preconceptions and investigate phenomena in their original nature, or whether one must begin by defining the object to be investigated, is an age-old problem. Kant's cogent arguments made explicit those forms of understanding which existed a priori in the mind and which could not be located originally in the data. Descartes' argument, however, was that the researcher must wipe away all past thoughts and commitments and start with a clean slate. The phenomenologist's argument is of the same order as Descartes' in modern form. And some participant observers, we have said, also function in this tradition of working with a radically open mind.

In the structured study, however, the participant observer assumes that his procedures and categories of knowing can be developed from theory and his study may thus become relevant to existing concepts of man. He assumes that his subject can be understood in its natural context within broadly defined categories. For example, the six general categories we have discussed as significant for field studies (time, place, circumstance, etc.) contain an implicit "theory" about meaning and the nature of man. The theory to which we have referred as structural-functionalism (or social action) and which prevails today among some sociologists contains postulates and models about sociocultural reality which can serve as part of a structured study. The adequacy of a theory is judged partly by how well it articulates with the reality found in field studies; the adequacy of a field study is judged partly by how well the theory was applied so that what are believed to be significant dimensions of original meanings have been thoroughly explored. Theory can never be fully separated from the processes of verification.

We will now bring together several categories deemed important in social action theory with the six dimensions we have stressed important to field studies in order to illustrate how a researcher may structure his study in participant observation. The relationship to action theory can only be suggested here because of our need to simplify our statement. If we were to follow action theory more exactly we would develop a paradigm based upon the two action categories—motivational and value orientation—with their three subdivisions—cognitive, cathetic, and evaluational processes which are said by action theorists to be a part of the life of any human collectivity. The researcher could then investigate how meanings appear in the "orientation system" of a particular "collectivity" by using these categories. For illustrative purposes we have chosen the categories of cognition, cathexis, and conduct and interpreted them in special ways we shall discuss shortly.[1]

The researcher should begin his research by defining the objectives and the categories of his investigation, for they are interdependent in his work and closely related to the problem of verification. If his objectives are exploratory, that is, if they outline the major forms of cultural life in a particular group, then his categories should be abstract and broadly defined. If the basic viewpoint of the people the researcher studies is already fairly well understood, he can begin with greater precision. In such a case he may focus upon a particular object or belief in the culture he plans to study and investigate the special meanings and connotations that surround it.

The focus of a research design could be on "the place of an object in the cultural context" studied; "the practical consequences" of something perceived in the experience of the people studied; the essence of a symbol as it is constituted in the minds of members of a particular culture; a word such as *freedom* or *justice* (if it has any meaning in the culture); the experiential referent of an objective sociological category such as "social class" as it may be found in special expressions such as "hoi poloi" (already described in community studies); or a "social role" such as the "right guy" or "silk stockings" or "wolves" (already studied as a part of prison cultures).[2]

The focus of a research design could be on particular ideas or beliefs which the researcher already knows are commonly held in a culture he wants to study but which are not understood in detail. For example, the meaning of democracy in the life-world of selected political groups, the meaning of nonviolence in the culture of civil rights workers, the meaning of capitalism in various corporate circles of businessmen are examples of beliefs of major importance in American culture, which have worldwide significance. These beliefs could be researched for their cultural meanings in other cultural settings, particularly in Russia, India, and South America, respectively. Beliefs function symbolically in the minds of people in ways

---

1 Certain processes by which a work of research is verified are too complicated and detailed to be discussed here. Each piece of work involves its own peculiar problems. If a *team* of observers is involved, for example, the way details are handled by a team must be assessed. This means evaluating the details of recording, assembling, and categorizing data as the team conceives collectively in the process of working together. If the research objective is limited, the problems of research differ from a case in which the objective is broadly stated. The study of motivational symbols of a criminal gang is much different from the study of the basic symbols of an entire community. Therefore, decisions about how to approach each living unit involve their own problems of validity. We suggest here only the general outline of how a study may be approached, based primarily on the categories which we have just mentioned are related to contemporary theory.

2 Examples of different foci of meaning such as some of these suggested here may be found in Charles K. Ogden and I. A. Richards, *The Meaning of Meaning* (New York: Harcourt, Brace & World, Inc., 1946), pp. 186–87.

that are different from formal philosophy, and an empirical description of how they differ could be an important contribution to sociological theory and understanding. Such studies are not normally conducted in the methodological traditions of social research because of the problems of verification and generalization.

While the general objective of the structured study may be to explore certain meanings in the "orientation system" of an occupational, religious, or political group, our focus here will be on the categories of investigation. In a structured study we know that even though theoretical categories will lead us to see cultural meanings logically related to the categories themselves and not fully original to the people studied, these broadly defined categories can still reflect important ways in which human meaning originally arises in any society. Therefore, we know that even though categories of inquiry limit the range of our observations and even partially shape what we observe and what we conclude about the people we study, these categories can, at the same time, be defined broadly enough to guide us toward discovering original meanings, largely as the culture itself reveals them. We also assume that the categories of investigation can be made specific enough to make verification feasible and at the same time we assume they can be of the kind relevant to sociological theory.

Charting Original Meanings through Theoretical Categories

In order to establish the basis for an experimental model which can be followed by successive researchers, let us assume that meanings which are important in the lives of any people are expressed through their capacity to think, feel, and act. (See Table 1.) Man is much more complex in his expressions than these categories as separately understood would indicate, but as preconceptions of how people express themselves meaningfully, the categories serve a useful function for relating our findings to contemporary theory.

The first category which refers to man's capacity to think we shall term *cognition*. This category should guide us in our search for how a sociocultural meaning is made intelligible among the people studied. We want to know if people think about this meaning, and if they do, how the meaning is considered according to the cognitive standards in the culture being studied. We want to know *how* people think as well as *what* they think about the meaning under investigation. Second, we shall refer to that dimension of man we have called by various terms such as sentiments, spirit, feelings, emotions, etc., as *cathexis*. There is no single scientific category that adequately includes the nuances in this complex capacity of man.

Table 1

Experimental Categories of Verification: Focus on Data

Categories of Data	Dimensions of Data					
	Time	Place	Circumstance	Language	Intimacy	Consensus
Cognition (How is the meaning made intelligible?)	How long has the meaning been intelligible?	Is it cognitively associated with the environs? How?	Is it associated with social roles and groups? How?	How is the meaning communicated?	Is it expressed in private? How is it conveyed intelligibly?	How is it confirmed?
Cathexis (What quality of feeling is associated with the meaning?)	How long has sentiment been associated and does time change it?	Is the sentiment associated with environs? How?	Is it felt differently in different roles and events?	How is the sentiment communicated?	How is it experienced privately?	How is the sentiment confirmed?
Conduct (What kind of social action accompanies the meaning? How many people are involved?)	How long have how many people participated?	In what places do how many people act accordingly?	How do people act in different groups?	How is it conveyed in action? (In sound or ritual?)	How do people behave behind the scenes?	How do people show agreement in action?

Cathexis generally refers to man's desires or to feelings of pleasure and pain. Talcott Parsons uses the term in this sense in referring to man's gratificational life, his positive and negative valences toward objects. But this is only one aspect of what we mean by the term. We assume that all those feelings which may lie significantly behind and within social meanings cannot be categorized by the term *desire* or *gratification*; they are to be discovered as they are in the cultural context being studied. Charles Cooley has reminded us that man has already linguistically cataloged his sentiments for us in such words as "kindly," "angry," and "humble." The vast number of types, shadings, and intensities of feeling qualities which are to be studied in this dimension of cathexis, then, are to be discovered phenomenologically in the culture under study. The third property of meaning we will term *conduct,* for we will assume that people everywhere act in certain ways to express meanings which are significant to them. The researcher is interested in observing both the behavior and the people who are behaving. While it is true that the participant observer is not interested in focusing on behavior primarily, it is still an important dimension of meaning about which he must be cognizant.

These three categories are interdependent and serve as checks on each other which must be examined for their validity. Man sometimes acts differently than he thinks, and feels differently than he acts. Sometimes he may not think of the meaning contained in his action; sometimes he acts without feeling; sometimes he thinks and feels and yet does not act. Nevertheless, we would suggest that there is a "strain toward consistency" among these three modes of man's being, and that in most cases significant meanings are found consistently expressed in all three modes. In any case, the researcher who discovers inconsistencies in these modes of being or content lacking in any one of them is able to comprehend better the true nature of those meanings which are existent in the culture he investigates.

In order to complete our table we shall draw upon those categories which we said earlier indicated some measure of the subjective adequacy of the observer. We may proceed, then, to ask questions about the data with regard to time, place, circumstance, language, intimacy, and consensus, and thus begin to delineate a workable guide for observers to follow in checking their findings. *These six dimensions represent the context within which meaning arises.* A brief interpretation of this context as represented in the form of an experimental verification table is appropriate here.

Given a specific meaning under investigation, we would first ask how long the meaning has been intelligibly communicated among those who are studied? Has it been rationalized in different ways at different times? While it is true that the immediate expression of a particular meaning in a single social event has validity for that context, we are interested in how that single context fits into the larger context. That is, we assume that in order to really understand social meanings, they must be seen with reference to a time period to give them perspective. If we can achieve at least an approximate understanding of the time elements involved in the meaning, the meaning must next be understood in relation to the physical environment. For example, do people think about a man-environs relationship in the way that Laurens Van der Post tells us the Bushmen think about fertility and droughts?

If we continue to move horizontally across the table we must next answer under what circumstances and in what social groups meaning is made intelligible. If an association is found here, we want to know how it is associated and with how many people. Next, how is the meaning rhetorically expressed so that it is made intelligible to those who share it? Then, how is the meaning conveyed in intimate or close contact? Is it more intelligible under these conditions? Finally, how is the meaning confirmed among the subjects studied? That is, in what ways do the subjects recognize that they mutually understand and accept the particular meanings? If the observer has the opportunity to intelligibly confirm the meanings with his subjects, then the question is, how does he do it?

If we move down to the next vertical category and move horizontally across the table we must ask other questions. The basic question here is, how do people feel about this meaning? Then, how long has this feeling been associated with this meaning? Does the quality vary at different times? Is the feeling experienced in association with the physical environment? In what way? Next, is there a different feeling in different social circumstances and in different social roles? How many people share it? How is the feeling communicated? Is there a different quality of feeling when privately communicated? Finally, how is the expression of this feeling confirmed in the social setting?

If we move to the last vertical category we must ask still other questions. We must ask how the meaning is expressed in action. We want to know how long people have expressed certain types of behavior associated with this meaning and if the behavior varies in time. Then, we want to know in what places people behave as they do. Do people act in this particular manner in special groups or only when they take certain social roles? Is the meaning communicated in ritual and ceremony? Do people act differently under intimate circumstances than in public? Finally, how do people demonstrate their agreement in action?

The categories in the experimental table are selected from a theory of culture which should lead us to an adequate understanding of original meanings as they exist within the framework of that theory. The dimensions set forth additional theoretical conditions wherein it is most probable that the true subjective character of the data will be revealed; and yet the data, as well as the dimensions themselves, have an objective character. This is because all social knowledge, in fact all human communication, has both an objective and a subjective dimension to it.

Questions which check the adequacy of the findings should also be directed toward the observer himself to determine how well he followed the rules. Thus, in Table 2 are listed the key questions which set the framework

Table 2

Experimental Categories of Verification: Focus on Observer

Criteria of Objective Observations	Criteria of Subjective Observations
Does the observer:	
	Time How long has the observer participated in the setting?
1. Relate his interpretations to empirical fact and structural theory?	
	Place Where has he participated in the physical setting?
2. Relate his study to other culturally associated contexts?	
	Circumstance In what social groups and social roles has he participated?
3. Manifest a lack of distortion in his reporting and sufficient distance from his subjects?	
	Language How well does he know the language?
4. Manifest illustrativeness and an objective style in his description?	*Intimacy* In what private social arrangements does he participate?
	Consensus How does he confirm what meanings he finds existing in the culture?

for judging the observer's ability to interpret subjective meanings in a culture accurately. These questions may serve as a countercheck with the questions in Table 1. Suppose, for example, the observer participated in a study for only one week, then claiming to have found that the meanings he investigated have lasted much longer than that; we would conclude without supplementary evidence that his findings are open to question on the basis of internal consistency in his study. In this way we can deal with methodological problems such as how long an observer must be in the culture to have adequately met the standard of this time requirement. The length of time an observer must be a part of the culture he studies depends upon the data he is studying and his research design.

These categories of knowing and dimensions of verification can be made more definitive and yet *they need not be quantified* to be understood at a level sufficient for social scientific purposes. The purpose in formulating more definitive categories would be only to place those qualitative requirements on the observer which are sufficient to make the meanings he finds clear and uncontestable. The categories themselves act as a screening device selecting data to be observed and therefore must be lucid and significantly related to the general character of social meanings which the researchers find important to study. Our verification of the findings, then, rests upon the social consensus of scientists that the data has been reported adequately within the confines of a reporting framework that sets the basis for revealing the meanings in clear outline.

In addition to checking adequacy at the subjective level, we must also check the objective level of the observer and his findings. We have said that, for our purposes, objectivity has two dimensions as it becomes a part of (1) knowledge and (2) consciousness. The questions associated with these two dimensions are posed in Table 2. We want to determine whether the observer has correctly related his findings to empirical facts and analytical theory. (If he uses structural-functional categories in his research design, he normally would relate his field experience to them.) Next we want to know how the observer has related his research focus to other social arrangements in the cultural environment he studies. The study cannot necessarily be judged to be subjectively prejudiced if the observer does not extend his observations to other associated cultural settings, but adequacy generally depends upon his intelligent grasp of these connections for his interpretations. As indicated, the assumption is that objectivity is gained as partial forms of knowledge become interconnected. Next, the consciousness of the observer is considered. The observer's ability to remain effectively neutral in his explications, that is, to remain free from making his own judgmental statements about the goodness or badness of the culture, must be examined. Finally, the observer must demonstrate how he maintained a respectable distance from his subjects to allow him full access to the data without becoming overinvolved with his subjects.

Charting for Discovery

There are various ways in which a study can be designed by participant observers, and each way will have some effect on the outcome and conclusions of the study. If the observer focuses his attention on specific hypotheses, or questions, or categories (such as cognition, cathexis, and conduct), he will see meanings within the framework of these preconditioning factors, but he will miss other meanings. These scientific factors will exclude other meanings which could be more important to people in the context of a culture. The researcher, then, who is interested in letting a culture "speak" to him more directly as it exists with its own "categories" and "values," can shape his study with this in mind. He can chart his research with more emphasis on the discovery of meanings in open encounter with his subjects, thereby moving, in one important sense, closer to the methodological viewpoint of writers such as Martin Heidegger in philosophy and C. Wright Mills in sociology.

By all rights, Heidegger and Mills represent totally different schools of thought in contemporary intellectual worlds. There is no indication that either had any interest in reading the works of the other. And yet both, strangely, show striking similarities in their vastly different fields of endeavor. They both had strong inclinations to discover knowledge about the world outside the past traditions structuring their disciplines. They were both concerned with how science in the modern world organizes our thought and therefore limits our capacity to interpret the world.

Martin Heidegger is a European philosopher who has traced the problem of knowing phenomenologically.[3] He has found that a major obstacle in the pursuit of knowledge exists in the structure of language and philosophic thought in western society. The structure of western language, for example, requires dividing subjects and objects in all "correct" sentences normatively conceived. Western man is forced to write and think in dualities, Heidegger said, which falsifies the original nature of truth. Martin Heidegger sought to go beyond the subject-object dichotomy to seek knowledge as it arose perceptively in fields of "pre-cognition."

Sociologist C. Wright Mills was also troubled with the language of his discipline. He traced the problem of knowing sociologically to rigidities in what he called "abstracted empiricism" and "grand theory" which kept the imaginative mind from opening itself to the realities of society. He boldly counseled social scientists to cast aside methodological requirements of the past that stunted the imagination. He was concerned with collective realities which were not a part of sociological theory and wanted to know how these realities related to problems of individuality. Mills felt that researchers should see society as it is actually constituted, but he wanted them to see it in a new light, outside the intellectual prisons of traditional social scientific thought.[4]

Researchers who want to break with tradition as Heidegger and Mills have done may be faced with the problem of verifiability of their work for some period of time, not simply because they are individualists, but because

---

[3] Martin Heidegger, *Being and Time* (New York: Harper & Row, Publishers, 1962).

[4] C. Wright Mills, *The Sociological Imagination* (New York: Oxford University Press, Inc., 1959).

they are in the process of revealing basically new perspectives which have no verificatory pattern for others to follow. Verification can take place only within a defined perspective (a theoretical framework) which sets down conditions for knowing those types of reality it is designed to explain. This is why, as we have indicated, verification must take place within the total scheme of contemporary theory, which is recognized as having some credence. Sociological realities which are discovered outside the framework of behaviorism, neo-positivism, or structural-functionalism and the methodological traditions accompanying them are incapable of being known scientifically by scientists who strictly adhere to these traditions. New discoverable realities would not be considered legitimate or "factual" to scientists who identify their science with prevailing theory and methodology.

The student who is interested in new discoveries about the sociocultural world of man must be willing to make discoveries which can be understood and verified by others at the level of his procedures without expectation of substantiation at other levels. Theoretical levels have not been providing the insights that are needed to meet the new demands of modern research. It is undoubtedly for this reason that C. Wright Mills called for a new slogan among social scientists with instinctive urgency: "Every man his own methodologist! Methodologists! Get to work!"[5]

In time, we would say that theory may eventually complete the circle of certainty and establish a scheme of thought which can interpret the new research and be understood at these other levels of knowing.

In order to constructively advance sociocultural knowledge the researcher must be willing to pare down his terms to a minimum and proceed to imaginatively experience the symbols and interpretive meanings of a culture as freshly as he can. Then he must clarify and reveal the character of these symbols and meanings.

If the participant observer proceeds *without* action categories he can stay within the general framework which we have indicated leads to verifiable knowledge. The objective standards (time, place, language, etc.) which we have suggested lead to adequate subjective interpretations can be elaborated and tested for their adequacy. The terms which we have used, such as "experience," "event," "social act," and "culture," all have their precedents in sociological, philosophical, anthropological, and historical theory. Nevertheless, they are still useful as sensitizing guides for the participant observer to open his mind and his emotions to the culture he seeks to know.[6]

---

5 *Ibid.,* p. 123.

6 The terms we use here to guide the observer's study are highly interdependent. It behooves us to give the reader a sense of orientation as to how these terms are interdependent in the tradition of symbolic theory, but we must caution against excessive concern over definition at the point of inquiry. It is better to keep in mind Edmund Husserl's imperative statement to philosophers: "To the things (*sache*)

In briefest fashion, the following outline illustrates some of the phases of this approach which we have indicated are of some importance in meeting methodological requirements of participant observation:

Field Data Guide: Aims, Methods, and Procedures

I. *Aim:* To discover, describe, and explain the culture of the people encountered in the study

II. *Method:*

    A. DISCOVERY

        To experience events that are important to the participants and realize how they interpret them

        To imaginatively take the role of participants in the process of experiencing events through social action

    B. DESCRIPTION

        To record the way events are interpreted by participants

        To record the interpretations (meanings) of participants in eventful social action

    C. EXPLANATION

        To reveal how these events and meanings exhibit a cultural character as in themes and values

        To reveal how this cultural character exhibits a configuration in action

        To reveal how this configuration exhibits analytical character (having reference to other cases) in categories and theories of man in society

---

themselves!" Translated into the language and method of participant observation, this would mean: "Look to the interpretations themselves for definitions of what is important to guide the study!"

The basic field unit of observation in our structured study is the interpretation (meaning) given to social acts in the context of events. An interpretation is the meaning of a social act (as observed by the people acting), but it also defines the nature of an event. A social act (in the sense of mutually aroused symbolic action as described by G. H. Mead) can be an event in itself. An event, on the other hand, can contain a number of social acts within a broader act of interpretation of what happens to people. An event is something that happens to people which they deem important by way of their interpretations. People interpret events in various ways which the observer discovers and reports in his journal.

The observer's own value interpretations (as Max Weber would call them) are not entirely ignored in the study. They are part of the analysis and they appear in the observer's synthetic judgments about the data. As we have noted, the observer first makes judgments about the interpretations of others by witnessing events within varying times, places, circumstances, languages, intimacies, and consensuses in the cultural context studied. These observations should be factual reports of the interpretations of participants. Second, the observer judges the relation between interpreted data and the character of the culture that appears within them. Third, the observer judges the relation between the culture studied and analytical categories and theories. Analytical theories contain premises derived and deduced separately from the culture studied for the purpose of explaining how man exists in general in the context of society. See the *Field Data Guide* for an illustration of how these concepts are used in research.

III. *Procedures:*

A. JOURNAL RECORD

1. Describe the way (process) in which events are interpreted by participants.

2. Describe the interpretations (meanings) themselves. Include intersubjective interpretations (collective meanings).

3. Describe how the interpretations of participants and the observer compare within the context of time, place, circumstance, language, intimacy, and consensus.

B. ANALYSIS (Examples are drawn from the study of the culture of a mental hospital.)[7]

1. List categories representing significant areas of interpretations (meanings).

(e.g.)   a. Patient subculture

b. Professional subculture

c. Employees' subculture

    (1) Patient-doctor contacts

    (2) Controlling patient behavior

    (3) Defining circumstances requiring punishment

    (4) Carrying on ward routine with minimum effort

2. Describe how interpretations exhibit a cultural character.

(e.g.)   a. *Hierarchy of values* in "patient subculture"

    (1) Going home

    (2) Residence in certain wards

    (3) Attention of doctors

    (4) Preference for certain jobs in hospital

        (a) Kitchen and dining hall in demand

        (b) Jobs contributing toward discharge, etc.

(e.g.)   b. *Themes* in "professional subculture"

    (1) "All patients must be classified in two weeks."

    (2) "All patients must work inside the institutions."

3. Describe the total configuration in action.

a. The *formal* design of how the subcultures and the organizations expressing them are an interrelating network of life-worlds and activities.

(e.g.)   b. The *dynamics* of the design as in professional and employee cultures conflicting in their separate orientations toward the patient; the professional orientation involves diagnostic treatment and release while the employees' orientation involves punishment and control of patients.

4. Describe the relationship of the design to analytical categories and theory.

a. An appropriate analytical category having reference to the configura-

---

7 S. Kirson Weinberg and H. Warren Dunham, *The Culture of a Mental Hospital* (Detroit: Wayne State University Press, 1960).

tion would be *bureaucracy*; another analytic category having reference to the data would be *norms*.
b. A general theory would be structural-functionalism; some of the
explanatory elements of this theory would include the functional
requirements for the survival of bureaucratic organizations in general
(with special reference in this case to psychiatric hospitals) and the
general processes of institutionalization in society.

The findings of a participant observer can seldom be judged as either
totally valid or invalid. Such findings are subject to the same kind of
"approximations" which we indicated affect statistical correlations in the
empirical tradition. Correlations are seldom perfect, and in some cases conclusions are hard to draw. Does a Pearson correlation coefficient of .6, for
example, indicate a significant relationship between the variables measured?
The confirmation of a single meaning in the field observation of a social
act may be easier to obtain than the statistical relationship between two
operationally defined variables. However, if a number of meanings are
involved, and a complicated relationship among them is being ascertained,
the findings become more difficult to validate. The meanings reported by
the observer as existing in one part of the culture studied may be adequate,
while the meanings he reports in another part may not be adequate. The
researcher's conclusion as to the nature of the larger configuration he studies
may be based upon meanings of which some have been validated while
others have not. The result can be functional for the purposes at hand
and still not be adequate to the perfecting requirements of the serious
researcher.

Absolute certainty is not a feature of scientific knowledge in the sense
that it might be a feature of some forms of philosophical and religious
beliefs. The scientist is guided by a desire for certainty, but he is aware
that he is in tension with the world that lies just beyond his current state
of knowledge. It is through his failure to reach certainty in any total sense
that he realizes the limits of his human perspective; it is through his engaging
discovery of new horizons of certainty that he realizes the expanding potential of it.

Phenomenological
Procedures

Since some readers of this book are probably not familiar with the method of phenomenology, and since we refer to this field as having some common ground with the methodology of participant observation, we include this appendix for further clarification. We have said that the method of participant observation does not follow empirical traditions in many ways, some of which are similar to phenomenology. A brief comparison of these two methods as they are jointly compared with traditional empiricism should prove helpful.

What we will say should indicate that a more systematic comparison of the traditional and the newer approaches to empiricism in human studies could reveal a conceptual link between what have become the great opposing theories of American and European thought. The method of participant observation is largely American (in its recent development, at least), and the phenomenological approach is of European origin. As relatively new approaches to human studies, both break with traditional empiricism in similar ways. And yet, it is difficult to compare these approaches accurately and briefly, since they are both complex modes of research containing different perspectives which would be defended by particular methodologists from each approach. The field of phenomenology especially contains many subperspectives which have yet to be reconciled within the larger phenomenological movement. We shall therefore select only one methodological model in phenomenology as our point of inquiry, recognizing that, in utilizing one model, we can make only a tentative statement of how the two methodologies may be comparable in selected respects.

If we choose Herbert Spiegelberg's description of the phenomenological method as our model we can capture certain salient features of the method and thus make our comparison brief and to the point.[1] Speigelberg describes seven different "stages" of knowing by way of the phenomenological method. While each step described is suggestive of a natural sequence, we must conclude that each step also has phases which interpenetrate with those of other steps, and to that extent must be considered to be only dimensions of the phenomenological method which guide the observer. These stages are:

1. Investigating particular phenomena
2. Investigating general essences
3. Apprehending essential relationships among essences
4. Watching modes of appearing
5. Watching the constitution of phenomena in consciousness
6. Suspending belief in the existence of the phenomena
7. Interpreting the meaning of phenomena

If we follow Spiegelberg's explanation of these steps we find that the first step involves three phases: (1) an intuitive grasp of the phenomena, (2) their analytic examination, and (3) their description. In the first phase, Spiegelberg notes, in order to obtain an intuitive grasp of the phenomena under study the observer must become highly aware of his subject and its surroundings. This heightened awareness or openness of the observer's consciousness is crucial to the method, and, we would add, is stressed repeatedly in the work of other phenomenologists. The observer must approach his subject with no structured expectations of how an object should be described. While we might argue that this is an impossible requirement, the phenomenologist feels that at least the observer seeks to reduce his preconceptions to a minimum so that he can receive an object as it is given to his consciousness. He must have no hypotheses to direct him as to what he should find in his investigation. The investigator goes into the situation to be studied with a totally open mind—open, in fact, in depth to all the stimuli that impinge upon his consciousness. He admits only that which is immediately experienced as he concentrates on the object of his inquiry.

This phenomenological rule seems to be in direct violation to what we have stated is important in all structured studies—systematically outlining what one seeks to know by gathering all the background information which is available in literature. The phenomenologist would contend, however, that while the general scheme of study can be outlined, he intends to open himself to the human realities which he studies in ways not customary

---

1 Herbert Spiegelberg, "The Essentials of the Phenomenological Method," in *The Phenomenological Movement: A Historical Introduction* (2nd ed.) (The Hague: Martinus Nijhoff, 1965), Vol. II, pp. 655–701. My extensive references to Spiegelberg's model are all drawn from this chapter (Chap. xiv).

to the observer in the empirical tradition. If the phenomenologist kept empirical hypotheses constantly in mind in the social situations in which he functions—a procedure which is basic to empirical investigation—he would probably create that very reality which he defines in his design. The phenomenologist would support the famous postulate of W. I. Thomas as appropriate for explaining the difference here: *What people define as real is real in its consequences.* And so the researcher may unintentionally "define into reality" that which he seeks without knowledge of his own involvement in the creation of the product.

In any event, this basic phenomenological principle is reflected in the writings of participant observers who have found that assumptions or hypotheses can be too strongly advanced in a research design, and may interfere with the accuracy of findings. In their study, *Boys in White,* Becker, Geer, Hughes, and Strauss stress this rule as basic to their methodology:

> This meant that we concentrated on *what* students learned as well as on *how* they learned it. Both of those assumptions committed us to working with an open theoretical scheme in which variables were to be discovered, rather than with a scheme in which variables decided on in advance would be located and their consequences isolated and measured.
>
> This commitment raises both theoretical questions and questions of method. To start with the latter, we necessarily had to use methods that would allow us to discover phenomena whose existence we were unaware of at the beginning of the research; our methods had to allow for the discovery of the variables themselves as well as relationships between variables. We were committed, therefore, to the use of unstructured techniques, particularly at the beginning. "Unstructured techniques" refers here, obviously, to techniques in which the data-gathering operations are not designed, for instance, to see which of two or more alternative answers to a question someone will pick, but rather which questions he himself will ask.[2]

There is clearly a similarity in emphasis in the work of the participant observer and the phenomenologist on this point; they contrast with the traditional empiricist. The traditional empiricist sets up preconceived realities which he seeks to verify; the observer and the phenomenologist show tendencies to reduce preconceptions of their subject to a minimum. While many participant observers have shown an interest in outlining a general design of their study beforehand, their research interests thereafter are clearly guided by their subject as it is given. As they become personally involved in the activities of the people they study, participant observers

---

2 Howard S. Becker, Blanche Geer, Everett C. Hughes, and Anselm L. Strauss, *Boys in White* (Chicago: University of Chicago Press, 1961), p. 18.

report the importance of following the activities as they exist, rather than following preconceptions. Causal relationships, for example, must not necessarily be anticipated as holding true between elements to be studied. The participant observer would say with the phenomenologist that one cannot interpret one factor as having "caused" another factor unless a "causal" relationship is found in the meanings existing in the context of the investigation. In such a case, this relationship is understood to be only experiential data which may be useful in later analyses of the interpretive meaning of cause.

In the second phase of Spiegelberg's first step we find that objects of consciousness are analyzed by tracing the elements of the observer's experience "as given" in their natural continuity. The observer does not interpret these objects of consciousness by means of any typology. The use of the term *analysis,* Spiegelberg notes, is different in phenomenology than in traditional empiricism. In phenomenology analysis refers simply to distinguishing the constituents of phenomena within the framework of consciousness, and then distinguishing the relations of the constituents to each other and to adjacent phenomena. (Spiegelberg illustrates each of these steps by analyzing the meaning of "force.") The third phase of the first step, "description," proceeds by first describing what a phenomenon is not (negation), and second, by describing the phenomenon by analogy; these techniques together, Spiegelberg notes, provide the basic guideposts which lead others to find the nature of phenomena.

The second stage of phenomenological investigation, investigating essences, grows out of the descriptive phase noted above in which the observer begins to order particular phenomena in his consciousness according to their similarities, and then proceeds to interpret intuitively what constitutes the "essence" of these phenomena when experienced together. In this stage, the basic question which the phenomenologist asks himself in determining what constitutes essence is: Can a phenomenon remain the same phenomenon without the elements deemed essential by the observer? For example, Spiegelberg states, can a triangle still remain a triangle without three sides and three angles? We have previously suggested that the term *essence* be used in participant observer research in the description of the basic forms of cultural experiences studied by the observer. While participant observers have not technically employed the term essence, so that no comparison can be drawn on this point, it is true that observers are dealing with data, like those of the phenomenologist, which are "constituting themselves in their consciousness," data which are not defined solely from the powers of reason or the reality of the senses.

The phenomenologist's aim in the third stage is to examine essential relations. In fact, the most important concern of the phenomenologist is not to identify separate essences, but to find the essential relations of these essences. Spiegelberg notes that to "break down" an essence into components is the usual meaning of analysis, but to find essential relations between essences is a synthetic process. However, the relationship of phenomenological terms such as "synthetic" and "essence" to terms in social research has yet to be studied carefully, and comparisons at this point are not easily made.

The fourth stage of "watching modes of appearing" is particularly apropos to the method of participant observation. The methodological principles which the phenomenologist must follow here remind him that: (1) he sees only a "side aspect" of what is actually whole, (2) he observes a "shading off" of the phenomenon in his field of awareness, and (3) he observes different "modes of clarity" in the phenomenon. For example, in looking at a cube-like object, the observer sees in his mind the whole cube with six sides. He does *not* see the cube as it would appear to him unconditioned by his image of it; he sees the essence of the cube as it exists in its wholeness when he looks at it because his mind unconsciously and directly supplies the unseen parts to complete the image. If he did not have this prior image to control his observation, he would see instead a trapezoid-like form with some parts distinct and other parts indistinct and still other parts invisible and therefore unknown to him. The sides of the cube which were not directly facing him would "shade off" into indistinctness, and he could not see the cube in its essentialness. And yet these modes of appearing must be described as part of the process of knowing phenomenologically.

In social research we would say that the experience is paralleled by what the participant observer would witness if he participated in the activities of only one particular class level but with a prior conception of the total class structure. The normal member of a social class experiences a "shading off" of classes directly and distantly opposite to him. When a member of the upper class socially observes the classes at his extreme opposite, they become indistinct and shade into a general group. Lower income people are all "on the other side of the tracks" or are "wage-earners." However, if an upper class member were to live among the lower classes he would find considerable differentiation among groups within the general group. (W. Lloyd Warner has already told us of this experiential phenomenon; he found class members of both upper and lower extremes failing to "see" the distinct differences among the subclasses of those classes opposite to them.) The participant observer who has been trained sociologically will normally supply the remaining portions of the class structure image to what would otherwise shade off in his conception of those classes opposite to his own, just as the observer of a cube supplies the remaining portion of the image in his mind. The methodological problem is one of recognizing the differences between "seeing" the class as a sociologist and as a member of a class whose knowledge "shades off," and then taking these meanings into consideration in findings and conclusions.

The fifth phase of the phenomenological method involves exploring the "constitution" of phenomena in the consciousness of the observer. A phenomenon, we should say, need not be fully identified before this phase can function; it is still emerging in the consciousness of the individual. In this phase the observer describes the experience as it begins to take form. Spiegelberg illustrates this process by describing how one obtains a "picture" of a new city which is visited for the first time. Such a depiction of what happens phenomenologically to the migrant entering a new city, we would add, is far from what an urban sociologist would normally find about the same subject. The form of the city, Spiegelberg notes, only gradually becomes understood in the migrant's consciousness:

> A first illustration of such a constitution can be the experience of getting oriented in a new city, whose "picture" gradually takes shape in our mind. Having arrived at night and having lost all our bearings in retiring to our quarters, with only a very confused idea as to how we got there, we may find ourselves awaking in a strange bed with the task of building up a new space pattern, thus far quite unrelated to our previous life spaces.... Perhaps the most important process here is how the "empty lots" of our new spatial pattern are more and more "built up" by corridors, stairs, streets, and houses that establish themselves more or less firmly until the pattern gets sedimented, usually after a good many upsets, which break up the first outlines as a result of disorientations, "getting lost," and similar adventures.[3]

The sixth step, which, incidentally, Husserl felt to be the primary phase of phenomenological research, Spiegelberg describes as "suspending belief in existence." The problem becomes that of detaching "the phenomena of our everyday experience from the context of our naive or natural living, while preserving their content as fully and as purely as possible." The exact position of this phase in phenomenological analysis today is disputed. Spiegelberg's inclusion of it at this stage of analysis is considered unorthodox.

The seventh and last step involves interpreting "concealed meanings." This involves what the social researcher would call moving to the theoretical level of interpreting data, and what Spiegelberg calls moving to ontological formulations of essences which illuminate phenomena for the observer. Ontological formulations have been made by Martin Heidegger and Jean-Paul Sartre and function, we would say, at a comparable level with "theory" in relation to the "data" of social research. Just as the social scientist seeks an adequate relationship between theory and facts, so the phenomenologist may

---

[3] Spiegelberg, "The Esssentials of the Phenomenological Method," p. 688.

look for relationships between ontological conceptions of the structures of being and the ontic meanings of everyday life. Not all phenomenologists would agree that this phase of the method should be included. The phenomenologist who does, however, would state that he is still *describing* a phenomenon ontologically, while the theoretician would more likely state that he is *explaining* it.

Husserl and succeeding phenomenologists would say that, technically speaking, phenomenology precedes empiricism (or underlies it) as a methodology, and therefore the two methodologies are not comparable as polarities. Nevertheless, it is worthwhile to summarize some of the differences which are manifest. Formulating these differences in terms of procedural rules we find the following:

Observing Phenomenologically

1. Investigate particular phenomena without definitive preconceptions of their nature.
2. Observe in phenomena that which appears immediately to consciousness.
3. Look for similarities in phenomena as given to consciousness; distinguish their essences and essential relations intuitively.
4. Explore how the phenomena constitute themselves in consciousness while continuing to suspend prior conceptions of their nature.
5. Examine what concealed meanings may be discovered through the application of ontological conceptions of reality.

Observing Empirically

1. Investigate particular phenomena with definitive preconceptions of their nature.
2. Observe in phenomena that which immediately appears to the senses.
3. Look for similarities and differences between what is observed and what is operationally defined; distinguish their correlations statistically.
4. Explore how the phenomena constitute themselves in reason relative to social typologies.
5. Examine what concealed meanings may be discovered through the application of theoretical conceptions of social action.

The difference between knowing what appears to one's *consciousness* and what appears to one's *senses* is basic. The phenomenologist, like the participant observer, assumes that there is something in the nature of human experience, other than sheer reason or sensory observation, which can produce knowledge. In the past, the empiricist has recognized "sudden revelations" or acquired valuable insight from outside the scientific framework of knowing, but he has never sought to explain the process systematically. We would say that the method of phenomenology and participant observation may contribute toward a valid explanation of this phenomenon. What the phenomenological method is describing here is actually the process which lies behind the revelation of new, testable knowledge, or what Robert Merton has called the "serendipity pattern" of social reseach:

> The serendipity pattern refers to the fairly common experience of observing an *unanticipated, anomalous, and strategic* datum which becomes the occasion for developing a new theory or extending an existing theory.[4]

What Merton calls surprising and unanticipated data in empirical studies are often produced when researchers have unintentionally followed the phenomenological method. The phases of this method have been an un-rationalized, yet experiential, part of the empirical process of research and actually have been the means by which significant social meanings have been discovered in empirical data. Such meanings become apparent to the empiricist as he participates in the processes of communication and symbolic life experienced by the people being studied. The empiricist who can design the major outlines of his sensory observations and yet remain open to new meanings given symbolically in the situations he studies is thus rewarded by finding new perspectives cast on his data.

The participant observer and the phenomenologist differ in their method-ologies in certain respects. The participant observer in the social sciences studies meanings which exist in the minds of people other than himself by empathically taking their roles as though they were his own; he participates in the natural processes of communication extant in the culture he studies. The phenomenologist in philosophy, however, studies objects as they con-stitute themselves independently in human consciousness; he studies the act of consciousness itself without necessarily judging objects in the conscious-ness of others. The phenomenologist in the social sciences has been more concerned with problems of "intersubjectivity," but he has not thoroughly examined the common ground he shares with the participant observer in the study of man in society.[5]

We have indicated some areas of common agreement between the par-ticipant observer and the phenomenologist when jointly compared with the traditional empiricist. We have said they agree that human meanings are not simply logically inferred from sense impressions even though this tradi-tional process may be important for gaining knowledge of a certain kind. In contrast to this process, the participant observer and the phenomenologist have both insisted upon the importance of intuition in developing knowledge

---

[4] Robert K. Merton, *Social Theory and Social Structure* (New York: Free Press of Glencoe, Inc., 1949), p. 98.

[5] Recent signs of a serious account being given to phenomenology in its relationship to American sociology are now visible, though too recent to be critically examined in this volume. Cf. Edward A. Tiryakian, "Existential Phenomenology," *American Sociological Review,* **30** (October 1965), 674–88. Critical appraisals of this article and a reply by Tiryakian may be found in *American Sociological Review,* **31** (April 1966), 258–64.

which fulfills the scientific requirement of certainty as well as or better than traditional forms of knowledge. The phenomenologist and the participant observer both stress the importance of intuitive apprehension of human meanings which reveal themselves in the consciousness of the observer. In these and other ways, the phenomenologist and the participant observer are methodologically parallel in their search for knowledge, but their methodologies are still in formative stages and the future is filled with the possibilities of their development in the study of man in society.

In Retrospect

New empiricists such as the participant observer in American society and the social phenomenologist in European society present a challenge to social scientists of the second half of the twentieth century: a challenge to complete the basis for what C.P. Snow points towards as the "third culture" of knowledge—the social sciences. It is a challenge no less momentous than that which lay before men in the second half of the eighteenth century when the culture of natural science was emerging. When the challenge was met by men such as Immanuel Kant, who helped define the basis for the scientific perspective, and by others who organized scientific knowledge, the effect on the outlook of modern man was enormous. In fact, the effect carried directly into the perspective of the social scientist, who sought to apply the scientific perspective wholeheartedly to the study of society. But society could not be treated only as an organism and cultural mores as though they were only like the forces of gravity. The truth about society was distorted in this image and an authentic part of man was lost. Thus, while the traditional scientific perspective continued to pervade the outlook of modern man, it has increasingly shown inadequacies in meeting man's need today to understand himself in the context of society.

A deep division was created in the philosophy of science between the natural and the moral worlds of man, and this division became worse in early scientific efforts to study society.[6] The naturalistic perspective could not be the basis for interpreting the moral world of man without serious misconceptions and unanticipated moral involvements, and so a new perspective had to be created. The natural and the moral perspective had to be recombined in some way by the social scientist into a new perspective of man, a perspective that reinstated him as a whole being. Constructive forces developed in the twentieth century to bring this about. Among these forces were studies in participant observation, which we have said have

---

6 The participant observer and the phenomenologist would jointly say that a division also was created between the worlds of "lived experience" and scientific concepts.

been bridging the great divide between the natural and moral worlds of man by helping build a human perspective.

The analogy of a divide and a bridge built between the moral and natural worlds in the creation of a human perspective has some value in relating the past with the present, but we must not take the analogy too seriously. As the bridge is built, we may very likely see an entirely new structure of knowledge developing among the major fields of learning which will make the analogy obsolete. The building of knowledge in modern society has become one of society's main tasks, and there is every indication that this emphasis will increase in the future. Knowledge-makers are in greater proportion than ever before, and the scale of the knowledge explosion is in competition only with the population growth itself. Social scientific knowledge is part of this explosion.

Social scientists today are in the process of developing a knowledge culture which brings into new relationship cultural opposites that have often stood separate in isolated contexts. Polar opposites such as subject and object or sacred and secular have often been conceived as basically irreconcilable ways of looking at the world. One is either a subject, or an object, for one cannot be both at the same time. Something is treated either as sacred or secular, but cannot be treated in the same way at the same time. Such polar opposites, however, now become an active, studied part of the methodology of social science. In participant observation the researcher must creatively combine the oppositional features of his role as participant, on the one hand, and observer, on the other, and in the process he forms a basis for studying and creatively conceiving other cultural opposites which have heretofore been outside the sphere of scientific inquiry. Science has usually identified with only one side of certain polarities in culture and as a result has become trapped in its efforts to understand them. In cultural studies the researcher is finding that if phenomena are to be accurately conceived they must be understood both subjectively and objectively; with this knowledge the researcher is finding that cultural opposites can have a complementary relationship. Understanding one member of a polarity can contribute insight into understanding the nature of the other.

As the social scientist continues to study man in society he is discovering a logos of culture, a new basis for understanding the world which radically penetrates the nature of man's being in the world. He is creating a process of understanding which opens people's minds and allows for the development of a new framework for viewing the world. The framework for the third culture is part of this development, and in the making of it a new image of man is emerging, an image which has significance beyond the scientific culture itself.

It is a special development, perhaps, of Saint Simon and Auguste Comte's third stage in man's explanation of his world. Comte endowed sociology in particular during the nineteenth century with the responsibility of discovering laws about society as the third and seemingly final stage of understanding. While the broad methodological elements of what Comte considered important—rational observation, experimentation, and comparison—are still roughly visible today, a new phase is in the process of being added. This phase includes the element of personal involvement in understanding through the method of participant observation.

This changes the Comtean perspective, even though much of Comte's thought remains. While the ultimate interest of the social scientist is still Comtean in range—he seeks knowledge about the whole of humanity rather than only a portion of it—aspirations of the social scientist today are more modest, tempered by a greater knowledge of how society works than Comte possessed. The social scientist today is not a humanist with a set of "ethics" and a world design to implement. He is a social observer with a set of principles and procedures devised for understanding the ethics and world designs of others as they emerge in the context of society. He does not ignore his own impact upon society, but recognizes himself as a fact-gatherer and an institutional analyst of society whose own ethics and designs are shaped by his primary interest in understanding man. He is thus expressing a new role and developing a new image not entirely without ethic, but not exactly with it either, in the formal sense.

The social scientist's ethics and social designs are built into his methodology. It is a methodology which is producing a scientific design of knowledge that transcends history and the particular social systems in which people live. At the same time, it is a methodology which retains the integrity of the values and beliefs of people living in these systems by means of expressive descriptions and accurate formulations of their cultural lives. Such a method has strong implications for the formal field of ethics and the applied fields of social design and planning. It is a scientific method with a challenging new perspective—a human perspective.

Index